THE CHRISTIAN WRITERS
MARKET GUIDE
2020

THE CHRISTIAN WRITERS
MARKET GUIDE

2020

Your Comprehensive Resource for Getting Published

STEVE LAUBE

THE CHRISTIAN WRITERS MARKET GUIDE 2020

ISBN – 978-162-184-0664 (paperback)
ISBN – 978-162-184-0732 (ebook)

Cover design and typesetting by Five J's Design (*fivejsdesign.com*)
Edited by Lin Johnson

Printed in the United States of America.

Visit The Christian Writers Institute at *www.ChristianWritersInstitute.com*.

E-mail: *admin@christianwritersmarketguide.com*

Disclaimer: The information in this guide is provided by the individuals or companies through online questionnaires and email inquiries, as well as their websites and writers guidelines. The individuals or companies do not pay to be listed in the *Guide*. The entries in the *Guide* are not necessarily endorsed by Steve Laube or The Christian Writers Institute. Steve Laube and The Christian Writers Institute make every attempt to verify the accuracy of the information provided. The entries in the *Guide* are for information only. Any transaction(s) between a user of the information and the individuals or companies listed is strictly between those parties.

TABLE OF CONTENTS

PART 5: SUPPORT FOR WRITERS 251

FOREWORD

WHAT A TREASURE TROVE YOU HOLD IN YOUR HANDS! And what a bargain!

Normally, I wouldn't write something so commercial. But since you're reading this book, you've already invested in it, so I don't have to sell you on it.

I invest in guides like this every year, without fail. I believe writers are either stagnating or they're lifelong learners—growing in their skills. And *The Christian Writers Market Guide* is a nonnegotiable asset to that end.

Why do I still do this, closing in on 200 published books? Couldn't I just coast at this point?

Sure I could, and so could you. But I want to finish well. Two-thirds of my published works are novels, meaning the remaining titles are nonfiction books of all stripes. Where else could I go to keep up with what's happening in the marketplace in both broad genres?

I'm not the first and won't be the last to hammer home that the publishing landscape is roiling with change as never before. We all wonder where it will land, but I also think we realize it may never settle again. With the miracles of technology we see every day, we have to strap in and hang on for a tumultuous ride.

Never has it been easier to find a publishing solution. I'm an enthusiastic proponent of traditional publishing, urging every hopeful author to exhaust all efforts to get paid for being published, rather than paying even a dime to be printed.

But I'm also a realist and know how stacked against you the odds are these days. There's hardly an excuse for *not* getting your manuscript published nowadays. You're more likely to self-publish than not, so do yourself a favor: Immerse yourself in this guide, and learn everything you need to know about *all* the available options.

Writing done well and stories well told still rise in the marketplace, so set yourself apart in the sea of competition and produce the absolute best work of which you're capable.

That you've chosen the *Christian* market guide tells me something. You have a message, something to say, a mission to accomplish. Welcome to the journey! I urge you to strive for excellence. Don't hide behind excuses or explanations that begin, "It's okay for a Christian book."

Because we have access to a power source the rest of the market lacks, we should be leading the way in quality writing. Settle for nothing less.

—Jerry B. Jenkins
www.JerryJenkins.com

INTRODUCTION

WRITING IS A SERIOUS CALLING. The privilege of having your words influence other people's thinking or inspiring their spirit is a wonderful thing. Numerous opportunities abound for great content from great authors. Traditional methods for publication remain, but the diversity of online opportunities are endless. In addition, independent-publication options have made it easier to see your byline on a book, a blog post, or an online magazine.

While it may seem like the Christian publishing industry is shrinking, it's not. In reality, it is simply changing. Therefore, you have to research more to find the best place for your work. The problem with online search engines is the immense number of results you receive. Then the results depend on that site's search-engine optimization. This market guide has curated the information for you. Now you can find what is targeted specifically for the Christian market and your areas of interest.

One of the biggest mistakes a writer can make is to ignore the guidelines of an agent, a publisher, or an editor. Some publications have dropped their listings in this guide due to writers failing to follow the instructions posted on their websites or in here. Editors are looking for writers who understand their periodicals or publishing houses and their unique approaches to the marketplace. This book will help you be such a writer. With a little time and effort, you can meet an editor's expectations, distinguish yourself as a professional, and sell what you write.

If you can, I recommend you attend a writers conference. (We have many listed inside.) It is good to meet new people and become familiar with the best teachers in the industry. If you cannot get to a conference, consider exploring the courses available online at *ChristianWritersInstitute. com*. There are more than 100 to choose from, and you can enjoy them at any time on any device.

If this is the first time you've used this guide, read the "How to Use This Book" section. If you run into an unfamiliar term, look it up in the "Publishing Lingo" section in back and learn the terminology.

Please be aware that the information in this guide is provided by the individuals or companies through online questionnaires and email inquiries, as well as their websites and writers guidelines. The individuals or companies do not pay to be listed in the *Guide*. The entries in the *Guide* are not necessarily endorsed by me or The Christian Writers Institute. We make every attempt to verify the accuracy of the information provided. The entries in the *Guide* are for information only. Any transaction(s) between a user of the information and the individuals or companies listed is strictly between those parties.

May God bless your writing journey. We are on a mission to change the world, word by word. To that end, strive for excellence and make your work compelling and insightful. Great writing is still in demand. But it must be targeted, crafted, edited, critiqued, polished, and proofread until it shines.

My thanks go to Lin Johnson whose incredible work makes this all possible. She keeps tabs all year on market changes, so every listing is accurate to the best of our information. (Our online version of this guide, *ChristianWritersMarketGuide.com*, is updated throughout the year.) As the administrator of the online and print editions, she is the genius behind the details. In addition, I would also like to acknowledge my wife, Lisa. Her love, support, and encouragement have been incalculable. We make a great team!

Steve Laube
President
The Christian Writers Institute
The Steve Laube Agency
24 W. Camelback Rd. A-635
Phoenix, AZ 85013
www.christianwritersinstitute.com
www.stevelaube.com

To update a listing or to be added to the next edition or online, go to *www.christianwritersinstitute.com*. Navigate to the market guide page, click on the Get Listed tab, and fill out the form.

For direct sales questions, email the publisher:
admin@christianwritersinstitute.com

For books and courses on the writing craft, visit The Christian Writers Institute: *www.christianwritersinstitute.com.*

HOW TO USE THIS BOOK

THE CHRISTIAN WRITERS MARKET GUIDE 2020 IS DESIGNED to make it easier for you to sell your writing. It will serve you well if you use it as a springboard to become thoroughly familiar with the markets best suited to your writing style and areas of interest and expertise.

Start by getting acquainted with the setup of this guide.

Part 1 lists Christian book publishers with contact information and what they are looking for. Notice that many houses accept manuscripts only from agents or through meeting with their editors at a writers conference. If you need an agent, check the agent listings in Chapter 16.

Since independent book publishing is a viable option today, Part 2 provides resources to help you. Chapter 2 lists independent book publishers, many of which provide all the services you need as packages or à la carte services. If you decide to publish on your own, Chapters 3 and 4 list design, production, and distribution services. You'll also want to hire a professional editor, so see Chapter 19 for help in this area.

Part 3 lists periodical—magazine, newspaper, and newsletter—publishers. Chapter 5 will help you find markets by topics (e.g., marriage, evangelism) and types (e.g., how-to, poetry, personal experience). Although these lists are not comprehensive, they provide a shortcut for finding appropriate markets for your ideas.

Cross-referencing may be helpful. For example, if you have an idea for a how-to article on parenting, look at the lists in both the how-to and parenting categories. Also, don't overlook writing on the same topic for different periodicals, such as money management for a general adult magazine, a teen magazine, a women's newsletter, and a magazine for pastors. Each would require a different slant, but you would get more mileage from one idea.

If you run into words in the listings that you are not familiar with, check the glossary at the back of the book.

In Part 4, "Specialty Markets," you'll find nonbook, nonperiodical markets like daily devotionals and drama. Here you can explore types of writing you may not have thought about but that can provide a steady writing income.

As a writer, you'll need support to keep going. Part 5 provides information for various kinds of support.

One of the best ways to get published today is to meet editors at writers conferences. Check out Chapter 17 for a conference or seminar near you or perhaps in a location you'd like to visit. Before deciding which conference to attend, check the websites for who is on faculty, what houses are represented, and what classes are offered that can help you grow your craft and writing business. You may also want to factor in the size of the conference. Don't be afraid to stretch outside your comfort zone.

For ongoing support and feedback on your manuscripts, join a writers group. Chapter 18 lists groups by state. If you can't find one near you, consider starting one or join an online group.

Since editors and agents are looking for polished manuscripts, you may want to hire a professional editor. See Chapter 19 for people who offer a variety of editorial services, including coaching.

Whether you publish your book with a royalty house or go the independent route, you'll need to do most, if not all, of the promotion. If you want to hire a specialist with contacts, check out Chapter 20, "Publicity and Marketing Services." And if you need accounting or legal help, check out Chapter 21.

One way to promote your message and your books is through speaking. If you need help in this area—and most writers do—see Chapter 22, "Speaking Services." There you will find organizations and conferences that train speakers and/or connect them with groups looking for speakers.

Since writers who stagnate don't get published, check out Chapter 23 for education resources to help you improve your writing style, write different types of manuscripts, and learn the business of writing and publishing. You'll find a variety of free and paid resources, including podcasts and classes.

Entering a writing contest can boost your sales, supplement your writing income, lead to publication, and sometimes give you valuable feedback on your writing. Check out Chapter 24 for a list of contests by genre. Many of them are not Christian oriented, but you can enter manuscripts with a Christian worldview.

Once you get acquainted with this guide, start using it. After you identify potential markets for your ideas and/or manuscripts, read their writers guidelines. If these are available on the website, the URL is included. Otherwise, email or send (with a SASE) for a copy. Also study at least one sample copy of a periodical (information to obtain one is given in most listings) or the book publisher's website to see if your idea truly fits there. Never send a manuscript without doing this market study.

Above all, keep in mind that this guide is only a starting point for your research and that change is the one constant in the publishing industry. It is impossible for any market guide to be 100 percent accurate since editors move around, publications and publishing houses close, and new ones open. But this guide is an essential tool for getting published in the Christian market and making an impact on God's Kingdom with your words.

PART 1

BOOK PUBLISHERS

BOOK PUBLISHERS

Before submitting your query letter or book proposal, it's critical that you read and follow a publisher's guidelines exactly. In most cases the guidelines are available on the website and a direct link is given in the listing. If you do not have a literary agent—and even if you do—check out a publisher thoroughly before signing a contract.

1517 MEDIA-BOOKS
See listings for Augsburg Fortress, Fortress Press, and Beaming Books.

AADEON PUBLISHING COMPANY
PO Box 223, Hartford, CT 06141
www.aadeonmedia.com

> **Submissions:** Mail only. Query first. Nonfiction 140-200,000 words. Responds in six weeks. Only considers manuscripts that have been edited by a professional book copy editor.
> **Types and topics:** cultural and moral makeup of society in the US and its impact on Christianity
> **Guidelines:** *www.aadeonmedia.com/submissions.html*

ABINGDON PRESS
2222 Rosa L. Parks Blvd., Nashville, TN 37228-1306 | 615-749-6000
www.abingdonpress.com
Constance Stella, Bible, leadership, and theology
Paul Franklyn, academic books

> **Parent company:** United Methodist Publishing House
> **Denomination:** United Methodist
> **Submissions:** Submit proposal with sample chapters through the website. Publishes 120 titles per year; receives 2,000 submissions annually. Fewer than 5% of books from first-time authors. Accepts manuscripts through agents only for Christian living. Bible: CEB.

Royalty: begins at 7.5% on net

Types and topics: seasonal for Advent, Christmas, Mother's Day, and Father's Day; spiritual and personal growth; devotional; gift books

Guidelines: *www.abingdonpress.com/submissions*

Tip: Looking for "any young and new voices that have active speaking and conference engagements, as well as blog and social-media followers."

AMBASSADOR INTERNATIONAL

411 University Ridge, Ste. B14, Greenville, SC 29601 | 864-751-4844, 864-751-4847

publisher@emeraldhouse.com | *www.ambassador-international.com*
Brenda Covert, editor

Mission statement: dedicated to spreading the gospel of Christ and empowering Christians through the written word

Submissions: Submit proposal with three chapters through the website. Publishes fifty titles per year; receives 750 submissions annually. First-time authors: 50%. Accepts manuscripts through agents or authors. Length: 144 pages minimum. Considers simultaneous submissions. Responds in one month. Bible: KJV, NIV, ESV, NKJV, NASB.

Royalty: 15-20% of net, 25% for ebooks, no advance

Types and topics: theology, devotionals, biography, inspirational, children's, business, finance, topical, Bible studies; fiction for teens, new adults, and adults

Guidelines: *ambassador-international.com/submission-guidelines*

Tip: "We're most open to a book that has a clearly defined market and the author's total commitment to the project. We do well with first-time authors. We have full international coverage. Many of our titles sell globally."

AMERICAN CATHOLIC PRESS

16565 State St., South Holland, IL 60473-2025 | 708-331-5485

acp@acpress.org | *www.acpress.org, www.leafletmissal.com*
Father Michael Gilligan, editorial director

Denomination: Catholic

Submissions: Publishes four titles per year; receives ten submissions annually. Query first via mail. Average first printing 3,000. Publication within one year. No simultaneous submissions. Responds in two months. Bible: NAS.

Royalty: pays $25-100 for outright purchases only

Types and topics: only publishes material on the liturgy

Guidelines: *www.americancatholicpress.org/faq.html#faq5*

AMG PUBLISHERS

6815 Shallowford Rd., Chattanooga, TN 37421 | 800-266-4977, 423-894-6060
sales@amgpublishers.com | *www.amgpublishers.com*
Amanda Jenkins, author liaison

Parent company: AMG International

Submissions: "God's Word to you is our highest calling." We are unique in that proceeds from our sales are funneled into world missions through our parent organization. Publishes one to five titles per year; receives 500 submissions annually. Email or mail query letter first. Accepts manuscripts through agents or authors. Length: 40-60,000 words (128-224 pages) for Bible studies, 60-100,000 words (208-400 pages) for trade nonfiction. Prefers accepted manuscript by email. Responds in one to four months. Bible version: prefers NASB 95, NKJV, ESV, or NIV.

Royalty: 10-20% of net, 30-40% for ebooks

Guidelines: *www.amgpublishers.com/main/pdf/Prospective_ Author_ Guidelines.pdf*

Types and topics: Bible studies (highly recommended that they fit the Following God series format), devotional, applied theology, apologetics, Bible reference, African-American, Hispanic

Also does: Bible software, Bible CD-ROMs

Imprints: Living Ink Books, God and Country Press

Tip: "Most open to an interactive workbook Bible study geared for small groups that effectively taps into a largely female audience. We are currently placing priority on books with strong bibliocentric focus."

ANCIENT FAITH PUBLISHING

PO Box 748, Chesterton, IN 46304
khyde@ancientfaith.com | *www.ancientfaith.com/publishing*
Katherine Hyde, editorial director, adult
Jane Meyer, children's book editor, jmeyer@ancientfaith.com

Mission statement: to embrace the fullness of the Orthodox Christian faith, encourage the discipleship of believers, equip the faithful for ministry, and evangelize the unchurched

Denomination: Eastern Orthodox

Submissions: Publishes twelve to sixteen adult titles per year; receives 100 submissions annually. First-time authors: 50%. Length: 40-100,000 words. Email query letter only. Responds in three months. Bible: NKJV.

Royalty: 10-15%, no advance

Types and topics: Orthodox life, marriage and family, theology, spirituality, church history, memoir, biography/hagiography, Bible commentary, worship and sacraments, patristics, contemporary issues—all from Eastern Orthodox perspective; children's/YA fiction, nonfiction, picture books

Also does: small booklets

Guidelines: *www.ancientfaith.com/publishing#af-resources*

Tip: "Read and follow the guidelines. Look through our website to see the kinds of books we publish. Do not submit material that is not intended specifically for an Eastern Orthodox audience."

ANEKO PRESS

PO Box 652, Abbotsford, WI 54405 | 855-489-7839
submit through website | www.anekopress.com
Jeremiah Zeiset, president

Parent company: Life Sentence Publishing, Inc.

Mission statement: helping the church reach the lost and disciple believers

Submissions: Niche is publishing ministry-related books. Publishes thirty-two titles per year; receives 100. First-time authors: 20%. Length: 40-50,000 words. Submit proposal with full manuscript through the website or mail. Responds in two weeks. Bible: Jubilee Bible, KJV, ESV, ASV. Agent not needed.

Types of books: offset paperback, hardcover, ebook, audiobook; print run 1,000-20,000

Royalty: 30% net, no advance

Types and topics: Christian living, commentary, biography

Guidelines: *anekopress.com/faq*

Tip: "Our authors tend to be in ministry."

ARMOUR BOOKS

PO Box 492, Corinda, QLD 4075, Australia
message through Facebook | www.facebook.com/armourbooks.au
Anne Hamilton

Mission statement: to publish quality books with a "kiss from God" at their heart

Submissions: Publishes three to five books per year; receives 50-100 submissions. Responds in two to four weeks. First-time authors: 50%. Length: maximum of 50,000 words. Inquire via email messenger first. No simultaneous submissions.

Type of books: POD

Royalty: 9-10%, sometimes offers advance

Types and topics: fantasy, science fiction, spiritual blockages to calling and healing

Guidelines: by email

Tip: "The golden rule: Support other authors as you would like to be supported."

ASCENDER BOOKS

proposals@newhopepublishers.com | www.ironstreammedia.com
Ramona Richards, acquisitions

Parent company: Iron Stream Media

Submissions: Authors must come from the Spirit-led community. Only accepts proposals through agents, author referrals, and conference meetings.

Types and topics: focused for a grace-inspired audience, spiritual growth, spiritual warfare, in-depth studies of Scripture, also includes online studies for churches and small groups

Guidelines: *www.ironstreammedia.com/submission-process*

ASPIRE PRESS

PO Box 3473, Peabody, MA 01961-3473 | 800-358-3111
info@hendricksonrose.com | www.hendrickson.com/content/aspire-press
Lynette Pennings, managing editor

Parent company: Hendrickson Publishers

Submissions: Publishes books that are "compassionate in their approach and rich with Scripture," giving "godly insight and counsel for those personally struggling and for believers who have a heart to minister and encourage others." Need credentials in helping others. Takes submissions only through agents or conferences.

Types and topics: Christian living, counseling

AUGSBURG FORTRESS

PO Box 1209, Minneapolis, MN 55440-1209 | 800-328-4648
afsubmissions@augsburgfortress.org | www.augsburgfortress.org
Suzanne Burke, director of development and senior editor

Parent company: 1517 Media-Books

Denomination: Evangelical Lutheran Church in America

Mission statement: committed to the development and publication of resources to support the ministry of congregations in the areas of worship and music, adult education, and leadership

Submissions: There is a continuing need to identify gifted writers for resources. If you would like to be considered as a writer, send an email indicating your area of interest. You will be contacted as to what sample writing we would like to see. Submit for consideration a letter of inquiry, proposal with outline, or manuscript. Accepts submissions only as email attachments in PDF or Microsoft Word. Responds in two months only if proposals fit publishing needs and catalog.

Types and topics: worship planning, leadership, preaching resources, Bible study, Christian living, all focused for Lutheran churches

Guidelines: *www.augsburgfortress.org/media/downloads/ Submission%20Guidelines.pdf*

AVE MARIA PRESS

PO Box 428, Notre Dame, IN 46556
submissions@mail.avemariapress.com | www.avemariapress.com
Heidi Hess Saxton, acquisitions editor

Parent company: Congregation of Holy Cross

Denomination: Catholic

Mission statement: to help people know, love, and serve God and to spread the gospel of Jesus through books and other resources

Submissions: Publishes forty to fifty books per year; receives hundreds. Email proposal with first chapter. Responds in four to six weeks. Accepts both agented and unagented proposals.

Types and topics: Catholic prayer and spirituality, family life, history, parish ministry, theology, no fiction or children's books

Guidelines: *www.avemariapress.com/manuscript-submissions*

B&H PUBLISHING GROUP

1 Lifeway Plaza, MSN 188, Nashville, TN 37234
www.bhpublishinggroup.com
Ashley Gorman, strategic acquisitions
Chris Thompson, academic acquisitions
Michelle Prater Burke, publisher, B&H Kids

Denomination: Southern Baptist

Parent company: LifeWay Christian Resources

Submissions: "Because we believe Every Word Matters, we seek to provide innovative, intentional content that is grounded in biblical truth." Agents only. Publishes ninety titles per year; receives thousands of submissions annually. First-time authors: 10%. Responds in two to three months. Bible version: CSB.

Royalty: on net, advance

Types and topics: Christian living, leadership, reference, women, Bible-study helps, church growth, college textbooks, evangelism, theology, marriage, parenting, worship, children's

Imprints: B&H Books, B&H Kids, B&H Academic, Holman Bible Publishers, Holman Reference, Broadman Church Supplies, B&H Español

Guidelines: none

Tip: "Be informed that the market in general is very crowded with the book you might want to write. Do the research before submitting."

BAAL HAMON PUBLISHERS

244 Fifth Ave., Ste. T279, New York, NY 10001 | 646-233-4017
publishers@baalhamon.com | *www.baalhamon.com*
Temitope Oyetomi, managing and acquisitions editor

Parent company: Joy and Truth Christian Ministry

Submissions: Publishes twenty to thirty books per year; receives 300 proposals annually. First-time authors: 30%. Length: 60,000 words. Email proposal with sample chapters. Responds in three to six weeks. Bible version: NKJV.

Royalty: 30% on net, advance sometimes

Guidelines: *www.baalhamonpublishers.com/guidelines.html*

Types and topics: fiction (general, historical), biographies, Christian living, devotionals, general nonfiction, theology, African-American

Tip: "For nonfiction, include a cursory highlight of your book's comparative advantage over similar books."

BAKER ACADEMIC

6030 E. Fulton Rd., Ada, MI 49301 | 616-676-9185
submissions@bakeracademic.com | *bakerpublishinggroup.com/bakeracademic*

Parent company: Baker Publishing Group

Submissions: Publishes fifty titles per year. First-time authors: 10%. Accepts manuscripts through agents, submission services, or editor's personal contacts at writers conferences.

Royalty: standard, advance

Types and topics: religious academic books, professional books for students and church leaders

Guidelines: *bakerpublishinggroup.com/bakeracademic/contact/submitting-a-proposal*

BAKER BOOKS

6030 E. Fulton Rd., Ada, MI 49301 | 616-676-9185
bakerpublishinggroup.com/bakerbooks
Rebekah Guzman, editorial director
Brian Thomasson, senior acquisitions editor
Rachel Jacobson, acquisitions editor

Parent company: Baker Publishing Group
Submissions: No unsolicited proposals. Agents only.
Types and topics: family, parenting, business, leadership, marriage, Christian living, spiritual growth, personal growth, self-help, memoir/personal narrative, biography, cultural engagement, theology, apologetics, church life, ministry resources
Guidelines: *bakerpublishinggroup.com/contact/submission-policy*

BARBOUR PUBLISHING, INC.

PO Box 719, Uhrichsville, OH 44683 | 740-922-6045
submissions@barbourbooks.com | *www.barbourbooks.com*
Annie Tipton, senior acquisitions editor

Submissions: Agents only.
Types and topics: fiction, popular Bible reference, devotions, gift books, Christian classics, children's, practical Christian living
Guidelines: *www.barbourbooks.com/frequently-asked-questions*

BEAMING BOOKS

510 Marquette Ave., Minneapolis, MN 55403
www.beamingbooks.com
Andrew DeYoung, director of product development

Parent company: 1517 Media-Books
Denomination: Evangelical Lutheran Church in America
Submissions: Publishes twenty-four books per year; receives 250. First-time authors: 50%. Length: 500 words for picture book. Submit proposal with sample chapters or full manuscript through the website. Responds in three months. Bible: NIV, CEB.
Royalty: varies, advance
Types and topics: board books for ages birth-3, picture books for ages 3-8, activity books for ages 3-8, early reader and first chapter books for ages 5-9, nonfiction books for ages 5-9 and 8-12, fiction for ages 8-12, activity books for families, devotionals for ages 0-12 and families
Guidelines: *beamingbooks.submittable.com/submit*
Tip: "Look at what we've published before. Read a few of our books before submitting."

BETHANY HOUSE PUBLISHERS

11400 Hampshire Ave. S., Bloomington, MN 55438 | 952-829-2500
bakerpublishinggroup.com/bethanyhouse
Raela Schoenherr, fiction acquisitions
Jeff Braun, nonfiction acquisitions

Parent company: Baker Publishing Group

Mission statement: to publish high-quality writings that represent historical Christianity and serve the diverse interests and concerns of evangelical readers

Submissions: Publishes seventy-five to eighty-five titles per year. Accepts manuscripts through agents only or writers met at conferences. No unsolicited submissions. Bible: NIV.

Types of books: offset paperback, hardcover, ebook

Royalty: varies by type of book and author, advance

Types and topics: devotionals, Christian living, family resources, theology, prayer; fiction: Amish, biblical, contemporary, contemporary and historical romance, historical, romantic suspense, Regency, fantasy

Guidelines: *bakerpublishinggroup.com/contact/submission-policy*

Tip: "The best opportunities for new authors come via literary agencies, conferences, writing communities, and author referrals. Get connected."

BLING!

100 Missionary Ridge, Birmingham, AL 35242 | 888-811-9934
editor@blingromance.com | *www.blingromance.com*
Jessica Nelson, acquisitions and managing editor

Parent company: Lighthouse Publishing of the Carolinas/Iron Stream Media

Submissions: Publishes eight books per year; receives forty proposals. First-time authors: 50%. Length: 80,000 words. Only accepts proposals from agents, author referrals, and conference meetings. Responds in three months. Bible: NIV.

Types of books: POD, ebook

Royalty: 40% net, no advance

Types and topics: romance fiction

Guidelines: *blingromance.com/submissions*

Tip: "At Bling! the first thing readers will notice is a solid, entertaining story. Think parables. The primary objective is to entertain and engage the contemporary reader. The stories are simultaneously character- and plot-driven, written by seasoned and debut novelists with unique voices. We seek clean, wholesome stories with God's moral truths woven into the story. Please avoid sermons in stories. Bling! sells into the general market."

BLINK

3900 Sparks Dr. S.E., Grand Rapids, MI 49546 | 616-698-3431
blinkyasubmissions@harpercollins.com | *www.blinkyabooks.com*

Parent company: HarperCollins Christian Publishing

Submissions: Query letter only via email, from agents only. All submissions must be PG or PG-13 content with no excessive profanity, violence, drug/alcohol use, etc. First-time authors: 20%. Length 60-90,000 words. Replies in four to six weeks. Bible: NIV.

Royalty: depends on the project, advance

Types and topics: YA fiction and nonfiction; novels with great contemporary love stories, serious issues with heart, fun summer reads, laugh-out-loud comedy, unique fantasy or magical realism, psychological suspense (but no horror), and stories featuring characters from diverse backgrounds; African-American and Hispanic audiences

Guidelines: none

Tip: "Please note that Blink books do not contain overt Christian content. These books are intended to be 'clean' teen reads aimed toward the ABA market. We seek established authors, authors with growing social-media platforms, and/or authors with strong literary connections. We look for novels that have bestseller or literary award potential. We look for nonfiction by well-known individuals with a strong platform to reach readers."

BMH BOOKS

PO Box 544, Winona Lake, IN 46590 | 800-348-2756, 574-372-3098
lcgates@bmhbooks.com | *www.BMHbooks.com*
Liz Cutler Gates, executive director

Denomination: Grace Brethren

Submissons: Shows preference to Grace Brethren authors who have important and worthwhile messages that need to be heard. Trinitarian theology, dispensational eschatology, emphasis on exegesis. Publishes three to five titles per year; receives thirty submissions annually. First-time authors: 50%. Query first; no unsolicited manuscripts. Requires accepted manuscripts by email. Length: 50-75,000 words or 128-256 pages. Prefers not to consider simultaneous submissions. Responds in three months. Bible version: prefers KJV, NIV.

Royalty: 8-10% on retail, rarely pays an advance

Types and topics: theology, the church, pastoral helps, Bible studies, Christian home, devotional studies, Christian living, deeper life

Guidelines: *bmhbooks.com/guidelines-submitting-manuscripts*

Tip: "Most open to a small-group study book or text for Bible college/ Bible institute and biblically based, timeless discipleship material."

BOLD VISION BOOKS

PO Box 2011, Friendswood, TX 77549-2011 | 832-569-4282
boldvisionbooks@gmail.com | www.boldvisionbooks.com
Karen Porter, senior acquisitions editor
Gloria Penwell-Holtzlander, acquisitions editor, BVBGloria@gmail.com

Mission statement: to help authors navigate the difficult and ever-changing publishing industry

Submissions: Publishes twelve to fourteen titles per year; receives 100. First-time authors: 80%. Length: 50-90,000 words. Email query only. Prefers submissions from agents and writers met at conferences. Responds in three months. Bible: NIV, NLT, NKJV.

Types of books: offset paperback, hardcover, POD, ebook; first print run 3,000-5,000

Royalty: 25-50%; advance sometimes

Types and topics: Christian living, women's, narrative nonfiction, fiction (contemporary, historical, romance, mystery), YA fiction

Imprints: Bold Vision Books (Christian living and fiction), Nuts 'n Bolts (craft books on writing, speaking, and leadership), Optasia Books (books from beloved pastors)

Guidelines: *www.boldvisionbooks.com/new-page-1*

Tip: "Send us a fresh approach to a timeless truth. Do your best work on your proposal. Show us you understand the industry and have invested in your growth as a writer."

BRAZOS PRESS

6030 E. Fulton Rd., Ada, MI 49301 | 616-676-9185
submissions@brazospress.com | bakerpublishinggroup.com/brazospress
Katelyn Beaty, acquisitions editor

Parent company: Baker Publishing Group

Submissions: Publishes books that creatively draw on the riches of our catholic Christian heritage to deepen our understanding of God's creation and inspire faithful reflection and engagement. Authors typically hold advanced degrees and have established publishing platforms.

Guidelines: *bakerpublishinggroup.com/brazospress/contact/submitting-a-proposal*

BRIDGE LOGOS

17750 N.W. 115th Ave., Bldg. 200, Ste. 220, Alachua, FL 32615 | 386-462-2525
swooldridge@bridgelogos.com | *www.bridgelogos.com*
Peggy Hildebrand, acquisitions editor, phildebrand@bridgelogos.com

Submissions: Publishes classics, books by Spirit-filled authors, and inspirational books that appeal to the general evangelical market. Publishes forty titles per year; receives 200 submissions annually. First-time authors: 30%. Accepts manuscripts through agents or authors. Email proposal with three to five chapters. Length: 250 pages. Responds in six weeks. Prefers accepted manuscripts by email.

Royalty: 10% on net, rarely pays advance

Types and topics: Bible study, biographies of notable Christians, business, finance, personal money management, Christian living, contemporary issues, devotionals/personal growth, encouragement, eschatology, evangelism, families and marriage, Messianic work, material on our nation's heritage (history and patriotism), men's issues, political issues, prayer, singles, social issues, Spirit-filled topics, timely topics, unusual outreach ministries, women's issues, youth, African American, Hispanic

Imprint: Synergy

Guidelines: *www.bridgelogos.com/Manuscript_Submission.html*

Tip: "Looking for well-written, timely books that are aimed at the needs of people and that glorify God. Have a great message, a well-written manuscript, and a specific plan and willingness to market your book. Looking for previously published authors with an active ministry who are experts on their subjects."

BRIMSTONE FICTION

1440 W. Taylor St., Ste. 449, Chicago, IL 60607 | 224-339-4159
brimstonefiction@gmail.com | *www.brimstonefiction.com*
Rowena Kuo, CEO and executive editor
Meaghan Burnett, CFO and marketing director

Submissions: Brimstone Fiction is geared for YA through adult readers who enjoy speculative fiction and chiller thrillers with supernatural or paranormal elements. Publishes eight to twelve books per year; receives sixty proposals. First-time authors: 60%. Length:

60-100,000 words. Submit proposal with sample chapters or full manuscript by email or through the website. Prefers submissions from agents. Responds in six to eight weeks. Bible: NIV.

Types of books: POD, ebook

Royalty: 30% of profits, no advance

Types and topics: science fiction, YA fantasy and science fiction, suspense, mystery, action and adventure, romance, supernatural, paranormal, paranormal romance, paranormal suspense, contemporary women's, historical/medieval fiction, time travel

Also does: short and full-length films

Guidelines: *brimstonefiction.com/submission-guidelines*

Tip: "We welcome new and multipublished authors and/or authors with or without agents. If you have a good story, come and meet us at writers conferences or through our website."

BROADSTREET PUBLISHING

8646 Eagle Creek Cir., Ste. 210, Savage, MN 55378 | 855-935-2000
proposals@broadstreetpublishing.com | *www.broadstreetpublishing.com*
Nina Derek, editor

Submissions: Prefers working with agents but will work directly with authors. Publishes more than 100 titles per year.

Types and topics: biographies, Majestic Expressions adult coloring books, Christian living, fiction, devotionals, and Bible promise books

Imprint: Belle City Gifts (women's journals, devotional journals, and planners)

Guidelines: *broadstreetpublishing.com/contact*

CANDLELIGHT ROMANCE

100 Missionary Ridge, Birmingham, AL 35242 | 888-811-9934
editor@candlelightfiction.com | *www.candlelightfiction.com*
Jessica Nelson, acquisitions editor

Parent company: Lighthouse Publishing of the Carolinas/Iron Stream Media

Submissions: Publishes four books per year; receives twenty proposals. First-time authors: 50%. Length: 55-80,000 words. Only accepts proposals from agents, author referrals, and conference meetings. Responds in three months. Bible: NIV.

Types of books: POD, ebook

Royalty: 40% net, no advance

Types and topics: inspirational contemporary romance fiction

Guidelines: *www.candlelightfiction.com/submissions*

Tip: "At Candlelight we agree that a romance novel should first entertain. In doing so, the story should have a strong action plot, emotional plot, and faith plot. Candlelight envisions romance as a novel incorporating depth of character as relationships develop. Romance can be exhibited in the worst of trials and circumstances or encased in a lovely evening of moonlight and roses. Candlelight stories may focus on a soft glow, an illumination of heart and soul, a flame of emotion, and/or a light to one's spiritual journey. Our realistic love stories are designed to entertain, encourage, inspire, and enlighten. We seek clean, wholesome stories with God's moral truths woven into the story. Please avoid sermons in stories. Candlelight sells into the general market."

CASCADE BOOKS

199 W. 8th Ave., Ste. 3, Eugene, OR 97401 | 541-344-1528
www.wipfandstock.com/imprint/cascade-3

Parent company: Wipf and Stock
Types of books: POD, ebook
Types and topics: theology, religion
Guidelines: *wipfandstock.com/submitting-a-proposal*

CASCADIA PUBLISHING HOUSE

126 Klingerman Rd., Telford, PA 18969
editor@CascadiaPublishingHouse.com | *CascadiaPublishingHouse.com*
Michael A. King, publisher, editor

Submissions: Query only by mail or email.
Types and topics: creative, thought-provoking, Anabaptist-related material
Guidelines: *www.cascadiapublishinghouse.com/submit.htm*
Tip: "All Cascadia books receive rigorous evaluation and some form of peer or consultant review."

CATHOLIC BOOK PUBLISHING CORP.

77 W. End Rd., Totowa, NJ 07572 | 973-890-2400
info@catholicbookpublishing.com | *www.catholicbookpublishing.com*
Anthony Buono, editor

Denomination: Catholic
Submissions: Primarily assigns books but will look at mailed queries. No simultaneous submissions or submissions from agents. Responds in two to three months. Publication in twelve to fifteen months.

Royalty: no royalty or advances, outright purchases
Imprint: Resurrection Press (see separate entry)
Types and topics: liturgical books, Bibles, missals, prayer books
Guidelines: *www.catholicbookpublishing.com/page/faq#manuscript*

CHALICE PRESS

483 E. Lockwood Ave., Ste. 100, St. Louis, MO 63119 | 800-366-3383
submissions@chalicepress.com | chalicepress.com
Brad Lyons, publisher

Submissions: Open to receiving any publishing proposal that "aligns with our mission to publish resources inviting all people into deeper relationship with God, equipping them as disciples of Jesus Christ, and sending them into ministries as the Holy Spirit calls them. Particularly interested in publishing content by and for women, young adults (age 18 to 35), and racial/ethnic cultures for our academic, congregational leadership, and general audiences." Send email query only initially.

Types and topics: academic (homiletics, biblical studies, theology, Christian education); congregational leadership (preaching, evangelism, hospitality, leadership development, discipleship/equipping ministries); general (faith and life, inspiration/devotion, Bible study/application, mission/evangelism)

Guidelines: *www.chalicepress.com/AuthorGuidelines.aspx*

Tip: "Our theological tradition is evangelistic (we share with others our experience of God), inclusive (we are guests at a table where everyone is welcome), and mission-oriented (our gratitude to God compels us to serve others)."

CHARISMA HOUSE

600 Rinehart Rd., Lake Mary, FL 32746 | 407-333-0600
charismahouse@charismamedia.com | www.charismahouse.com
Maureen Eha, acquisitions editor

Mission statement: to inspire and equip people to live a Spirit-led life and walk in the divine purpose for which they were called

Submissions: Accepts proposals only through agents. Publishes 150 titles per year; receives 1,500 submissions annually. First-time authors: 65%. Reprints books. Length: 55,000 words. Responds in one to two months.

Royalty: on net or outright purchase, advance

Topics and types: Charisma House: Charismatic/Pentecostal perspective on Christian living, work of the Holy Spirit, prophecy, prayer, Scripture, adventures in evangelism and missions, popular theology. Siloam: living in good health—body, mind, and spirit, including alternative medicine; diet and nutrition; and physical, emotional, and psychological wellness; prefers manuscripts from certified doctors, nutritionists, trainers, and other medical professionals. Frontline: contemporary political and social issues from a Christian perspective. Realms: adult Christian fiction in the supernatural, speculative genre, 80-120,000 words; also considers historical or biblical fiction if supernatural element is substantial. Excel: targeted toward success in the workplace and businesses. Casa Creación: books in Spanish; contact: 800-987-8432; *casacreacion@charismamedia.com*; *www.casacreacion.com*.

CHICKEN SOUP FOR THE SOUL BOOKS
See listing in the periodicals section, "**Adult Markets**."

CHOSEN
6030 E. Fulton Rd., Ada, MI 49301 | 616-676-9185
bakerpublishinggroup.com/chosen
Jane Campbell, editorial director
Kim Bangs, senior acquisitions editor
David Sluka, acquisitions editor

Parent company: Baker Publishing Group
Mission statement: to publish thoughtful, accessible books that recognize the gifts and ministry of the Holy Spirit and help readers live more empowered and effective lives for Jesus Christ
Submissions: Publishes thirty to forty books annually. First-time authors: 10-15%. Length: 40-50,000 words. Email query letter or proposal with sample chapters. Responds in one to two months.
Types of books: offeset paperback, hardcover, ebook
Royalty: starts at 16%, advance
Types and topics: Charismatic, prayer, prophecy, healing, spiritual warfare
Guidelines: *bakerpublishinggroup.com/chosen/contact/preparing-a-proposal-for-chosen-books*
Tip: "Today, with almost no retail bookshelves left, the author's platform has become the new bookshelf; and we are partnering with authors who are growing their platforms. So tell us about your monthly/annual website traffic; number of followers on Facebook, Instagram, and Twitter; size of email list; number of people you address annually; countries outside the US where you speak."

CHRISTIAN FOCUS PUBLICATIONS

Geanies House, Fearn, Tain, Ross-shire IV20 1TW, Scotland, UK |
01862 871011
submissions@christianfocus.com | *www.christianfocus.com*
Willie MacKenzie, director
Catherine MacKenzie, children's editor, Catherine.Mackenzie@christianfocus.com

> **Submissions:** Submit proposal with two chapters by email or mail.
>
> **Types and topics:** Christian Focus: popular works, including biographies, commentaries, basic doctrine, and Christian living. Mentor: written at a level suitable for Bible college and seminary students, pastors, and other serious readers, including commentaries, doctrinal studies, examination of current issues, and church history. Christian Heritage: classic writings from the past. Children's: Bible story books, devotionals, craft books, puzzle books, activity books, game books, material for family devotions, biography series (Trailblazers for ages 9-14, retells the stories of well-known Christians past and present; Torchbearers for ages 8-11 about real martyrs), and several fiction series
>
> **Imprint:** CF 4 Kids
>
> **Guidelines:** adults: *www.christianfocus.com/about/adult-guidelines* | children: *www.christianfocus.com/about/childrens-guidelines*
>
> **Tip:** "Read our website please. Don't send us stuff we don't publish."

CISTERCIAN PUBLICATIONS

dutton@ohio.edu | *www.cistercianpublications.org*
Marsha L. Dutton, executive editor

> **Submissions:** Prefers a proposal. All submissions must be accompanied by a summary form that's available on the website. Before submitting a manuscript, request the style sheet and instructions.
>
> **Types and topics:** studies on the Christian monastic tradition and monographs reflecting contemplative monastic spirituality
>
> **Guidelines:** *www.cistercianpublications.org/Contact/manuscript*

CLADACH PUBLISHING

PO Box 336144, Greeley, CO 80633 | 970-371-9530
cathy@cladach.com | *www.cladach.com*
Catherine Lawton, publisher, editor

> **Submissions:** Publishes four titles per year; receives fifty proposals. First-time authors: 50%. Considers book proposals from authors

met at writers conferences. Email query letter only. Length: 120-300 pages. Responds in three months. Bible: NIV, NRSV.

Types of books: offset and POD paperback, ebook, audiobook

Royalty: 10-20%, $100 advance

Types and topics: creative nonfiction, memoir, poetry, fiction (frontier, literary), nature writings, devotional, inner healing/wholeness

Guidelines: *cladach.com/authors*

Tip: "We are accepting very few unsolicited manuscripts."

CLC PUBLICATIONS

PO Box 1449, Fort Washington, PA 19034 | 215-542-1242
submissions@clcpublications.com | www.clcpublications.com
Dave Fessenden, editorial coordinator

Parent company: CLC Ministries International

Mission statement: books for the deeper life

Submissions: Publishes twelve titles per year; receives 200 submissions. First-time authors: 30%. Length: 144-320 pages, 35,000-80,000 words. Submit proposal with sample chapters or full manuscript via email, mail, or website form. Prefers submissions from agents and writers met at conferences. Cold contacts from authors: Use the website form. Responds in one to two months. Bible: ESV.

Types of books: offset paperback, ebook, audiobook; first print run 2,000-3,500

Royalty: 12-14% net, advance sometimes

Types and topics: Christian living, Christian growth, deeper life

Guidelines: *www.clcpublications.com/about/prospective-authors-submissions*

Tip: "We prefer a book that speaks to an international audience, not only North America."

COLLEGE PRESS PUBLISHING

PO Box 1132, 2111 N. Main St., Ste. C, Joplin, MO 64801 | 800-289-3300
collpressjoplin@gmail.com | www.collegepress.com

Denomination: Christian Churches/Churches of Christ

Submissions: Requires a query or proposal first. Responds in two to three months.

Types and topics: Bible studies, topical studies (biblically based), apologetic studies, historical biographies of Christians

Guidelines: *www.collegepress.com/pages/for-authors*

CONCORDIA PUBLISHING HOUSE

3558 S. Jefferson Ave., St. Louis, MO 63118-3968 | 314-268-1080
ideas@chph.org | *www.cph.org*
Rev. Paul T. McCain, publisher, executive director of editorial,
paul.mccain@cph.org

Denomination: Lutheran Church, Missouri Synod
Submissions: Send proposal and sample chapters. Publication within two years. Responds in six weeks.
Types and topics: nonfiction, fiction, no longer looking for children's books
Guidelines: *www.cph.org/t-about-faq.aspx*

CROSSLINK PUBLISHING

558 E. Castle Pines Pkwy., Ste. B4117, Castle Rock, CO 80108 | 888-697-4851
publisher@crosslinkpublishing.com | *www.crosslinkpublishing.com*
Rick Bates, managing editor

Parent company: CrossLink Ministries
Submissions: As a small publisher, it is author focused, processes are nimble, and it prides itself on having the most transparent and participative publishing process in the industry. Publishes thirty-five titles per year. Receives 500 submissions annually. First-time authors: 85%. Requires manuscript submission on the website. Length: 12-60,000 words. Responds in a week.
Royalty: 10% of retail, 20% for ebooks, no advance
Types and topics: adult fiction, Bible studies, devotional, inspirational, meditations, spiritual-growth areas
Imprint: New Harbor Press
Guidelines: *www.crosslinkpublishing.com/submit-a-manuscript*
Tip: "We are particularly interested in providing books that help Christians succeed in their daily walk (inspirational, devotional, small groups, etc.)."

CROSSRIVER MEDIA GROUP

PO Box 187, Brewster, KS 67732 | 785-269-4730
submissions@crossrivermedia.com | *www.crossrivermedia.com*
Debra L. Butterfield, editorial director, deb@crossrivermedia.com

Mission statement: to glorify God by providing high-quality books and materials that ignite a woman's relationship with God and inspire her to lead a life that honors Him
Submissions: Publishes four to eight titles per year; receives more than 100 submissions annually. First-time authors: 50%. Accepts

but doesn't require submissions through agents. Length: 60-80,000 words. Email proposal with sample chapters. Responds in four to five months. Bible: any except NIV.

Types of books: POD, ebook
Royalty: 8-12%, negotiable, no advance
Types and topics: inspirational fiction for adults (contemporary, historical, biblical, mystery/suspence, romance), Bible studies, Christian living, family and marriage, inspirational, women's
Guidelines: *www.crossrivermedia.com/about/manuscript-submissions*
Tip: "Know how your book fits our mission statement and include that information in your proposal."

THE CROSSROAD PUBLISHING COMPANY
submissions@crossroadpublishing.com | www.crossroadpublishing.com

Submissions: Open to unsolicited proposals; email submissions only. Responds in six to eight weeks. Accepts submissions from agents or authors.
Royalty: yes, no advance
Types and topics: spirituality, Christian living, theology
Guidelines: *www.crossroadpublishing.com/crossroad/static/for-authors*

CROSSWAY
1300 Crescent St., Wheaton, IL 60187 | 630-682-4300
submissions@crossway.org | www.crossway.org
Jill Carter, editorial administrator (submit to her)

Parent company: Good News Publishers
Submissions: Publishes eighty titles per year; receives more than 1,000 annually. First-time authors: 1%. Length: 25,000 words and up. Email a query first. Responds in six to eight weeks. Bible: ESV.
Royalty: varies, variable advance
Types and topics: biblical studies, Christian living, current issues, academic, professional
Guidelines: *www.crossway.org/submissions*
Tip: "Be sure to look at our guidelines and see if your project fits. A well-written proposal is vital."

CSS PUBLISHING GROUP, INC.
5450 N. Dixie Hwy., Lima, OH 45807-9559 | 419-227-1818
editor@csspub.com | www.csspub.com
Missy Cotrell, managing editor

Submissions: Serves the needs of pastors, worship leaders, and parish program planners in the broad Christian mainline of the American church. Prefers query first but will also look at proposals with a sample chapter(s) by email or mail. Publishes fifteen titles per year; receives 500-1,000 submissions annually. First-time authors: 50%. Length: 100-125 pages. Responds in three weeks to six months. Bible version: NRSV.

Royalty: none, no advance, outright purchase

Types and topics: lectionary-based resources for worship, preaching, group study, drama, and use with children (but not children's books); sermons, preaching, and worship resources for special seasons and days of the church year and special themes or emphasis; children's object lessons and sermons; resources for working with youth; pastoral aids, such as materials to assist in counseling; easy-to-perform dramas and pageants for all age groups, primarily for Advent/Christmas/Epiphany and Lent/Easter (no full-length plays); parish-tested materials for use in education, youth ministry, stewardship, and church growth; a few general titles

Guidelines: *store.csspub.com/page.php?Custom%20Pages=10*

Imprints: Fairway Press (see separate listing in "Independent Book Publishers"), B.O.D. (Books On Demand)

Tip: "We're looking for authors who will help with the marketing of their books."

DAVID C. COOK

4050 Lee Vance Dr., Colorado Springs, CO 80918 | 719-536-0100
www.davidccook.org
Michael Covington, senior acquisitions and development editor
Susan McPherson, acquisitions (women, familiy)
Stephanie Bennett, acquisitions (teens, youth leaders)

Mission statement: to equip the Church with Christ-centered resources for making and teaching disciples

Submissions: Only proposals from agents and writers met at conferences. Publishes forty books per year; receives 1,200 proposals. First-time authors: 10%. Responds in one month. Bible: any. Length: 45-50,000 words.

Types of books: offset paperback, hardcover, POD, ebook

Also does: Sunday school curriculum, Standard Lesson Commentary

Royalty: 12-22%, advance varies

Types and topics: Christian living, spiritual growth, discipleship, leadership, marriage, parenting, women's, men's, church resources, some picture books

Guidelines: *shop.davidccook.org/pages/frequently-asked-questions*

Tip: "We look for significant platform, excellent writing, and relevant content."

DIVINE MOMENTS BOOKS

See listing in periodicals section, "**Adult Markets.**"

DOVE CHRISTIAN PUBLISHERS

PO Box 611, Bladensburg, MD 20710-0611 | 240-342-3293
editorial@dovechristianpublishers.com | www.dovechristianpublishers.com
Raenita Wiggins, acquisitions editor

Parent company: Kingdom Christian Enterprises

Mission statement: "We entertain, edify, equip and encourage people through products that glorify and honor Jesus Christ and His kingdom. In addition, we provide new and emerging Christian authors with a forum for their creative and kingdom-building voices."

Submissions: Submit proposal with full manuscript through the website. Publishes ten books per year; receives 300 proposals. First-time authors: 95%. Responds in three to four weeks. Length: 100-220 pages. Bible: NIV.

Books: POD, ebooks, hardcover

Royalty: 10-25%, no advance

Types and topics: Christian living, self-help, devotionals, relationships, fiction (romance, fantasy, suspense, historical, thrillers, biblical, adventure), children's, African-American

Guidelines: *www.dovechristianpublishers.com/publish-with-us*

Tip: "Author should establish a platform and familiarize themselves with book marketing and promotion prior to submission."

EERDMANS BOOKS FOR YOUNG READERS

4035 Park East Ct. S.E., Grand Rapids, MI 49546 | 800-253-7521
kmerz@eerdmans.com | www.eerdmans.com/youngreaders
Kathleen Merz, acquisitions and managing editor

Parent company: Wm. B. Eerdmans Publishing Co.

Mission statement: to engage young minds with books—books that are honest, wise, and hopeful; books that delight us with their storyline, characters, or good humor; books that inform, inspire, and entertain

Submissions: Submit by mail; prefers from agents. Send a proposal with three chapters for book length or complete manuscript for picture books. Publishes sixteen to twenty titles per year; receives 1,500 submissions annually. First-time authors: 5-10%. Length: picture books, 1,000 words; middle-grade books, 15-30,000 words. Publication within one year for novels, two to three years for picture books. Responds in four months if interested. Ethnic books: African-American.

Types of books: hardcover, ebook, audiobook

Royalty: on net, advance varies

Types and topics: picture books: animal, contemporary, folktales, history, humor, multicultural, nature/environment, poetry, religion, special needs, social issues; middle grade: adventure, contemporary, history, humor, multicultural, nature/environment, religion, social issues

Guidelines: *www.eerdmans.com/Pages/YoungReaders/EBYR-Guidelines.aspx*

Tip: "We strongly encourage writers and illustrators to become familiar with our publications and the general trade children's book market before submitting any material. Please review our books in our catalog, on our website, or at your local library or bookstore to determine whether your manuscript is appropriate for us."

WM. B. EERDMANS PUBLISHING CO.

4035 Park East Ct. S.E., Grand Rapids, MI 49546 | 800-253-7521, 616-459-4591
info@eerdmans.com | *www.eerdmans.com*
James Ernest, editor

Submissions: Publishes about 100 titles per year. Accepts manuscripts through agents or authors. Email proposal only. Responds in six weeks.

Royalty: yes, some advances

Topics and types: adult nonfiction, textbooks, reference, biblical studies, theology, religious history and biography, ethics, spirituality, Christian living, ministry, social issues, contemporary cultural issues

Imprint: Eerdmans Books for Young Readers (see separate listing)

Guidelines: *www.eerdmans.com/Pages/About/Submission-Guidelines. aspx*

Tip: "Review submission guidelines carefully and check website for suitability. Target readerships range from academic to semipopular. We are publishing a growing number of books in Christian life, spirituality, and ministry."

eLECTIO PUBLISHING

4206 S. Mentor Ave., Springfield, MO 65804 | 972-987-0015
submissions@electiopublishing.com | *www.electiopublishing.com*

Submissions: Publishes sixty to 100 titles per year; receives 1,000 annually. First-time authors: 70-80%. Length: 25-100,000 words. Email full manuscript. Responds in three months.

Royalty: 20%, no advance

Types and topics: Christian living, fiction (historical, romance, mystery), Bible studies, memoir, YA, African-American, Hispanic

Guidelines: *www.electiopublishing.com/submit/submission-guidelines*

Tip: "Please read carefully the submissions guidelines listed on website."

ELK LAKE PUBLISHING, INC.

35 Dogwood Dr., Plymouth, MA 02360-3166 | 508-746-1734
Deb@ElkLakePublishingInc.com | *ElkLakePublishingInc.com*
Deb Haggerty, publisher & editor-in-chief
Linda Rondeau, senior acquisitions editor—fiction,
   LindaRondeau@gmail.com
Susan K. Stewart, senior acquisitions editor—nonfiction,
   SKStewart@elklakepublishinginc.com

Mission statement: to captivate our readers and carry them to places of escape, encouragement, education, and entertainment—to broaden their horizons and urge them to new heights. More than anything else, we want to point people to Jesus Christ.

Submissions: Publishes fifty titles per year; receives 150 plus. First-time authors: 85%. Length: fiction, 80-100,000 words. Email proposal with sample chapters, or submit them through the website form. Prefers submissions from agents or writers met at conferences. Replies in one month. Bible: NLT, ESV.

Types of books: POD, ebook, hardcover, audiobook

Royalty: 40%, no advance

Types and topics: romance to speculative fiction, contemporary to historical, children's, middle-grade, young adult; nonfiction with a twist; no Amish fiction, westerns, Bible studies, devotionals, poetry

Guidelines: *www.elklakepublishinginc.com/choose-best-publisher*

Tip: "Ensure the style sheet is followed as well as the guidelines. Ensure the proposal is free of errors and follows the guidelines completely."

EMPOWERED PUBLICATIONS, INC.

529 County Road 31, Millry, AL 36558 | 251-754-9335
editor@empoweredpublicationsinc.com | www.empoweredpublicationsinc.com

Denomination: Conservative Pentecostal (Assemblies of God, Church of God, independent Pentecostals)

Submissions: Publishes thirty-six titles per year; receives 500 annually. First-time authors: 80%. Length: 35,000 for nonfiction, 65-80,000 for fiction. Email or mail proposal with full manuscript. Replies in two weeks. Bible version: KJV.

Royalty: 8-30%

Types and topics: Christian living; theology; biographies; pneumatology; historical, biblical, contemporary fiction for all ages

Guidelines: *www.empoweredpublicationsinc.com/about-us.html*

Tip: "We prefer submissions from those with an established ministry, but will consider works from a lay person recommended by a minister personally known to us. Potential authors must agree with our Statement of Faith. No prosperity preaching."

ENCLAVE PUBLISHING

24 W. Camelback Rd. A-635, Phoenix, AZ 85013
acquisitions@enclavepublishing.com | www.enclavepublishing.com
Steve Laube, publisher and acquisitions editor

Submissions: Enclave is a focused publisher of Christian fantasy and science fiction. Publishes twelve titles per year; receives more than 300 submissions annually. Responds in two to three months. First-time authors: 20-30%. Submit proposal and full manuscript through the website form. Length: 70-150,000 words.

Royalty: varies

Types and topics: only speculative fiction (sci-fi, fantasy, supernatural) for adults and YA

Guidelines: *www.enclavepublishing.com/guidelines*

Tip: "Keep word count above 70,000 words and below 150,000. Too often we are sent books that are either far too short or extremely long."

EVERGREEN PRESS

5601-D Nevius Rd., Mobile, AL 36619 | 251-861-2525
brian@evergreenpress.com | www.evergreenpress.com
Brian Banashak and Kathy Banashak, editors-in-chief

Parent company: Genesis Communications

Mission statement: publishes books that empower people for breakthrough living by being practical, biblical, and engaging

Submissions: Publishes thirty titles per year; receives 250 submissions annually. First-time authors: 40%. Accepts manuscripts through agents or authors. Submit proposal, query, or full manuscript with the "Author and Book Submission Form" on the website. Length: 96-160 pages. Responds in four to six weeks.

Royalty: on net, no advance

Types and topics: Christian living, family and parenting, personal growth, business and finances, humor and pets, children's picture books, youth books, devotional and prayer, health and fitness, and recovery; fiction: allegory, historical, fantasy and science fiction, mystery, romance, youth

Also does: booklets

Imprints: Gazelle Press, Axiom Press (POD for short runs)

Guidelines: *evergreenpress.com/for-authors*

Tip: "Most open to books with a specific market (targeted, not general) that the author is qualified to write for and that is relevant to today's believers and seekers. Author must also be open to editorial direction."

FAITH ALIVE CHRISTIAN RESOURCES

1700 28th St. S.E., Grand Rapids, MI 49508-1407 | 800-333-8300, 616-224-0728
rvanderhart@crcna.org | *www.faithaliveresources.org*
Ruth Vanderhart, managing editor

Denomination: Christian Reformed

Submissions: Submit by mail or email. Responds in one month.

Types and topics: educational curricula for children, teens, and adults; Bible studies; church leadership and training materials

FAITHWORDS

1 Franklin Park, 6100 Tower Cir., Ste. 210, Franklin, TN 37067 | 615-221-0996
www.faithwords.com

Parent company: Hachette Book Group

Submissions: Through agents only. Publishes seventy-five books per year; receives 350 proposals. First-time authors: 50%. Length: 50,000 words. Responds in one month. Bible: ESV, NIV.

Types of books: offset paperback, hardcover, ebook

Royalty: 10% and up, advance

Types and topics: for Christian women ages 25-45: parenting, marriage, Christian living, social issues, spiritual issues, African-American, Hispanic

Guidelines: *www.hachettebookgroup.com/about/faqs/#submissions*
Tip: "Have a clear, well-written proposal and a solid platform."

FATHER'S PRESS

590 N.W. 1921 St. Rd., Kingsville, MO 64061-9312 | 816-566-0654
mike@fatherspress.com | *www.fatherspress.com*
Mike Smitley, editor

> **Submissions:** Accepts manuscripts only through authors; no agents. Send proposal. Responds in four weeks. Bible versions: KJV, ESV.
>
> **Types and topics:** fiction (contemporary or historical), historical nonfiction, reference, children's books, biblical studies, theology, ethics, literature, religious history, regional history, cookbooks, self-help, Christian counseling
>
> **Guidelines:** *fatherspress.com/submission-guidelines*
>
> **Tip:** "Father's Press is a rapidly-growing, full-service publishing company dedicated to publishing well-written works by dynamic, energetic new authors who are frustrated with the endless barriers that have historically locked talented authors out of the writing profession."

FIREFLY SOUTHERN FICTION

100 Missionary Ridge, Birmingham, AL 35242 | 888-811-9934
fireflysouthernfiction@aol.com | *lpcbooks.com/firefly-southern-fiction*
Eva Marie Everson, managing editor

> **Parent company:** Lighthouse Publishing of the Carolinas/Iron Stream Media
>
> **Submissions:** Publishes four to six books per year; receives twenty-five proposals. First-time authors: 50%. Length: 75-85,000 words. Only accepts proposals from agents, author referrals, and conference meetings. Responds in three months. Bible: NIV, KJV, RSV.
>
> **Types of books:** POD, ebook
>
> **Royalty:** 40% net, no advance
>
> **Types and topics:** southern fiction
>
> **Guidelines:** *lpcbooks.com/firefly*
>
> **Tip:** "Write well. Edit well. Do not send first drafts. Remember that writing is a business as well as a craft."

FIRST STEPS PUBLISHING

PO Box 571, Gleneden Beach, OR 97388 | 541-961-7641
rj@FirstStepsPublishing.com | *www.FirstStepsPublishing.com*

RJ McRoberts, senior acquisitions editor

> **Submissions:** Publishes three to five titles per year; receives 400-500 submissions. First-time authors: 90%. Length: children's, 700 words minimum; fiction and nonfiction, 50-80,000 words. Email proposal with sample chapters through the website. Prefers to work with agents but occasionally accepts unsolicited submissions for specific genres. Responds in two to three months but only to writers who adhere to proper submission guidelines. Bible: NKJV, NIV.
>
> **Types:** offset paperback, POD, ebook, audiobook
>
> **Royalty:** 15-35%, higher for special cases, no advance
>
> **Types and topics:** fiction: action/adventure, mystery, thriller, historical; adventure; true stories; memoir; biography; creative nonfiction
>
> **Imprints:** White Parrot Press (children), West Wind Press (middle grade, young adult)
>
> **Guidelines:** *www.firststepspublishing.com/get-published*
>
> **Tip:** "Our acquisition editors are the first readers who decide whether a manuscript is worth pursuing. Put your best foot forward, and edit your manuscript until you are happy with every single word. This includes your query letter and proposal. If these concepts are foreign to you, learn them. If you just 'wing it,' we'll know; and your submission will be rejected. Do you know your target audience? Why would your book sell? Do you have a platform? Taking the time to learn what a publisher is looking for in an author will improve your chances of acquisition."

FOCUS ON THE FAMILY

8605 Explorer Dr., Colorado Springs, CO 80995 | 719-531-5181
www.focusonthefamily.com
Larry Weeden, acquisitions

> **Submissions:** Accepts manuscripts only via established literary agents or manuscript services.
>
> **Types and topics:** family advice topics, including resources about specific elements of marriage and parenting, encouragement for women, and topics for seniors

FORTRESS PRESS

PO Box 1209, Minneapolis, MN 55440-1209
www.fortresspress.com
Valerie Weaver-Zercher, acquisitions editor

Lil Copan, senior acquisitions editor

> **Denomination:** Evangelical Lutheran Church in America
> **Parent company:** 1517 Media-Books
> **Submissions:** Submit via the online form.
> **Types and topics:** scholarly works in biblical studies, theology, Christian history, spirituality, social justice, wisdom traditions, spiritual practices, Christian living, creativity, culture
> **Guidelines:** *fortresspress.com/submissions*
> **Tip:** "People in all stages of life hunger for meaning, understanding, spiritual growth, and to make a difference in the world. Fortress Press seeks to be an informed, valuable, and delightful companion—a change maker in readers' spiritual and intellectual journeys and a leader in key conversations. With fresh perspectives, compelling stories, and fearless explorations, our books inspire readers to build a better world."

FORWARD MOVEMENT

412 Sycamore St., Cincinnati, OH 45202-4110 | 800-543-1813
editorial@forwardmovement.org | *www.forwardmovement.org*
Richelle Thompson, managing editor, rthompson@forwardmovement.org

> **Denomination:** Episcopal
> **Submissions:** Focuses on discipleship. Submit through email. Responds in four to six weeks.
> **Also does:** PDF downloads, smartphone applications
> **Types and topics:** prayer, spiritual practices, stewardship, church traditions, emerging trends, Bible study
> **Guidelines:** *www.forwardmovement.org/Pages/About/Writers_ Guidelines.aspx*

THE FOUNDRY PUBLISHING

PO Box 419527, Kansas City, MO 64141
thefoundrypublishing.com
René McFarland, consumer product editor

> **Denomination:** Nazarene
> **Submissions:** Mail proposal to Attn: Product Development.
> **Types and topics:** Christian living, spiritual growth, ministry resources
> **Guidelines:** *www.nph.com/nphweb/html/bhol/FAQ.jsp*

FOUR CRAFTSMEN PUBLISHING

PO Box U, Lakeside, AZ 85929-0585 | 928-367-2076
info@fourcraftsmen.com | *www.fourcraftsmen.com*

CeCelia Jackson, editor in chief; Martin Jackson, publisher
> **Mission statement:** publishing truth that works for Christian readers
> **Submissions:** Publishes four to six books per year; receives five proposals. First-time authors: 100%. Length: 40-80,000 words. Submit proposal with sample chapters or full manuscript by email or mail. Responds in two weeks. Bible: NASB, NKJV, TLB, TEV.
> **Types of books:** POD, ebook, offset paperback, hardcover; print run 500
> **Royalty:** 10-60%, no advance
> **Types and topics:** testimony, Scripture studies, Christian living, finances, Bible analysis, spiritual warfare
> **Guidelines:** *fourcraftsmen.com/additional-info*
> **Tip:** "Original work, not compilation of source quotes. Necessary quotes correctly attributed and permissions provided."

FRANCISCAN MEDIA

28 W. Liberty St., Cincinnati, OH 45202 | 800-488-0488, 513-241-5615
info@franciscanmedia.org | www.FranciscanMedia.org
Mark Lombard, director, acquisitions, MLombard@FranciscanMedia.org
> **Denomination:** Catholic
> **Submissions:** Seeks manuscripts that inform and inspire adult Catholics, other Christians, and all who are seeking to better understand and live their faith. Goal is to help people "Live in love. Grow in faith." Not accepting unsolicited manuscripts. Publishes twenty to thirty books per year. Submit proposal by email or mail. Responds in one to three months. Length: 25,000-50,000 words or 100-250 pages. Bible: NRSV. No simultaneous submissions.
> **Royalty:** 10-14% on net, advance $1,000-3,000
> **Topics and types:** Christian living, spiritual growth, fiction
> **Guidelines:** *tinyurl.com/y29kt4do*

FRIENDS UNITED PRESS

101 Quaker Hill Dr., Richmond, IN 47374 | 765-962-7573
friendspress@fum.org | friendsunitedmeeting.org
Kristina Evans, managing editor
> **Denomination:** Quaker
> **Mission statement:** to energize and equip Friends through the power of the Holy Spirit to gather people into fellowships where Jesus Christ is known, loved, and obeyed as Teacher and Lord

Submissions: Email proposal with two or three chapters; responds in one to three months. Publishes two to five books per year; receives twenty-five proposals. First-time authors: 50%. Length: 120-350 pages.

Types of books: offset paperback, POD, hardcover, ebook

Royalty: 10-15%, no advance

Types and topics: nonfiction, fiction (historical, juvenile), children, juvenile, Quakerism, Quaker history, Quaker thought

Guidelines: by email

Tip: "Must relate to the Religious Society of Friends (Quakers), currently or in the past, or be strongly related to the work of Friends United Meeting."

GRACE ACRES PRESS

PO Box 22, Larkspur, CO 80118 | 303-681-9995
Anne@GraceAcresPress.com | www.GraceAcresPress.com
Anne R. Fenske, publisher

Mission statement: Growing Your Faith One Page at a Time

Submissions: Publishes six books per year; receives twenty. First-time authors: 75%. Length: 100-300 pages. Email or mail query letter only; or submit through the website. No agents. Responds in one month. Bible: NKJV, NIV.

Types of books: offset and POD paperback, hardcover, ebook; print run 500-2,000

Royalty: 10-15%, no advance

Types and topics: Bible study, evangelism, discipleship, missions, biography/memoir

Guidelines: by email

Tip: "Explain your contribution as a copartner in marketing your book."

GRACE PUBLISHING

PO Box 1233, Broken Arrow, OK 74013-1233 | 918-346-7960
editorial@grace-publishing.com | www.grace-publishing.com
Terri Kalfas, publisher

Parent company: The Jomága Group, LLC

Mission statement: to develop and distribute—with integrity and excellence—biblically based resources that challenge, encourage, teach, equip, and entertain Christians in their personal journeys

Submissions: Publishes eight titles per year; receives 200 submissions. First-time authors: 10%. Length: varies, fiction 40-80,000 words. For unsolicited work, email query only. However, for a completed manuscript accepts a two-page, double-spaced synopsis, three consecutive sample chapters (double-spaced), and a proposal as email attachments. Responds in six months. Bible: any. First-time authors: 10%.

Types of books: offset and POD paperback, ebook

Royalty: 12%, some flat fees, no advance

Types and topics: Christian living, Bible studies, fiction, devotional, compilation, counseling

Imprint: Jomága House

Guidelines: *grace-publishing.com/manuscript-submission*

Tip: "Need strong writing and a good platform."

GROUP PUBLISHING, INC.

1515 Cascade Ave., Loveland, CO 80538 | 970-669-3836
PuorgBus@group.com | *www.group.com*

Mission statement: We create experiences that help people grow in relationship with Jesus and each other.

Submissions: Publishes thirty titles per year; receives 200 submissions annually. First-time authors: 10%. Length: 128-250 pages. Email or mail proposal with sample chapters. Responds in three months. Bible: NLT.

Types of books: offset paperback, hardcover, ebook; print run 3,000

Royalty: 8-10% net, $2,000 advance sometimes

Topics and types: church resources, Christian living, curriculum

Guidelines: *grouppublishingps.zendesk.com/hc/en-us/articles/211878258-Submissions*

Tip: "Most open to innovative and practical resources involving active/interactive learning that will help change lives. Tell our readers something they don't already know in a way that they've not seen before."

GUARDIAN ANGEL PUBLISHING, INC.

12430 Tesson Ferry Rd. #186, St. Louis, MO 63128 | 314-276-8482
editorial_staff@guardianangelpublishing.com |
www.guardianangelpublishing.com

Submissions: Publishes thirty-six to seventy titles per year; receives 100+ submissions annually. First-time authors: 5-10%. Length: picture book, 100 words; storybook, up to 5,000 words; chapter book, up to 25,000 words. Email complete manuscript. Responds in one to three months. Bible: no preference. Submit only during August.

Types of books: POD, ebook, CD, hardcover

Royalty: 30%, advance sometimes

Types and topics: all kinds of books for kids ages 2-12, nonfiction and fiction, Spanish and bilingual, ethnic audiences

Imprints: Wings of Faith, Chapbooks for Tweens, Littlest Angels, Academic Wings, Health & Hygiene, Animals & Pets, Angelic Harmony, Angel to Angel

Guidelines: *www.guardianangelpublishing.com/submissions.htm*

Tip: "Send your best story. Follow the directions and suggestions."

GUIDEPOSTS BOOKS

110 William St., Ste. 901, New York, NY 10038 | 212-251-8100
bookeditors@guideposts.org | *www.guideposts.org*
Jon Woodhams, fiction editor

Submissions: Extremely limited acquisitions. Accepts manuscripts through agents only. Publishes twenty to thirty titles per year.

Types and topics: inspirational memoir; Christian living; contemporary women's fiction focusing on faith, family, and friendships

GUIDING LIGHT WOMEN'S FICTION

100 Missionary Ridge, Birmingham, AL 35242 | 888-811-9934
submissions@guidinglightfiction.com | *shoplpc.com/guiding-light*
Karin Beery, managing editor

Parent company: Lighthouse Publishing of the Carolinas/Iron Stream Media

Mission statement: to publish compelling stories, beautifully written

Submissions: Publishes maximum of eight books per year; receives 100 proposals. First-time authors: 50%, enjoys working with. Length: 80-90,000 words. Only accepts proposals from agents, author referrals, and conference meetings. Responds in one to three months. Bible: NIV.

Types of books: POD, ebook, audiobook

Royalty: 40% net, no advance

Types and topics: women's fiction

Guidelines: *shoplpc.com/guiding-light-1*

Tip: "Be teachable. A willingness to learn will get you far."

HARAMBEE PRESS

100 Missionary Ridge, Birmingham, AL 35242 | 888-811-9934
harambeepresslpcbooks@gmail.com | *shoplpc.com/harambee-press*

Edwina Perkins, managing editor

> **Parent company:** Lighthouse Publishing of the Carolinas/Iron Stream Media
>
> **Mission statement:** giving voice to ethnic writers
>
> **Submissions:** Publishes four to eight books per year; receives sixty proposals. First-time authors: 50%. Length: 40-90,000 words. Email proposal with sample chapters. Only accepts proposals from agents, author referrals, and conference meetings. Responds in three months. Bible: NIV.
>
> **Types of books:** POD, ebook, audiobook
>
> **Royalty:** 40% on net, no advance
>
> **Types and topics:** marriage, Christian living, devotionals, memoirs, parenting; fiction: women's, romance, suspense, mystery; books for African-American, Hispanic, and Asian audiences
>
> **Guidelines:** *shoplpc.com/harambee*
>
> **Tip:** "Follow any additional instructions when asked."

HARBOURLIGHT BOOKS

PO Box 1738, Aztec, NM 87410
inquiry@harbourlightbooks.com | *www.pelicanbookgroup.com*
Nicola Martinez, editor-in-chief

> **Parent company:** Pelican Book Group
>
> **Submissions:** Novels 25-80,000 words. Interested in series ideas. Accepts unagented submissions. Responds to queries in one month, full manuscript in three months. Email submissions through the website form.
>
> **Royalty:** 40% on download, 7% on print, nominal advance
>
> **Types and topics:** fiction: action-adventure, mystery (cozy or other), suspense, crime drama, police procedural, family saga, westerns, women's
>
> **Guidelines:** *pelicanbookgroup.com/ec/index.php?main_page=page&id=57*

HARPERCOLLINS CHRISTIAN PUBLISHING

See Blink, Thomas Nelson, Tommy Nelson, Zonderkidz, and Zondervan.

HARPERONE

353 Sacramento St. #500, San Francisco, CA 94111-3653 | 415-477-4400
harperone.com
Gideon Weil, editorial director

> **Parent company:** HarperCollins Publishing
>
> **Submissions:** Requires manuscripts through agents only. Publishes

seventy-five titles per year; receives 10,000 submissions annually. First-time authors: 5%. Length: 160-256 pages. Responds in three months.

Royalty: 7.5-15% on retail, advance $20-100,000

Types and topics: religion, spirituality

HARVEST HOUSE PUBLISHERS

PO Box 41210, Eugene, OR 97404-0322 | 800-547-8979
harvesthousepublishers.com
Kathleen Kerr, acquisitions editor
Kyle Hatfield, acquisitions editor, children and family
Ruth Samsel, senior acquisitions editor

Submissions: Requires submissions through agents.

Types and topics: self-help (relationships, family, Christian living), Bible resources (Bible studies, topical studies), and full-color gift and children's books

Imprint: Harvest House Kids (children)

Guidelines: *www.harvesthousepublishers.com/about/manuscript-submissions*

HENDRICKSEN PUBLISHERS

137 Summit St., PO Box 3473, Peabody, MA 01961
rbrown@hendrickson.com | *www.hendrickson.com*
Rick Brown, publisher

Submissions: Works only through agents or direct contact at various conferences editors attend throughout the year (most notably, the AAR/SBL annual meeting).

Types and topics: academic, Bible studies, marriage and parenting resources, new media and the arts, biblical studies and reference works for both pastors and thoughtful laypersons, devotionals, classic fiction, Christian classics, and prolife resources

Imprints: Aspire Books, Rose Publishing, RoseKidz

Guidelines: *www.hendrickson.com/content/getting-published*

HERITAGE BEACON FICTION

100 Missionary Ridge, Birmingham, AL 35242 | 888-811-9934
LPCHistorical@gmail.com | *shoplpc.com/heritage-beacon-historical-fiction*
Ann Tatlock, managing editor

Parent company: Lighthouse Publishing of the Carolinas/Iron Stream Media

Submissions: Publishes six books per year; receives twenty proposals.

First-time authors: 75%. Length: 65-80,000 words. Only accepts proposals from agents, author referrals, and conference meetings. Responds in one to two months. Bible: NIV.

Types of books: POD, ebook, audiobook

Royalty: 40% net, no advance

Types and topics: historical fiction

Guidelines: *shoplpc.com/heritage-beacon*

Tip: "Romance should be a subplot, rather than the main plot."

HOWARD BOOKS

1230 Avenue of the Americas, New York, NY 10020 | 212-698-7329
simonandschusterpublishing.com/howard-books
Peter Borland, acquisitions editor

Parent company: Simon & Schuster, Atria Publishing Group

Submissions: Does not accept, review, or return unsolicited manuscripts, except through agents. Publishes twenty-five books per year; receives 400 submissions. First-time authors: 25%. Responds in two months.

Types of books: offset paperback, hardcover, ebook, audiobook

Royalty: standard, advance

Types and topics: fiction, memoir, Christian living, spiritual growth

Guidelines: none

Tip: "Have a great idea, a large platform, and strong writing."

ILLUMINATEYA

100 Missionary Ridge, Birmingham, AL 35242 | 888-811-9934
illuminateYAsubmission@gmail.com | *www.illuminateya.com*
Tessa Emily Hall, acquisitions editor

Parent company: Lighthouse Publishing of the Carolinas/Iron Stream Media

Mission statement: Our goal is to shed light on positive and inspiring books that engross readers in an entertaining journey from beginning to end. We don't shy away from reflecting today's authentic youth culture, yet we do so in a way that promotes good morals and values. Our stories touch teens' deepest needs, answer their life questions, sweep them away in a can't-put-me-down adventure, and portray their world with a thread of hope.

Submissions: Publishes four books per year; receives twenty-five proposals. First-time authors: 50%. Length: 50-95,000 words. Email proposal with sample chapters. Only accepts submissions from agents, author referrals, and conference meetings. Responds in one to three months. Bible: NIV.

Types of books: POD, ebook, audiobook

Royalty: 40% net, no advance

Types and topics: YA contemporary, historical, romance, fantasy, speculative, sci-fi

Guidelines: *www.illuminateya.com/submissions*

Tip: "Our YA novels are clean reads; no vulgar language or sex scenes. IlluminateYA seeks to change our culture by publishing books with strong moral values. We will consider inspirational themes but prefer stories that can reach the young, general-market reader."

IMAGE BOOKS

1745 Broadway, New York, NY 10019 | 212-782-9000
imagebooks@randomhouse.com |crownpublishing.com/imprint/ image-catholic-books
Gary Jansen, director

Parent company: Crown Publishing Group, which is part of Penguin Random House

Denomination: Catholic

Submissions: Takes submissions only from agents.

IRON STREAM BOOKS

100 Missionary Ridge, Birmingham, AL 35242 | 888-811-9934
proposals@newhopepublishers.com | www.ironstreammedia.com
Ramona Richards, acquisitions

Parent company: Iron Stream Media

Submissions: Only accepts proposals through agents, author referrals, and conference meetings. Email proposal. Length: 50,000-90,000. Responds in four months. Bible: NASB.

Types and topics: leadership, spiritual growth, business as mission, millennials, and specialty markets

Royalty: no advance

Guidelines: *www.ironstreammedia.com/submission-process*

Tip: "All submissions must follow the guidelines. No query letters."

IRON STREAM MEDIA

See Iron Stream Books; New Hope Publishers; and the imprints of Lighthouse Publishing of the Carolinas: Bling!, Candlelight Romance, Firefly Southern Fiction, Guiding Light Women's Fiction, Harambee Press,

Heritage Beacon Fiction, IlluminateYA, Lamplighter Mysteries & Suspense, Smitten Historical Romance, Sonrise Devotionals, Straight Street Books, Trailblazer Western Fiction

IVP

PO Box 1400, Downers Grove, IL 60515-1426 | 630-734-4000
email@ivpress.com | *www.ivpress.com*
Al Hsu, senior editor and acquisitions, IVP Books
Jon Boyd, editorial director, academic

> **Parent company:** InterVarsity Christian Fellowship
>
> **Submissions:** Publishes 100 titles per year; receives more than 1,000 submissions annually. First-time authors: 15%. Accepts manuscripts through agents or if you have had direct contact with an editor. Length: 50,000 words or 200 pages. Bible: NIV, NRSV.
>
> **Royalty:** negotiable on retail or outright purchase, negotiable advance
>
> **Types and topics:** IVP books are characterized by a thoughtful, biblical approach to the Christian life that transforms the hearts, souls, and minds of readers in the university, church, and the world, on topics ranging from spiritual disciplines to apologetics, to current issues, to theology. Especially looking for ethnic writers (African-American, Hispanic, Asian-American).
>
> **Imprints:** IVP Academic, IVP Books, IVP Connect (Bible studies and small-group resources), IVP Formatio (spiritual formation), IVP Cresendo (women's books), IVP Praxis (ministry)
>
> **Guidelines:** *www.ivpress.com/submissions*
>
> **Tip:** "Most open to books written by pastors (though not collections of sermons) or other church staff, by professors, by leaders in Christian organizations. Authors need to bring resources for publicizing and selling their own books, such as a website, an organization they are part of that will promote their books, speaking engagements, well-known people they know personally who will endorse and promote their book, writing articles for national publication, etc."

JOURNEY FICTION

2657 Rungsted St., Las Vegas, NV 89142 | 702-570-3433
contact@journeyfiction.com | *www.journeyfiction.com*
Jennifer L. Farey, publisher

> **Mission statement:** Specializes in series fiction. We encourage binge reading.
>
> **Submissions:** Publishes twelve books per year; receives forty. First-

time authors: 90%. Length: 70-80,000 words. Email proposal with sample chapters. Prefers series. Responds in two weeks. Bible: NKJV.

Types of books: POD, ebook, audiobook

Royalty: 50% of net sales, no advance

Types and topics: fiction only: contemporary and historical, romance, suspense, mystery, speculative

Guidelines: *www.journeyfiction.com/for-authors*

Tip: "We're looking for great characters with compelling stories. Let us see characters live out their faith (or struggle with it), rather than break out into sermons."

JOURNEYFORTH BOOKS

1430 Wade Hampton Blvd., Greenville, SC 29609 | 864-546-4600
journeyforth@bjupress.com | *www.journeyforth.com*
Nancy Lohr, acquisitions editor

Parent company: BJU Press

Mission statement: We publish youth fiction and biographies as well as teen and adult nonfiction that reflect a solidly biblical worldview and encourage Christians to live out their faith.

Submissions: Publishes six to eight titles per year; receives 250-300 submissions. First-time authors: 40%. Length: varies, see guidelines. Email or mail proposal with sample chapters; no multiple submissions. Agent not necessary. Responds in three to four months. Bible: KJV, NKJV, ESV, NASB.

Types of books: offset paperback, ebook

Royalty: 10-15%, variable advance

Types and topics: youth fiction: adventure, contemporary stories, historical fiction, mystery, family stories, animal stories, classic fantasy; youth biographies; teen and adult Bible study and Christian living; specific Bible passages or timely topics like marriage and family, meditation, sanctification; ethnic characters for broad range of readers

Guidelines: *www.bjupress.com/books/freelance.php*

Tip: "We are looking for fresh writing that leads to engaging text for the target reader."

JUDSON PRESS

1075 First Ave., King of Prussia, PA 19406
editor@judsonpress.com | *www.judsonpress.com*
Rebecca Irwin-Diehl, editor

Parent company: American Baptist Home Mission Societies

Denomination: Baptist

Mission statement: committed to producing Christ-centered leadership resources for the transformation of individuals, congregations, communities, and cultures

Submissions: Publishes twelve titles per year; receives 300 submissions. First-time authors: 25%. Email or mail proposal with sample chapters. Responds in three to six months. Length: 128-244 pages. Bible: NRSV.

Types of books: offset paperback, ebook, POD; print run 2,500

Royalty: 10-15% net, advance sometimes

Types and topics: church resources, pastoral resources, Christian living, devotional, Baptist identity and history, worship resources, African-American, Asian, Hispanic, multicultural

Guidelines: *www.judsonpress.com/Pages/Info/For-Authors.aspx*

Tip: "Be clear about your audience; be proactive as a promotional partner; be passionate about what makes your project unique and compelling."

KENDALL NEFF PUBLISHING

PO Box 22, Talladega, AL 35160 | 256-368-1559
publr@KendallNeff.com | *www.KendallNeff.com*
Dr. Tana N. Thompson, publisher

Submissions: Publishes fewer than ten titles per year.

Types and topics: projects that are spiritual, secular, or educational in nature, ranging from print books to digital downloads of audio, video, or text media, including children's picture books, devotionals, self-help works, and children's activity pages

KREGEL PUBLICATIONS

2450 Oak Industrial Dr. N.E., Grand Rapids, MI 49505 | 616-451-4775
kregelbooks@kregel.com | *www.kregel.com*
Janyre Tromp, development and acquisitions editor

Submissions: Does not accept unsolicited proposals or manuscripts for review. Submit only through agents or manuscript-review services.

Types and topics: biblical studies, biography, Bible reference, children's, Christian living, church/ministry, fiction (YA, historical, romance, romantic suspense), marriage and family, theology, women's issues, self-help, parenting, Bible studies (prefers topical), discipleship, devotionals

Guidelines: *www.kregel.com/contact-us/submissions-policy*

LAMPLIGHTER MYSTERIES & SUSPENSE

100 Missionary Ridge, Birmingham, AL 35242 | 888-811-9934
lamplighterlpc@gmail.com | *shoplpc.com/lamplighter-1*
Darla Crass, managing editor

> **Parent company:** Lighthouse Publishing of the Carolinas/Iron Stream Media
> **Submissions:** Publishes five books per year; receives twenty proposals. First-time authors: 80%. Length: 65-80,000 words. Email proposal with sample chapters. Prefers submissions from agents and writers met at conferences. Responds in one month. Bible: NIV.
> **Types of books:** POD, ebook, audiobook
> **Royalty:** 40% net, no advance
> **Types and topics:** mystery, suspense
> **Guidelines:** *shoplpc.com/pages.php?pageid=22*
> **Tip:** "A good handle on plot and structure will be a strong advantage."

LEAFWOOD PUBLISHERS

ACU, PO Box 29138, Abilene, TX 79699 | 325-674-2720
manuscriptsubmissions@groupmail.acu.edu | *www.leafwoodpublishers.com*
Dr. Jason Fikes, editor

> **Parent company:** Abilene Christian University
> **Denomination:** Churches of Christ
> **Mission statement:** to publish deeper books that make faith practical
> **Submissions:** Publishes fifteen to twenty books per year; receives 100 proposals. First-time authors: 35%. Length: 55,000 words. Prefers working with agents. Response time: three to six months. Bible: NIV, ESV.
> **Types of books:** offset paperback, ebook
> **Royalty:** 14-16%, advance
> **Types and topics:** Christian living, spirituality, social issues, leadership, church history, theology
> **Guidelines:** *tinyurl.com/ybgt6bew*
> **Tips:** "Know your readers. Your book is not for everyone. Be practical. Don't be afraid to go deep."

LEXHAM PRESS

1313 Commercial St., Bellingham, WA 98225
editor@lexampress.com | *www.lexhampress.com*
Dr. Brannon Ellis, publisher

> **Parent company:** FaithLife Corporation, makers of Logos Bible Software

Submissions: Publishes print, ebooks, and innovative resources for Logos Bible Software. Will work directly with authors. Submit proposal and sample chapters through the website.

Types and topics: evangelical scholarly and pastoral works in the areas of biblical studies, including Bible reference and original language resources; biblical, historical, and systematic theology; and ministry resources

Guidelines: *www.lexhampress.com/manuscript-submission*

LIGHTHOUSE PUBLISHING

754 Roxholly Walk, Buford, CA 30518 | 770-709-2268
info@lighthousechristianpublishing.com |
www.lighthousechristianpublishing.com
Sylvia Charvet, acquisitions editor

Parent company: Lighthouse eMedia and Publishing

Submissions: Publishes thirty books annually; receives 200. First-time authors: 80%. Length: 300-320 pages for fiction. Email proposal with full manuscript. Responds in four to six weeks. Bible: NAS.

Types of books: POD, ebook, audiobook

Royalty: 50%, no advance

Types and topics: all fiction and nonfiction, also African-American and Hispanic audiences

Imprint: Lone Oak Publishing (general market)

Tip: Looking for unique stories.

LIGHTHOUSE TRAILS PUBLISHING, LLC

PO Box 908, Eureka, MT 59917 | 406-889-3610
david@lighthousetrails.com | *www.lighthousetrails.com*
David Dombrowski, acquisitions editor

Mission statement: publishes books that bring clarity and light to areas of spiritual darkness or deception

Submissions: Publishes two to four titles per year; receives fifty to seventy-five submissions annually. First-time authors: 30%. Accepts manuscripts directly from authors. Length: 160-300 pages. Email proposal with two sample chapters as attachment, or mail it. Responds in two months. Bible: KJV.

Royalty: 12-17% of net, 20% of retail

Types and topics: stories of Christians who have risen above incredible and unusual challenges and even their own failures to illustrate God's amazing grace and strength to overcome, books about or by missionaries, fiction for all ages

Guidelines: *www.lighthousetrails.com/content/11-submit-manuscript*

Tip: "Any book we consider will not only challenge the more scholarly reader, but also be able to reach those who may have less experience and comprehension. Our books will include human interest and personal experience scenarios as a means of getting the point across. Read a couple of our books to better understand the style of writing we are looking for. We also have a doctrinal statement on our website that helps to define us."

LION HUDSON

Wilkinson House, Jordan Hill Rd., Oxford OX2 8DR, UK
SubmissionstoLionBooksMonarchLionFiction@LionHudson.com |
www.lionhudson.com
Jon Oliver, senior commissioning editor

Parent company: AFD Group

Submissions: Publishes internationally; distributed in the US by Kregel Publications. Email or mail a proposal and sample chapters or manuscript; mail only for children's books. If no response in three months, consider it a rejection.

Types and topics: Lion Books, Lion Children's Books, Lion Fiction: accessible books that reflect a Christian worldview to a general audience. Candle Books, Monarch Books: support Christian families, individuals, and communities in their devotional and spiritual lives

Guidelines: *www.lionhudson.com/page/submissions*

LITTLE LAMB BOOKS

PO Box 211724, Bedford, TX 76095 | 817-505-8719
subs@littlelambbooks.com | *www.littlelambbooks.com*
Rachel Pellegrino, managing editor, publisher

Parent company: Lamb Publishing, LLC

Mission statment: to shepherd the next generation of readers by encouraging their faith in God, inspiring their love of reading, and delighting their imaginations through colorful and creative literary works

Submissions: Publishes four to six books per year; receives 125-175 proposals. First-time authors: 75%. Length: picture books, 500 words; chapter books, 1,500-5,000 words; middle grade, 30-60,000 words; YA, 50-80,000 words. Email proposal with sample chapters. Prefers submissions from writers met at conferences. Responds in three to four months. Bible: NIV.

Types of books: offset paperback, hardcover, ebook, POD

Royalty: varies, no advance

Types and topics: picture books, chapter books, middle-grade and YA novels, comedy/humor, sweet romance, mystery, action, adventure, fantasy and fables, contemporary, historical, holidays/seasonal, character values, etc.

Guidelines: *littlelambbooks.com/subs*

Also does: digital printables, T-shirts, coffee mugs, coloring books, stickers

Tip: "We're seeking original stories from a biblical worldview that entertain, inspire, and engage young readers. Authors should follow the guidelines; but also be sure that your query is attention-grabbing and includes the synopsis, a few comp titles, platform notes, and a hook."

LITURGICAL PRESS

2950 St. John's Rd., PO Box 7500, Collegeville, MN 56321-7500
submissions@litpress.org | *www.litpress.org*

Denomination: Catholic

Submissions: Email or mail proposal, using the downloadable "Project Summary Form" and "Author Biography Form" from the website.

Types and topics: biography, vocation, commentaries, chidren's, church, discipleship, liturgy, marriage and family, prayer, preaching, Bible reference books, theology, spirituality

Guidelines: *www.litpress.org/Authors/submit_manuscript*

LOVE INSPIRED

195 Broadway, 24th floor, New York, NY 10007 | 212-207-7900
harlequin.submittable.com/submit | *www.loveinspired.com*
Tina James, executive editor
Melissa Endlich, senior editor
Emily Rodmell, editor
Shana Asaro, editor
Dina Davis, assistant editor

Parent company: Harlequin, a division of HarperCollins Publishers

Mission statement: From contemporary romance to heart-stopping romantic suspense, Love Inspired books celebrate wholesome, inspirational romances that enrich the lives of each reader.

Submissions: Publishes 144 titles per year; receives 500-1,000. First-time authors: 15%. Submit proposal with sample chapters or full manuscript through the website. Agent not required. Responds in three months. Length: 55,000 words. Bible: KJV.

Royalty: on retail, competitive advance

Type of books: mass-market paperback

Types and topics: Love Inspired: contemporary romance; Love Inspired Suspense: contemporary romantic suspense

Guidelines: *harlequin.submittable.com/submit*

Tip: "We're looking for compelling stories with engaging characters, a sustained conflict, and an emotionally satisfying romance. The focus must always be on the hero and heroine as they overcome the obstacles in their paths to find love together."

LOVE2READLOVE2WRITE PUBLISHING, LLC
(L2L2 PUBLISHING)

PO Box 103, Camby, IN 46113

editor@love2readlove2writepublishing.com | *www.love2readlove2writepublishing.com*

Michele Israel Harper, acquisitions editor

Submissions: Publishes four to six titles per year; receives 150-200 proposals. 20% from first-time authors. Length: 60-90,000. Email proposal with full manuscript. Replies in two to three months. Bible: NKJV. Agent not required though welcome.

Type of book: POD

Royalty: 50% of net, $50 advance

Types and topics: Christian or clean speculative fiction only: YA, fantasy, paranormal, supernatural, dystopian, science fiction; unique writing guides

Guidelines: *www.love2readlove2writepublishing.com/submissions*

Tip: "Be professional, be succinct, and know your audience."

LOYOLA PRESS

3441 N. Ashland Ave., Chicago, IL 60657 | 773-281-1818, 800-621-1008

durepos@loyolapress.com | *www.loyolapress.com*

Joseph Durepos, acquisitions editor

Denomination: Catholic

Submissions: Publishes twenty titles per year; receives 500 submissions annually. Accepts manuscripts directly from authors. Email proposal with sample chapters. Length: 25-75,000 words or 150-300 pages. Considers first-time authors without agents. Responds in three months. Bible: NRSV (Catholic edition).

Royalty: standard, reasonable advance

Types and topics: books that help people experience God in their lives more directly, that introduce the dynamics of the Spiritual Exercises and the Ignatian process of discernment and decision-making, and that open up Scripture as a way of encountering Jesus; books that introduce and explain Catholic tradition and the richness of our faith

Guidelines: *www.loyolapress.com/general/submissions*

Tip: "Looking for books and authors that help make Catholic faith relevant and offer practical tools for the well-lived spiritual life."

MANTLE ROCK PUBLISHING, LLC

2879 Palma Rd., Benton, KY 42025 | 270-493-1560
mantlerockpublishing@gmail.com | *mantlerockpublishingLLC.com*
Erin Howard, acquisitions, Erin@mantlerockpublishingLLC.com
Kathy Cretsinger, owner, kathy@mantlerockpublishingLLC.com
Pam Harris, editor, Pam@mantlerockpublishingLLC.com

Submissions: Publishes ten to fifteen books per year; receives thirty. First-time authors: 99%. Length: 70-80,000 words. Submit through the website a proposal with sample chapters. Prefers submissions from agents. Responds in two to four weeks. Bible: NKJV.

Royalty: 12% retail on print, 50% of publisher's royalty on ebook, no advance

Types and topics: Christian fiction only: contemporary romance, historical romance, romantic suspense, fantasy/speculative

Guidelines: *mantlerockpublishingLLC.com/submissions-and-guidelines*

Tip: "Follow our guidelines, write a clean manuscript with few grammar or punctuation errors, use the font we state in the guidelines, and only send the genres we publish."

MASTER BOOKS

PO Box 726, Green Forest, AR 72638 | 800-999-3777
submissions@nlpg.com | *www.masterbooks.com*
Craig Froman, acquisitions editor

Parent company: New Leaf Publishing Group

Submissions: Publishes thirty to thirty-five titles per year. First-time authors: 10%. Accepts manuscripts directly from authors. Requires email submission with "Author's Proposal Document" on the website. Responds within three months or isn't interested. No simultaneous submissions.

Royalty: varies on net, no advance

Types and topics: young-earth creation material for all ages, including apologetics, homeschool resources, science and the Bible, reference titles, and children's literature

Guidelines: *www.nlpg.com/submissions*

MOODY PUBLISHERS

820 N. LaSalle Blvd., Chicago, IL 60610 | 800-678-8812
www.moodypublishers.com
Judy Dunagan, acquisitions editor, judy.dunagan@moody.edu
Drew Dyck, acquisitions editor, drew.dyck@moody.edu
John Hinkley, acquisitions editor, john.hinkley@moody.edu
Duane Sherman, acquisitions editor, duane.sherman@moody.edu
Amy Simpson, acquisitions editor, amy.simpson@moody.edu

Parent company: Moody Bible Institute

Mission statement: to resource the church's work of discipling all people

Submissions: Publishes fifty to sixty titles per year; receives thousands of submissions annually. First-time authors: 20%. Does not accept unsolicited manuscripts in any category; must be submitted by a literary agent, an author who has published with Moody, a Moody Bible Institute employee, or a contact at a writers conference. Responds in one to two months. Bible: NASB, ESV, NKJV.

Royalty: on net, advances begin at $500

Types and topics: books need to fit one of these categories: marriage and family resources—how to be a better mom, dad, grandparent, etc.; church leaders—pastors, community care, leading in a church context; Bible study materials—how to better study God's Word, primarily for women and young people; Christian living—how to help people take that next step in the Christian life; and ministry partners—those who work to make a better world in some way from orphan care to responsible finances

Guidelines: *www.moodypublishers.com/about/contact*

Tip: "Most open to books that (1) have a great idea at the core, (2) are executed well, and (3) can demonstrate an audience clamoring for the content."

MOUNTAIN BROOK INK

White Salmon, WA | 509-493-3953
mountainbrookink@gmail.com | *www.mountainbrookink.com*
Miralee Ferrell, lead acquisitions editor

Mission statement: fiction you can believe in that embodies restoration and/or renewal for a woman's heart

Submissions: Publishes twelve titles per year; receives fifty proposals. First-time authors: 75%. Length: minimum 80,000 words, 75,000-90,000 words for YA. Email query letter if not a traditionally published book author. If traditionally published, email proposal with sample chapters. Accepts submissions from agents and directly from authors. Replies in two months. Bible: KJV, NKJV, NIV.

Types of books: POD, ebook, audiobook

Royalty: 30-45%, no advance

Types and topics: fiction only—women's, historical, historical romance, contemporary romance, YA, mystery, suspense/thrillers, biblical, speculative

Guidelines: *mountainbrookink.com/submission-guidelines-for-inquiries*

Tip: "Send the best work you've done, preferably that's been edited so it shines."

MY HEALTHY CHURCH

1445 N. Boonville Ave., Springfield, MO 65802 | 800-641-4310, 417-831-8000
newproducts@myhealthychurch.com | *www.myhealthychurch.com*
Julie Horner, senior director of publishing and marketing

Denomination: Assemblies of God

Submissions: Does not accept unsolicited manuscripts unless represented by an agent. Responds in two to three months.

Types and topics: church resources for kids, youth, and adults; small group studies

Guidelines: *myhealthychurch.com/store/startcat.cfm?cat=tWRITGUID*

Tip: "The content of all our books and resources must be compatible with the beliefs and purposes of the Assemblies of God."

NAVPRESS

3820 N. 30th St., Colorado Springs, CO 80904 | 719-598-1212
inquiries@navpress.com | *www.navpress.com*
Caitlyn Carlson, acquisitions editor
David Zimmerman, acquisitions editor

Parent company: The Navigators

Submissions: Publishes twenty titles per year; receives 1,000 proposals annually. First-time authors: 40%. Length: 40,000 words. Submissions only from agents, current authors, or authors known to the editors. Responds in two months.

Royalty: 16-22%, advance

Types and topics: Christian living, spiritual growth, devotionals, marriage, prayer, discipleship, parenting/grandparenting, leadership, counseling/psychology, evangelism, missions, apologetics, theology, church/ministry, women, men, relationships, dating, home/family, Bible studies

Guidelines: *www.navpress.com/faq*

Tip: "Proposals with strong discipleship elements are preferred. Authors should have a ministry platform that supports their discipleship elements. NavPress does not accept unsolicited manuscripts."

NEW GROWTH PRESS

PO Box 4485, Greensboro, NC 27404 | 336-378-7775
submissions@newgrowthpress.com | *www.newgrowthpress.com*
Cheryl White, director of acquisitions

Mission statement: to empower individuals, families, and churches to grow in their love for God, their love for others, and their ability to bring healing and hope to the world

Submissions: Will work directly with authors and agents.

Types and topics: small-group resources, family, parenting, counseling issues, sexual-identity issues, missions, renewal, fiction, illustrated children's books

Also does: minibooks, short, 24-page booklets that address one specific felt need

NEW HOPE PUBLISHERS

100 Missionary Ridge, Birmingham, AL 35252 | 866-266-8399
proposals@newhopepublishers.com | *www.newhopepublishers.com*
Ramona Richards, acquisitions, managing editor

Parent company: Iron Stream Media

Submissions: Publishes twenty to twenty-five nonfiction and ten to fifteen fiction titles per year; receives more than 100. First-time authors: 20%. Length 40-50,000 words. Only accepts proposals through agents, author referrals, and conference meetings. Responds in four months. Bible: any.

Royalty: 12-14%; sometimes variable advance, depending on publishing history

Types and topics: spiritual growth, personal growth, leadership, Bible studies, fiction (women's, suspense, romantic suspense, contemporary and historical romance, seasonal, speculative), parenting, family

Imprint: New Hope Kidz (picture and board books for preschool and early readers, storybooks and Bibles for boys and girls)

Guidelines: *www.newhopepublishers.com/proposals*

Tip: "Proposals must be polished and free of errors. Marketing plans in proposal must show author's knowledge of market, platform, and genre. Please include previous sales figures (if any) and author's biography as related to book topic."

NEW LEAF PRESS

PO Box 726, Green Forest, AR 72638-0726 | 870-438-5288
submissions@newleafpress.net | *www.nlpg.com/imprint/new-leaf-press*
Craig Froman, acquisitions editor

Parent company: New Leaf Publishing Group

Submissions: Publishes thirty to thirty-five titles per year; receives 1,000 submissions annually. First-time authors: 10%. Accepts manuscripts directly from authors. Requires email submission with "Author's Proposal Document" on the website. Responds within three months or isn't interested.

Royalty: on net, no advance

Types and topics: Christian living, stewardship, reference titles, church ministry, family issues, some materials in Spanish

Guidelines: *www.nlpg.com/submissions*

Tip: "Always follow our online guidelines before submitting."

NORTH WIND PUBLISHING

PO Box 3655, Brewer, ME 04412 | 207-922-8435
info@northwindpublishing.com | *www.northwindpublishing.com*
Janet Robbins, publisher

Submissions: Email or mail proposal with sample chapters. No agents. Responds in three months. Publishes one or two titles per year; receives ten. First-time authors: 70%. Length: 150 pages. Bible: NIV.

Type of books: POD

Royalty: 10-20%, no advance

Types and topics: devotionals, Christian living

Guidelines: none

Tip: "Manuscripts must have already been professionally edited."

NORTHWESTERN PUBLISHING HOUSE

1250 N. 113th St., Milwaukee, WI 53226 | 800-662-6022, 414-615-5710

braunj@nph.wels.net | *www.nph.net*
John Braun

> **Denomination:** Wisconsin Evangelical Lutheran Synod
> **Submissions:** Mail proposal and manuscript, Attn: Manuscript Submissions.
> **Types and topics:** devotions, family and personal guidance, church history, Scripture studies like the popular People's Bible commentary series and the People's Bible Teachings series on doctrine
> **Guidelines:** *online.nph.net/manuscript-submission*

OLIVIA KIMBRELL PRESS

PO Box 470, Fort Knox, KY 40121-0470 | 859-577-1071
admin@oliviakimbrellpress.com | *www.oliviakimbrellpress.com*
Heather McCurdy, editor
Gregg Bridgeman, editor-in-chief

> **Submissions:** Specializes in true-to-life, meaningful Christian fiction and nonfiction titles intended to uplift the heart and engage the mind. Primary focus on "Roman Road" small-group guides or reader's guides to accompany nonfiction and fiction. Fiction: finished manuscript only. Nonfiction: primarily completed and an outline. Email submission.
> **Types and topics:** adult devotionals, family, Christian living, healthy living, cookbooks, fasting/feasts; fiction: speculative/science fiction, fantasy
> **Imprints:** CAVË (historical fiction from the periods immediately before, during, or after the time of Christ), Sign of the Whale (biblical and/or Christian fiction primarily with speculative fiction, science fiction, fantasy, or other futuristic and/or supernatural themes), House of Bread (biblical and/or traditional foods; clean foods; fasting; feasts; and healthy, nutritious information presented in an educational and entertaining manner)
> **Guidelines:** *www.oliviakimbrellpress.com/submission.html*
> **Tip:** "Must meet our stated editorial standards. Follow our submission guidelines. Fiction series preferred over standalone titles. Complete manuscripts only."

OUR DAILY BREAD PUBLISHING

3000 Kraft Ave. S.E., Grand Rapids, MI 49512 | 800-653-8333
submissions@dhp.org | *www.ourdailybreadpublishing.org*
Dawn Anderson, senior editor

Parent company: Our Daily Bread Ministries

Mission statement: to publish resources that feed the soul with the Word of God

Submissions: Publishes forty-five titles per year; receives 1,000 submissions annually. First-time authors: 10-20%. Accepts manuscripts through agents or authors. Send proposal with sample chapters by email. Responds in six to eight weeks. Length: 50,000 words for nonfiction. Bible: NIV.

Types of books: offset paperback, hardcover, POD, ebook

Royalty: 12% on net, advance $2,500-7,500; flat fee for Bible reference and children's books

Types and topics: Christian living, popular Bible reference, children's, African-American

Imprint: Voices (for African-Americans)

Guidelines: *ourdailybreadpublishing.org/faq-dhp*

Tip: "Ask yourself, 'How does my book feed the soul with the Word of God?'"

OUR SUNDAY VISITOR, INC.

200 Noll Plaza, Huntington, IN 46750-4303 | 260-356-8400, 800-348-2440

www.osv.com

Greg Willits, editorial director

Mission statement: to assist Catholics to be more aware and secure in their faith and capable of relating their faith to others

Submissions: Submit proposal through the website. Publishes thirty to forty titles per year; receives more than 500 submissions annually. First-time authors: 10%. Prefers not to work through agents. Responds in six to eight weeks.

Royalty: 10-12% of net, average advance $1,500

Also does: pamphlets and booklets

Types and topics: prayer—books and devotionals that help readers draw nearer to God; Scripture—books about how to read, understand, pray, and apply Scripture; family and marriage—books that reflect on the nature of marriage and practical books on family life; saints and heritage—informative and inspiring stories about Mary, the saints, and Catholic identity; faith and culture—books about the intersection of faith and contemporary culture; service—practical application of the call to serve the needy and love our neighbor; evangelization, apologetics, and catechetics—books that help readers explain, defend, and share their faith with others; worship—books about understanding and experiencing

the graces of the sacraments, especially the eucharist; parish—
books that help pastors, leaders, and parishioners conduct parish
life more effectively

Guidelines: *osv.submittable.com/submit*

Tip: "All books published must relate to the Catholic Church;
unique books aimed at our audience. Give as much background
information as possible on author qualification, why the topic was
chosen, and unique aspects of the project. Follow our guidelines. We
are expanding our religious education product line and programs."

P&R PUBLISHING

1102 Marble Hill Rd., Phillipsburg, NJ 08865 | 908-454-0505
acquisitions@prpbooks.com | *www.prpbooks.com*
David Almack, acquisitions director
Amanda Martin, editorial director
Melissa Craig, children's editor

Denomination: Reformed

Submissions: Devoted to stating, defending, and furthering the
gospel in the modern world. Download the submission form from
the website, and email it with an outline and two or three chapters.
Publishes forty-five titles per year; receives 400 submissions
annually. First-time authors: fewer than 10%. Length: 140-240
pages. Responds in one to four months.

Royalty: 10-15% net, advance

Types and topics: apologetics, Bible study aids, biography, Christian
issues and ethics, Christian living, church history, church
resources, commentary, counseling, fiction for children and teens,
theology, women's resources, youth resources

Guidelines: *www.prpbooks.com/manuscript-submissions*

Tip: "Direct biblical/Reformed content. Clear, engaging, and
insightful applications of Reformed theology to life. Offer us fully
developed proposals and polished sample chapters. Check our
website to see the categories we publish."

PACIFIC PRESS

PO Box 5353, Nampa, ID 83653-5353 | 208-465-2500
booksubmissions@pacificpress.com | *www.pacificpress.com*
Scott Cady, acquisitions editor

Denomination: Seventh-day Adventist

Submissions: Books of interest and importance to Seventh-day
Adventists and other Christians of all ages. Publishes thirty-five to

forty titles per year; receives 500 submissions annually. First-time authors: 5%. Email or mail query. Accepts manuscripts directly from authors. Length: 40-90,000 words, 128-320 pages. Responds in one to three weeks. Requires requested proposal with three chapters by email or mail, manuscript by email.

Royalty: 12-16% net, advance $1,500

Also does: booklets

Types and topics: adults: inspiration/Christian life, prayer, doctrine and Bible study, church history, Ellen White, topics and issues, biographies and true stories, story collections, cookbooks, health and nutrition, marriage and parenting, books for sharing and gospel outreach; children: picture books illustrating a distinctive Adventist belief for ages 1-3; true or based-on-truth, contemporary or historical stories with Christian themes (usually in a series) for ages 6-8 and 9-12; sets of Bible stories for ages 8-108

Guidelines: *www.pacificpress.com/authors_artists/submission-guidelines*

Tip: "Most open to spirituality, inspirational, and Christian living. Our website has the most up-to-date information, including samples of recent publications. Do not send full manuscript unless we request it after reviewing your proposal."

PARACLETE PRESS

PO Box 1568, Orleans, MA 02653 | 508-255-4685
submissions@paracletepress | www.paracletepress.com
Jon Sweeney, publisher and editor-in-chief

Denomination: Catholic and Protestant

Submissions: Email proposal and two or three sample chapters as single, attached Word file. Responds in one month.

Types and topics: prayer, faith formation, spirituality, grief, Advent/Christmas or Lent/Easter picture books; poetry by invitation only

Guidelines: *www.paracletepress.com/pages/submission-guidelines*

PARSONS PUBLISHING HOUSE

PO Box 410063, Melbourne, FL 32941 | 850-867-3061
diane@parsonspublishinghouse.com | www.parsonspublishinghouse.com
Diane Parsons, senior editor

Mission statement: empowering Christians to walk with God in a deeper way on a daily basis

Submissions: Email proposal. Responds in six to eight weeks. Publishes six to eight titles per year; receives twenty-five submissions annually. First-time authors: 80%. Length: 42-62,000 words. No agents. Bible: NKJV, NLT.

Types of books: offset and POD paperback, hardcover, ebook; print run 1,000

Royalty: 10%, no advance

Types and topics: Christian living, spiritual warfare, spiritual growth, Charismatic interests

Guidelines: click Submissions tab

Tip: "Must be biblical and positive/uplifting."

PAULINE BOOKS & MEDIA

50 Saint Paul's Ave., Boston, MA 02130-3491 | 617-522-8911
editorial@paulinemedia.com | www.pauline.org
Sean Mayer, FSP, acquisitions editor, adults
Marilyn Monge, FSP, and Jaymie Stuart Wolfe, editors, children and teens

Denomination: Catholic/Daughters of St. Paul

Submissions: Publishes twenty titles per year; receives more than 300 submissions annually. First-time authors: 10%. Accepts manuscripts directly from authors. Length: 10-60,000 words. Email proposal as an attachment, or mail it. Responds in two months. Bible: NRSV.

Royalty: 5-10% net, advance

Types and topics: adults: spirituality, prayer, lives of saints, faith formation, theology, family life; children: prayer books, lives of saints, Bible stories, activity books, easy reader and middle-grade fiction, board books, picture books; YA: fiction and nonfiction

Guidelines: *www.pauline.org/Publishing/Submit-a-Manuscript*

Tip: Looking for well-documented historical fiction and graphic novels for middle grade and YA.

PAULIST PRESS

997 Macarthur Blvd., Mahwah, NJ 07430-9990
submissions@paulistpress.com | www.paulistpress.com
Trace Murphy, editorial director

Denomination: Catholic

Submissions: Email proposal and sample chapters, pages for children's chapter books, or full manuscript for other children's books. Responds in two months.

Types and topics: academic, children's, popular, and professional or clergy books

Guidelines: *www.paulistpress.com/Pages/Center/auth_res_0.aspx*

PELICAN BOOK GROUP

See Harbourlight Books, Prism Book Group, Pure Amore, Watershed Books, and White Rose Publishing.

PRAYERSHOP PUBLISHING

2800 Poplar St., Ste. 43-L, Terre Haute, IN 47803 | 812-238-5504
jon@prayershop.org | *www.prayershop.org*
Jonathan Graf, publisher

Parent company: Harvest Prayer Ministries, Church Prayer Leaders Network

Mission statement: to help churches become houses of prayer by discipling and equipping individuals in the aspects of prayer since a praying believer is a kingdom believer who will be an asset to his or her local church

Submissions: We only do resources that will move an individual or church deeper in prayer. Publishes eight to ten titles per year; receives twenty submissions annually. First-time authors: 35%. Accepts manuscripts directly from authors. Length: 20,000-30,000 words, 128-144 pages. Email or mail proposal with sample chapters or full manuscript. Reports in six to twelve weeks. Bible: NIV, ESV.

Types of books: offset paperback, hardcover, POD, ebook; first print run 3,500-5,000

Royalty: 10% net, no advance

Types and topics: prayer, revival, Christian living

Guidelines: *www.prayerleader.com/prayershop-publishing/submissions*

Also does: booklets and brochure-formatted prayer guides

Tip: "We are looking for authors who understand prayer and can encourage their readers to desire a deeper prayer life and can equip them to pray more effectively."

PRISM BOOK GROUP

contact@prismbookgroup.com | *www.prismbookgroup.com*
Jacqueline Hopper, acquisitions editor, jhopper@prismbookgroup.com
Susan Baganz, acquisitions editor, sbaganz@prismbookgroup.com
Paula Mowery, acquisitions editor, pmowery@prismbookgroup.com

Parent company: Pelican Book Group

Submissions: Publishes clean and wholesome fiction. Publishes twenty-four to sixty titles annually. Submit proposal through the website form.

Royalty: paid quarterly

Types and topics: fiction: romance, Christian romance, Christian fiction, young adult

Imprints: Prism Lux (Christian), Prism CW (clean and wholesome)

Guidelines: *pelicanbookgroup.com/ec/index.php?main_page=page&id=55*

Tip: "Our books offer clean and compelling reads for the discerning reader. We will not publish graphic language or content and look for well-written, emotionally charged stories, intense plots, and captivating characters. We are especially interested in western/cowboy romances, regency romance, romantic suspense, and contemporary romance in both imprints. We would also love to see more historical, biblical fiction."

PURE AMORE

PO Box 1738, Aztec, NM 87410
customer@pelicanbookgroup.com | *pelicanbookgroup.com*
Nicola Martinez, editor-in-chief

Parent company: Pelican Book Group

Submissions: Length: 40-45,000 words. Accepts unagented submissions. Responds to queries in one month, full manuscripts in four months. Email submissions only through the website.

Royalty: yes, advance

Types and topics: only contemporary Christian romance, sweet in tone and in conflict, emotionally driven tales of youthful Christians between the ages of 21 and 33 who are striving to live their faith in a world where Christ-centered choices may not fully be understood

Guidelines: *pelicanbookgroup.com/ec/index.php?main_page=page&id=69*

Tip: "Pure Amore romances emphasize the beauty in chastity, so physical interactions, such as kissing or hugging, should focus on the characters' emotions, rather than heightened sexual desire; and scenes of physical intimacy should be integral to the plot and/or emotional development of the character or relationship."

RANDALL HOUSE PUBLICATIONS

114 Bush Rd., Nashville, TN 37217 | 615-361-1221
michelle.orr@randallhouse.com | *www.randallhouse.com*
Michelle Orr, senior acquisitions editor

Denomination: Free Will Baptist

Mission statement: to emphasize generational discipleship with creative excellence, communicating the Word of God with absolute integrity

Submissions: Email or mail proposal with sample chapters. Responds in ten to twelve weeks. Publishes twelve to fifteen titles per year; receives 300 submissions annually. First-time authors: 35%. Accepts manuscripts directly from authors. Length: 128-180 pages. Bible: ESV.

Types of books: offset paperback, ebook; first print run 5,000-10,000

Royalty: 14-18%, advance sometimes

Types and topics: Christian living, parenting, family ministry, small-group studies, church leadership, theology, academic, commentaries, marriage, counseling

Guidelines: *www.randallhouse.com/other/BookProposalGuide.pdf*

Tip: "Review the categories we publish, and do not submit other categories."

RESOURCE PUBLICATIONS

199 W. 8th Ave., Ste. 3, Eugene, OR 97401 | 541-344-1528
www.wipfandstock.com/imprint/resource-2

Parent company: Wipf and Stock

Types of books: POD, ebook

Types and topics: personal growth, textbooks, novels, poetry, sermon collections, biographies

Guidelines: *wipfandstock.com/submitting-a-proposal*

RESURRECTION PRESS

77 West End Rd., Totowa, NJ 07572 | 973-890-2400
info@catholicbookpublishing.com | *www.catholicbookpublishing.com*
Anthony Buono, editor

Denomination: Catholic

Parent company: Catholic Book Publishing Corp.

Submissions: Mail proposal and two chapters. Responds in four to six weeks.

Royalty: negotiable

Types and topics: prayer, healing, spirituality, pastoral and liturgical resources

Guidelines: *www.catholicbookpublishing.com/page/faq#manuscript*

REVELL BOOKS

6030 E. Fulton Rd., Ada, MI 49301 | 616-676-9185

www.bakerpublishinggroup.com/revell
Andrea Doering, editorial director
Rachel McRae, acquisitions editor
Kelsey Bowen, acquisitions editor
Vicki Crumpton, acquisitions editor

> **Parent company:** Baker Publishing Group
> **Submissions:** Publishes inspirational fiction and nonfiction for the broadest Christian market. Accepts proposals only through agents, meeting an editor at a writers conference, or *ChristianBookProposals.com*.
> **Types and topics:** apologetics/world religions, Bible study, biography/memoir, Christian living, Christianity and culture, church life, marriage and family, Spirit-filled, fiction, children and youth fiction and nonfiction
> **Guidelines:** *bakerpublishinggroup.com/contact/submission-policy*

ROSE PUBLISHING

PO Box 3473, Peabody, MA 01961-3473 | 800-358-3111
info@hendricksonrose.com | www.hendricksonrose.com
Lynette Pennings, managing editor

> **Parent company:** Hendrickson Publishers
> **Mission statement:** publishes resources that help believers love God by deepening their understanding of who God is
> **Submissions:** Submit through *ChristianBookProposals.com*.
> **Types and topics:** reference products packed with charts, timelines, and simple summaries to make the Bible and its teachings easy to understand
> **Also does:** pamphlets, wall charts

ROSEKIDZ

PO Box 3473, Peabody, MA 01961-3473 | 800-358-3111
info@hendricksonrose.com | www.hendricksonrose.com
Brenda Noel, managing editor

> **Parent company:** Hendrickson Publishers
> **Submissions:** Email samples of work first.
> **Types and topics:** reproducible Bible lesson material for children, including age-appropriate Sunday-school activities, instant Bible lessons, girls and boys devotionals, fiction; nursery, toddler, preschool, kindergarten, elementary, and preteen

SALEM BOOKS

300 New Jersey Ave., N.W., Ste. 500, Washington, DC 20001
www.salembooks.com
Tim Peterson, acquisitions

Parent company: Regnery Publishing, Salem Media Group
Mission statement: to enrich the lives of Christians and proclaim the gospel of Jesus to the world through the written word
Submissions: Only accepts manuscripts and proposals from agents.
Types and topics: Christian living

SCEPTER PUBLISHERS

PO Box 360694, Strongsville, OH 44136 | 800-322-8773, 212-354-0670
info@scepterpublishers.org | www.scepterpublishers.org

Denomination: Catholic
Mission statement: to publish Catholic books that help men and women find God in ordinary life and realize sanctity in their work, family life, and everyday activities
Submissions: Send a one- or two-page proposal with cover letter by mail or email.

SLANT

199 W. 8th Ave., Ste. 3, Eugene, OR 97401 | 541-344-1528
www.wipfandstock.com/imprint/slant-7

Parent company: Wipf and Stock
Types of books: POD, ebook
Types and topics: literary fiction
Guidelines: *wipfandstock.com/submitting-a-proposal*

SMITTEN HISTORICAL ROMANCE

100 Missionary Ridge, Birmingham, AL 35252 | 866-266-8399
smitten@lpcbooks.com | shoplpc.com/smitten-historical-romance
Pegg Thomas, managing editor

Parent company: Lighthouse Publishing of the Carolinas/Iron Stream Media
Mission statement: to engage the reader from the first paragraph to the last in a story that touches the mind, heart, and spirit
Submissions: Publishes eight books per year; receives fifty proposals. First-time authors: 30%. Length: 75-85,000 words. Only accepts proposals through agents, author referrals, and conference meetings. Responds in three to twelve weeks.
Types of books: POD, ebook, audiobook

Royalty: 40% net, no advance

Types and topics: historical romance

Guidelines: *shoplpc.com/smitten*

Tip: "Submit stories steeped in real history/places populated by fascinating characters and a happily-ever-after ending that satisfies the reader. The history and Christian content should be organic to the time period, never preachy, and not overshadow the story. Implied Christian content without overt evangelism is preferred."

SMYTH & HELWYS BOOKS

6316 Peake Rd., Macon, GA 31210-3960 | 478-757-0564
proposal@helwys.com | *www.helwys.com*

Submissions: Submit both a hard and digital copy of the complete proposal and two to four sample chapters. Responds in several months.

Types and topics: Christian living, ministry/leadership, biblical studies

Guidelines: *www.helwys.com/submit-a-manuscript*

SONFIRE MEDIA PUBLISHING, LLC

120 W. Grayson St., Ste. 350, Galax, VA 24333 | 276-233-0276
www.sonfiremedia.com
Larry Van Hoose, creative director

Submissions: Publishes two to five titles per year. Receives fifty per year. First-time authors: 95%. Length: 40-80,000 for nonfiction, 70-100,000 for fiction. Email query letter only. Replies in one to two months. Bible: prefers NIV but open to others.

Type of book: POD

Royalty: 10-20%

Types and topics: devotionals; Christian living; writing instruction; YA and adult fantasy, science fiction, speculative; open to other types of fiction except romance

Imprints: Sonfire Media (nonfiction), Taberah Press (fiction)

Guidelines: *www.sonfiremedia.com/submit.html*

Tip: "We are open to new writers if they are serious about their craft, understand the need for author marketing, and have a 'message that matters.'"

SONRISE DEVOTIONALS

100 Missionary Ridge, Birmingham, AL 35252 | 866-266-8399
csproleslpcacquisitions@gmail.com | *www.sonrisedevotionals.com*

Cindy Sproles, managing editor

> **Parent company:** Lighthouse Publishing of the Carolinas/Iron Stream Media
>
> **Mission statement:** to present books that shine a light into a dark world
>
> **Submissions:** Publishes five books per year; receives fifty proposals. First-time authors: 50%. Length: 30-70,000 words. Only accepts proposals from agents, author referrals, and conference meetings. Responds in six months. Bible: any. Welcomes submissions from ethnic writers.
>
> **Types of books:** POD, ebook, audiobook
>
> **Royalty:** 50% net, no advance
>
> **Types and topics:** daily devotionals, Hispanic audiences
>
> **Guidelines:** *shoplpc.com/sonrise*
>
> **Tip:** "Looking for devotions that move away from niche audiences and return to devotions that address everyone at any season in their lives."

STONE TABLE BOOKS

39 Archer St., North Adelaide, SA 5006, Australia
editor@stonetablebooks.com | *stonetablebooks.com*
Mark Worthing, senior editor

> **Types of books:** paperback (ebook coming soon)
>
> **Submissions:** Publishes six to twelve books per year.
>
> **Types and topics:** speculative fiction
>
> **Tip:** "Check the website for a list of things you can do to make your text more likely to succeed."

STRAIGHT STREET BOOKS

100 Missionary Ridge, Birmingham, AL 35252 | 866-266-8399
csproleslpcacquisitions@gmail.com | *shoplpc.com/straight-street-books*
Cindy Sproles, managing editor

> **Parent company:** Lighthouse Publishing of the Carolinas/Iron Steam Media
>
> **Mission statement:** to provide wholesome reading, leaning to both general and Christian markets
>
> **Submissions:** Publishes six books per year; receives fifty proposals. First-time authors: 85%. Length: 60-80,000 words. Only accepts proposals through agents, author referrals, and conference meetings. Responds in six months. Bible: any. Welcomes submissions from ethnic writers.
>
> **Types of books:** POD, ebook, audiobook

Royalty: 40% net, no advance

Types and topics: Christian living, pastoral help, marriage, disabilities, Christian walk

Guidelines: *shoplpc.com/straight-street*

Tip: "Fresh and unique subjects. We do not accept memoirs."

THOMAS NELSON PUBLISHERS

PO Box 141000, Nashville, TN 37214-1000 | 615-889-9000

www.thomasnelson.com

Becky Monds, acquisitions editor, fiction

Debbie Wickwire, acquisitions, W Publishing

Jessica Wong, nonfiction acquisitions, Thomas Nelson

Joel Kneedler, publisher, Emanate Books

Parent company: HarperCollins Christian Publishing

Submissions: Only accepts proposals through agents or direct contact with editors. Does not accept or review any unsolicited queries, proposals, or manuscripts. Publishes fewer than 100 titles per year.

Types and topics: Christian living, church and ministry resources, Bible reference, commentaries, Bible book studies, business and leadership, biography, women's devotionals, fiction for adults and YA, gift books

Imprints: Nelson Books (spiritual growth and practical living), W Publishing Group (memoir, help and hope for doing life better, and leading pastoral voices, with select practical living), Grupo Nelson (Spanish), Tommy Nelson (children and teens; see separate entry), Emanate Books (Charismatic)

TOMMY NELSON

PO Box 141000, Nashville, TN 37214-1000 | 615-889-9000

www.tommynelson.com

Mackinzie Howard, children's acquisitions editor

Parent company: Thomas Nelson Publishers

Submissions: Only accepts proposals through agents or direct contact with editors. Does not accept or review any unsolicited queries, proposals, or manuscripts.

Types and topics: board books, picture books, Bible storybooks, devotionals for middle grade and teens

TRAILBLAZER WESTERN FICTION

100 Missionary Ridge, Birmingham, AL 35252 | 866-266-8399

trailblazerwesterns@gmail.com | *trailblazerwesterns.com*

Jennifer Uhlarik, managing editor

Parent company: Lighthouse Publishing of the Carolinas/Iron Stream Media

Mission statement: to recapture the glory days of the Western, but with an updated feel that will ignite the hearts and minds of a new generation of readers

Submissions: Publishes four books annually. Length to 90,000 words. Only accepts proposals through agents, author referrals, and conference meetings. Responds in three months. Bible: NIV.

Types of books: POD, ebook, audiobook

Royalty: 40% net, no advances

Types and topics: contemporary and historical westerns

Guidelines: *shoplpc.com/trailblazer*

Tip: "Trailblazer is looking for quality fiction in the style of past greats like Louis L'Amour and Zane Grey, as well as new twists on the genre."

THE TRINITY FOUNDATION

PO Box 68, Unicoi, TN 37692 | 423-743-0199
tjtrinityfound@aol.com | www.trinityfoundation.org
Thomas W. Juodaitis, president

Mission statement: to publish books based on the truth that the Bible alone is the Word of God

Submissions: Publishes one to three titles per year; receives four proposals. First-time authors: 5%. Length: 60-300 pages. Email or mail a proposal with sample chapters. Responds in two to four weeks. Bible version: KJV, NKJV.

Types of books: offset paperback, ebook; print run 500-1,000

Royalty: none, no advance, $2,000 flat fee

Types and topics: theology, philosophy

Guidelines: by email

Tip: "Books must be in line with the theology and philosophy of The Trinity Foundation."

TWINTEUM PUBLISHING CO.

PO Box 211191, St. Louis, MO 63121-9191 | 314-309-1716
Iskindertioliendo@gmail.com
Teo Tioliendo, editor in chief

Submissions: Publishes ten books per year; receives 2,000 proposals. First-time authors: 10%. Length: 50-150 pages. Query letter from agents only. Responds in one month. Bible: KJV.

Types of books: offset paperback, ebook; print run 50-500
Royalty: 5-15%, no advance
Types and topics: fiction: action, fantasy; drama; Christian living; marriage; sexuality; understanding the Bible; spiritual warfare; prayer; about the body, soul, and spirit; time and the spiritual realm; inner life; ethnic audiences: African-American, Hispanic, Ethiopian, Asian, Native American, Latin
Also does: art prints, clothing, merchandise
Imprint: Art Arrow Star (Christians around the world and their work in other countries)
Guidelines: none
Tip: "Pray and ask God's guidance."

TYNDALE HOUSE PUBLISHERS

351 Executive Dr., Carol Stream, IL 60188 | 630-668-8300
www.tyndale.com
Sarah Atkinson, senior acquisitions, nonfiction
Jon Farrar, acquisitions director, devotionals
Jan Stob, fiction acquisitions

Submissions: Publishes more than 100 titles per year. First-time authors: 5%. Only reviews manuscripts submitted by agents, Tyndale authors, authors known to them from other publishers, or other people in the publishing industry. Responds in three to six months. Bible: NLT. Fiction length: 75-100,000 words.
Types of books: offset paperback, hardcover, ebook
Types and topics: home and family, Christian beliefs, finance, leadership, career, parenting, marriage, memoir, biography, devotionals, counseling; fiction with evangelical message: biblical, contemporary, futuristic, historical, romance, suspense/thriller
Imprint: Tyndale Kids (see separate entry), Tyndale Español (Spanish)
Guidelines: *www.tyndale.com/faq*

TYNDALE KIDS

351 Executive Dr., Carol Stream, IL 60188 | 630-668-8300
www.tyndale.com
Linda Howard, acquisitions editor

Submissions: Publishes twenty to twenty-five books per year. Proposals only from agents, Tyndale authors, authors known to them from other publishers, or other people in the publishing industry.

Types and topics: picture books, first-chapter books, middle grade, YA, Bible stories, fiction, nonfiction
Imprint: Wander (YA)
Guidelines: *www.tyndale.com/faq*

WARNER PRESS

2902 Enterprise Dr., Anderson, IN 46013 | 765-644-7721
rfogle@warnerpress.org | *www.warnerpress.org*
Robin Fogle, kids and family ministry editor
Karen Rhodes, church ministry editor, krhodes@warnerpress.org

Denomination: Church of God (Anderson)
Mission statement: produces resources to equip the church, to advance the Kingdom, and to give hope to future generations
Submissions: Publishes three to five books annually; receives fifty plus proposals. First-time authors: 50%. Email or mail proposal with sample chapters or full manuscript. Accepts manuscripts directly from authors. Responds in six to eight weeks. Bible: KJV, NIV.
Types of books: offset paperback, ebook
Royalty: based on the author and type of book, advance sometimes
Types and topics: Bible studies, Christian living, books for pastors, group and personal studies, ministry booklets, family and children's teaching resources; also see entry in "Miscellaneous."
Guidelines: *www.warnerpress.org/submission-guidelines*
Tip: "Do your research and visit our website to view what we already produce."

WATERBROOK MULTNOMAH

10807 New Allegiance Dr., Ste. 500, Colorado Springs, CO 80921 | 719-590-4999
info@waterbrookmultnomah.com | *www.waterbrookmultnomah.com*
Andrew Stoddard, acquisitions editor
Paul Pastor, editor
Becky Nesbitt, executive editor, WaterBrook acquisitions

Parent company: Penguin Random House
Submissions: Publishes sixty books annually; receives 300 proposals. First-time authors: 15%. Length: 208-400 pages. Proposals from agents only. Responds in one to two months. Bible: ESV.
Types of books: offset and POD paperback, hardcover, ebook, audiobook
Royalty: advance
Types and topics: fiction: Amish, romantic suspense, historical,

period; children's; creative, interactive books and journals; Christian living; spiritual growth; relationships; personal growth; devotional; inspirational; motivational; home and lifestyle

Guidelines: *waterbrookmultnomah.com/submissions*

Tip: "We recommend working with an agent whose clientele aligns with your strengths as a writer."

WATERSHED BOOKS

PO Box 1738, Aztec, NM 87410
customer@pelicanbookgroup.com | *www.pelicanbookgroup.com*
Nicola Martinez, editor-in-chief

Parent company: Pelican Book Group

Submissions: Email submissions only through the website. Length: 25-60,000 words. Accepts unagented submissions. Responds to queries in one month, full manuscript in three months. Email submissions only.

Royalty: 40% on download, 7% on print, nominal advance

Types and topics: young-adult fiction that features young-adult characters; action-adventure, mystery (amateur sleuth or other), romance, science fiction, fantasy, supernatural, suspense, crime drama, police procedural, teen angst, coming-of-age, westerns; interested in series ideas

Guidelines: *pelicanbookgroup.com/ec/index.php?main_page=page&id=60*

WESTMINSTER/JOHN KNOX PRESS

100 Witherspoon St., Louisville, KY 40202-1396
submissions@wjkbooks.com | *www.wjkbooks.com*
Jessica Miller Kelley, acquisitions editor
David Dobson, editorial director

Denomination: Presbyterian

Parent company: Presbyterian Publishing Corporation

Submissions: Publishes approximately sixty books and other resources each year. Prefers emailed proposals but will take them by mail. Responds in two to three months.

Types and topics: children, theology, biblical studies, preaching, worship, ethics, religion and culture, and other related fields for four main markets: scholars and students in colleges, universities, seminaries, and divinity schools; preachers, educators, and counselors working in churches; members of mainline Protestant congregations; and general readers

Imprints: Flyaway Books (children), Geneva Press (books specifically related to the Presbyterian Church USA)

Guidelines: *www.wjkbooks.com/Pages/Item/1345/Author-Relations.aspx*

WHITAKER HOUSE

1030 Hunt Valley Cir., New Kensington, PA 15068 | 724-334-7000

publisher@whitakerhouse.com | *www.whitakerhouse.com*

Tom Cox, managing editor

Denomination: Charismatic

Submissions: Only reviews proposals from agents or by request from a house representative. Email a proposal or mail to Author Liaison. Responds in six months. Publishes seventy titles per year; receives 100 submissions annually. First-time authors: 15-20%. Length: 40-70,000 words, 96-336 pages.

Royalty: 6-20% net, 25% ebooks, variable advance

Types and topics: biography/autobiography, Charismatic interest, Christian living, devotions, fiction, gender-specific issues for men or women, inspiration, marriage, family, relationships, prayer, spiritual growth, spiritual warfare, theology, African-American, Hispanic

Imprints: Banner Publishing, Resolute Books, Smart Kidz

Guidelines: *www.whitakerhouse.com/contact,* click View Guidelines link

Tip: "Looking for quality nonfiction and fiction by authors with a national marketing platform. Most open to high-quality, well-thought-out, compelling pieces of work. Review the guidelines and submit details as thoroughly as possible for publication consideration."

WHITE ROSE PUBLISHING

PO Box 1738, Aztec, NM 87410

customer@pelicanbookgroup.com | *www.pelicanbookgroup.com*

Nicola Martinez, editor-in-chief

Parent company: Pelican Book Group

Submissions: Email submissions only through the website. Length: short stories, 10-20,000 words (ebook); novelettes, 20-35,000 words (ebook); novellas, 35-60,000 words (ebook); novels, 60-80,000 words (ebook and print). Accepts unagented submissions. Responds to queries in one month, full manuscript in three months. Email submissions only.

Royalty: 40% on download, 7% on print, nominal advance

Types and topics: only romance, interested in series ideas

Guidelines: *pelicanbookgroup.com/ec/index.php?main_
page=page&id=58*

WHITEFIRE PUBLISHING

13607 Bedford Rd. N.E., Cumberland, MD 21502 | 866-245-2211
r.white@whitefire-publishing.com | *www.whitefire-publishing.com*
Roseanna White, senior fiction editor

Mission statement: to deliver strong books that embody the motto of
"Where Spirit Meets the Page" because stories change the world

Submissions: Publishes twelve to eighteen titles per year; receives 150
annually. First-time authors: 50%. Email query letter only. Replies
in three months. Bible: KJV for historicals, no preference for
contemporaries.

Types of books: POD, hardcover, ebook, audiobook

Royalty: 50% on ebooks, 10-15% on print, advance sometimes

Types and topics: contemporary women's fiction, contemporary
romance, romantic suspense, historical, historical romance,
suspense, all genres of middle grade and young adult, picture
books, homeschool curriculum, Christian living, marriage, family,
hiking and adventure, inspirational

Imprint: Ashberry Lane (romance, including contemporary, historical,
and romantic suspense); WhiteSpark (picture books, middle
grade, and YA)

Guidelines: *whitefire-publishing.com/submissions*

Tip: "We're looking for a strong hook and for authors who know who
their audience is."

WILD HEART BOOKS

733 Flamingo Rd., Clover, SC 29710 | 704-363-0360
submissions@wildheartbooks.org | *www.wildheartbooks.org*
Misty M. Beller, managing editor

Parent company: Misty M. Beller Books, Inc.

Mission statement: Wild Heart Books publishes exciting historical
romance stories, complete with heroes to make readers swoon,
strong heroines, and inspirational messages to encourage their
faith. We publish to a very small niche, and that's part of what
makes us successful.

Submissions: Publishes ten books per year; receives seventy-five
proposals. First-time authors: 50%. Length: 55-75,000 words.
Email proposal with sample chapters. Works with agents and
directly with writers. Responds in two weeks. Bible: KJV.

Types of books: POD, ebook, audiobook
Royalty: 35-50%, advance sometimes
Types and topics: historical romance only
Guidelines: *wildheartbooks.org/submissions.html*
Tip: "A good strong story (that fits with what we publish) will always snag our attention."

WILLIAM CAREY LIBRARY

626-720-8210
submissions@WCLBooks.com | www.missionbooks.org

Submissions: Publishes scholarly and professional or educational books, all related to missions. "We especially seek to assist the work of the mission executive, field missionary, church leader, and the student of world mission." Responds in three to six months. Send a maximum two-page query letter initially. No unsolicited manuscripts.
Types and topics: ethnography, biography, educational, nonfiction, missions, missiology
Guidelines: *missionbooks.org/pages/submission-guidelines*
Tip: "Read our publishing focus carefully. We only publish literature promoting world missions, specifically among unreached and unengaged peoples."

WINGED PUBLICATIONS

PO Box 8047, Surprise, AZ 85374 | 623-910-4279
cynthiahickey@outlook.com | www.wingedpublications.com
Cynthia Hickey, editor

Mission statement: Where Your Stories Take Flight
Submissions: Publishes fifty books per year. First-time authors: 25%. Length: at least 50,000 words. Email proposal with sample chapters. Prefers agent submissions. Also open to writers met at conferences. Responds in two weeks. Bible: NIV.
Types of books: POD, ebook
Royalty: 60%, no advance
Types and topics: contemporary romance, historical romance, fantasy, young adult, science fiction, dystopian, speculative, thriller, romantic suspense, memoir, devotional
Guidelines: *wingedpublications.com/submissions*
Also offers: author services
Tip: "Send the cleanest proposal you can."

WIPF AND STOCK PUBLISHERS

199 W. 8th Ave., Ste. 3, Eugene, OR 97401-2960 | 541-344-1528
proposal@wipfandstock.com | www.wipfandstock.com
Rodney Clapp, editor, rodney@wipfandstock.com
Dr. Chris Spinks, editor, chris@wipfandstock.com

Submissions: Email proposal with proposal form from the website. Responds in eight weeks. It is your responsibility to submit a manuscript that has been fully copyedited by a professional copy editor. Publishes more than 400 books per year.

Types of books: short-run, ebooks

Types and topics: primarily academic

Guidelines: *wipfandstock.com/submitting-a-proposal*

WORTHY KIDS / IDEALS

6100 Tower Cir., Ste. 210, Franklin, TN 37067 | 615-932-7600
IdealsInfo@worthypublishing.com |
worthypublishing.com/imprint/hachette-nashville/worthy-books
Peggy Schaefer, publisher

Parent company: Hachette Book Group

Mission statement: helping kids experience the heart of God

Submissions: Publishes forty titles per year; receives 500 annually. First-time authors: 1-5%. Length: 200 words for board books, 800 words for picture books. Mail proposal with full manuscript. Responds only to manuscripts of interest. Prefers submissions from agents. Bible: no preference.

Types of books: hardcover, board

Royalty: 5-7%, advance

Types and topics: fiction, nonfiction, holiday

Tip: "Carefully study the types of books we have published and submit manuscripts that complement our product line but do not duplicate."

WORTHY PUBLISHING GROUP

6100 Tower Cir., Ste. 210, Franklin, TN 37067 | 615-932-7600
www.worthypublishing.com
Marilyn Jansen, acquisitions, Worthy Inspired

Parent company: Hachette Book Group

Submissions: Publishes thirty-six titles per year. Requires submission by agents; unsolicited manuscripts returned unopened.

Royalty: for Worthy Books, flat fee for some of Worthy Inspired, advance

Types and topics: broad spectrum of genres, including current events, pop culture, biography, fiction, spiritual growth, and Bibles; Worthy Inspired: felt-need personal growth, inspirational, devotional, for professional women

Imprints: Worthy Books, Worthy Inspired, Worthy Kids/Ideals (see separate listing), Ellie Claire (gifts, see separate listing), Museum of the Bible Books (engagement with the Bible)

WRITE INTEGRITY PRESS

PO Box 702852, Dallas, TX 75370 | 214-676-9974
MarjiLaine@WriteIntegrity.com | *www.WriteIntegrity.com*
Marji Laine Clubine, senior editor

Mission statement: to provide clean and wholesome fiction and uplifting nonfiction

Submissions: Publishes one to two dozen titles per year; receives 100-200. First-time authors: 60%. Length: 60-90,000 words. Email proposal with first three chapters. Responds in one to three months. Bible: ESV.

Types of books: POD, ebook

Royalty: 40-50%, no advance

Types and topics: Christian living; devotional; Bible studies; YA adventure, coming of age, fantasy; middle grade adventure; fiction: contemporary, romance, historical, romantic suspense, cozy mystery

Imprints: Favored Books (heartwarming stories and clean romance), Pursued Books (mystery and suspense), Emerged Books (YA and middle grade), Entrusted Books (Christian living, devotional, Bible studies)

Guidelines: *www.writeintegrity.com/submissions*

Tip: "Write Integrity Press insists on books that adhere to our readers' expectations of clean, wholesome, and uplifting. Therefore, any manuscripts containing cursing, gratuitous sex, or behavior contrary to a Christian lifestyle will not be considered."

YWAM PUBLISHING

PO Box 55787, Seattle, WA 98155 | 800-922-2143
books@ywampublishing.com | *www.ywampublishing.com*

Parent company: Youth With A Mission

Submissions: Email or mail proposal, following the template on the website. Will not respond to submissions that deviate from proposal guidelines.

Types and topics: evangelism, mission adventures, missions for kids,

Bible studies, devotionals, leadership, relationships; no longer accepts fiction or children's literature

Guidelines: *www.ywampublishing.com/topic.aspx?name=submission*

ZONDERKIDZ

3900 Sparks Dr. S.E., Grand Rapids, MI 49512 | 616-698-6900

ZonderkidzSubmissions@harpercollins.com | www.zonderkidz.com

Parent company: HarperCollins Christian Publishing

Submissions: Requires submissions only through agents.

Types and topics: children's fiction and nonfiction, teen fiction and nonfiction, children's Bibles

Guidelines: none

Tip: "We are seeking fresh fiction and nonfiction for children ages 0-18. Under our Zonderkidz and Zondervan imprints, we look for engaging picture books and board books, timeless storybook Bibles, faith-centric fiction from established authors, and nonfiction from key voices in the Christian sphere."

ZONDERVAN

3900 Sparks Dr. S.E., Grand Rapids, MI 49512 | 616-698-6900

www.zondervan.com

Carolyn McCready, executive editor

Andrew Rogers, nonfiction acquisitions editor

Parent company: HarperCollins Christian Publishing

Submissions: Requires submissions only through agents. Publishes 120 trade titles per year. Bible version: NIV.

Types and topics: spiritual growth, marriage, family, social issues, leadership, finance, biography, commentaries, church and ministry, fiction (contemporary, mystery, historical, romance, science fiction, fantasy, suspense)

Imprints: Zonderkidz (see separate entry), Editorial Vida (Spanish), Zondervan Academic

Guidelines: none

Christian Writers Institute Courses
2020 Publisher Bundle

Courses in this bundle:
- The Elements of an Effective Book Proposal
- How to Get Published
- How to Sell Everything You Write
- What Editors Won't Tell You
- The Power Book Proposal
- 12 Ways to Please an Editor

Normal price: $62
Savings: 52%
Market Guide price $29.76

https://cwmg.link/publisher2020

How to Scan QR Codes
Use the camera on your smartphone to focus on the above QR code to activate the discount. It will give you the option to visit the site, which you will want to accept. If you are using an older smartphone, you may need to download a QR code scanning app. You can also visit the URL below the code to activate the discount on your computer.

PART 2

INDEPENDENT BOOK PUBLISHING

2

INDEPENDENT BOOK PUBLISHERS

PUBLISHING A BOOK YOURSELF NO LONGER CARRIES THE STIGMA self-publishing has had in the past—if you do it right. Even some well-published writers are now hybrid authors, with independently published books alongside their royalty books. Others have built their readerships with traditional publishers, then moved to independent publishing where it is possible to make more money per sale.

Independent book publishers require the author to pay for part of the publishing costs or to buy a certain number of books. They call themselves by a variety of names, such as book packager, cooperative publisher, self-publisher, custom publisher, subsidy publisher, or simply someone who helps authors get their books printed. Services vary from including different levels of editing and proofreading to printing your manuscript as is.

Whenever you pay for any part of the production of your book, you are entering into a nontraditional relationship. Some independent publishers also offer a form of royalty publishing, so be sure you understand the contract they give you before signing it.

Some independent publishers will publish any book, as long as the author is willing to pay for it. Others are as selective about what they publish as a royalty publisher is. Some independent publishers will do as much promotion as a royalty publisher—for a fee. Others do none at all.

If you are unsuccessful in placing your book with a royalty publisher but feel strongly about seeing it published, an independent publisher can make printing your book easier and often less expensive than doing it yourself. POD, as opposed to a print run of 1,000 books or more, could save you upfront money, although the price per copy is higher. Having your manuscript produced only as an ebook is also a less-expensive option.

Entries in this chapter are for information only, not an endorsement of publishers. For every complaint about a publisher, there can be several other authors who sing the praises of it. Before you sign with any company, get more than one bid to determine whether the terms you are offered are competitive. A legitimate independent publisher will provide a list of former clients as references. Also buy a couple of the publisher's previous books to check the quality of the work—covers, bindings, typesetting, etc. See if the books currently are available through any of the major online retailers.

Get answers before committing yourself. You may also want someone in the book-publishing industry to review your contract before you sign it. Some experts listed in the "**Editorial Services**" chapter review contracts.

If you decide not to use an independent publisher but do the work yourself, at least hire an editor, proofreader, cover designer, and interior typesetter-designer. The "**Editorial Services**" and "**Design and Production Services**" chapters will help you locate professionals with skills in these areas, as well as printing companies. Plus the "**Distribution Services**" and "**Publicity and Marketing Services**" chapters can help you solve one of the biggest problems of independent publishing: getting your books to readers.

ACW PRESS

PO Box 110390, Nashville, TN 37222 | 800-21-WRITE
acwriters@aol.com | *www.acwpress.com*
Reg A. Forder, publisher

> **Types:** hardcover, offset and POD paperback, gift book
> **Services:** design, substantive editing, copyediting, proofreading, packages of services
> **Production time:** two to four months
> **Tip:** "We offer a high-quality publishing alternative to help Christian authors get their material into print. High standards, high quality. If authors have a built-in audience, they have the best chance to make self-publishing a success."

ALTEN INK

1888 Montara Way, San Jacinto, CA 92583 | 951-327-3698
AltenInk3@gmail.com | *www.AltenInk.blogspot.com*
Deborah L. Alten

> **Types:** paperback, ebook, picture book
> **Services:** substantive editing, proofreading, design, promotional materials, online bookstore, publishing packages of services, à la carte options
> **Production time:** six months
> **Tip:** "Email us. You will get a quicker response."

AMPELOS PRESS

951 Anders Rd., Lansdale, PA 19446 | 484-991-8581
mbagnull@aol.com | *writehisanswer.com/ampelospress*
Marlene Bagnull, publisher

Types: ebook, POD

Services: manuscript evaluation, design, substantive editing, copyediting, proofreading

Production time: six months

Books per year: one or two

Tip: "Especially interested in helping authors independently publish books about missions, issues, and the needs of children. Not actively soliciting manuscripts, but accepts them from writers she meets at conferences."

BK ROYSTON PUBLISHING, LLC

PO Box 4321, Jeffersonville, IN 47131 | 502-802-5385
bkroystonpublishing@gmail.com | *www.bkroystonpublishing.com*
Julia Royston, CEO

Types: hardcover, offset and POD paperback, ebook, audiobook, picture book

Services: manuscript evaluation, design, substantive editing, copyediting, proofreading, promotional materials, marketing, distribution, author websites, online bookstore, packages of services, à la carte options

Production time: two to three months

Books per year: twenty-five to thirty

Also does: ghostwriting, coaching, royalty contracts

Production time: one to four months

Tip: "Visit *www.getstartedwithroyston.com* to get submission guidelines."

BOOKBABY

7905 N. Crescent Blvd., Pennsauken, NJ 08110 | 877-961-6878
info@bookbaby.com | *www.bookbaby.com*

Types: paperback, hardcover, ebook, offset and POD paperback, gift book, picture book, cookbook, comic book, yearbook, many other formats

Services: manuscript evaluation, design, substantive editing, copyediting, proofreading, promotional materials, marketing, distribution, author website, online bookstore

Production time: as quick as five days

Tip: Has ebook and printed book distribution network for self-published authors around the globe.

BROWN CHRISTIAN PRESS

16250 Knoll Trail Dr., Ste. 205, Dallas, TX 75248 | 972-381-0009
email through website | *www.brownbooks.com/christian.php*

Types: hardcover, paperback, gift book, ebook

Services: substantive editing, copyediting, proofreading, ghostwriting, design, marketing, distribution, author website

Publication time: six months

Tip: "We are a relationship publisher and work with our authors from beginning to end in the journey of publishing."

CARPENTER'S SON PUBLISHING

307 Verde Meadow Dr., Franklin, TN 37067 | 615-472-1128
larry@christianbookservices.com | *www.carpenterssonpublishing.com*
Larry Carpenter, president-CEO, editor

Types: offset and POD paperback, hardcover, ebook, audiobook, gift book, picture book

Services: manuscript evaluation, design, substantive editing, copyediting, proofreading, indexing, promotional materials, marketing, distribution, author website, à la carte options

Production time: three to six months

Books per year: 100

Tip: "Make sure someone is selling your book to the bookstores."

CASTLE GATE PRESS

244 E. Glendale Rd., St. Louis, MO 63119 | 314-962-1940
p.wheeler@castlegatepress.com | *www.castlegatepress.com*
Phyllis Wheeler, owner

Types: POD, ebook, audiobook

Services: manuscript evaluation, design, substantive editing, copyediting, proofreading, à la carte options

Publication time: depends on manuscript editing needs

Books per year: one or two

Tip: "Castle Gate Press was a traditional publisher from 2013-2018. One of our books is an Amazon genre bestseller, and another won a Selah Award for Christian fiction in the speculative category. Yet another was a finalist for Selah and also for the Realm Award, and another a finalist for the Grace Award. In short, we provide award-winning editing."

CHRISTIAN FAITH PUBLISHING

832 Park Ave., Meadville, PA 16335 | 800-955-3794
contact@christianfaithpublishing.com | www.Christianfaithpublishing.com
Chris Rutherford, president; Jason Murray, executive vice president

Types: offset and POD paperback, hardcover, ebook
Services: manuscript evaluation, design, copyediting, indexing, promotional materials, marketing, distribution, author website, packages of services, à la carte options
Also offers: royalty contracts
Production time: eight to ten months
Books per year: 1,200
Tip: "Be mindful of the fact that it is quite challenging to publish a book and have commercial success."

CLM PUBLISHING

Building G, Ste. 5, Countryside Shopping Village, Box 1217 GT, Grand Cayman, Cayman Islands KY11108 | 345-926 2507
production@clmpublishing.com | www.clmpublishing.com
Karen E. Chin, managing editor

Types: hardcover, ebook, offset and POD paperback, gift book, picture book
Services: manuscript evaluation, design, substantive editing, copyediting, proofreading, promotional materials, marketing, distribution, author website, online bookstore, publishing packages of services, à la carte options
Production time: three months
Also does: royalty contracts
Tip: "Even after many rejection letters, never stop writing. There is always a publisher for you."

COVENANT BOOKS, INC.

11661 Hwy. 707, Murrells Inlet, SC 29576 | 843-507-8373
contact@covenantbooks.com | www.covenantbooks.com
Denice Hunter, president; Kasha Foret, vice president

Types: offset and POD paperback, hardcover, ebook
Services: design, copyediting, marketing, distribution, online bookstore, promotional materials, author website, packages of services, à la carte options

Also does: royalty contracts
Production time: six months
Books per year: 1,000
Tip: "Publishing a book can be a fun and enlightening process. Take your time, and choose a publisher you feel comfortable with."

CREATIVE ENTERPRISES STUDIO

1507 Shirley Way, Ste. A, Bedford, TX 76022-6737 | 817-312-7393
AcreativeShop@aol.com | *CreativeEnterprisesStudio.com*
Mary Hollingsworth, publisher and managing director

Types: offset and POD paperback, hardcover, ebook, audiobook, gift book, picture book
Services: manuscript evaluation, design, substantive editing, copyediting, proofreading, indexing, promotional materials, marketing, distribution, author website, online bookstore, à la carte options, warehousing, fulfillment, book trailers, Bible language experts, Spanish translation
Production time: six months
Books per year: six to ten
Tip: "Contact us by email first."

CREDO HOUSE PUBLISHERS

2200 Boyd Ct. N.E., Grand Rapids, MI 49525-6714 | 616-363-2686
publish@credocommunications.net | *www.credohousepublishers.com*
Timothy J. Beals, publisher

Types: offset and POD paperback, hardcover, ebook, audiobook, gift book, picture book
Services: manuscript evaluation, design, substantive editing, copyediting, proofreading, indexing, promotional materials, marketing, distribution, author website, online bookstore, packages of services, à la carte options
Also offers: royalty contracts
Production time: three months
Books per year: thirty
Tip: "Come prepared. Be persistent. Get published."

CROSSHAIR PRESS

PO Box 154, Haven, KS 67543 | 316-214-9818
acquisitions@crosshairpress.com | *www.crosshairpress.com*
Amy Davis, acquisitions manager

Types: ebook, audiobook, POD

Services: manuscript evaluation, design, substantive editing, copyediting, proofreading, distribution

Production time: one year

Tip: "View our submission guidelines online for our reading period dates. Email submissions only."

DCTS PUBLISHING

PO Box 40216, Santa Barbara, CA 93140 | 805-570-3168
dennis@dctspub.com | *www.dctspub.com*
Dennis Hamilton, publisher

Types: offset paperback

Services: manuscript evaluation, design, substantive editing, indexing, proofreading, promotional materials, packages of services

Production time: two to three months

Books per year: five

Tip: "Edit, edit, and edit."

DEEP RIVER BOOKS

PO Box 310, Sisters, OR 97759 | 541-549-1139
submit@deepriverbooks.com | *www.deepriverbooks.com*
Andy Carmichael, publisher

Types: hardcover, offset and POD paperback, ebook, audiobook

Services: manuscript evaluation, design, substantive editing, copyediting, proofreading, promotional materials, marketing, distribution, packages of services

Production time: nine to twelve months

Books per year: thirty to thirty-five

Tip: "Deep River Books is a full-service partner publisher. Unlike self/vanity publishers, we not only provide editing, cover design, and all production, we also provide full marketing, sales, and distribution. We have a sales team that makes face-to-face calls on bookstore buyers who represent more than 2,000 stores. We also provide up to two hours of one-on-one social-media coaching for every author we publish. We carefully select only the manuscripts we feel have a strong chance to see success in retail sales."

DEEPER REVELATION BOOKS

PO Box 4260, Cleveland, TN 37320-4260 | 423-478-2843
info@deeperrevelationbooks.org | *www.deeperrevelationbooks.org*
Mike Shreve, CEO

Types: offset and POD paperback, hardcover, ebook, gift book, picture book

Imprints: Pure Heart Publication (fiction), Children of Promise (children)

Services: manuscript evaluation, design, substantive editing, copyediting, proofreading, promotional materials, distribution, marketing, author website, online bookstore, à la carte options

Also offers: royalty contracts

Production time: six months

Books per year: eight to twelve

Tip: "Visit the Deeper Revelation Books website, and read the beginning articles. Also visit author's corner to read about good writing skills."

DESTINY IMAGE

167 Walnut Bottom Rd., Shippensburg, PA 17257 | 717-532-3040
manuscripts@norimediagroup.com | norimediagroup.com/pages/submit-your-manuscript
Mykela Krieg, executive acquisitions director

Types: hardcover, paperback, ebook

Services: evaluation, editing (whatever level is necessary), proofreading, design, marketing

Production time: one year

Tip: Requires prepurchase of 1,000 to 3,000 copies. Major topics include dreams/dream interpretation, supernatural God encounters, healing/deliverance, and prophecy. No poetry, art, or children's stories; limited fiction. Prefers 40,000-60,000 words. "Most open to books on the deeper life or of Charismatic interest."

EABOOKS PUBLISHING

1567 Thornhill Cir., Oviedo, FL 32765 | 407-712-3431
info@eabookspublishing.com | www.eabookspublishing.com
Cheri Cowell, publisher
Michelle Booth, managing editor

Types: POD, ebook, audiobook, gift book, hardcover

Services: manuscript evaluation, design, substantive editing, copyediting, proofreading, marketing, distribution, author website, packages of services

Also offers: royalty contracts

Production time: two months

Books per year: thirty

Tip: "Let us help you understand your options. Meet us at writers conferences; or send us an email, and we'll get back to you."

EBOOK LISTING SERVICES

PO Box 57, Glenwood, MD 21738 | 443-280-5077
sales@taegais.com | *ebooklistingservices.com*
Amy Deardon, CEO

> **Types:** POD, ebook
> **Services:** design, packages of services, à la carte options, promotional materials, marketing, distribution
> **Production time:** one to three months
> **Books per year:** ten
> **Tip:** "There's no reason you can't be successfully published even if you don't go the traditional route. Write a great book, and research your markets—who will purchase your book and ebook. We develop your book and show you how to become an independent self-publisher. Our company motto is 'We treat you the way we'd like to be treated,' and we take that seriously."

ELECTRIC MOON PUBLISHING, LLC

PO Box 466, Stromsburg, NE 68666 | 402-366-2033
info@emoonpublishing.com | *www.emoonpublishing.com*
Laree Lindburg, owner

> **Types:** offset and POD paperback, hardcover, ebook, audiobook, gift book, picture book
> **Services:** manuscript evaluation, design, substantive editing, copyediting, proofreading, promotional materials, marketing, distribution, author website, packages of services, à la carte options
> **Production time:** six to eight months
> **Books per year:** twelve plus
> **Tip:** "Ask the publisher for submission guidelines, and follow them. Take your time with your book, and do all steps with excellence. You will never regret a well-executed project."

ELM HILL

836 S. Western Dr., Bloomington, IN 47403 | 800-254-2735
email through website | *elmhillbooks.com*

> **Types:** POD, hardcover, ebook
> **Services:** manuscript evaluation, substantive editing, copyediting, design, marketing, promotional materials, author website, video

trailer, distribution assistance, packages of services, à la carte options

Tip: Parent company is Harper-Collins Christian Publishing in collaboration with Accurance, a production services company.

ESSENCE PUBLISHING

20 Hanna Ct., Belleville, ON K8P 5J2, Canada | 800-238-6376, 613-962-2360

info@essence-publishing.com | www.essence-publishing.com
Sherrill Brunton, manager of publishing department

Types: offset and POD paperback, gift book, ebook, picture book

Services: manuscript evaluation, design, substantive editing, copyediting, proofreading, indexing, promotional materials, marketing, distribution, online bookstore

Production time: three months

Books per year: 100-150

Tip: "Submit a copy of your manuscript for your free evaluation."

FAIRWAY PRESS

5450 N. Dixie Hwy., Lima, OH 45807-9559 | 800-241-4056, 419-227-1818

david@csspub.com | www.fairwaypress.com
Missy Cotrell, acquisitions editor

Types: hardcover, offset and POD paperback, ebook

Services: mechanical edit (spelling, grammar, punctuation, etc.), formatting, proofreading, cover design, printing (average print run five hundred copies, minimum fifty), ISBN, bar coding, copyright filing

Production time: six to nine months

Books per year: ten to fifteen

Tip: This is the subsidy division of CSS Publishing Company. No longer does color illustrations or four-color books.

FAITH BOOKS & MORE PUBLISHING

PO Box 1024, Athens, OH 45701 | 678-232-6156

publishing@faithbooksandmore.com | www.faithbooksandmore.com
Nicole Antoinette Smith, author advocate

Types: hardcover, offset and POD paperback, picture book

Services: manuscript evaluation, design, substantive editing, copyediting, proofreading, promotional materials, marketing, distribution, author website, packages of services, à la carte options

Also does: author coaching, ghostwriting

Production time: three months

Books per year: ten

Tip: "Understand the anatomy of a book, and develop a marketing plan for your book."

FIESTA PUBLISHING

PO Box 44984, Phoenix, AZ 85064 | 602-795-5868
julie@fiestapublishing.com | www.fiestapublishing.com
Julie Castro, owner

Types: offset paperback, ebook

Services: manuscript evaluation, substantive editing, copyediting, proofreading, marketing, distribution, online bookstore, à la carte options, author website

Production time: eight to ten weeks if ready to print

Books per year: three or four

Tip: "Don't look at the cost to publish a book, as touching one person is priceless."

FILLED BOOKS

529 County Road 31, Millry, AL 36558 | 888-278-2547
editor@empoweredpublications.com | www.filledbooks.com
Bridgett Henson, acquisitions editor

Types: offset and POD paperback, hardcover, ebook

Services: manuscript evaluation, design, substantive editing, copyediting, proofreading, promotional services, marketing, distribution, author website, online bookstore, packages of services, à la carte options

Also does: royalty contracts

Production time: five weeks

Books per year: six

Tip: "We are a conservative, Pentecostal publisher for ministers who agree with our trinitarian statement of faith. All authors must submit their testimonies of salvation and baptism of the Holy Ghost."

FIRESIDE PRESS

PO Box 571, Gleneden Beach, OR 97388
contact@firesidepress.com | www.FiresidePress.com
Suzanne Parrott, president and lead designer

Types: offset and POD paperback, hardcover, ebook, audiobook, gift book, picture book

Services: manuscript evaluation, design, substantive editing, copyediting, proofreading, indexing, promotional materials, marketing, distribution, author websites, online bookstore, packages of services, à la carte options

Also does: royalty contracts

Production time: six months to two years

Tip: "Fireside Press offers professional, personal, and affordable services every author deserves."

FIRST STEPS PUBLISHING

PO Box 571, Gleneden Beach, OR 97388 | 541-961-7641
publish@firststepspublishing.com | *www.FirstStepsPublishing.com*
Suzanne Fyhrie Parrott, publisher

Types: POD, hardcover, ebook

Services: manuscript evaluation, design, substantive editing, copyediting, proofreading, promotional materials, marketing, online bookstore

Also does: royalty contracts

Production time: twelve to eighteen months

Books per year: four to five

Tip: "Our goal is to publish books of high quality, including those that may have trouble finding homes in traditional markets. We love working with authors who are passionate about their work and have a desire to publish to the world. Are you writing a book you would like to see published? We have years of publishing experience as well as being authors ourselves. We know the quality and service you want from a publisher; and as your publisher, we seek to work with undiscovered and talented authors with the desire and potential to grow to success, whose work is exciting and fresh."

FOREFRONT BOOKS

info@forefront books.com | *www.forefrontbooks.com*
Jonathan Merkh, publisher

Services: ghostwriting, editing, sales, distribution

FRUITBEARER PUBLISHING, LLC

PO Box 777, Georgetown, DE 19947 | 302-856-6649
info@fruitbearer.com | *www.fruitbearer.com*
Candy Abbott, owner

Types: offset and POD paperback, hardcover, ebook, gift book, picture book

Services: manuscript evaluation, design, substantive editing, copyediting, proofreading, indexing, promotional materials, marketing, distribution, online bookstore, author websites, à la carte options

Also does: royalty contracts

Production time: three to six months

Books per year: six

Tip: "Content doesn't have to be overtly religious but must be uplifting and suitable for a Christian audience."

HEALTHY LIFE PRESS

702 S. Wolff St., Denver, CO 80219 | 877-331-2766
info@healthylifepress.com | *www.HealthyLifePress.com*
Dr. David Biebel, publisher

Types: hardcover, POD, ebook, gift book, picture book

Services: manuscript evaluation, design, substantive editing, copyediting, proofreading, promotional materials, marketing, online bookstore

Also does: royalty contracts

Production time: three to six months

Books per year: eight to twelve

Tip: "Healthy Life Press is a cooperative (author-subsidized) and collaborative company, sharing costs and net proceeds equitably. We welcome well-written, edited, and ready-for-design manuscripts on topics the author is passionate about and about which he or she is able to provide a new, different, unique, or original perspective. Submit book proposal plus three sample chapters; inquiries and manuscripts by email only. Do not inquire by phone, except for clarification."

HOLY FIRE PUBLISHING

5016 Spedale Ct., Ste. 199, Spring Hill, TN 37174 | 843-285-3130
publisher@holyfirepublishing.com | *www.holyfirepublishing.com*
Vanessa Hensel, COO

Types: hardcover, paperback, ebook

Services: design, copyright service, bookstore advertising, distribution, online bookstore, packages of services

Tip: "Our contract can be canceled at any time for any reason with a 60-day written notice. It's that simple."

HONEYCOMB HOUSE PUBLISHING LLC

New Cumberland, PA
dave@fessendens.net | davefessenden.com
David E. Fessenden, publisher

Types: POD, ebook
Services: manuscript evaluation, design, substantive editing, copyediting, proofreading, promotional materials, marketing, distribution, author website, packages of services, à la carte options
Production time: three to six months
Tip: "Prepare a book proposal, even if you plan to self-publish, and use it as a guideline for your book project."

HONEYDROP KIDS

2108 Dallas Parkway, Ste. 214-206, Plano, TX 75093 | 866-375-2525
honeydropkids@gmail.com | www.HoneydropKids.com
Tracee Jones, owner

Types: POD, hardcover, ebook, audiobook, Sunday school and school curriculum, picture book
Services: design, promotional materials, marketing, distribution, author websites, online bookstore, packages of services
Production time: three to six months
Tip: "Write for the sake of getting the gospel out, not for the money. When choosing a cover or illustrator, make sure your design looks like something that is in major retail stores."

IMMORTALISE

Australia
info@immortalise.com.au | immortalise.com.au
Ben Morton, senior editor

Types: POD, ebook
Services: writing coaching, manuscript assessment, editing, proofreading, typesetting, illustration, cover design, à la carte options

LOGOS PUBLICATIONS, LLC

Lampter, PA 17537 | 717-681-8452
customerservice@logospub.com | www.logospub.com
Lois Robinson, author support

Types: paperback, POD, hardcover, ebook, audiobook
Services: manuscript evaluation, substantive editing, proofreading, promotional materials, marketing, author website, online bookstore

Also offers: royalty contracts
Production time: six months
Books per year: one to three
Tip: "Present your story to readers who will give you honest feedback during the creation process."

MCDOUGAL PUBLISHING

PO Box 3595, Hagerstown, MD 21742 | 301-797-6637
publishing@mcdougal.org | www.mcdougalpublishing.com

Types: POD, offset printing
Services: manuscript critiquing, editing, cover design, typesetting

MORGAN JAMES PUBLISHING

5 Penn Plaza, 23rd Floor, New York City, NY 10001 | 516-900-5711
terry@morganjamespublishing.com | www.morganjamespublishing.com
W. Terry Whalin, acquisitions editor, Morgan James Faith

Types: hardcover, offset and POD paperback, ebook, audiobook, picture book
Services: design, distribution, marketing, promotional materials, online bookstore
Also does: royalty contracts
Production time: three to six months
Books per year: 150
Tip: "General-market publisher that does 45 to 50 Christian books per year. Our books have been on *The New York Times* bestseller list more than twenty-five times (broad distribution). For nonfiction, requires authors to purchase 2,500 copies at print costs plus $2 over lifetime of agreement. Pays 20-30% royalties on sales; pays small advance. Email proposal with sample chapters or full manuscript. Only 30% of authors have agents."

NORDSKOG PUBLISHING

4562 Westinghouse St., Ste. E, Ventura, CA 93003 | 805-642-2070
email through website | nordskogpublishing.com
Michelle Shelfer, editor

Types: paperback, hardcover
Services: editing, design, marketing
Tip: "Looking for the best in sound theological and applied Christian faith books, both nonfiction and fiction."

PARSON PLACE PRESS

PO Box 8277, Mobile, AL 36689-0277 | 251-643-6985
info@parsonplacepress.com | www.parsonplacepress.com
Michael L. White, managing editor

> **Types:** POD, hardcover, ebook
> **Services:** substantive editing, proofreading, distribution
> **Production time:** four months
> **Tip:** "Peruse website thoroughly before making submissions."

REDEMPTION PRESS

1730 Railroad St., Enumclaw, WA 98022 | 360-226-3488
athena@redemption-press.com | www.redemption-press.com
Athena Dean Holtz, publisher

> **Types:** offset and POD paperback, hardcover, ebook, audiobook, gift book, picture book
> **Services:** manuscript evaluation, design, substantive editing, copyediting, proofreading, indexing, promotional materials, marketing, distribution, author website, online bookstore, à la carte options, coaching, ghostwriting
> **Production time:** three to eight months
> **Books per year:** 75-100
> **Tip:** "Contract for professional coaching to provide your best content. Plan ahead with the training you need to accomplish the most effective book launch possible. Your message should travel well beyond your natural sphere of influence. Your work should be the best that it can be, so if you're going to self-publish to get to market sooner and provide the needed resources for others, the last thing you want to do is look or read self-published! Don't cut corners. Produce your message with excellence (Colossians 3:17)."

SALVATION PUBLISHER AND MARKETING GROUP

PO Box 40860, Santa Barbara, CA 93140 | 805-252-9822
opalmaedailey@aol.com
Dr. Opal Mae Dailey, editor

> **Types:** hardcover, offset paperback, ebook
> **Services:** manuscript evaluation, design, substantive editing, copyediting, proofreading
> **Production time:** six to nine months
> **Books per year:** five to seven
> **Tip:** "Turning taped messages into book form for pastors is a specialty

of ours. We do not accept any manuscript we would be ashamed to put our name on."

SERMON TO BOOK

424 W. Bakerview Rd., Ste. 105 #215, Bellingham, WA 98226 | 360-223-1877
info@sermontobook.com | *www.sermontobook.com*
Caleb Breakey, lead book director

> **Types:** offset and POD paperback, ebook, audiobook
> **Services:** design, substantive editing, copyediting, proofreading, indexing, promotional materials, marketing, distribution, author website, online bookstore, packages of services, manuscript evaluation
> **Production time:** seven to nine months
> **Books per year:** sixty
> **Tip:** "Check out our materials at SermonToBook.com."

SPLASHDOWN BOOKS

Auckland, New Zealand
grace@splashdownbooks.com | *www.splashdownbooks.com*
Grace Bridges, owner

> **Types:** ebook, POD
> **Services:** manuscript evaluation, substantive editing, copyediting, proofreading, à la carte options, hybrid publishing
> **Production time:** as needed
> **Books per year:** four to eight
> **Tip:** "Be an excellent indie author with support. Steep discounts on editing for well-critiqued work. Use of Splashdown branding may be offered after edits to qualifying. mainstream-compatible science-fiction and fantasy works."

STONE OAK PUBLISHING

PO Box 2011, Friendswood, TX 77549 | 832-569-4282
stoneoakpublishing@gmail.com | *www.stoneoakpublishing.com*
Karen Porter, editor

> **Types of books:** POD and offset paperback, hardcover, ebook, gift book
> **Services:** manuscript evaluation, design, substantive editing, copyediting, proofreading, indexing, promotional materials, marketing, distribution, author website, online bookstore, packages of services, à la carte options

Production time: six to eight months

Books per year: ten

Tip: "Our goal is to give you the highest-quality book with the best service. We hope to make your experience with Stone Oak Publishers better than you expected. To work with our excellent editors, designers, artists, and marketers, begin by contacting us with your book idea; and we will help you take it to the highest level."

STONEHOUSE INK

Boise, ID | 208-608-8325

stonehousepress@hotmail.com | stonehouseink.com

Aaron Patterson, editor-publisher

Types: paperback, ebook

Tip: Specializes in fiction, including thrillers, mystery, and YA. Interested in published authors looking to publish backlist titles or to rebrand and relaunch titles.

STRONG TOWER PUBLISHING

PO Box 973, Milesburg, PA 16863 | 814-206-6778

strongtowerpubs@aol.com | www.strongtowerpublishing.com

Heidi L. Nigro, publisher

Types: ebook, POD

Services: manuscript evaluation, copyediting, proofreading, substantive editing, design, online bookstore

Production time: three to four months

Books per year: one or two

Tip: Specializes in books on end-times topics from the prewrath rapture perspective.

TEACH SERVICES, INC.

11 Quartermaster Cir., Fort Oglethorpe, GA 30742-3886 | 706-504-9192

publishing@teachservices.com | www.teachservices.com

Timothy Hullquist, author advisor

Types: offset and POD paperback, hardcover, ebook, gift book, picture book, landscape hardback, mechanical binding

Services: manuscript evaluation, design, substantive editing, copyediting, proofreading, indexing, promotional materials, marketing, distribution, author websites, online bookstore, packages of services, à la carte options

Also does: royalty contracts

Production time: one to four months

Tip: "We specialize in marketing our titles to Seventh-day Adventists."

TESTIMONY PUBLICATIONS, LLC

5625 Pearl Dr., Ste. F-123, Evansville, IN 47712 | 812-602-3031
mkough@testimonypublications.com | *www.testimonypublications.com*
Marj Kough, CEO

Types: hardcover, ebook, POD
Services: manuscript evaluation, design, substantive editing, copyediting, proofreading, promotional materials, marketing, distribution, author websites, online bookstore, packages of services, à la carte options
Also does: royalty contracts
Production time: three to six months
Tip: "We publish fiction or nonfiction books or materials with a Christian focus."

TMP BOOKS

3 Central Plaza, Ste. 307, Rome, GA 30161
info@tmpbooks.com | *www.TMPbooks.com*
Tracy Ruckman, publisher

Types: POD, ebook, picture book, hardcover
Services: manuscript evaluation, design, substantive editing, copyediting, proofreading, promotional materials, marketing, distribution, packages of services, à la carte options, author websites
Production time: six months
Books per year: twenty
Tip: "We offer affordable, professional self-publishing options, including one package that allows the author to retain 100% of the royalties. Read testimonials from our clients on our website."

T2PNEUMA PUBLISHERS LLC

PO Box 230564, Centreville, VA 20120 | 703-973-8898
T2Pneuma@gmail.com | *www.T2Pneuma.com*
Stephen W. Hiemstra, publisher

Types: paperback, ebook
Service: manuscript evaluation
Production time: one year
Tip: "We focus on nonfiction, Christian books in English and Spanish. Check website for details before submitting manuscript ideas."

TRACT PLANET

1155 Fountain Coin Loop, Orlando, FL 32828 | 877-778-7228
support@tractplanet.com | *www.tractplanet.com*
Andy Lawniczak

Type: Gospel tracts
Services: design, promotional materials
Production time: varies
Tip: "We focus on Gospel tracts that follow the Way of the Master method of evangelism."

TRAIL MEDIA

PO Box 387, La Mirada, CA 90637
admin@ChisholmTrailMedia.com | *www.chisholmtrailmedia.com*
Christine "CJ" Simpson, director of publishing

Types: POD, ebook, gift book, picture book
Services: manuscript evaluation, substantive editing, copyediting, proofreading, promotional materials, marketing, packages of services, à la carte options
Production time: negotiable
Tip: "Our goal is to help new authors publish their work by coordinating the services needed with experts in the field and publishing in a co-op fashion under the Trail Media imprint, so 100% of the revenue generated goes to ministry of the authors. In many cases, we find scholarships and grants to help missionaries and those in the persecuted church. Trail Media is a ministry of modified tentmaking models."

TRUTH BOOK PUBLISHERS

800 S. Main St., Jacksonville, IL 62650 | 217-243-8880
truthbookpublishers@yahoo.com | *www.truthbookpublisher.com*
JaNell Lyle, owner

Types: offset paperback, hardcover, ebook, picture book
Services: design, copyediting, proofreading, promotional materials, distribution, à la carte options
Production time: one month
Books per year: forty
Tip: "Be sure to have the book edited."

TULPEN PUBLISHING

11043 Depew St., Westminster, CO 80020 | 303-438-7276

tulpenpublishing@gmail.com | TulpenPublishing.com
Sandi Rog, acquisitions editor

> **Types:** ebook, POD
>
> **Services:** manuscript evaluation, design, substantive editing, copyediting, proofreading, distribution, online bookstore, marketing
>
> **Production time:** twelve to twenty months
>
> **Tip:** Only accepts submissions via email. See the website for submission guidelines.

WESTBOW PRESS

1663 Liberty Dr., Bloomington, IN 47403 | 866-928-1240
email through website | www.westbowpress.com

> **Types:** hardcover, paperback, ebook, audiobook
>
> **Services:** manuscript evaluation, substantive editing, copyediting, design, illustrations, indexing, Spanish translation, marketing, video trailer, distribution
>
> **Tip:** Independent publishing division of Thomas Nelson and Zondervan.

WORD ALIVE PRESS

131 Cordite Rd., Winnipeg, MB R3W 1S1, Canada | 866-967-3782
publishing@wordalivepress.ca | www.wordalivepress.ca

> **Types:** hardcover, offset and POD paperback, ebook, gift book
>
> **Services:** packages of services, editing, design, marketing, distribution, online bookstore
>
> **Production time:** four to five months

XULON PRESS

2301 Lucien Way, Ste. 415, Maitland, FL 32751 | 407-339-4217, 866-381-2665
email through website | www.xulonpress.com
Donald Newman, director of sales

> **Types:** hardcover, offset and POD paperback, ebook
>
> **Services:** manuscript review, editorial critique, developmental editing, copyediting, design, packages of services, à la carte options, color illustrations, back-cover copy, ghostwriting, translation, marketing, promotional materials, publicity, video trailer, 100% net royalty, online bookstore
>
> **Production time:** three to six months

YO PRODUCTIONS, LLC

PO Box 32329, Columbus, OH 43232 | 614-452-4920
info_4u@yoproductions.net | *www.yoproductions.net*
Yolonda Tonette Sanders, founder and CEO

> **Types:** POD, ebook
> **Services:** manuscript evaluation, design, substantive editing, copyediting, proofreading, packages of services, à la carte options
> **Also does:** royalty contracts
> **Production time:** three to six months, six months to a year royalty
> **Books per year:** six plus, two royalty
> **Tip:** "Books considered for traditional publishing must be exceptionally well-written prior to submission. In addition, manuscripts cannot contain any foul or vulgar language."

ZOË LIFE PUBLISHING

PO Box 871066, Canton, MI 48187 | 888-400-4922
info@zoelifepub.com | *www.zoelifepub.com*
Sabrina Adams, publisher

> **Types:** hardcover, paperback, ebook
> **Services:** packages of services, editing, design, rights and registrations, warehousing, promotion, distribution and fulfillment, online bookstore
> **Production time:** one year

Christian Writers Institute Courses 2020 Indie Publishing Bundle

Courses in this bundle:

- How to Get Published
- Independent Publishing Basics
- Indie Publishing Technical How-To's
- How to Find Your Readers as an Indie Author
- Independent Publishing Subsidiary Rights
- Newsletter Marketing for Independent Authors
- SMART Copywriting for Independent Authors

Normal price: $140
Savings: 72%
Market Guide price $39.20

https://cwmg.link/indie2020

How to Scan QR Codes
Use the camera on your smartphone to focus on the above QR code to activate the discount. It will give you the option to visit the site, which you will want to accept. If you are using an older smartphone, you may need to download a QR code scanning app. You can also visit the URL below the code to activate the discount on your computer.

3

DESIGN AND PRODUCTION SERVICES

AUTHOR SUPPORT SERVICES | RUSSELL SHERRARD

Carmichael, CA | 916-967-7251
*russellsherrard@reagan.com | www.sherrardsebookresellers.com/WordPress/
author-support-services-the-authors-place-to-get-help*

> **Contact:** email
>
> **Services:** Kindle ebook formatting, ebook linked table of contents,
> PDF creation, book-cover design
>
> **Charges:** flat fee
>
> **Credentials/experience:** Writing and editing since 2009; currently
> providing freelance services for multiple clients.

BETHANY PRESS INTERNATIONAL

6820 W. 115th St., Bloomington, MN 55438 | 888-717-7400
info@bethanypress.com | www.bethanypress.com

> **Contact:** email, phone, website form
>
> **Services:** short-run digital printing and long-run (minimum 500
> copies) printing, only with files created by a professional book
> designer; ebook conversion, only with corresponding print order
>
> **Charges:** flat fee
>
> **Credentials/experience:** Printer for the majority of Christian
> publishing houses since 1997. "We partner with publishers and
> ministries to create, produce, and distribute millions of life-
> changing Christian books each year. We invest our proceeds in
> training and sending missionaries through Bethany International."

BLUE LEAF BOOK SCANNING

618 Crowsnest Dr., Ballwin, MO 63021 | 314-606-9322
blue.leaf.it@gmail.com | www.blueleaf-book-scanning.com

> **Contact:** email, phone, website form

Services: book and document scanning to multiple formats, ebook and audio conversions

Charges: flat fee

Credentials/experience: The first book-scanning service for consumers. Accurate optical character recognition (more than 99.6% accurate on ideal conditions) with excellent format retention. Can scan nearly 200 languages.

BOB CRUM

Kenosha, WI

bob@mrbobcrum.com | mrbobcrum.com

Contact: email

Services: book-cover design, book-interior design, illustrations

Charges: flat fee

Credentials/experience: A full-time illustrator and designer with more than twenty years of experience with authors in the young-adult fiction market, as well as graphic novels and comics.

BOOK WHISPERS

Capalaba QLD 4157, Australia | +61 7 3167 6513

info@bookwhispers.com.au | www.bookwhispers.com.au

Contact: website form, phone

Services: cover design; interior design; typesetting; preparing print-ready files; promotional materials, including bookmarks, banners, and flyers

BREADBOX CREATIVE | ERYN LYNUM

1437 N. Denver Ave. #167, Loveland, CO 80538 | 970-308-3654

eryn@breadboxcreative.com | www.breadboxcreative.com/creators

Contact: website form

Services: website design, social-media assistance

Charges: flat fee

Credentials/experience: "At Breadbox Creative, we have more than twenty years of experience in web design. The owner, Eryn Lynum, is an author herself and marries her passion for writing with her passion for web design to come alongside writers and speakers and help them further spread the messages God has laid on their hearts. Breadbox Creative works with businesses, writers, and speakers by creating professional WordPress websites, as well as assisting with SEO and social-media platforms. We also offer assistance with preparing book proposals and writing consulting."

BRENDA WILBEE

4631 Quinn Ct., 202 | Bellingham, WA 98226

brenda@brendawilbee.com | brendawilbee.com

> **Contact:** email, website form
>
> **Services:** book-cover design, book-interior design, typesetting, printing, bookmarks, flyers, sell sheets, postcards, calendars, photo enhancement, files ready for offset printing or digital publication
>
> **Charges:** flat fee, hourly rate, custom rate
>
> **Credentials/experience:** "I've been helping writers find their voice for more than 20 years and now help them get their manuscripts into print. I have a passion for combining narrative and images. To that end, I hold an MA in Professional Writing, a BA in Creative Writing, an AA in Visual Communications. I've written ten books, with over 700,000 copies sold. I taught college and university composition for seven years, and some of my design clients include Habitat for Humanity, Whatcom Community College, Edirol, self-published writers, and service organizations. See my portfolio at BrendaWilbee.com/designer. My goal is to help all writers realize their full potential as a force for good in a troubled world."

BROOKSTONE CREATIVE GROUP | SUZANNE KUHN

PO Box 211, Evington, VA 24550 | 302-514-7899

www.brookstonecreativegroup.com

> **Contact:** website form
>
> **Services:** book-cover design, book-interior design, offset and POD printing, distribution, website design, promotional materials
>
> **Charges:** flat fee
>
> **Credentials/experience:** Suzanne has more than thirty years of book-specific experience. Brookstone is an expansion of her business, SuzyQ, with a team of almost two dozen professionals who bring a wide range of knowledge and experience to help you get published.

BUTTERFIELD EDITORIAL SERVICES |
DEBRA L. BUTTERFIELD

4810 Gene Field Rd. #2, St. Joseph, MO 64506 | 816-752-2171

deb@debralbutterfield.com | DebraLButterfield.com

> **Contact:** email
>
> **Services:** book-cover design, book-interior design, ebook conversion
>
> **Charges:** custom rate
>
> **Credentials/experience:** "Our team has more than eight year's experience in book design."

CASTELANE, INC. | KIM MCDOUGALL

Whitehall, PA | 647-281-1554
kimm@castelane.com | www.castelane.com

> **Contact:** email
> **Services:** book-cover design, ebook conversion, book video trailers
> **Charges:** flat fee
> **Credentials/experience:** "I have made more than five hundred book video trailers and three hundred book covers since 2009. Samples and references are available on the website."

CELEBRATION WEB DESIGN | BRUCE SHANK

PO Box 471068, Celebration, FL 34747 | 610-989-0400
info@celebrationwebdesign.com | CelebrationWebDesign.com

> **Contact:** email, phone, website form
> **Service:** website design
> **Charges:** flat fee, hourly rate, custom rate
> **Credentials/experience:** "Celebration Web Design offers tailor-made websites. If you can dream it, we can build it. Our vision is to work with you in creating a high-quality, visually engaging, full-featured website that exceeds your every expectation. Partnering with our team will revolutionize your web presence. Our goal is to take care of all the tech stuff, so you can focus on what you do best. We are committed to providing the best possible service at the lowest possible price. Our staff is dedicated to furthering the Kingdom of God by partnering with authors, ministries, missionaries, and churches to create websites with purpose."

CHRISTIANPRINT.COM

6820 W. 115th St., Bloomington, MN 55438 | 888-201-1322
www.christianprint.com

> **Contact:** phone, website form
> **Services:** prints ancillary products, such as business cards, brochures, booklets, banners, postcards, posters, and signs
> **Charges:** flat fee
> **Credentials/experience:** A division of Bethany Press, founded in 1997.

CONCEPTARTDESIGNINC | JIM COLLINS

9 Lorne St., Chatham, Ontario | 519-437-0485
jacartcreations@hotmail.com | conceptartdesigninc.patternbyetsy.com

> **Contact:** email
> **Services:** book-cover design, illustrations

Charges: flat fee or hourly, depending on job requirements
Credentials/experience: "Thirty plus years as fine art/commerical artist; published fine-art prints, biblical calendar, children's book illustration; art gallery representation; owned an art gallery. Customer service is priority one and meeting deadlines. Bachelor of Commerce degree in marketing."

CREATIVE EDITORIAL SOLUTIONS | CLAUDIA VOLKMAN

North Fort Myers, FL | 203-645-5600
cvolkman@mac.com | creativeeditorialsolutions.com

Contact: email
Services: book-interior design, typesetting
Charges: flat fee
Credentials/experience: "I have over thirty-five years of experience in the book-publishing industry, and I love both finessing content and then creating book interiors that complement it. I'm happy to send samples on request."

DESIGN CORPS | JOHN WOLLINKA

Colorado Springs, CO | 719-260-0500
john@designcorps.us | designcorps.us

Contact: email
Services: book-cover design, book-interior design, typesetting, ebook conversion, illustrations, website design, printing, marketing
Charges: flat fee
Credentials/experience: Design Corps has been serving Christian publishers, denominations, ministries, and organizations for more than twenty years.

THE DESIGN IN YOUR MIND | MARY C. FINDLEY

Tulsa, OK | 918-805-0669
mjmcfindley@gmail.com | elkjerkyforthesoul.wordpress.com

Contact: email
Services: book-cover design, book-interior design, ebook conversion, illustrations
Charges: flat fee
Credentials/experience: Designer and formatter for seven years for many indie authors and many genres, including illustrated children's books, graphics in layouts, illustrated ebooks, print for fiction, and curriculum.

DIGGYPOD | KEVIN OSWORTH

301 Industrial Dr., Tecumseh, MI 49286 | 877-944-7844
kosworth@diggypod.com | www.diggypod.com

> **Contact:** email, website form, phone
> **Services:** book-cover design, printing
> **Charges:** based on the number of books/pages being printed; website
> has an active quote calculator that provides 100% accurate pricing
> **Credentials/experience:** DiggyPOD has been printing books since
> 2001. All facets of the book printing take place in its facility.

EDENBROOKE PRODUCTIONS | MARTY KEITH

Franklin, TN | 615-415-1942
johnmartinkeith@gmail.com | www.edenbrookemusic.com/booktrailers

> **Contact:** email
> **Service:** book trailers with custom music
> **Charges:** flat fee
> **Credentials/experience:** Has produced music for everyone from CBS
> TV to Discovery Channel.

FISTBUMP MEDIA, LLC | DAN KING

Sarasota, FL | 941-780-4179
dan@fistbumpmedia.com | fistbumpmedia.com

> **Contact:** email
> **Services:** book-cover design, book-interior design, typesetting, ebook
> conversion, website design
> **Charges:** flat fee, hourly rate
> **Credentials/experience:** See the website for references and portfolio.
> Specializes in design and formatting for print-on-demand.

FIVE J'S DESIGN | JOY A. MILLER

info@fivejsdesign.com | fivejsdesign.com

> **Contact:** email, website form
> **Services:** book-cover design, book-interior design, typesetting
> **Charges:** hourly rate, flat fee, custom rate
> **Credentials/experience:** "We have been designing and typesetting
> books since 2008, including the cover design and interior layout
> for *The Christian Writers Market Guide*."

THE FOREWORD COLLECTIVE, LLC |
MOLLY KEMPF HODGIN, NICOLE CORSE LEVINE

1726 Charity Dr., Brentwood, TN 37027
info@theforewordcollective.com | www.theforewordcollective.com

Contact: email, website form
Service: book-cover design
Charges: custom rate
Credentials/experience: "We employ a wide variety of creative professionals on a per-project basis, including editors, copyeditors, designers, writers, photographers, marketers, and public-relations pros. We have more than thirty years of publishing experience between us, and we want to put that experience to work for you. Molly was most recently the associate publisher for the specialty division of HarperCollins Christian Publishing, directing the design of some of the most-coveted covers in the Christian market. Nicole was most recently the editorial director at InSight Publishing, directing the design of books for kids and teens."

GRACE BRIDGES
New Zealand
gracebridges1@gmail.com | www.gracebridges.kiwi/hire-me
Contact: email
Services: book-cover design, book-interior design, typesetting, ebook conversion
Charges: custom fee, flat fee according to project requirements, hourly rate on changes requested after client approval
Credentials/experience: "Designed dozens of print interiors to top-publishing quality. Cover designs and ebook conversions are basic standard and priced accordingly. Contact for examples."

IMMORTALISE | BEN MORTON
Australia
info@immortalise.com.au | www.immortalise.com.au
Contact: email
Services: typesetting, illustrations, cover design
Credentials/experience: Published author, creative-writing teacher, experienced editor and publisher, MA fiction writing supervisor.

JOANNA MARIE ART | JOANNA MARIE
PO Box 30664, Mesa, AZ 85275 | 520-686-1088
joanna@joanamarieart.com | www.joannamarieart.com
Contact: email
Services: book-cover design, illustrations, website design
Charges: flat fee
Credentials/experience: More than ten years in fine art/illustration work, five years web design.

KELLIE BOOK DESIGN | KELLIE PARSONS

Perth, WA, Australia | 0412 591 687

hello@kelliemaree.com | facebook.com/kelliebookdesign

Contact: email

Services: book-cover design, book-interior design, typesetting, ebook conversion, print liaison

Charges: flat fee

Credentials/experience: "Kellie Book Design has been doing graphic design for churches, ministries, and nonprofit organizations for over 10 years and has specialized in book design since 2015."

KEN RANEY

1848 Georgia St., Cape Girardeau, MO 63701 | 316-737-9724

kenraney@mac.com | kenraney.com

Contact: email

Services: book-cover design, book-interior design, ebook conversion, illustrations

Charges: flat fee, hourly rate

Credentials/experience: "Ken is president of Raney Day Creative, LLC, a producer of illustration and graphic design, and Raney Day Press. He is the author/illustrator of two children's picture books and has more than forty-five years of experience in graphic design, illustration, advertising, and marketing."

LAURA PACE GRAPHIC DESIGN | LAURA PACE

1287 Gambel Oaks Pl., Elizabeth, CO 80107 | 303-906-8850

pacelauradesign@gmail.com | Laurapacedesign.com

Contact: email, phone

Services: book-cover design, full-cover layouts, business cards, bookmarks, table tents, postcards, fliers

Charges: flat fee

Credentials/experience: "Freelance designer specializing in book-cover and full-cover layouts, as well as a large variety of print material for promotional and advertising purposes. I enjoy working directly with both authors and publishing companies."

MADISON BOOK COVER DESIGNS | RUTH DERBY

220 W. Elm St., Hanford, CA 93230 | 559-772-2489

rmadison_1@hotmail.com | www.ruthiemadison.com

Contact: email, website form

Services: book-cover design

Charges: flat fee

Credentials/experience: More than three years of experience and has had mentors in this field.

MARTIN PUBLISHING SERVICES | MELINDA MARTIN

Palestine, TX | 903-948-4893

support@melindamartin.me | *melindamartin.me*

Contact: email

Services: book-cover design, book-interior design, typesetting, ebook conversion

Charges: flat fee

Credentials/experience: Five years of working with clients' manuscripts to achieve a design that is best for their platforms.

MCLENNAN CREATIVE | ALISON MCLENNAN

1933 Geraldson Dr., Lancaster, PA 17601 | 717-572-2585

alison@mclennancreative.com | *www.mclennancreative.com*

Contact: email, phone, website contact form

Services: book-cover design, ebook conversion, website design

Charges: flat fee, hourly rate, customized packages

Credentials/experience: More than twenty years of experience in the publishing industry.

MEADE AGENCY | KRIS MEADE

460 King St. #200, Charleston, SC 29403 | 843-206-3871

kris@meadeagency.cc | *www.meadeagency.cc*

Contact: email, phone

Service: video production

Charges: custom fee

Credentials/experience: "Meade Agency is a professional video production company specializing in book trailers, branding videos, and online course creation. We have mastered the production of web-based, on-demand video education. Online courses are a powerful way to monetize a platform, and we've got you covered from filming lessons to the web development of your course. We have worked with a variety of leaders in the industry, such as Proverbs 31 Ministries, HarperCollins, Thomas Nelson, and David C. Cook Publishing."

MISSION AND MEDIA | MICHELLE RAYBURN

11510 County Highway M, New Auburn, WI 54757 | 715-382-6030

info@missionandmedia.com | *www.missionandmedia.com*

Contact: email

Services: book-cover design, book-interior design, typesetting, ebook conversion

Charges: flat fee, hourly rate, free consultation

Credentials/experience: "Michelle works with indie and self-published authors to design a quality book cover and interior. She also coaches those who want to create their own imprint with full control of their own publishing process. Her area of specialty is with Amazon KDP (formerly CreateSpace). Michelle worked for a marketing and advertising agency for 3 years, and also has 17 years of experience on the writing and editing side of publishing. Portfolio and additional information are available on the website."

PROFESSIONAL PUBLISHING SERVICES | CHRISTY CALLAHAN

PO Box 461, Waycross, GA 31502 | 912-809-9062
professionalpublishingservices@gmail.com | *www.ChristyCallahan.com*

Contact: email

Services: book-interior design, typesetting, ebook conversion

Charges: flat fee, custom rate

Credentials/experience: "We offer typesetting with quick turnaround times and reasonable rates to traditional and independent book publishers, as well as indie authors. Christy graduated Phi Beta Kappa from Carnegie Mellon University, where she first learned how to use Adobe software and worked as an assistant in the Language Learning Resource Center and the psychology department. While she earned her MA in Intercultural Studies from Fuller Seminary, she edited sound files for distance-learning classes for the Media Center and designed ads as Women's Concerns Committee chairperson. Christy is proficient in using Adobe InDesign software, leveraging her expertise as an editor and proofreader and extensive knowledge of *Chicago* style to create professional-looking interior book layouts."

RICK STEELE EDITORIAL SERVICES | RICK STEELE

26 Dean Rd., Ringgold, GA 30736 | 706-937-8121
rsteelecam@gmail.com | *steeleeditorialservices.myportfolio.com*

Contact: email, website form

Services: book-interior design, typesetting

Charges: flat fee based on page count and complexity of layout

Credentials/experience: "More than twenty years of working for Christian publishing houses has led me to wear many hats, including typesetting and page-layout duties. I have more than two decades of experience using page-layout software programs, such as Adobe InDesign and QuarkXPress. I've performed layout duties for countless trade fiction and nonfiction books, workbook Bible studies, devotionals, and prayer journals."

ROSEANNA WHITE DESIGNS | ROSEANNA WHITE
roseannamwhite@gmail.com | www.RoseannaWhiteDesigns.com
    Contact: email, website form
    Services: book-cover design, book-interior design, typesetting, ebook conversion, illustrations
    Charges: flat fee, hourly rate, custom fee
    Credentials/experience: "Roseanna has been designing and typesetting books for nearly ten years, combining her keen eye and artistic skills with her insider knowledge of the industry. As an author herself, she knows how important it is for the appearance of a book to match the words and strives to bring your story to life at a single glance. She has worked for publishing houses and independently for some of Christian fiction's top authors."

SCREE, LLC | LANDON OTIS
Sandpoint, ID | 208-290-4624
landon@scree.it | scree.it

    Contact: email
    Services: website design, website development
    Charges: hourly rate
    Credentials/experience: Professional, full-time web developer at a local design and marketing firm. Websites include *veritasincorporated.com* and *mineralchurch.org*.

STARCHER DESIGNS | KARA STARCHER
Chloe, WV | 330-705-3399
info@starcherdesigns.com | www.starcherdesigns.com

    Contact: email
    Services: book-interior design, typesetting
    Charges: custom fee
    Credentials/experience: BA in publishing, professional designer with more than fifteen years of experience.

SUZANNE FYHRIE PARROTT
PO Box 571, Gleneden Beach, OR 97388
author@suzannefyhrieparrott.com | www.SuzanneFyhrieParrott.com
    Contact: email, website form

Services: book-cover design, book-interior design, ebook conversion, illustrations

Also does: publication and marketing

Charges: flat fee, hourly rate, custom fee

Credentials/experience: "Suzanne graduated from the University of Washington in 1981 and has earned several Montana Addy Awards for design excellence, working with such clients as Yellowstone Park, Old West Trail, Columbia Paint, Winston Fly Rod Company, and Montana Power Company. She is currently the lead designer for First Steps Publishing, Fireside Press, Penman Productions, and several other publishing companies. Her primary design focus is book design and publication, producing original layouts/designs in print and digital (ebook/audio), as well as creating a complete marketing plan for your publication success."

TLC BOOK DESIGN | TAMARA DEVER

Austin, TX

tamara@tlcbookdesign.com | www.TLCBookDesign.com

Contact: website form

Services: book-cover design, book-interior design, typesetting, ebook conversion, printing

Charges: custom rate

Credentials/experience: "TLC provides award-winning book design, editorial, printing, and guidance with a personal touch that takes the stress out of book creation and gives serious authors and publishers high-quality books they are proud to represent. The recipients of over 200 industry awards, we've been joyfully serving the publishing industry for twenty-five years."

TRILION STUDIOS | BRIAN WHITE

Lawrence, KS | 785-841-5500

brian@TriLionStudios.com | www.TriLionStudios.com

Contact: email, phone

Services: book-cover design, illustrations, web design

Charges: flat fee, hourly rate

Credentials/experience: Twenty years in the design/web design/ branding industry. Has worked with nonprofits and churches for more than fifteen years.

VIVID GRAPHICS | LARRY VAN HOOSE

221 S. Main St., Ste. 200, Galax, VA 24333 | 276-233-0276

larry@vivid-graphics.com | www.vivid-graphics.com

Contact: email
Services: book-cover design, book-interior design, ebook conversion, typesetting, website design, book trailers
Charges: hourly rate, flat fee, custom fee
Credentials/experience: "Executive editor for local magazine, graphic design, creative, marketing, research. Managed creative teams with more than twenty-five years of experience in technical and marketing design, copywriting, communications, and publishing. Specialties: creative direction; technical and nonfiction writing; editing; publishing; web, graphic, book, and magazine design."

WRITER'S TABLET AGENCY | TERRI WHITEMORE
4371 Roswell Rd. #315, Marietta, GA 30062 | 770-648-4101
WritersTablet@gmail.com | www.WritersTablet.org

Contact: email
Services: book-cover design, book-interior design, typesetting, ebook conversion, illustrations, website design
Charges: flat fee
Credentials/experience: Graphic design, BS in computer science, testimonials from local and national businesses and authors. Copywriter for G5. Six years of experience.

YO PRODUCTIONS, LLC | YOLONDA TONETTE SANDERS
PO Box 32329, Columbus, OH 43232 | 614-452-4920
info_4u@yoproductions.net | www.yoproductions.net

Contact: email, phone, website form
Services: book-interior design, typesetting, ebook conversion
Charges: flat fee, custom fee
Credentials/experience: More than thirteen years of professional experience, editor and writer for a national publication, traditionally published author.

Note: See **"Editorial Services"** and **"Publicity and Marketing Services"** for help with these needs.

Christian Publishing Show
Featured Episode

Podcast episode: How to Avoid the #1 Cause of Bad Book Covers: Design by Committee
Market Guide price FREE

https://cwmg.link/design2020

How to Scan QR Codes
Use the camera on your smartphone to focus on the above QR code to activate the discount. It will give you the option to visit the site, which you will want to accept. If you are using an older smartphone, you may need to download a QR code scanning app. You can also visit the URL below the code to activate the discount on your computer.

4

DISTRIBUTION SERVICES

CHRISTIAN BOOK DISTRIBUTORS

PO Box 7000, Peabody, MA 01961-7000 | 800-247-4784
customer.service@christianbook.com | *www.christianbook.com*
Sometimes distributes independently published books.

NOVELLA DISTRIBUTION

Unit 3, 5 Currumbin Ct., Capalaba, QLD 4157 Australia |
+ 617 3167 6519

info@novelladistribution.com.au | *faith.novelladistribution.com.au*
Provides warehousing and distribution to trade bookstores (Christian and general market), as well as library and educational suppliers and major online retailers. Also operates a specialist division that is the supplier of choice for many Christian schools in Australia.

PATHWAY BOOK SERVICE

34 Production Ave., Keene, NH 03431 | 800-345-6665
pbs@pathwaybook.com | *www.pathwaybook.com*
Provides warehousing, order fulfillment, and trade distribution. It is a longtime distributor to Ingram and Baker & Taylor, the vendors of choice for most bookstores. Pathway uploads new-title spreadsheets to *Ingram and Baker & Taylor*, as well as to *Amazon.com*, Barnes & Noble, and Books-A-Million and databases on a weekly basis. Distribution outside of North America is available through Gazelle Book Services in the United Kingdom. Also provides the option of having Pathway add titles to its Amazon Advantage account, which is at a lower discount and often a lower shipping cost per book than individual accounts.

PART 3

PERIODICAL PUBLISHERS

5

TOPICS AND TYPES

This chapter is not an exhaustive list of types of manuscripts and topics editors are looking for, but it is a starting place for some of the more popular ones. For instance, almost all periodicals take manuscripts in categories like Christian living, so they are not listed here. Plus writers guidelines tend to outline general areas, not every specific type and topic an editor will buy.

CONTEMPORARY ISSUES
Brio
Catholic Sentinel
The Christian Herald
Christianity Today
City Light News
The Covenant Companion
Faith Today
Focus on the Family
Holiness Today
Light + Life Magazine
Ministry
New Frontier Chronicle
Now What?
Our Sunday Visitor Newsweekly
Presbyterians Today
St. Anthony Messenger
War Cry

DEVOTIONS
Focus on the Family
The Gem
Gems of Truth
Girlz 4 Christ Magazine

Keys to Living
ParentLife
Presbyterians Today
Reach Out, Columbia

ESSAY
America
The Canadian Lutheran
Catholic Digest
The Christian Century
Christian Communicator
Christian Leader
The Christian Librarian
Commonweal
The Cresset
CrossCurrents
Faith Today
Image
Liguorian
Love Is Moving
Lutheran Witness
Our Sunday Visitor Newsweekly
Poets & Writers Magazine
Relief Journal

Sharing
Story Embers
U.S. Catholic
The Writer
The Writer's Chronicle
Writer's Digest

EVANGELISM
Christian Leader
Christian Research Journal
CommonCall
Decision
Evangelical Missions Quarterly
Facts & Trends
Indian Life
Just Between Us
Lutheran Witness
Message of the Open Bible
Net Results
New Identity Magazine
On Mission
Outreach
War Cry

FAMILY
Boundless
Celebrate Life Magazine
Christian Leader
Columbia
CommonCall
Evangelical Missions Quarterly
Faith & Friends
Focus on the Family
HomeLife
Joyful Living Magazine
Ministry
The Mother's Heart
ParentLife
Power for Living
St. Anthony Messenger

Southwest Kansas Faith
and Family
Thrive Connection
YouthMinistry.com

FICTION
See **Short Story**.

FILLERS
Angels on Earth
Bible Advocate
Children's Ministry
The Christian Herald
Christian Living in
the Mature Years
Creation Illustrated
Eternal Ink
FellowScript
Focus on the Family Clubhouse
Focus on the Family Clubhouse Jr.
Freelance Writer's Report
Girlz 4 Christ Magazine
Guideposts
Indian Life
LIVE
The Lutheran Digest
The Mother's Heart
War Cry
Words for the Way
YouthMinistry.com

FINANCES/MONEY
Boundless
Children's Ministry
Christian Living in
the Mature Years
Christian Standard
Columbia
Joyful Living Magazine
Just Between Us
MTL Magazine

Net Results
WritersWeekly.com

HOW-TO

Canada Lutheran
Catechist
Catholic Digest
Celebrate Life Magazine
Charisma Leader
Children's Ministry
Christian Communicator
The Christian Herald
*Christian Living in
the Mature Years*
Christian Standard
CommonCall
Creation Illustrated
Evangelical Missions Quarterly
Facts & Trends
Faith Today
Focus on the Family
Focus on the Family Clubhouse
Girlz 4 Christ Magazine
Homeschooling Today
InSite
Journal of Adventist Education
Joyful Living Magazine
Just Between Us
Leading Hearts
LIVE
Lutheran Witness
Ministry
The Mother's Heart
MTL Magazine
Mutuality
Net Results
New Identity Magazine
Outreach
ParentLife

Parish Liturgy
Poets & Writers Magazine
Prayer Connect
Psychology for Living
SAConnects
Story Embers
Teachers of Vision
Vibrant Life
The Writer
The Writer's Chronicle
Writer's Digest
Writing Corner
YouthMinistry.com

INTERVIEW/PROFILE

The Alabama Baptist
The Arlington Catholic Herald
Brio
byFaith
Cadet Quest
Canada Lutheran
Catholic Sentinel
Celebrate Life Magazine
Charisma
Charisma Leader
Christ Is Our Hope
The Christian Century
Christian Communicator
The Christian Herald
The Christian Journal
Christian Leader
Christianity Today
City Light News
Columbia
CommonCall
The Covenant Companion
Creation
The Cresset
DTS Magazine

Eternal Ink
Evangelical Missions Quarterly
Faith & Friends
Faith Today
Focus on the Family Clubhouse
Focus on the Family Clubhouse Jr.
Friends Journal
Gems of Truth
Girlz 4 Christ Magazine
History's Women
Homeschooling Today
Image
InSite
International Journal
of Frontier Missiology
Joyful Living Magazine
Kansas City Metro Voice
Leading Hearts
LEAVES
Leben
Light + Life Magazine
Liguorian
Love Is Moving
Lutheran Witness
The Mother's Heart
MTL Magazine
Our Sunday Visitor Newsweekly
Outreach
Parish Liturgy
Peer
Poets & Writers Magazine
Point
Power for Living
Reach Out, Columbia
St. Anthony Messenger
St. Mary's Messenger
Story Embers
Testimony/Enrich

Today's Christian Living
U.S. Catholic
Vibrant Life
War Cry
The Writer's Chronicle
Writer's Digest

LEADERSHIP/MINISTRY

Charisma Leader
Children's Ministry
Christian Leader
Christian Standard
CommonCall
Facts & Trends
Holiness Today
Just Between Us
Message of the Open Bible
Ministry
Mutuality
Net Results
Outreach
YouthMinistry.com

MARRIAGE

Boundless
Catholic Digest
Christian Leader
Converge Magazine
Faith & Friends
Focus on the Family
Joyful Living Magazine
The Mother's Heart
St. Anthony Messenger
Thrive Connection

NEWSPAPER

The Alabama Baptist
The Anglican Journal
The Arlington Catholic Herald
Catholic New York
Catholic Sentinel

Christian Courier
The Christian Herald
Christian News Northwest
City Light News
The Good News (Florida)
The Good News (New York)
The Good News Journal
Indian Life
Kansas City Metro Voice
The Messianic Times
New Frontier Chronicle
Our Sunday Visitor Newsweekly
Prairie Messenger
Southwest Kansas Faith and Family

PARENTING

Catholic Digest
City Light News
Columbia
Focus on the Family
Just Between Us
The Light Magazine
The Mother's Heart
Parenting Teens
ParentLife
Reach Out, Columbia
War Cry

PERSONAL EXPERIENCE

Angels on Earth
The Anglican Journal
Bible Advocate
The Breakthrough Intercessor
Canada Lutheran
Catholic Digest
Catholic New York
Catholic Sentinel
Celebrate Life Magazine
Chicken Soup for the

Soul Book Series
  Christ Is Our Hope
  Christian Leader
  Christian Living in the Mature Years
  Christian Standard
  Christianity Today
  Converge Magazine
  Creation Illustrated
  Decision
  Divine Moments Book Series
  DTS Magazine
  Facts & Trends
  Faith & Friends
  Friends Journal
  The Gem
  Guideposts
  Highway News
  Holiness Today
  Journal of Adventist Education
  Joyful Living Magazine
  Just Between Us
  Keys to Living
  Leading Hearts
  LEAVES
  LIVE
  The Lutheran Digest
  Lutheran Witness
  Message of the Open Bible
  The Mother's Heart
  MTL Magazine
  Mutuality
  Mysterious Ways
  New Identity Magazine
  Now What?
  Point
  Power for Living
  Prayer Connect

Psychology for Living
Purpose
SAConnects
Sharing
Shattered Magazine
Standard
Story Embers
Teachers of Vision
Testimony/Enrich
Thrive Connection
Today's Christian Living
Vibrant Life
Victorious Women in Christ
Words for the Way

POETRY

America
Bible Advocate
Chicken Soup for the
Soul Book Series
The Christian Century
Christian Communicator
Christian Courier
Commonweal
Creation Illustrated
The Cresset
CrossCurrents
Eternal Ink
Focus on the Family Clubhouse Jr.
Friends Journal
The Gem
Gems of Truth
Girlz 4 Christ Magazine
Image
Keys to Living
LEAVES
LIVE
The Lutheran Digest
The Lutheran Journal

Lutheran Witness
The Messenger
Mutuality
Poets & Writers Magazine
Power for Living
Purpose
Relief Journal
St. Anthony Messenger
St. Mary's Messenger
Sharing
Sojourners
Story Embers
Teachers of Vision
Time Of Singing
U.S. Catholic
Victorious Women in Christ
Words for the Way

PROFILE

See **Interview**.

REVIEWS

The Anglican Journal
byFaith
The Canadian Lutheran
Canadian Mennonite
Charisma
The Christian Century
Christian Communicator
Christian Courier
The Christian Herald
The Christian Journal
Christian Librarian
Christian Retailing
Christianity Today
The Covenant Companion
Creation Research Journal
Faith Today
FellowScript
Girlz 4 Christ Magazine

The Good News (New York)
Indian Life
Journal of Adventist Education
Kansas City Metro Voice
Leading Hearts
LEAVES
The Living Church
Love Is Moving
The Messianic Times
Ministry
MTL Magazine
Mutuality
New Frontier Chronicle
On Mission
Sojourners
Story Embers
Time Of Singing
U.S. Catholic

SCIENCE

Answers
Creation
Nature Friend

SEASONAL

The Anglican Journal
Answers
Brio
Canadian Lutheran
Catechist
Catholic Digest
Catholic New York
Celebrate Life Magazine
Charisma
Children's Ministry
The Christian Century
Christian Courier
Christian Leader
*Christian Living in
the Mature Years*

Christian Standard
Columbia
Decision
Divine Moments Book Series
DTS Magazine
EFCA Today
Eternal Ink
Faith Today
Focus on the Family Clubhouse
Focus on the Family Clubhouse Jr.
Freelance Writer's Report
The Gem
Gems of Truth
Girlz 4 Christ Magazine
Guide
Indian Life
Insight
InSite
Keys to Living
Liguorian
LIVE
The Lutheran Digest
Message of the Open Bible
The Messenger
The Mother's Heart
Nature Friend
Our Little Friend
Outreach
Poets & Writers Magazine
Presbyterians Today
Primary Treasure
Reach Out, Columbia
St. Anthony Messenger
St. Mary's Messenger
Standard
Testimony/Enrich
Time Of Singing
U.S. Catholic

War Cry
Words for the Way
Writer's Digest
WritersWeekly.com

SHORT STORY/ FICTION

The Anglican Journal
Brio
Cadet Quest
CrossCurrents
Focus on the Family Clubhouse
Focus on the Family Clubhouse Jr.
The Gem
Gems of Truth
Girlz 4 Christ Magazine
Image
The Kids' Ark
Liguorian
LIVE
Nature Friend
Relief Journal
St. Anthony Messenger
St. Mary's Messenger
Standard
Story Embers

Teachers of Vision
U.S. Catholic
Victorious Women in Christ
War Cry

TAKE-HOME PAPER

The Gem
Gems of Truth
Guide
LIVE
Our Little Friend
Power for Living
Primary Treasure
Purpose
Standard

THEOLOGY

byFaith
The Canadian Lutheran
Christianity Today
Faith & Friends
Lutheran Witness
Mature Living
The Messenger
Presbyterians Today

6

ADULT MARKETS

THE ALABAMA BAPTIST

3310 Independence Dr., Birmingham, AL 35209 | 205-870-4720
news@thealabamabaptist.org | *www.thealabamabaptist.org*
Janet Erwin, executive editor

> **Parent company:** Alabama Baptist State Convention
> **Denomination:** Southern Baptist
> **Type:** weekly print and PDF newspaper; circulation 55,000 print, 3,000 PDF
> **Audience:** general
> **Purpose:** to empower readers to live out discipleship in their personal, professional, and church life, equipping them with resources and information
> **Submissions:** Most articles and columns are assigned but open to freelance submissions. Email, or use the online form at *www.the alabamabaptist.org/submissions/reader-submissions*.
> **Types of manuscripts:** news, profiles of individuals and churches
> **Tip:** "Each week, the content is chosen with our readers' Christian walk in mind, as well as resources for living out that walk in their personal, professional and church life. The paper also provides concise and balanced reporting of events from the world of religion, and moral and ethical issues are examined from a biblical standpoint."

AMERICA

106 W. 56th St., New York, NY 10019-3803 | 212-581-4640
articles@americamagazine.org | *www.americamagazine.org*
Kevin Clarke, senior editor
Joseph Hoover, S.J., poetry editor, jhoover@americamagazine.org

> **Denomination:** Catholic
> **Parent company:** America Media, Jesuit Conference of the United States and Canada

Type: weekly print magazine plus online content, circulation 46,000

Audience: primarily Catholic; two-thirds are laypeople, college educated

Purpose: to provide a smart Catholic take on faith and culture

Submissions: Only accepts complete manuscripts submitted through the website. Unsolicited freelance: 100%. Responds in two weeks.

Types: Articles, 2,500 words maximum. "Faith in Focus," personal essays, 800 to 1500 words. "Short Take" opinion essays, 500-600 words. Poetry, 30 lines maximum.

Topics: Catholic take on a political, social, cultural, economic, or ecclesial news event or historical/cultural trend; essays on joys and challenges of living out one's faith in the midst of real life

Rights: first, electronic

Payment: competitive rates, on acceptance

Guidelines: *americamedia.submittable.com/submit*

Sample: download from the website

Tip: "We are known across the Catholic world for our unique brand of excellent, relevant, and accessible coverage. From theology and spirituality to politics, international relations, arts and letters, and the economy and social justice, our coverage spans the globe."

ANGELS ON EARTH

110 William St., Ste. 901, New York, NY 10038 | 212-251-8100
www.guideposts.org/angels-on-earth
Colleen Hughes, editor-in-chief

Parent company: Guideposts

Type: bimonthly print and digital magazine, circulation 550,000

Purpose: to tell true stories of heavenly angels and earthly ones who find themselves on a mission of comfort, kindness, or reassurance

Submissions: Submit complete manuscript through the website; click the tab Tell Your Story. Responds in two months or isn't interested. Unsolicited freelance: 90%. Articles to 1,500 words, 40- 60 per year; short anecdotes similar to full-length articles, 50-250 words. All stories must be true.

Types of manuscripts: personal experience, recipes, fillers

Topics: true stories about God's angels and humans who have played angelic roles on earth; "Angel Sightings," pictures of angels

Rights: all

Payment: $25-500, on publication, 20% kill fee on assignments

Guidelines: *www.guideposts.org/writers-guidelines*

Sample: 7x10 SASE with four stamps

Tip: "We are not limited to stories about heavenly angels. We also accept stories about human beings doing heavenly duties."

THE ANGLICAN JOURNAL

80 Hayden St., Toronto, ON M4Y 3G2, Canada | 416-924-9199
jthomas@national.anglican.ca | *www.anglicanjournal.com*
Janet Thomas, assistant to editor

Denomination: Anglican
Parent company: Anglican Church of Canada
Type: monthly (except July and August) print and digital newspaper, circulation 123,000, takes ads
Audience: denomination
Purpose: to share compelling news and features about the Anglican Church of Canada and the Anglican Communion and religion in general
Submissions: No unsolicited manuscripts; email query as attachment. Length: 500-600 words. Freelance: 5%. Seasonal at least two months in advance. Responds in two weeks. Bible: NRSV.
Types of manuscripts: personal experience, short stories, news, reviews
Topics: Christian life, spiritual issues
Rights: first
Payment: $75-100, on acceptance
Guidelines: *www.anglicanjournal.com/about-us/writers-guidelines*
Sample: on website
Tip: Looking for "local church/parish news stories, book reviews, spiritual reflection."

ANSWERS

PO Box 510, Hebron, KY 41048 | 800-350-3232
editor@answersmagazine.com | *answersingenesis.org/answers/magazine*
Mike Matthews, editor in chief

Parent company: Answers in Genesis
Type: bimonthly print and digital magazine, circulation 50,000, takes ads
Audience: Christian laypeople interested in a biblical worldview from a young-earth creation perspective
Purpose: to illustrate the importance of Genesis in building a creation-based worldview and to equip readers with practical answers, so they can confidently communicate the gospel and biblical authority with accuracy and graciousness

Submissions: Email query letter. Once accepted, email article as an attachment. Responds in two weeks. Length: 300-2,500 words. Seasonal six months in advance. Buys ninety articles per year. Bible: ESV.

Types of manuscripts: teaching, wide range of scientific and theological analysis

Topics: creation-evolution, biblical authority

Rights: all

Payment: varies, on publication, kill fee sometimes

Sample: email Connie Par-Due at *conniep@answersingenesis.org*

Tip: "Science writing from a knowledge of young-earth creationism. We normally carry articles by specialists in a scientific field. We do not carry devotionals or general apologetics for creation over evolution. Rather, we cover specific topics from a biblical creation perspective."

THE ARLINGTON CATHOLIC HERALD

200 N. Glebe Rd., Ste. 600, Arlington, VA 22203 | 703-841-2590
editorial@catholicherald.com | *www.catholicherald.com*
Ann M. Augherton, editor

Denomination: Catholic

Parent company: Arlington, VA Diocese

Type: weekly print and digital newspaper, circulation 70,000, takes ads

Audience: denomination

Purpose: to support the Church's mission to evangelize by providing news from a Catholic perspective

Submissions: Email a query with a story idea.

Types of manuscripts: news, feature articles, profiles

Sample: on the website

BIBLE ADVOCATE

PO Box 33677, Denver, CO 80233
bibleadvocate@cog7.org | *baonline.org*
Sherri Langton, associate editor

Denomination: Church of God (Seventh Day)

Type: bimonthly print and digital magazine, circulation 13,000

Audience: denomination, general

Purpose: to advocate the Bible and represent the Church of God

Submissions: Email complete manuscript as attachment or in body of message. Unsolicited freelance: 25-30%. Buys ten to twenty manuscripts per year. Length: 600-1,300 words. Responds in four to ten weeks. No Christmas or Easter manuscripts. Bible: NKJV, NIV.

Types: teaching, poetry, personal experience, fillers, testimony

Topics: theme related, Christian life

Rights: first, reprint (tell when/where appeared), electronic

Payment: articles, $25-65; poems and fillers, $20; on publication

Guidelines and theme list: *baonline.org/write-for-us*

Sample: 9x12 envelope with three stamps

Tip: "Please read past issues of the magazine before you submit and become familiar with our style. No Christmas or Easter manuscripts."

THE BREAKTHROUGH INTERCESSOR

PO Box 121, Lincoln, VA 20160-0121 | 540-338-4131
breakthrough@intercessors.org | *www.intercessors.org*
Noelle Garnier, editor

Parent company: Breakthrough

Type: quarterly print magazine, circulation 4,000

Audience: adults interested in growing their prayer lives

Purpose: to encourage people to pray and to equip them to do so more effectively

Submissions: Email complete manuscript. Length: articles, 600-1,000 words.

Types of manuscripts: personal experience, teaching

Topic: prayer

Rights: first, onetime, nonexclusive electronic

Payment: none

Guidelines: *www.intercessors.org/media/downloads/Guidelines%20 &%20PermissionForm.pdf*

Sample: download from the website

byFAITH

1700 N. Brown Rd., Ste. 105, Lawrenceville, GA 30043 | 678-825-1005
editor@byfaithonline.com | *byfaithonline.com*
Dick Doster, editor, ddoster@byfaithonline.com

Denomination: Presbyterian Church in America (PCA)

Type: online magazine

Audience: denomination

Purpose: to provide news of the PCA, to equip readers to become a more active part of God's redemptive plan for the world, and to help them respond biblically and intelligently to the questions our culture is asking

Submissions: Email complete manuscripts. Articles 500-3,000 words.

Types: profiles, teaching, reviews, news

Topics: true stories of people living out their faith, practical theology, biblical perspective on arts and culture, reviews of current books and movies, Christian living, PCA news

Guidelines: *byfaithonline.com/about*

Tip: "Theologically, the writers are Reformed and believe the faith is practical and applicable to every part of life. Most of our writers (though not all) come from the PCA."

CANADA LUTHERAN

600-177 Lombard Ave., Winnipeg, MB R3B 0W5, Canada | 888-786-6707

www.elcic.ca

British Columbia Synod, Jude Whaley, editor, deacjudy09@yahoo.ca

Synod of Alberta and the Territories, Colleen McGinnis, editor, mail@caelinartworks.com

Saskatchewan Synod, sksynod@elcic.ca

Manitoba/Northwestern Ontario Synod, Rick Scherger, editor, rscherger@elcic.ca

Eastern Synod, Beverley Cunningham, editor, beverley@cunninghamcommunications.ca

Denomination: Evangelical Lutheran Church in Canada

Type: monthly print magazine (8x), circulation 14,000

Audience: denomination

Purpose: to engage the Evangelical Lutheran Church in Canada in a dynamic dialogue in which information, inspiration, and ideas are shared in a thoughtful and stimulating way

Submissions: Especially looking for articles for "Practising Our Faith," stories and ideas about how you or the people around you handle life's challenges and opportunities through faith. Length: 700-1,200 words. Also takes documentary articles and profiles of people of interest to readers (normally ELCIC members), seasonal, advice in how-to lists, and articles highlighting ministry in the synods. Email submissions.

Types of manuscripts: personal experience, profile, documentary, how-to

Topics: seasonal, Christian living, ELCIC ministries

Rights: onetime

Guidelines: *www.elcic.ca/clweb/contributing.html*

Tip: "As much as is possible, the content of the magazine is chosen from the work of Canadian writers. The content strives to reflect the Evangelical Lutheran Church in Canada in the context of our Canadian society."

THE CANADIAN LUTHERAN

3074 Portage Ave., Winnipeg, MB R3K 0Y2, Canada | 800-588-4226, 204-895-3433

editor@lutheranchurch.ca | www.lutheranchurch.ca/canluth.php
Matthew Block, editor-in-chief

Denomination: Lutheran Church—Canada

Type: bimonthly print magazine, circulation 20,000

Audience: denomination

Purpose: to inspire, motivate, and inform

Submissions: Email complete manuscript with "Canadian Lutheran article" in the subject line. Looking for Christian reflections on current events, teaching articles about our theology, discussions of contemporary culture in the light of faith, and more.

Types of manuscripts: news, teaching, essay

Topics: theology, contemporary culture, congregational and district news (submit to appropriate district editor and include photo)

Rights: first (but reserves the right to reprint)

Payment: none for unsolicited manuscripts

Sample: download from the website

Tip: "All feature articles with doctrinal content must go through doctrinal review to ensure fidelity to the Scriptures. As a result, authors may occasionally be asked to rewrite some sections of their article before publication."

CANADIAN MENNONITE

490 Dutton Dr., Unit C5, Waterloo, ON N2L 6H7, Canada | 519-884-3810

submit@canadianmennonite.org | www.canadianmennonite.org
Ross W. Muir, managing editor

Denomination: Mennonite Church Canada

Type: biweekly print magazine

Audience: denomination

Purpose: to educate, inspire, inform, and foster dialogue on issues facing Mennonites in Canada as they share the good news of Jesus Christ from an Anabaptist perspective

Submissions: Email query first. Email manuscripts as attachments or mail them.

Types: theological reflections, sermons, opinion pieces, letters, reviews (books, music, movies), personal stories, news

Topics: theme-related

Payment: none for unsolicited articles, 10¢/word for solicited articles

Guidelines and theme list: *www.canadianmennonite.org/submissions*

Sample: download from the website

CATECHIST

2 W. Hill Dr., Worcester, MA 01609
pat.gohn@bayard-inc.com | *www.catechist.com*
Pat Gohn, editor

Parent company: Bayard, Inc.

Type: monthly (7x during school year) print and digital magazine, digital newsletter; print circulation 42,000; takes ads

Audience: catechists, directors of religious education, catechetical leaders

Purpose: to support the work of catechists through formation, lessons, activities, and resources

Submissions: Must be Catholic-focused. Freelance: 10%. Buys 200 manuscripts per year. Seasonal six months in advance. Query first. Email as an attachment. Responds in one week. Length: 500-1,500 words. Bible: NABRE.

Types of manuscripts: lessons and activities for K-12 students or adults

Topics: Catholic faith, sacraments, liturgical year

Rights: first

Payment: $75-350, on acceptance

Guidelines: *www.catechist.com/about-catechist*

Sample: on the website

Tip: "Query editor with your ideas first. We work most with writers who are catechists themselves or specialists in this field."

CATHOLIC DIGEST

1 Montauk Ave., New London, CT 06320
queries@catholicdigest.com | *www.catholicdigest.com*
Paul McKibben, managing editor

Denomination: Catholic

Type: print magazine, 9x a year; takes ads

Audience: denomination

Purpose: to encourage and support Catholics in a variety of life stages and circumstances

Submissions: Query for feature articles. Accepts simultaneous submissions. Articles 1,500 words. Seasonal four to five months ahead. Departments: "Last Word" personal essay, 550-700 words; "Open Door" first-person stories about conversion to or recovering the Catholic faith, 350-600 words; send to *opendoor@ catholicdigest.com*. Email complete manuscript for departments.

Types of manuscripts: how-to, essay, personal experience

Topics: marriage, practical spirituality, parish/work, parenting, grandparenting, homemaking, relationships, beauty

Rights: first

Payment: $100-500, on publication

Guidelines: *www.catholicdigest.com/writers-guidelines*

CATHOLIC NEW YORK

1011 First Ave., Ste. 1721, New York, NY 10022 | 212-688-2399
jwoods@cny.org | *www.cny.org*
John Woods, editor-in-chief

Denomination: Catholic

Parent company: Ecclesiastical Communications Corp.

Type: biweekly print newspaper, circulation 127,000, takes ads

Audience: denomination

Purpose: to publish news and information of interest to Catholics in the Archdiocese of New York

Submissions: Email query or complete manuscript as attachment. Unsolicited freelance: 2%. Accepts five to ten manuscripts per year. Length: 600 words. Responds in one month. Seasonal two weeks in advance. Bible: NAB.

Types of manuscripts: news reports, personal experience, teaching

Topics: state news, Christian living, moral issues

Rights: onetime

Payment: $125, on publication

Guidelines: none

Sample: written request

Tip: "We use freelancers from New York to cover evening and weekend events."

CATHOLIC SENTINEL

5536 N.E. Hassalo, Portland, OR 97213 | 503-281-1191
sentinel@CatholicSentinel.org | *www.CatholicSentinel.org*

Ed Langlois, managing editor

Denomination: Catholic

Parent company: Archdiocese of Portland

Type: bimonthly print newspaper

Audience: Catholics who live in Oregon

Purpose: to feature Oregon people and Oregon issues that relate to Catholics

Submissions: Articles 600-1,500 words. Query first. Feature stories about Catholics living out their faith. Columns about local, national, or international issues of interest with a local connection.

Types of manuscripts: profiles, personal experience

Topics: Christian living, issues

Payment: variable rates for articles, none for columns

Guidelines: *catholicsentinel.org/Content/About-Us/About-Us/Article/Article-Submission/15/60/11770*

CELEBRATE LIFE MAGAZINE

PO Box 1350, Stafford, VA 22555 | 540-659-4171
clmag@all.org | *www.clmagazine.org*
William Mahoney, editor

Denomination: Catholic

Parent company: American Life League

Type: quarterly print and digital magazine, circulation 7,500, takes ads

Audience: pro-life

Purpose: to inspire, encourage, and educate pro-life activists

Submissions: Email complete manuscript as an attachment. Freelance: 25%. Accepts six manuscripts per year. Length: 800-1,800 words. Seasonal six months ahead. Responds in one to two months. Bible: *Jerusalem Bible*.

Types of manuscripts: personal experience, interviews, how-to, teaching

Topics: matters concerning the sanctity of life and human personhood in harmony with the teachings of the Catholic Church; see specific list in guidelines

Rights: first

Payment: 10-25¢/word, on publication, sometimes kill fee

Guidelines: *www.clmagazine.org/submission-guidelines*

Sample: email for copy

Tip: "Most in need of timely investigative reports and personal experiences."

CHARISMA

600 Rinehart Rd., Lake Mary, FL 32746 | 407-333-0600
charisma@charismamedia.com | *www.charismamag.com*
Christine D. Johnson, managing editor

> **Denomination:** Pentecostal/Charismatic
> **Type:** monthly print and digital magazine, circulation 90,000
> **Audience:** passionate, Spirit-filled Christians
> **Purpose:** to empower believers for life in the Spirit
> **Submissions:** Query only through the online form. If accepted, prefers email submission. Responds in two to three months. Seasonal five months ahead. Assigned: 80%. Needs articles that reflect on the work of a particular ministry, Christian author, or artist, 700 words maximum; product reviews of newly released books, music, and movies/DVDs (assigned); in-depth feature stories to 2,600 words. Bible: MEV. Prefers third-person.
> **Types:** profiles, interviews, reviews, feature stories
> **Topics:** prayer, healing, spiritual warfare, end times, the prophetic and Israel, Christmas, Easter
> **Rights:** all
> **Payment:** on publication
> **Guidelines:** *www.charismamag.com/about/write-for-us*
> **Sample:** on the website
> **Tip:** "Please take time to read—even study—at least one or two of our recent issues before submitting a query. Sometimes people submit their writing without ever having read or understood our magazine or its readers, and sometimes people will have read our magazine years ago and think it's the same as it has always been; but magazines undergo many changes through the years."

CHARISMA LEADER (FORMERLY MINISTRY TODAY)

600 Rinehart Rd., Lake Mary, FL 32746 | 407-333-0600
chris.johnson@charismamedia.com | *www.ministrytodaymag.com*
Christine D. Johnson, managing editor

> **Denomination:** Pentecostal/Charismatic
> **Parent company:** Charisma Media
> **Type:** quarterly print and digital magazine, circulation 30,000
> **Audience:** pastors, ministry leaders, business leaders
> **Purpose:** to inspire and assist ministry leaders
> **Submissions:** Email query through the online submission form. If no response in two weeks, assume not interested. Email (preferred) or mail manuscript after query if requested. Bible version: MEV. Most

open to departments: "Ministry Life," "Leadership," "Outreach," and "Facilities." Length: to 700 words. Also buys more in-depth features; length to 2,500 words.

Types of manuscripts: how-to, interviews, teaching

Topics: anything related to church ministry and leadership

Rights: all

Payment: unspecified, on publication

Guidelines: *ministrytodaymag.com/write-for-us*

Tip: "Most open to departments. Please take time to read—even study—at least one or two of our recent issues before submitting a query."

CHICKEN SOUP FOR THE SOUL BOOK SERIES

PO Box 700, Cos Cob, CT 06807
www.chickensoup.com
Amy Newmark, editor-in-chief

Parent company: Chicken Soup for the Soul Publishing, LLC

Type: trade paperback books, about a dozen yearly

Purpose: to share happiness, inspiration, and hope

Submissions: Submit complete manuscript only through the website. Unsolicited freelance: 98%. Length: 1,200 words maximum. "A Chicken Soup for the Soul story is an inspirational, true story about ordinary people having extraordinary experiences. . . . These stories are personal and often filled with emotion and drama." Poems tell a story; no rhyming. Accepts submissions from children and teens for some books. No reprints.

Types: personal experiences, poetry

Topics: *www.chickensoup.com/story-submissions/possible-book-topics*

Payment: $200, one month after publication, plus ten copies of the book

Tip: "The most powerful stories are about people extending themselves or performing an act of love, service, or courage for another person."

CHILDREN'S MINISTRY

1515 Cascade Ave., Loveland, CO 80538 | 970-669-3836
puorgbus@group.com | *childrensministry.com/about-us*
Jennifer Hooks, managing editor

Parent company: Group

Type: bimonthly print and digital magazine; circulation 20,000, 210,000 hits monthly; takes ads

Audience: children's ministry workers

Purpose: to help leaders make Jesus irresistible to kids

Submissions: Feature articles, 1,000-2,200 words; teacher and parent tips, 200 words; games, crafts, activities, 200-500 words. Unsolicited freelance: 10%. For assignments: Know the magazine, start with smaller ideas, and submit with previously published clips; offer pitches for new and unique article ideas. Buys 250 manuscripts per year. Seasonal six months in advance. Email complete manuscript as attachment with cover letter or query. Responds in eight weeks. Bible: NLT. Accepts submissions from teens.

Types of manuscripts: how-to, tips, crafts, activities, sidebars, columns

Topics: leadership, ideas to use with children in ministry; regular columns on age-level development, outreach, family ministry, leading volunteers, special needs, and discipline

Rights: all

Payment: features $75-400, tips and fillers $40; on acceptance

Guidelines: *grouppublishingps.zendesk.com/hc/en-us/articles/211878258-Submissions*

Theme list: by email

Sample: *childrensministry.com/subscribe*

Tip: "We need practical, fresh articles. Do not submit unless you're familiar with the magazine. Biggest reason for a rejection is that the writer is unaware of what we actually publish, so submits fiction, poetry, etc."

CHRIST IS OUR HOPE

16555 Weber Rd., Crest Hill, IL 60403 | 815-221-6100
magazine@dioceseofjoliet.org |
www.dioceseofjoliet.org/magazine/sectioncontent.php?secid=1
Carlos Briceño, editor

Denomination: Catholic

Parent company: Diocese of Joliet, Illinois

Purpose: to tell inspiring stories of faith and share information with the goal of educating and evangelizing others

Type: monthly print magazine

Submissions: Query by email.

Types: news, personal experiences, profiles

Topics: Catholic life, local news

Payment: none

Sample: on the website

THE CHRISTIAN CENTURY

104 S. Michigan Ave., Ste. 1100, Chicago, IL 60603-5901 | 312-263-7510

submissions@christiancentury.org | *www.christiancentury.org*

David Heim, editor in chief

Elizabeth Palmer, books editor

Jill Peláez Baumgaertner, poetry editor, poetry@christiancentury.org

Type: biweekly print magazine, takes ads

Audience: ecumenical, mainline ministers, educators, and church leaders

Purpose: to explore what it means to believe and live out the Christian faith in our time

Submissions: Email query first. Responds in four to six weeks. Unsolicited freelance: 90%. Seasonal four months in advance. Articles 1,500-3,000 words, buys 150 per year; poetry (free verse, traditional) to twenty lines. Bible version: NRSV.

Types of manuscripts: essays, humor, interviews, opinion, book reviews (assigned), poetry

Topics: poverty, human rights, economic justice, international relations, national priorities, popular culture, critiques of individual religious communities

Rights: all, reprint (tell where/when published)

Payment: articles $100-300, poems $50, reviews to $75, on publication

Guidelines and theme list: *www.christiancentury.org/submission-guidelines*

Sample: $3.50

Tip: "Keep in mind our audience of sophisticated readers, eager for analysis and critical perspective that goes beyond the obvious. We are open to all topics if written with appropriate style for our readers."

CHRISTIAN COURIER

2 Aiken St., St. Catherines, ON L2N 1V8, Canada | 800-969-4838, 905-937-3314

editor@christiancourier.ca | *www.christiancourier.ca*

Angela Reitsma Bick, editor-in-chief, editor@christiancourier.ca

Amy MacLachlan, features editor, features@christiancourier.ca

Brian Bork, review editor, bbork41@gmail.com

Denomination: Christian Reformed

Type: biweekly print newspaper, circulation 2,500, takes ads

Purpose: to connect Christians with a network of culturally savvy partners in faith for the purpose of inspiring all to participate in God's renewing work with His creation

Submissions: Email queries and manuscripts to the appropriate editor. Articles 700-1,200 words, book and movie reviews 750 words. Responds in one to two weeks, only if accepted. Seasonal three months ahead. Accepts simultaneous submissions. Uses some sidebars. Prefers NIV.

Types of manuscripts: editorials, reviews, columns, features, news, poetry

Rights: onetime, reprint (tell when/where appeared)

Payment: $45-$70, 30 days after publication; no pay for reprints

Guidelines: *christiancourier.ca/about/category/write-for-us*

Tip: "Suggest an aspect of the theme which you believe you could cover well, have insight into, could treat humorously, etc. Show that you think clearly, write clearly, and have something to say that we should want to read. Have a strong biblical worldview and avoid moralism and sentimentality."

THE CHRISTIAN HERALD

PO Box 68526, Brampton, ON L6R 0J8, Canada | 905-874-1731
info@christianherald.ca | www.christianherald.ca
Fazal Karim, Jr., editor-in-chief

Type: monthly (11x) print newspaper, circulation 27,000, takes ads

Purpose: to keep Southern Ontario's Christian community informed and aware of Christian news and events

Audience: Southern Ontario's Christian community

Submissions: Email query letter as attachment or in body of message. Gives assignments. Unsolicited freelance: 10%. Buys six to twelve articles per year. Length: 500-900 words. Seasonal six weeks in advance. Bible: ESV.

Types of manuscripts: how-to, news story, feature story, interview, travel destination, book/music/movie review, sidebars, columns, filler

Topics: variety

Rights: first, reprint (tell when/where published)

Payment: 15¢/per word on publication, kill fee sometimes

Guidelines: by email

Sample: email for digital copy

Tip: Primarily needs feature stories, personal interviews, travel destinations, and Christian book/music/movie reviews.

THE CHRISTIAN JOURNAL

1032 W. Main, Medford, OR 97501 | 541-773-4004
info@thechristianjournal.org | *www.TheChristianJournal.org*
Chad McComas, senior editor

Type: monthly print and digital magazine
Audience: both Christians and non-Christians
Purpose: to share encouragement with the body of Christ in the Rogue Valley, Oregon
Submissions: Each article needs to inspire the reader to reconnect with God and his or her faith. Length: 300–500 words, average around 400 words. Email manuscript.
Types of manuscripts: feature articles, testimonies, profiles, reviews
Topics: hope, encouragement, theme-related articles, profiles of local ministries and Christian personalities, children's stories
Rights: onetime
Payment: none
Guidelines: *thechristianjournal.org/writers-information/guidelines-for-writers*

CHRISTIAN LEADER

PO Box 155, Hillsboro, KS 67063
editor@usmb.org | *christianleadermag.com*
Connie Faber, editor

Denomination: Mennonite Brethren
Parent company: U.S. Conference of Mennonite Brethren Churches
Type: bimonthly print magazine, circulation 9,800
Audience: denomination
Purpose: to inspire, inform, educate, and challenge church members and attendees, as well as to provide a "kitchen table" around which our diverse denomination can gather
Submissions: Email manuscripts. Prefers writers from North American Mennonite Brethren congregations, ministries, and educational institutions and Anabaptist and Mennonite family of denominations. Length: feature articles, 800-1,200 words; columns, 550 words. Bible: NIV.
Types of manuscripts: first-person testimony, opinion essay, feature
Topics: evangelism, disciple-making, leadership development, networking, Anabaptist/evangelical distinctives, Christian living, marriage and family, social issues, Bible exposition, seasonal
Rights: first
Payment: on publication

Guidelines: *christianleadermag.com/about-cl/cl-history*

THE CHRISTIAN LIBRARIAN

PO Box 4, Cedarville, OH 45314 | 937-766-2255
tcl@acl.org | www.acl.org
Garrett Trott, editor-in-chief

Parent organization: Association of Christian Librarians
Type: biannual print journal
Audience: primarily Christian librarians in institutions of higher learning
Purpose: to publish articles, provide a membership forum, and encourage writing
Submissions: Mail or email manuscripts. Shorter articles, 1,000-3,000 words, are generally preferable for practical and nonresearch papers; scholarly articles to 5,000 words, some longer. Include a 100-word abstract.
Types of manuscripts: teaching, reviews, bibliographies
Topics: Christian interpretation of librarianship, theory and practice of library science, bibliographic essays, reviews, and human-interest articles relating to books and libraries
Rights: first, with signed grant of license
Payment: none
Guidelines: *www.acl.org/index.cfm/publications/the-christian-librarian/tcl-author-guidelines-4-24-18*

CHRISTIAN LIVING IN THE MATURE YEARS

2222 Rosa L Parks Blvd., Nashville, TN 37228
matureyears@umpublishing.org | matureyears.submittable.com/submit
Rachel Mullen, features and acquisitions editor

Denomination: United Methodist
Parent company: United Methodist Publishing House
Type: quarterly print magazine
Audience: ages 50 and older
Purpose: to help older adults with opportunities and challenges related to aging
Submissions: Submit through the website. Responds in two to four months. Seasonal one year in advance. Length: 250-2,000 words. Buys fifty manuscripts per year. Unsolicited freelance: 100%. Bible: CEB.
Types of manuscripts: how-to, short memoir, personal experience, recipe, religious reflection/meditation, filler, puzzle

Topics: grandparenting, Christian life, general interest, health, money, retirement, aging, Bible lessons

Rights: onetime

Payment: 7¢/word, on acceptance

Guidelines: *matureyears.submittable.com/submit*

Sample: email for a PDF

Tip: "Our 'Fragments of Life' section always needs new writers. It is a short memoir section; four pieces needed each quarter. We do not accept articles about 'the good old days' or pieces that focus on negativity and death over health, wellness, and life."

CHRISTIAN NEWS NORTHWEST

PO Box 974, Newberg, OR 97132 | 503-537-9220
cnnw@cnnw.com | www.cnnw.com
John Fortmeyer, publisher and editor

Parent company: Christian News Northwest Ministries Inc.

Type: monthly print newspaper, circulation 28,000, ads

Audience: evangelical Christians in western and central Oregon and southwest Washington

Purpose: to inform and encourage the evangelical Christian community in our part of the Pacific Northwest

Submissions: Email (as attachment or in body of message) or mail complete manuscript, or use the website form. Unsolicited freelance: 10%. Length: 700 words. Responds in several days. Bible: NIV.

Types of manuscripts: news

Topics: all focused on church and ministry

Rights: onetime

Payment: none

Guidelines: by email

Sample: via email

Tip: "Our strongest focus is on ministry news in the Northwest."

CHRISTIAN RESEARCH JOURNAL

PO Box 8500, Charlotte, NC 28271-8500 | 704-887-8200
response@equip.org | www.equip.org/christian-research-journal
Melanie Cogdill, managing editor

Parent company: Christian Research Institute

Type: quarterly print journal

Audience: thoughtful laypeople, academics, scholars

Purpose: to equip Christians with the information they need to discern doctrinal errors; to evangelize people of other faiths; to present a strong defense of Christian beliefs and ethics; and to provide comprehensive, definitive responses to contemporary apologetic concerns

Submissions: Email query or a manuscript that follows formatting guidelines. Responds in four months. Articles should reflect a command of the subject at hand, including its history, the key personalities involved, the beliefs and/or practices surrounding the controversy, and the criticisms that have been made concerning the subject. Feature articles 2,200 or 3,500 words as assigned; include 250-300-word synopsis with main facts and arguments. Summary critique review 1,700 words, effective evangelism 1,700 words, viewpoint 1,700 words. All articles must be within 25 words of these word counts.

Types of manuscripts: feature articles, news stories, viewpoint, summary critiques

Topics: apologetics, evangelism, cults and new religions, the occult, New Age movement, aberrant Christian movements and teachings

Rights: first, reprint

Payment: $175-325, kill fee 50%

Guidelines: *www.equip.org/wp-content/uploads/2019/09/Writers-Guidelines.SEPT-2019.PDF*

Tip: "Almost nothing can better prepare you to write for the *Christian Research Journal* than familiarity with the journal itself. If you are not a regular reader of the journal, you should read all the articles in recent issues that correspond to the type of article you wish to write."

CHRISTIAN RETAILING

600 Rinehart Rd., Lake Mary, FL 32746 | 407-333-0600
retailing@charismamedia.com | www.christianretailing.com
Christine D. Johnson, editor, chris.johnson@charismamedia.com

Parent company: Charisma Media

Type: bimonthly print and digital trade journal

Audience: retailers, church bookstores, publishers, music labels, distributors, and others working and volunteering in the Christian products industry

Purpose: to champion the world of Christian resources and to provide critical information and insight to advance business and ministry

Submissions: Query only. Prefers third-person point of view. Bible: MEV.

Types of manuscripts: features, news stories, columns, reviews

Topics: all aspects of running a bookstore, trends in publishing, new-product reviews

Payment: varies by assignment
Guidelines: *christianretailing.com/index.php/general/28335-writers-guidelines-christian-retailing*

CHRISTIAN STANDARD

16965 Pine Ln., Ste. 202, Parker, CO 80134 | 800-543-1353
CS@christianstandardmedia.com | *www.christianstandard.com*
Michael C. Mack, editor
Jim Nieman, managing editor

Denomination: Christian Churches, Churches of Christ
Parent company: Christian Standard Media
Type: monthly print and digital magazine, circulation 13,000
Audience: Christian leaders
Purpose: to resource Christian leaders
Submissions: Email queries and manuscripts as attachments. Length: 500-1,800 words. Freelance: 5-10%. Buys fifteen manuscripts per year. Seasonal six to eight months in advance. Responds in one to three months. Bible: NIV.
Types of manuscripts: how-to, meditations, sidebars
Topics: theme-related, church and ministry leadership, church finances, intergenerational ministry, urban and rural ministry, international ministry and missions, Communion meditations
Rights: first, reprint (tell when/where published)
Payment: $50-250, on acceptance, kill fee sometimes
Guidelines: *www.christianstandard.com/contact-us/submit-articles*
Theme list: *www.christianstandard.com/wp-content/uploads/2019/07/2020-Theme-List.pdf*
Sample: by email
Tip: "We are looking for well-written articles especially by and about independent Christian churches (Restoration Movement churches). Success stories are great, of course, but we want real stories about real people who rely on God's grace and power to overcome adversity and grow in Christlikeness. How is the church/ministry/leader living out and carrying out the mission?"

CHRISTIANITY TODAY

465 Gundersen Dr., Carol Stream, IL 60188-2498 | 630-260-6200
editor@christianitytoday.com | *www.christianitytoday.com*
Ted Olsen, editorial director
Matt Reynolds, books editor, mreynolds@christianitytoday.com

Type: monthly (10x) print and digital magazine, 4.3 million page views per month, takes ads

Audience: Christian leaders throughout North America

Purpose: equipping Christians to renew their minds, serve the church, and create culture to the glory of God

Submissions: Query first through email. Unsolicited freelance: small percentage. Length: 300-1,800 words. Bible: NIV.

Types of manuscripts: profiles, interviews, feature stories, book reviews, opinion pieces

Topics: see the website

Rights: first

Payment: varies on acceptance, kill fee sometimes

Guidelines: *www.christianitytoday.com/ct/help/about-us/writers-guidelines.html*

Sample: articles are on the website

Tip: "The most successful pitches combine Christian formation and credible information. We seek pieces that offer not just new ideas and opinions, but research, reporting, and biblical analysis to back them up."

THE CHURCH HERALD & HOLINESS BANNER

7407 Metcalf, Overland Park, KS 66212
editor@heraldandbanner.com | *www.heraldandbanner.com*
Dr. Gordon L. Snider, editor

Denomination: Church of God (Holiness)

Parent company: Herald and Banner Press

Type: monthly print and digital magazine

Audience: denomination

Submissions: Email through the website for current needs. Includes various teaching articles each month that will inspire you in your Christian walk, help you understand more about a biblical topic, etc. Also featured are various articles promoting Christian ideals, such as the importance to live with gratitude.

Types of manuscripts: teaching

Topics: biblical teaching, Christian living from a holiness perspective

CITY LIGHT NEWS

20218 Fraser Highway, #200, Langley, BC V3A 4E6, Canada | 604-510-5070
editor@lightmagazine.ca | *www.citylightnews.com*
Steve Almond, editor

Parent company: Light Christian Media

Type: monthly print and digital newspaper, circulation 10,000, takes ads

Audience: Christians in Calgary, Red Deer, and Southern Alberta

Purpose: inspiring faith for everyday life

Submissions: Email in body of message. Freelance: 10%. Contact editor to get assignments. Buys twenty-four manuscripts per year. Seasonal two months in advance. Responds in one week. Length: 800 words maximum. Bible: no preference.

Types of manuscripts: lifestyle, news, testimony

Topics: parenting, senior life, Christian living, travel

Rights: first, reprint

Payment: 10¢/word on publication, kill fee sometimes

Guidelines: *alberta.lightmagazine.ca/about-us*

Sample: by email

Tip: "Looking for Christian lifestyle, local news; Canadian experience helpful."

COLUMBIA

1 Columbus Plaza, New Haven, CT 06510-3326 | 203-752-4398
columbia@kofc.org | www.kofc.org/Columbia
Alton J. Pelowski, editor-in-chief

Denomination: Catholic

Parent company: Knights of Columbus

Type: monthly print and digital magazine, circulation 1.7 million

Audience: general Catholic family

Submissions: Query first by email or mail. Length: 700-1,500 words. Seasonal six months in advance.

Types of manuscripts: feature articles, profiles

Topics: current events, social trends, family life, parenting, social problems, health and nutrition, finances, Catholic practice and teaching, church programs, institutions, personalities

Rights: first, electronic

Payment: varies, on acceptance

Guidelines: *www.kofc.org/un/en/columbia/guidelines.html*

Sample: *www.kofc.org/un/en/columbia/archive/columbia.html#*

COMMONCALL

PO Box 259019, Plano, TX 75025 | 214-630-4571 x1012
kencamp@baptiststandard.com | www.baptiststandard.com
Ken Camp, managing editor

Denomination: Baptist

Type: quarterly print magazine

Purpose: to aid and support the denomination

Submissions: Looking for stories about everyday Christians who are putting their faith into action.

Types of manuscripts: profiles, how-to
Topics: missions, evangelism, family life, leadership, effective church ministry, Texas Baptist history

COMMONWEAL

475 Riverside Dr., Rm. 405, New York, NY 10115 | 212-662-4200
editors@commonwealmagazine.org | *www.commonwealmagazine.org*
Paul Baumann, editor

Denomination: Catholic
Type: biweekly (20x) print and digital magazine
Audience: educated, committed Catholics, as well as readers from other faith traditions
Purpose: to provide a forum for civil, reasoned debate on the interaction of faith with contemporary politics and culture
Submissions: Submit through the website. Mail poetry; buys thirty per year. Articles fall into these categories: (1) "Upfronts," 1,000-1,500 words, brief, newsy, and reportorial, giving facts, information, and some interpretation behind the headlines of the day. (2) Longer articles, 2,000-3,000 words, reflective and detailed, bringing new information or a different point of view to a subject, raising questions, and/or proposing solutions to the dilemmas facing the world, nation, church, or individual. (3) "Last Word" column, a 750-word reflection, usually of a personal nature, on some aspect of the human condition: spiritual, individual, political, or social.
Types of manuscripts: essays, features, news with interpretation, poetry
Topics: public affairs, religion, literature, the arts
Rights: all
Payment: on publication
Guidelines: *www.commonwealmagazine.org/contact-us*
Sample: $5
Tip: "Articles should be written for a general but well-educated audience. While religious articles are always topical, we are less interested in devotional and churchy pieces than in articles which examine the links between 'worldly' concerns and religious beliefs."

CONVERGE MAGAZINE

107 E. 3rd Ave., Vancouver, BC V5T 1C7, Canada | 604-558-1982
editor@convergemagazine.com | *www.convergemagazine.com*

Leanne Janzen, editor

Type: quarterly print and digital magazine

Audience: millennials

Purpose: to influence a growing number of people through daily content that is intelligent, is authentic, and stimulates hope in God

Submissions: Email queries and manuscripts. Articles 500-1,000 words. If no response in six weeks, assume no interest.

Types of manuscripts: personal experience

Topics: life, relationships, experiences, work, culture, faith

Guidelines: *convergemagazine.com/write*

Sample: see link at *convergemagazine.com/magazine*

Tip: "We write for those in transition: between school and work, singleness and marriage, freedom and responsibility, doubt and faith. We write as friends on the journey together, rather than one coaching another down the path. We share what we've learned through experience, rather than what we've heard or been taught. Our stories, like our lives, don't need to be tidy, with all the right answers."

THE COVENANT COMPANION

8303 W. Higgins Rd., Chicago, IL 60631 | 773-907-3328

cathy.norman.peterson@covchurch.org | *covenantcompanion.com*

Cathy Norman Peterson, director of editorial services

Denomination: Evangelical Covenant Church

Type: monthly (10x) print magazine

Audience: denomination

Purpose: to inform, stimulate thought, and encourage dialogue on issues that impact the church and its members

Submissions: Email or mail. Length: 1,200-1,800 words.

Types of manuscripts: news, profiles, book reviews

Topics: Christian life, the church (local, denominational, and universal), spirituality, contemporary issues, social justice, outreach ministry

Rights: onetime

Payment: $35-100, two months after publication

Guidelines: *covenantcompanion.com/submit-story*

Tip: "We are interested in what is happening in local churches, conferences, and other Covenant institutions and associations, as well as reports from missionaries and other staff serving around the world. Human interest stories are also welcome."

CREATION

PO Box 4545, Eight Mile Plains, QLD 4113, Australia | 073-340-9888
editors@creation.info | creation.com
Margaret Wieland, magazine coordinator

Parent company: Creation Ministries International
Type: quarterly print and digital magazine, circulation 50,000
Audience: families, homeschoolers
Purpose: to support the effective proclamation of the gospel by providing credible answers that affirm the reliability of the Bible, in particular its Genesis history
Submissions: Email manuscript as an attachment or mail it; cover letter required. Length: maximum 1,500 words. Buys more than 100 manuscripts per year. Responds in a few days. Bible: ESV.
Types of manuscripts: interviews with creationists, teaching
Topics: creation science, evolution's errors
Rights: first
Payment: none
Guidelines: *creation.com/creation-magazine-writing-guidelines*
Sample: on the website
Tip: "Except in technical articles, we like to see simple words, short sentences, and short paragraphs."

CREATION ILLUSTRATED

PO Box 7955, Auburn, CA 95604 | 530-269-1424
CI@creationillustrated.com | www.creationillustrated.com
Jennifer Ish, associate editor

Type: quarterly print and digital magazine, circulation 20,000, takes ads
Audience: families
Purpose: to share the wonders of God's creation
Submissions: Email queries (preferred) and manuscripts. Length: 700-1,500 words; children's stories 500-1,500 words. Bible: KJV, ESV, NKJV. Unsolicited freelance: 75%. Buys thirty-two manuscripts per year. Seasonal at least four months in advance. Responds in two to four weeks.
Types of manuscripts: teaching, personal experience, children's stories, profile, how-to
Topics: nature, outdoor adventures, creatures, a creation day from Genesis; each story needs to be able to support strong, visual illustrations as we place many high-end photos with each story
Rights: first, electronic, reprint (tell when/where published)
Payment: articles $100, children's stories $50-75, poetry $15; 30 days after publication; kill fee 25% sometimes

Guidelines and theme list: *www.creationillustrated.com/writer--photographer-guidelines*

Sample: on the website

Tip: "We strongly encourage all writers to read the magazine before writing to see how the Christian character lessons and scriptures are woven into each story, how God's creation is "illustrated," how biblical nature stories are focused on the features we currently are publishing. Write for the reader. Inspire the reader to be in awe of the Creator. Make your story uplifting and positive, rather than confrontational or argumentative."

THE CRESSET

Lindwood House, Valparaiso University, 1320 S. Campus Dr., Valparaiso, IN 46383

cresset@valpo.edu| thecresset.org

Heather Grennan Gary, editor

Marci Rae Johnson, poetry editor

Parent company: Valparaiso University

Type: print journal, 5-6x per year

Audience: general readers interested in religious matters, mostly college teachers

Purpose: to comment on literature, the arts, and public affairs and explore ideas and trends in contemporary culture from a perspective grounded in the Lutheran tradition of scholarship, freedom, and faith while informed by the wisdom of the broader Christian community

Submissions: Email query first. Prefers submissions through the website but also takes them by email or mail.

Types of manuscripts: essays, poetry, interviews

Guidelines: *thecresset.org/submissions.html*

Sample: on the website

Tip: "The Cresset is not a theological journal, but a journal addressing matters of import to those with some degree of theological interest and commitment. Authors are encouraged to reflect upon the religious implications of their subject."

CROSSCURRENTS

475 Riverside Dr., Ste. 1945, New York, NY 10115 | 212-864-5439

cph@crosscurrents.org | www.aril.org

Charles Henderson, executive editor

Parent company: The Association for Religion and Intellectual Life

Type: quarterly print magazine

Audience: thoughtful activists for social justice and church reform
Submissions: Accepts emailed and mailed submissions with SASE. Responds in four to eight weeks. No unsolicited book reviews, reprints. Articles 3,000-5,000 words.
Types of manuscripts: essays, poetry, fiction
Payment: none
Guidelines: *www.aril.org/submissions.htm*
Sample: on the website

CRW MAGAZINE

PO Box 300, Pasadena, CA 91129 | 800-309-4466
managing.editor@ptm.org | *www.ptm.org/magazine*
Greg Albrecht, senior editor

Parent company: Plain Truth Ministries
Type: quarterly print and digital magazine
Audience: general
Purpose: to combat legalism and give hope, inspiration, and encouragement to those burned out by religion
Submissions: Queries only.
Types of manuscripts: teaching
Guidelines: by email
Sample: on the website

DECISION

PO Box 668886, Charlotte, NC 28262 | 704-401-2426
decision@bgea.org | *billygraham.org/decision-magazine*
Bob Paulson, editor

Parent company: Billy Graham Evangelistic Association
Type: monthly (11x) print and digital magazine
Audience: general
Purpose: to set forth the Good News of salvation in Jesus Christ with such clarity that readers will be drawn to make a commitment to Christ; to encourage, teach, and strengthen Christians to walk daily with Christ and reach out to others for Christ; and to inform readers about the ministry of the Billy Graham Evangelistic Association
Submissions: Query first. Freelance: 5%. Articles 400-1,500 words. "Finding Jesus" (people who became Christians through Billy Graham ministries), 500-900 words. Prefers queries. Seasonal six months in advance.
Types of manuscripts: testimonies, personal experience
Topics: salvation, evangelism

Payment: $200-500, on publication

DIVINE MOMENTS BOOK SERIES
102 Corbett Ln., Black Mountain, NC 28711 | 828-231-1963
yvonnelehman3@gmail.com | *www.yvonnelehman.com/moments*
Yvonne Lehman, compiler and editor

Parent company: Grace Publishing
Purpose: to show how faith works in everyday life experiences
Audience: general and Christian
Type: two books per year
Submissions: Accepts fifty articles per book. Email complete manuscript as attachment. Length: 500-2,000. Seasonal six months in advance. Responds in one day. Bible: no preference.
Types of manuscripts: personal experience
Topics: theme-related, Christmas, romance, brokenness, questioning
Rights: onetime
Payment: none, royalties donated to Samaritan's Purse
Guidelines and theme list: *www.yvonnelehman.com/moments-2*
Tip: Needs stories for these books: *Christmas 2020, Grandma's Cookie Jar Moments, Broken Moments, Lost Moments, Can Sir! Moments.*

DTS MAGAZINE
3909 Swiss Ave., Dallas, TX 75204
rwroten@dts.edu | *www.dts.edu/magazine*
Raquel Wroten, editor

Parent company: Dallas Theological Seminary (DTS)
Type: quarterly print and digital magazine
Audience: evangelical laypeople, students, alumni, donors, and friends
Purpose: to offer articles rich in biblical and theological exposition, tell stories of how God is working through students and alumni, and update friends on God's work at DTS
Submissions: Email query first. Responds in six to eight weeks. Seasonal six months in advance. Articles: alumni profiles; exposition, usually authored by DTS faculty or similarly qualified individuals; Christian living, personal experience that encourages average Christians in how to live out their faith in the world and includes some exposition that ends with application of truth. Length: 1,500-2,000 words.
Types: profiles, teaching, personal experience
Rights: first, reprint
Payment: up to $500 for first, $150 for reprints

Guidelines: *dts.edu/magazine/editorial-policies*
Sample: see the link on the website
Tip: "DTS Magazine is a ministry of Dallas Theological Seminary. We prefer articles written by our alumni, faculty, students, staff, board members, donors and their families."

ETERNAL INK

4706 Fantasy Ln., Alton, IL 62002
sonsong@charter.net
Mary-Ellen Grisham, editor
Gary James Smith, poetry editor, garyjamessmith2005@yahoo.ca

Type: biweekly print newsletter, circulation 400
Audience: general
Purpose: to share Christian inspiration
Submissions: Email manuscript in the body of the message. Email editor for assignments. Unsolicited freelance: 10%. Accepts twenty-five manuscripts per year. Length: 400-600 words. Seasonal two months in advance. Responds in two weeks. Bible: NIV. Some themes that follow the Christian year.
Types of manuscripts: devotions, meditations, feature articles, poetry, fillers, humor, reviews, columns
Topics: Christian life, Christian witness, profile or character sketch
Rights: all
Payment: none
Guidelines and theme list: by email
Sample: by email
Tip: Looking for features and brief devotions.

EVANGELICAL MISSIONS QUARTERLY

PO Box 398, Wheaton, IL 60187 | 770-457-6677
emq@missionexus.org | missionexus.org/emq
Peggy E. Newell, managing editor

Parent company: Missio Nexus
Type: quarterly digital journal
Audience: missionaries; mission executives, scholars, professors, students, pastors, and supporters; missionary candidates; lay leaders
Purpose: to increase the effectiveness of the evangelical missionary enterprise
Submissions: Email manuscript as attachment. Articles 2,000-3,000 words.

Types of manuscripts: reports, profiles, how-to
Topics: world missions, evangelism, missionary family life
Rights: first
Guidelines: *missionexus.org/emq/submit-an-article-to-emq*

FACTS & TRENDS

1 Lifeway Plaza, Nashville, TN 37234 | 615-251-2000
factsandtrends@lifeway.com | *www.factsandtrends.net*
Joy Allmond, managing editor
Aaron Earls, online editor

> **Denomination:** Southern Baptist
> **Parent company:** LifeWay Christian Resources
> **Type:** daily digital magazine, 200,000 hits per month, takes ads
> **Audience:** church leaders
> **Purpose:** to help pastors and other Christian leaders navigate the issues and trends impacting the church by providing information, insights, and resources for effective ministry
> **Submissions:** Email query as attachment. Gives assignments; to get one, email introduction, ask for writers guidelines, and pitch an idea. Unsolicited freelance: 40%. Length: 800-1,000 words. Seasonal three months in advance. Responds in one week. Bible: CSB.
> **Types of manuscripts:** personal experience, research analysis, practical/how-to, columns
> **Topics:** culture, leadership, discipleship, evangelism, ministry trends, missions, outreach, worship, church health, preaching, stewardship
> **Rights:** commissioned text with nonexclusive license to writer
> **Payment:** varies, on acceptance, kill fee sometimes
> **Guidelines:** by email
> **Sample:** on the website
> **Tip:** "Become a devoted reader of *Facts & Trends*, so you can better understand our audience and our mission for the publication."

FAITH & FRIENDS

The Salvation Army, 2 Overlea Blvd., Toronto, ON M4H 1P4, Canada | 416-422-6226
faithandfriends@can.salvationarmy.org | *salvationist.ca/editorial-publications/faith-and-friends*
Ken Ramstead, editor

> **Denomination:** Salvation Army
> **Type:** monthly print magazine
> **Audience:** general

Purpose: to show Jesus Christ at work in the lives of real people and to provide spiritual resources for those who are new to the Christian faith

Submissions: Email query or manuscript as attached file. Looking for stories about people whose lives have been changed through an encounter with Jesus: conversion, miracles, healing, faith in the midst of crisis, forgiveness, reconciliation, answered prayers, and more. Profiles of people who have found hope and healing through their ministries, including prisoners, hospital patients, nursing-home residents, single parents in distress, addicts, the unemployed, or homeless. Length: 750-1,200 words. Ten departments with 750-word narratives. Bible: TNIV.

Types of manuscripts: testimonies, personal experience, profiles

Topics: changed lives, marriage, family relationships, missionaries, theology

Payment: none

Guidelines: *salvationist.ca/files/salvationarmy/Magazines/FAITH-FRIENDS.pdf*

Sample: on the website

FAITH TODAY

PO Box 5885, West Beaver Creek PO, Richmond Hill, ON
L4B 0B8, Canada
editor@faithtoday.ca | www.faithtoday.ca
Bill Fledderus, senior editor
Karen Stiller, senior editor

Parent company: The Evangelical Fellowship of Canada

Type: bimonthly print and digital magazine, print circulation 20,000, takes ads

Audience: Canadian evangelicals

Purpose: to connect, equip, and inform Canada's four million evangelical Christians from Anglican and Baptist to Pentecostal and Salvation Army

Submissions: Email query with clips first. Responds in one week. Seasonal four months in advance. Length: 300-1,800. Freelance: 10%. Buys one hundred manuscripts per year.

Types of manuscripts: analysis of trends in church and society, news, profiles, reviews of books and music, tips for lay ministry, how-to, journalistic features, essays

Topics: societal issues and trends, church issues and trends

Rights: first, onetime, electronic, reprint (tell when/where published)

Payment: 15-25¢ per word CAD, on acceptance, kill fee sometimes

Guidelines: *www.faithtoday.ca/writers*

Sample: *www.faithtoday.ca/digital*
Tip: "What is the Canadian angle? How does your approach include diverse Canadian voices from different churches, regions, generations, etc.?"

FOCUS ON THE FAMILY

8605 Explorer Dr., Colorado Springs, CO 80920
focusmagsubmissions@family.org | www.focusonthefamily.com/magazine
Michael Ridgeway, editorial director

Parent company: Focus on the Family
Type: bimonthly print magazine
Audience: parents, primarily of ages 4-12
Purpose: to encourage, teach, and celebrate God's design for the family
Submissions: Email or mail to submissions editor. Responds in eight weeks or not interested. Departments: "Family Stages," 50-200 words, practical applications for parents of preschoolers, school-aged children, tweens, and teens; send complete manuscript. "Family Faith," 150 words, devotionals that explore how a biblical principle applies to marriage, 1,200-word articles that show how to help kids understand important biblical truths; send complete manuscript. Features, 1,200-1,500 words; send complete manuscript. "Family Living," 450 words on marriage and parenting; query.
Types of manuscripts: how-to, devotional, teaching
Topics: marriage, parenting
Rights: first
Payment: 25¢/word, $50 for "Family Stages," on acceptance
Guidelines: *www.focusonthefamily.com/magazine/call-for-submissions*
Tip: "Looking for stories about how parents have dealt with challenges and come up with active, practical ways (beyond explaining or talking) of solving those problems."

FRIENDS JOURNAL

1216 Arch St., Ste. 2A, Philadelphia, PA 19107 | 215-563-8629
martink@friendsjournal.org | www.friendsjournal.org
Martin Kelly, senior editor

Denomination: Religious Society of Friends
Type: monthly (11x) print and downloadable journal
Audience: denomination
Purpose: to communicate Quaker experience in order to connect and deepen spiritual lives
Submissions: Submit poetry through the website, maximum three.

Feature articles 1,200-2,500 words, related to themes. Departments, around 1,500 words or fewer: "Celebration," "Earthcare," "Faith and Practice," "First-day School," "Friends in Business," "History," "Humor," "Life in the Meeting," "Lives of Friends," "Pastoral Care," "Q&A," "Reflection," "Religious Education," "Remembrance," "Service," "Witness."

Types of manuscripts: poetry, testimonies, teaching, profiles, personal experience

Topics: most issues are themed

Rights: first

Payment: none

Guidelines: *www.friendsjournal.org/submissions*

Theme list: on the website

THE GEM

PO Box 926, Findlay, OH 45839-0926 | 419-424-1961
gem@cggc.org | *www.cggc.org*
Rachel Foreman, editor, rachelf@cggc.org
Jenn Schlumbohm, assistant editor, jenns@cggc.org

Denomination: Churches of God, General Conference

Type: weekly take-home paper, circulation 3,000

Audience: denomination

Purpose: to encourage readers with inspiring stories

Submissions: Articles 200-1,200 words. Seasonal four months in advance. For fiction, it is important that characters are true to life and solutions to problems are genuine. Email complete manuscript as Word attachment or in body of message. Responds in one month. Simultaneous OK. Accepts manuscripts from children and teens too. Freelance: 95%. Buys 100 manuscripts per year. Bible: NIV.

Types of manuscripts: personal experiences, devotionals, short stories, poetry, fillers

Topics: see themes on website

Rights: all

Payment: $10-30 on publication

Guidelines and theme list: *www.cggc.org/ministries/denominational-communications/the-gem*

Sample: #10 envelope with first-class postage

Tip: "We prefer true-to-life stories."

GEMS OF TRUTH

7407 Metcalf Ave., Overland Park, KS 66204 | 913-432-0331
www.heraldandbanner.com/product/gems-truth

Denomination: Church of God (Holiness)

Type: weekly take-home paper
Audience: denomination
Submissions: Send complete manuscript or query. Email through the website. Fiction 1,000-2,000 words. Seasonal six to eight months in advance. Bible: KJV.
Types of manuscripts: biography, profile, short story, devotional, poetry, teaching

GOOD NEWS

PO Box 132076, The Woodlands, TX 77393-2076 | 832-813-8327
info@goodnewsmag.org | www.goodnewsmag.org
Steve Beard, editor

Denomination: United Methodist
Type: bimonthly print magazine
Audience: Methodists seeking spiritual renewal
Purpose: to encourage United Methodist renewal
Submissions: Articles 1,500-1,850 words. Email for current needs.
Rights: onetime
Payment: $100-150, on publication

THE GOOD NEWS (FLORIDA)

PO Box 670368, Coral Springs, FL 33067 | 954-564-5378
ShellyP@goodnewsfl.org | www.goodnewsfl.org
Shelly Pond, editor

Type: monthly print and digital newspaper
Audience: Dade, Broward and Palm Beach, Florida areas
Submissions: Query through the website. Articles 500-800 words.
Payment: 10¢/word
Sample: on the website

THE GOOD NEWS (NEW YORK)

PO Box 18204, Rochester, NY 14618 | 585-271-4464
info@TheGoodNewsNewYork.com | www.thegoodnewsnewyork.com
Alexandre V. Boutakov, editor

Type: bimonthly print newspaper, circulation 10,000
Audience: New York state
Submissions: Email query.
Types: articles, reviews
Sample: on the website

THE GOOD NEWS JOURNAL

PO Box 170069, Austin, TX 78717-0069 | 512-260-1800
goodnewsjournal10@gmail.com | *www.thegoodnewsjournal.net*
Bill Myers, editor

> **Type:** bimonthly print and digital newspaper
> **Audience:** Capital MetroPlex and Central Texas areas
> **Purpose:** to provide leadership to individuals and corporations with a positive, patriotic, godly perspective
> **Submissions:** Articles 350 words. Email query first.
> **Payment:** none
> **Sample:** on the website

GRACECONNECT

PO Box 544, Winona Lake, IN 46590 | 574-268-1122
lcgates@bmhbooks.com | *www.graceconnect.us*
Liz Cutler Gates, executive director

> **Denomination:** Grace Brethren
> **Type:** quarterly print and digital magazine
> **Audience:** pastors, elders, and other leaders
> **Purpose:** to build bridges of communication between the people and churches of the denomination
> **Submissions:** Email through the website. Feature stories should have a Grace Brethren connection. Length: 1,000-1,500 words, sometimes 600-800 words or up to 2,000 words.
> **Topics:** theme-related
> **Guidelines:** *graceconnect.us/grace-stories/submit-a-story-idea*
> **Sample:** on the website

GUIDEPOSTS

110 William St., Ste. 901, New York, NY 10038 | 212-251-8100
www.guideposts.org/our-magazines/guideposts-magazine
Edward Grinnan, editor

> **Type:** bimonthly print and digital magazine
> **Audience:** general
> **Purpose:** to help readers find peace of mind, solve tough personal problems, and build satisfying relationships
> **Submissions:** Publishes true, first-person stories about people who have attained a goal, surmounted an obstacle, or learned a helpful lesson through their faith. A typical story is a first-person narrative with a spiritual point the reader can apply to his or her own life.

Buys forty to sixty per year. Length: 1,500 words. Submit queries and manuscripts through the online form at *guideposts.org/tell-us-your-story-2*. If no answer in two months, not interested. Freelance: 40%. Short anecdotes similar to full-length articles, 50-250 words, for departments: "Someone Cares," stories of kindness and caring, *sc@guideposts.com*; "Mysterious Ways," "Family Room," "What Prayer Can Do." Also takes inspiring quotes for "The Up Side," *upside@guideposts.com*.

Types of manuscripts: personal experiences
Rights: all
Payment: $100-500, on acceptance, kill fee: 20% but not to first-time freelancers
Guidelines: *www.guideposts.org/writers-guidelines*
Tip: "Be able to tell a good story with drama, suspense, description, and dialog. The point of the story should be some practical spiritual help that the subject learns through his or her experience. Use unique spiritual insights, strong and unusual dramatic details."

HEARTBEAT
PO Box 9, Hatfield, AR 71945 | 870-389-6196
heartbeat@cmausa.org | *www.cmausa.org/cma_national/heartbeat.asp*
Misty Bradley, editor

Parent company: Christian Motorcyclists Association
Type: monthly print and digital magazine
Purpose: to inspire leaders and members to be the most organized, advanced, equipped, financially stable organization, full of integrity in the motorcycling industry and the Kingdom of God
Submissions: Email manuscript.
Topics: related to motocycling

HIGHWAY NEWS
PO Box 117, Marietta, PA 17547-0117 | 717-426-9977
editor@transportforchrist.org | *www.transportforchrist.org/highway*
Inge Koenig, managing editor

Parent company: Transport for Christ, International
Type: monthly print and digital magazine, circulation 18-20,000
Audience: truck drivers and their families
Purpose: to lead truck drivers, as well as the trucking community, to Jesus Christ and help them grow in their faith
Submissions: Email manuscript as attachment or in the body of the message, or mail it. Simultaneous OK. Unsolicited freelance:

10-20%. Only responds if interested. Length: 800-1,000 words. Seasonal six months in advance. Bible: prefers ESV.

Types of manuscripts: personal experience, reports, short features

Topics: anything related to trucking life

Rights: first, reprint

Payment: none

Guidelines: by email

Sample: by email

Tip: "Articles submitted for publication do not have to be religious in nature; however, they should not conflict with or oppose guidelines and principles presented in the Bible."

HISTORY'S WOMEN

22 Williams St., Batavia, NY 14020 | 585-297-3009
patty.chadwick@juno.com | *www.historyswomen.com*
Patti Chadwick, editor

Type: monthly print newsletter, circulation 21,000

Audience: women

Purpose: to make history come alive for women from a Christian worldview

Submissions: Looking for articles highlighting the extraordinary achievements of women throughout history that have made life better for their families and the societies in which they lived. Articles 400-1,200 words. Requires email submissions with no attachments; put "Article Submission" in the subject line.

Types of manuscripts: profiles, interviews

Topics: women of faith, social reformers, the Arts, early America, women rulers, life lessons for women, amazing moms, women in sports

Payment: none but offers alternative compensation

Guidelines: *historyswomen.com/writers-guidelines*

Tip: "Interviews or features about women who are making a difference in their world today are also welcomed and probably the most sought after."

HOLINESS TODAY

17001 Prairie Star Pkwy., Lenexa, KS 66220 | 913-577-0500
holinesstoday@nazarene.org | *www.holinesstoday.org*
Dr. Frank Moore, editor in chief
Jordan Eigsti, assistant editor

Denomination: Nazarene

Type: bimonthly print and digital magazine, circulation 11,000, takes ads

Audience: Nazarene laity

Purpose: to connect Nazarenes with their heritage, vision, and mission through stories of God at work in the world

Submissions: Email manuscript as attachment. Also accepts submissions from children and teens. Freelance: 30%. Buys six to eight manuscripts per year. Length: 700-1,100 words. Responds in one day. Bible: NIV.

Types of manuscripts: personal experience, sidebars, columns

Topics: Christian ministry, theological teaching, denominational insights on real-world issues

Rights: first, reprint (tell when/where published)

Payment: $135, on publication, pays kill fee

Guidelines and theme list: by email

Sample: self-addressed 9x12 envelope with two stamps

Tip: "We are always interested in hearing from Nazarene pastors, lay leaders, and experts in their fields. We are a Nazarene publication that wants our articles to be relevant and applicable to real-life scenarios and the world we live in."

HOMELIFE

1 Lifeway Plaza, Nashville, TN 37234-0172 | 615-251-2196
homelife@lifeway.com | www.lifeway.com/en/product-family/homelife-magazine?intcmp=SRDR-homelife
David Bennett, managing editor

Parent company: LifeWay Christian Resources

Denomination: Southern Baptist

Type: monthly print magazine

Audience: families

Purpose: to equip and challenge families to experience dynamic, healthy, Christ-centered homes

Submissions: Manuscripts by assignment. Email résumé, bio, and clips. Offers practical, real-world solutions toward maintaining the spiritual health of family members amid school, sports, work, play, and more.

Payment: unspecified

Guidelines: by email

Sample: on the website

HOMESCHOOLING TODAY

PO Box 1092, Somerset, KY 42502 | 606-485-4105
ashley@homeschoolingtoday.com | *homeschoolingtoday.com*
Ashley Wiggers, executive editor

> **Type:** quarterly print and digital magazine, circulation 5-6,000, takes ads
> **Audience:** homeschooling parents
> **Purpose:** to encourage the hearts of homeschoolers and give them tools to instill a love of learning in their children
> **Submissions:** Does not accept queries; email full manuscript as an attachment with "Article Submission" in the subject line. Responds in six months or not interested. Feature articles include information about a topic, unit study, encouragement, challenge, or an interview, 900-1,200 words. Departments: "Faces of Homeschooling," true stories about real homeschooling families, 600-900 words; "The Home Team," physical education, 600-900 words; "Homeschooling around the World," 600-900 words; "Language Learning," foreign languages, 600-900 words; "Thinking," logic, critical thinking, 600-900 words; "Unit Study," 800-1500 words; "Family Math," 600-900 words.
> **Types of manuscripts:** how-to, unit studies, profiles, interviews
> **Topics:** education, homeschooling
> **Rights:** first, nonexclusive electronic
> **Payment:** 10¢/published word
> **Guidelines:** *homeschoolingtoday.com/write-for-us*

IMAGE

3307 Third Ave. W., Seattle, WA 98119 | 206-281-2988
mkenagy@imagejournal.org | *imagejournal.org*
Mary Kenagy Mitchell, executive editor
Shane McCrae, poetry editor
Lauren F. Winner, creative nonfiction editor
Nick Ripatrazone, culture editor

> **Type:** quarterly print literary journal
> **Purpose:** to demonstrate the continued vitality and diversity of contemporary art and literature that engage with the religious traditions of Western culture
> **Submissions:** Email queries. Submit manuscripts through the website. Responds in three months. Accepts simultaneous submissions. Poetry: no more than five poems or ten pages total. Fiction, essays, and other nonfiction: 3,000-6,000 words.

Types of manuscripts: poetry, fiction, essays, interviews, artist profiles
Topics: related to art and literature
Rights: first
Payment: unspecified
Guidelines: *imagejournal.org/journal/submit*
Tip: "All the work we publish reflects what we see as a sustained engagement with one of the western faiths—Judaism, Christianity, or Islam. That engagement can include unease, grappling, or ambivalence as well as orthodoxy; the approach can be indirect or allusive, but for a piece to be a fit for *Image*, some connection to faith must be there."

INDIAN LIFE

188 Henderson Hwy., Winnipeg, MB R2L 1L6, Canada | 800-665-9275, 204-661-9333
ilm.editor@indianlife.org | *www.newspaper.indianlife.org*
Jeanette Littleton, editor

Parent company: Indian Life Ministries
Type: bimonthly print and digital newspaper, circulation 12,000, takes ads
Audience: Native Americans, First Nations, and interested parties; also distributed in prisons and on reservations
Purpose: to present positive news of the First Nations/Native American world, encourage, and evangelize
Submissions: Email as attachment the complete manuscript or query letter with clips. Accepts simultaneous submissions. Unsolicited freelance and number of manuscripts accepted: open. Seasonal six months in advance. Response time varies. Bible: First Nations, NIV.
Types of manuscripts: news, features, reviews, columns, fillers, testimonies
Topics: evangelism, issues related to Native Americans/First Nations
Rights: onetime
Payment: varies from donation to small stipend, on publication
Guidelines: by email
Sample: on website
Tip: "Testimonies from Native Americans/First Nations are the ones we need most. The difference between our newspaper and other Native-focused newspapers is that we also want the reader to know about Christ and grow in the grace and knowledge of Christ."

INSITE

PO Box 62189, Colorado Springs, CO 80962-2189 | 719-260-9400
editor@ccca.org | www.ccca.org/ccca/Publications.asp
Jen Howver, editor

Parent company: Christian Camp and Conference Association
Type: bimonthly print and digital magazine, circulation 8,500
Audience: camp leaders
Purpose: to help our members maximize their ministries by learning and staying inspired while serving God's people
Submissions: Email query first. Responds within one week. Seasonal six months ahead. Profiles and features, 1,200-1,500 words; how-to articles, 1,000-1,200 words; sidebars, 250-500 words. Unsolicited freelance: 1-2%; email for assignment. Bible: NIV.
Types of manuscripts: profiles, interviews, how-to, sidebars
Topics: Christian camping, leadership, children and teen discipleship and development, legal, facilities, business operations
Rights: all
Payment: $300 on publication, sometimes pays kill fee
Guidelines and theme list: download from *www.ccca.org/ccca/ Publications.asp*
Sample: via email
Tip: "All articles must be applicable to camps and conference centers."

INTERNATIONAL JOURNAL OF FRONTIER MISSIOLOGY

1605 E. Elizabeth St., Pasadena, CA 91104 | 734-765-0368
editors@ijfm.org | www.ijfm.org
Brad Gill, editor

Parent company: International Society for Frontier Missiology
Type: quarterly print journal
Audience: mission professors, executives, and researchers; missionaries; young-adult mission mobilizers
Purpose: to cultivate an international fraternity of thought in the development of frontier missiology
Submissions: Query first. Articles 2,000-6,000 words.
Types: profiles, teaching
Topics: missiological perspective and principles, calls to commitment and involvement in frontier missions
Payment: none
Guidelines: *www.ijfm.org/author_info.htm*
Sample: download from website

JOURNAL OF ADVENTIST EDUCATION
12501 Old Columbia Pike, Silver Spring, MD 20904 | 301-680-5069
mcgarrellf@gc.adventist.org | *jae.adventist.org*
Faith-Ann McGarrell, editor

Denomination: Seventh-day Adventist

Parent company: General Conference of Seventh-day Adventists

Type: quarterly print and digital journal, circulation 10-16,000, takes ads

Audience: educators and administrators

Purpose: to aid professional teachers and educational administrators worldwide, kindergarten to higher education

Submissions: Submit complete manuscript through the website form. Unsolicited: 10%. Buys thirty-two articles per year. Length: 1,500-2,500 words. Seasonal six months in advance. Responds in four to six weeks. Bible: NIV.

Types of manuscripts: how-to, personal experience, sidebars, reviews

Topics: pedagogy, educational administration, integration of faith and learning, philosophy of education

Rights: first, reprint (tell where/when published)

Payment: $100-250, on publication

Guidelines: *jae.adventist.org/en/for-authors*

Sample: on the website

Tip: Wants "articles on best practices for teaching and pedagogy that can be applied in education settings both nationally and internationally."

JOYFUL LIVING MAGAZINE
PO Box 311, Palo Cedro, CA 97073 | 530-247-7500
joyfullivingmagazineredding@gmail.com | *joyfullivingmagazine.com*
Cathy Jansen, editor-in-chief

Type: quarterly print and digital magazine, takes ads

Audience: general

Purpose: to share encouragement and hope, to help readers grow spiritually and emotionally, and to help them in their everyday lives with practical issues

Submissions: Email articles as attachments. Length: 200-700 words.

Types of manuscripts: profiles, personal experience, recipes, how-to

Topics: making dreams come true, family, marriage, work, singleness, recovery, finances, health, dealing with loss, depression, aging, physical fitness, overcoming obstacles, healthy eating, and more

Payment: none

Guidelines: *www.joyfullivingmagazine.com/writers-info*
Sample: download from website

JUST BETWEEN US

777 S. Barker Rd., Brookfield, WI 53045 | 262-786-6478
jbu@justbetweenus.org | *www.justbetweenus.org*
Shelly Esser, executive editor

Parent organization: Elmbrook Church
Type: quarterly print magazine, circulation 8,000
Audience: women
Purpose: to encourage and equip women for a life of faith and service
Submissions: Prefers emailed manuscripts as attachments but also takes them by mail. Responds in six to eight weeks. Articles, 500 1,500 words; testimonies, 450 words. Bible version: NIV.
Types of manuscripts: how-to, testimony, personal experience
Topics: balance, intimacy with Christ, handling criticism, friendship, conflict, faith, church life, prayer, evangelism, change, Spirit-filled living, finances, forgiveness, God's will, spiritual warfare, staying committed to Christ no matter what, parenting, pain, fighting weariness, church wounds, ministry helps
Payment: none
Guidelines: *justbetweenus.org/writers-guidelines*
Sample: *justbetweenus.org/sample-issue*
Tip: "Articles should be personal in tone, full of real-life anecdotes as well as quotes/advice from noted Christian professionals, and be biblically based. Articles need to be practical and have a distinct Christian and serving perspective throughout."

KANSAS CITY METRO VOICE

PO Box 1114, Lee's Summit, MO 64063 | 816-524-4522
dwight@metrovoicenews.com | *www.metrovoicenews.com*
Dwight Widaman, editor

Type: monthly print and digital newspaper, takes ads
Audience: Kansas City metropolitan area and Topeka/Northeast Kansas
Purpose: to inform and encourage the evangelical community in the area
Submissions: Email for current needs. Takes articles and reviews.
Types of manuscripts: profiles, reviews, opinion pieces, news reports
Sample: download from the website

KEYS TO LIVING

253 Steffens Rd., Danville, PA 17821
owcam@verizon.net
Connie Mertz, editor and publisher
Collesce Beck, associate editor

> **Type:** quarterly print newsletter
> **Audience:** nature enthusiasts
> **Purpose:** to glorify God through nature and present inspirational writing for Christians
> **Submissions:** Email complete manuscript in body of message. Accepts simultaneous submissions. Unsolicited freelance: 30%. Buys twelve manuscripts per year. Length: 500 words maximum. Also considers high-quality photos to accompany devotionals. Responds in one month. Bible: NIV. Accepts manuscripts from teens.
> **Type of manuscripts:** devotionals, personal experience, poetry
> **Topics:** Christian living
> **Rights:** reprint
> **Payment:** none
> **Guidelines:** by email
> **Sample:** by email
> **Tip:** "Poetry is welcome but limited to one page maximum. Should have a religious slant."

LEADING HEARTS

PO Box 6421, Longmont, CO 80501 | 303-835-8473
amber@leadinghearts.com | *leadinghearts.com*
Amber Weigland-Buckley, editor

> **Parent company:** Right to the Heart Ministries
> **Type:** bimonthly digital magazine, circulation 60,000, takes ads
> **Audience:** women who lead hearts at home, church, work, and community; ages 35-50
> **Submissions:** Articles on assignment only. To audition for an assignment, email an article of 1,200 words maximum and a short résumé. Gives preferred consideration to members of AWSA. Articles 800 words maximum. Columns 250-500 words. Bible version: NIV.
> **Types of manuscripts:** personal experience, how-to, profiles, reviews
> **Topics:** based on theme list
> **Rights:** first, reprint
> **Payment:** none
> **Guidelines:** *leadinghearts.com/?page_id=32*

Sample: download from the website

LEAVES

PO Box 87, Dearborn, MI 48121-0087 | 313-561-2330
leaves-mag@mariannhill.us | *www.mariannhill.us/leaves.html*
Rev. Thomas Heier, editor-in-chief

> **Parent company:** Mariannhill Mission Society
> **Denomination:** Catholic
> **Type:** bimonthly print magazine , circulation 10,000
> **Audience:** Catholics, primarily in the Detroit, Michigan, area
> **Purpose:** to promote devotion to God and testimony of His blessings
> **Submissions:** Email or mail complete manuscript. Responds in one week. Accepts forty manuscripts per year. Length: 250 words. Unsolicited freelance: 50%. Bible: RSV Catholic edition.
> **Types of manuscripts:** personal experience, testimonies, reviews, poetry
> **Topics:** Christian life, pursuit of holiness
> **Rights:** first, reprint
> **Payment:** none
> **Sample:** write, email, or call for a copy
> **Tip:** Greatest need is for personal testimonies.

LEBEN

2150 River Plaza Dr., Ste. 150, Sacramento, CA 95833 | 916-473-8866
editor@leben.us | *www.leben.us*
Wayne C. Johnson, editor

> **Parent company:** City Seminary of Sacramento, California
> **Type:** quarterly print journal
> **Audience:** general
> **Purpose:** to tell the stories of the people and events that make up the Reformation tradition
> **Submissions:** We are a popular history publication that aims at a general readership. Query first. Length: 500-2500 words.
> **Types of manuscripts:** profiles
> **Topics:** Protestant Reformers and those who have followed in their footsteps
> **Payment:** not specified
> **Guidelines:** *leben.us/write-for-leben*
> **Tip:** "Focus on lesser-known events and people. We have no shortage of submissions about Luther, Calvin, Zwingli, etc."

THE LIGHT MAGAZINE

20218 Fraser Highway, #200, Langley, BC V3A 4E6, Canada |
604-510-5070
editor@lightmagazine.ca | *www.lightmagazine.ca*
Steve Almond, editor

> **Parent company:** Light Christian Media
> **Type:** monthly print and digital magazine, circulation 18,000, takes ads
> **Audience:** greater Vancouver Christian community
> **Purpose:** to inspire faith for everyday life
> **Submissions:** Email in body of message. Freelance: 10%. Contact editor to get assignments. Buys twenty-four manuscripts per year. Seasonal two months in advance. Length: 800 words maximum. Responds in one week. Bible: no preference.
> **Types of manuscripts:** lifestyle, news, testimony
> **Topics:** parenting, senior life, Christian living, travel
> **Rights:** first, reprint
> **Payment:** 10¢/word on publication, kill fee sometimes
> **Guidelines:** *lightmagazine.ca/about-us*
> **Sample:** by email
> **Tip:** "Canadian experience is helpful; otherwise all areas are open to freelancers."

LIGHT + LIFE MAGAZINE

770 N. High School Rd., Indianapolis, IN 46214 | 317-244-3660
jeff.finley@fmcusa.org | *lightandlifemagazine.com*
Jeff Finley, executive editor
Cynthia Schnereger, managing editor

> **Denomination:** Free Methodist
> **Type:** monthly print magazine, circulation 15,000
> **Audience:** general
> **Purpose:** to offer encouragement, provide resources, deal with contemporary issues, share denominational news, and offer faith to unbelievers
> **Submissions:** Articles: main article that provides a more detailed examination of the issue's theme, approximately 2,100 words, primarily in third person; action article that shares the story of someone living out the theme and sometimes serves as an instructional piece detailing how to take action, 1,000 words; discipleship, for use by a weekly small group or for individual study, 800 words, reflecting the theme plus two or three group

discussion questions. Query first. Responds in two months. Unsolicited freelance: 50%. Bible: NIV.

Types of manuscripts: teaching, profile, Bible study

Topics: theme-related

Rights: first, onetime, occasional reprint (tell when/where appeared)

Payment: $100 for feature articles, $50 for others, on publication

Guidelines: *lightandlifemagazine.com/writers*

Themes: email through the website

Tip: "We search for authors who write competently, provide clear information, and employ contemporary style and illustrations."

LIGUORIAN

1 Liguori Dr., Liguori, MO 63057 | 636-223-1538
liguorianeditor@liguori.org | www.liguorian.org
Elizabeth Herzing, editor

Denomination: Catholic

Type: monthly print and digital magazine

Audience: denomination

Purpose: to reinforce spiritual beliefs with inspiration and insight

Submissions: Articles must not exceed 2,200 words. Personal essays should be limited to 1,000. Fiction submissions should be approximately 2,000 words. Seasonal articles and stories must be received eight months in advance. Email query. Email manuscripts as attachments. Responds in two to three months.

Types of manuscripts: essay, feature, short stories, interviews

Topics: explanations of Church teachings, theological insights, Christian living

Rights: first

Payment: 12-15¢/published word, on acceptance

Guidelines: *www.liguorian.org/submissions-and-rights-and-permissions*

Sample: 9x12 SASE with three stamps

LIVE

1445 N. Boonville Ave., Springfield, MO 65802-1894 | 417-862-2781
wquick@ag.org
Wade Quick, editor

Denomination: Assemblies of God

Type: weekly take-home paper, circulation 12,000

Audience: denomination

Purpose: to encourage Christians in their faith and to apply biblical principles to everyday problems

Submissions: Email submissions as attachments. Stories should be encouraging, challenging, and/or humorous. Even problem-centered stories should be upbeat. Stories should not be preachy, critical, or moralizing. They should not present pat, trite, or simplistic answers to problems. No Bible fiction or sci-fi. Length: maximum 1,200 words; inside stories, 200-600 words; poetry, 12-25 lines. Seasonal eighteen months in advance. Unsolicited freelance: 100%. Receives 100 manuscripts per year. Bible: NIV.

Types of manuscripts: personal experiences, short stories, how-to from first-person point of view, poetry, fillers

Topics: Christian life/testimony

Rights: first, reprint, electronic

Payment: 10¢/word for first, 7¢/word for reprint, $42-60 for poetry; on acceptance

Guidelines: via email

Samples: 5x8 SASE with $2.20 postage

Tip: "Make sure the stories have a strong Christian element, are written well, have strong takeaways, but do not preach."

THE LIVING CHURCH

PO Box 510705, Milwaukee, WI 53203-0121 | 414-292-1241
jschuessler@livingchurch.org | *www.livingchurch.org*
John Schuessler, managing editor

Denomination: Episcopal

Type: biweekly print magazine

Audience: denomination

Purpose: to seek and serve the Catholic and evangelical faith of the one Church, to the end of visible Christian unity throughout the world

Submissions: Email for current needs.

Types: articles, reviews

THE LOOKOUT

16965 Pine Ln., Ste. 202, Parker, CO 80134 | 800-543-1353
soverstreet@christianstandardmedia.com | *www.lookoutmag.com*
Sheryl Overstreet, managing editor

Parent company: Christian Standard Media

Type: monthly print and digital magazine, circulation 40,000

Audience: ordinary Christians who want to grow in their faith

Purpose: to provide Christian adults with true-to-the-Bible teaching to help them mature as believers and live in the world as faithful witnesses of Christ

Submissions: Assignment only. Email editor for possible assignments. Bible: NIV.

Topics: theme-related

Rights: first

Payment: up to 11¢/word

Sample: *www.lookoutmag.com/sample*

THE LUTHERAN DIGEST

PO Box 100, Princeton, MN 55371

editor@lutherandigest.com | www.lutherandigest.com

> **Denomination:** Lutheran
>
> **Type:** quarterly print magazine
>
> **Audience:** denomination
>
> **Purpose:** to entertain and encourage believers and to subtly persuade nonbelievers to embrace the Lutheran-Christian faith
>
> **Submissions:** Prefers manuscripts by mail with SASE but will look at emailed submissions as attachments and respond only if accepted. Unsolicited freelance: 30%. Will consider simultaneous submissions but prefers not to. Length: 3,000-7,000 characters. Popular stories show how God has intervened in a person's life to help solve a problem. Seasonal six months in advance. Poetry one or two stanzas. Interested in poems that can be sung to the melodies of familiar hymns. Submit maximum three poems in a month.
>
> **Types of manuscripts:** personal experience, seasonal, poetry, recipes, jokes
>
> **Topics:** Christian living, God's presence in nature
>
> **Rights:** onetime, reprint (tell when/where last appeared)
>
> **Payment:** $35, on publication, none for poetry and fillers
>
> **Guidelines:** *lutherandigest.com/write-for-us*
>
> **Tip:** "Stories frequently reflect a Lutheran-Christian perspective but are not intended to be 'lecturing' sermonettes."

LUTHERAN FORUM

PO Box 327, Delhi, NY 13753-0327 | 607-746-7511

lutheranforum.com

R. David Nelson, editor

> **Denomination:** Lutheran
>
> **Parent company:** American Lutheran Publicity Bureau
>
> **Type:** quarterly print journal
>
> **Submissions:** Articles 2,000-3,000 words. Submit manuscript through online form. Responds in three months.

Rights: first
Payment: none
Guidelines: *alpb.org/writers-guidelines*
Sample: download from the website
Tip: "Prospective writers are encouraged to reflect on what moves them most, intellectually and spiritually, and then, armed with adequate research and forethought, put their ideas to paper."

THE LUTHERAN JOURNAL

PO Box 28158, Oakdale, MN 55128 | 651-702-0176
christianad2@msn.com | *thelutheranjournal.com*
Roger Jensen, editor

Denomination: Lutheran
Type: annual print magazine
Audience: families
Purpose: to provide wholesome and inspirational reading for the enjoyment and enrichment of Lutherans
Submissions: Email for current needs.
Types of manuscripts: articles, poetry, prayers
Payment: none
Sample: download from the website

LUTHERAN WITNESS

1333 S. Kirkwood Rd., St. Louis, MO 63122-7226 | 800-248-1930
lutheran.witness@lcms.org | *blogs.lcms.org/category/lutheran-witness*
Rachel Bomberger, managing editor, rachel.bomberger@lcms.org

Denomination: Luthern Church Missouri Synod (LCMS)
Type: monthly (11x) print and digital magazine, circulation 185,000
Audience: denomination
Purpose: to provide Missouri Synod laypeople with stories and information that complement congregational life, foster personal growth in faith, and help interpret the contemporary world from a Lutheran Christian perspective
Submissions: Prefers complete manuscript instead of a query. Submit by email or mail. Length: 500, 1,000, or 1,500 words. Bible: ESV.
Types of manuscripts: profiles, how-to, teaching, humor, personal experience, Bible studies, essays, poetry
Topics: current events; theology; LCMS missions, ministries, members, history; evangelism, outreach, spiritual growth
Rights: first, electronic
Guidelines and themes: *blogs.lcms.org/writers-guidelines-for-the-lutheran-witness*

Sample: on the website

Tip: "Because of the magazine's long lead time and because main features are planned at least six months in advance of the publication date, your story should have a long-term perspective that keeps it relevant several months from the time you submit it."

MATURE LIVING

1 Lifeway Plaza, MSN 136, Nashville, TN 37234-0175 | 615-251-2000
matureliving@lifeway.com |
www.lifeway.com/en/product-family/mature-living-magazine
Debbie Dickerson, managing editor

Parent company: LifeWay Christian Resources
Denomination: Southern Baptist
Type: monthly print magazine
Audience: ages 55 and older
Purpose: to equip mature adults as they live a legacy of leadership, stewardship, and discipleship
Submissions: Email for possible assignment. Not accepting unsolicited manuscripts or queries.
Types of manuscripts: personal experience, how-to, teaching, devotional, short stories, recipes
Topics: marriage, caregiving, evangelism, theology, relationship with adult children, grandchildren
Sample: on the website

MESSAGE OF THE OPEN BIBLE

2020 Bell Ave., Des Moines, IA 50315 | 515-288-6761
andrea@openbible.org | www.openbiblemessage.org
Andrea Johnson, managing editor

Denomination: Open Bible Churches
Type: bimonthly print and digital magazine, circulation 3,300, takes ads
Audience: denomination
Purpose: to inform, educate, and inspire
Submissions: Email as attachment. Freelance: 1%. Accepts thirty manuscripts per year. Length: 600 words. Seasonal four months in advance. Responds in three weeks. Bible: NIV.
Types of manuscripts: personal experience, sidebar
Topics: Christian life, discipleship, outreach, evangelism, leadership development
Rights: onetime
Payment: none
Guidelines: by email

Sample: SASE

Tip: Looking for "well-written articles that target people not accustomed to church."

THE MESSENGER

440 Main St., Steinbach, MB R5G 1Z5, Canada | 204-326-6401
messenger@emconference.ca | *www.emconference.ca/messenger*
Terry Smith, editor, tsmith@emconference.ca
Andrew Walker, assistant editor

Denomination: Evangelical Mennonite Conference (EMC)

Type: monthly print and digital magazine, circulation 2,300

Audience: denomination

Purpose: to inform concerning events and activities in the denomination, instruct in godliness and victorious living, and inspire to earnestly contend for the faith

Submissions: Email as attachment or mail query or complete manuscript. Simultaneous submissions OK. Unsolicited freelance: 25%. Buys thirty manuscripts per year. Also accepts manuscripts from children and teens. Length: 1,200 words maximum. Seasonal two months in advance. Responds in one week. Bible: modern translation.

Types of manuscripts: articles, poetry

Topics: theology, Christian life

Rights: first

Payment: $150 CAD for 1,200 words, on publication, kill fee always

Guidelines: *www.emconference.ca/the-messenger/submission-guidelines*

Theme list: not available but follow the church year

Sample: *www.emconference.ca/the-messenger/past-issues*

Tip: Looking for Evangelical Anabaptist perspectives.

THE MESSIANIC TIMES

50 Alberta Dr., Amherst, NY 14226 | 866-612-7770
editor@messianictimes.com | *www.messianictimes.com*
Sheila Fisher, editorial coordinator

Parent company: Times of the Messiah Ministries

Denomination: Messianic

Type: bimonthly print and digital newspaper

Audience: Messianic community

Purpose: to provide accurate, authoritative, and current information to unite the international Messianic Jewish community, teach Christians the Jewish roots of their faith, and proclaim that Yeshua is the Jewish Messiah

Submissions: Query preferred. Email for current needs.
Types of manuscripts: analysis; opinion pieces; book, music, and film reviews; news

METHODIST HISTORY JOURNAL

36 Madison Ave., Madison, NJ 07940 | 973-408-3189
atday@gcah.org | *www.gcah.org/research/methodist-history-journal*
Alfred T. Day, III, general secretary

Denomination: United Methodist
Type: annual print journal
Audience: denomination
Submissions: Only email manuscripts as attachments. Articles on the history of other denominations and subjects will be considered when there are strong ties to events and persons significant to the history of the United Methodist tradition. Manuscripts pertaining to strictly local, as opposed to national or international interest, are not accepted. Length: maximum 5,000 words.
Topics: United Methodist history
Payment: none
Guidelines: *www.gcah.org/resources/guidelines-for-publication*

MINISTRY

12501 Old Columbia Pike, Silver Spring, MD 20904 | 301-680-6518
ministrymagazine@gc.adventist.org | *www.ministrymagazine.org*
Pavel Goia, editor

Denomination: Seventh-day Adventist
Type: monthly print and digital magazine, circulation 18,000
Audience: pastors, professors, administrators, chaplains, pastoral students, lay leaders of all denominations
Purpose: to deepen spiritual life, develop intellectual strength, and increase pastoral and evangelistic effectiveness of all ministers in the context of the three angels' messages of Revelation 14:6-12
Submissions: For all submissions, include completed biographical information form. Send all submissions as email attachments. Articles to 2,500 words, book and resources reviews to 500 words.
Types of manuscripts: biblical studies, how-to, teaching, reviews
Topics: personal needs of the minister (spiritual, physical, emotional), pastor-spouse team and ministry relationships, pastoral family needs, pastoral skills, biblical studies for sermon preparation, theological studies, worship, current issues
Rights: all

Payment: not specified, on acceptance
Guidelines: *www.ministrymagazine.org/article-submissions*
Sample: click Archives page on the website
Tip: "Writers should ask themselves: What do I expect the reader to do with my manuscript?"

THE MOTHER'S HEART

PO Box 275, Tobaccoville, NC 27050
kim@tmhmag.com | www.the-mothers-heart.com
Kym Wright, editor and publisher

Parent company: alWright! Publishing
Type: bimonthly digital magazine, monthly hits 100,000, takes ads
Audience: mothers, wives, homeschoolers
Purpose: to serve and encourage mothers in the many facets of staying at home and raising a family, with the underlying theme of Family First
Submissions: Email query as attachment (preferred) or in the body of the message. Seasonal six months ahead. Unsolicited freelance: 50%. Buys fifty manuscripts per year. Length: 800-1,500 words. Responds in four to six months. Bible: any.
Types of manuscripts: personal experience, sidebar, filler, columns
Topics: mothering, homeschooling, parenting, marriage, organization, time management
Rights: first, reprint (tell when/where published), on publication
Payment: $15-75 on publication
Guidelines: *the-mothers-heart.com/Writers%20Guidelines%202016-2019.pdf*
Sample: *the-mothers-heart.com/subscribe.htm*
Tip: "Looking for "uplifting personal stories about family, mothering, homeschooling, God, faith.""

MTL (MORE TO LIFE) MAGAZINE

200 W. Bay Dr., Largo, FL 33770 | 727-596-7625
info@mtlmagazine.com | mtlmagazine.com
Andrea Stock, editor

Parent company: Munce Marketing Group
Type: online magazine with five print issues a year, takes ads
Audience: women
Purpose: to address the felt needs of women and connect those to products at local Christian bookstores
Submissions: Query ideas.

Types of manuscripts: personal experiences, testimonies, how-to, interviews, reviews
Topics: finances, home, relationships, spiritual growth, health
Sample: on the website

MUTUALITY

122 W. Franklin Ave., Ste. 218, Minneapolis, MN 55404 | 612-872-6898
cbe@cbeinternational.org |
www.cbeinternational.org/content/mutuality-magazine
Tim Krueger, editor

Parent company: Christians for Biblical Equality
Type: quarterly print magazine
Audience: evangelicals in professional and volunteer ministry, seminary faculty and students, male and female leaders, and laypeople interested in egalitarian theory (Bible and theology) and practice (application in churches and homes)
Purpose: to provide inspiration, encouragement, and information on topics related to a biblical view of mutuality between men and women in the home, church, and world
Submissions: Query first through the online contact form. Also submit requested manuscript through that form. Responds in one month or more. Length: first-person narratives and feature articles, 800-1,800 words; book, movie, or music reviews, 500-800 words. Bible: NIV.
Types of manuscripts: personal experience, how-to, biblical reflection, poetry, reviews
Topics: theme-related
Rights: first with electronic
Payment: one-year CBE membership ($49–$59 value) or up to three CBE recordings (up to $30 value)
Guidelines: *www.cbeinternational.org/content/mutuality-writers-guidelines*
Theme list: *www.cbeinternational.org/content/upcoming-mutuality-themes*
Sample: download PDF from guidelines page

MYSTERIOUS WAYS

110 William St., Ste. 901, New York, NY 10038 | 212-251-8100
www.guideposts.org/our-magazines/mysterious-ways-magazine
Edward Grinnan, editorial director

Parent company: Guideposts

Type: bimonthly print and digital magazine

Audience: general

Purpose: to encourage through true stories of extraordinary moments and everyday miracles that reveal a spiritual force at work in our lives

Submissions: Submit complete manuscript through the online form. Looking for true stories of unexpected and wondrous experiences that reveal a hidden hand at work in our lives. The best stories are those that present a credible, well-detailed account that can even leave skeptics in awe and wonder. Length: 750-1,500 words. Also buys news stories and short material, 50-350 words, for recurring features like "Wonderful World," "His Humorous Ways," and "Dreams & Premonitions."

Types of manuscripts: personal experiences

Payment: varies, after scheduled for publication

Guidelines: *www.guideposts.org/write-for-mysterious-ways*

Tip: "A typical *Mysterious Ways* story is written in dramatic style, with an unforeseen twist that inspires the reader to look for miracles in his or her own life. It may be told from a 1st-person or 3rd-person perspective, and can be your own experience or someone else's story. We are also on the lookout for recent experiences."

NET RESULTS

308 West Blvd. N., Columbia, MO 65203 | 888-470-2456
billtb@netresults.org | *netresults.org*
Bill Tenny-Brittian, managing editor

Parent company: The Effective Church Group

Type: bimonthly print and digital magazine

Audience: pastors, church volunteers, and Christian organizations

Purpose: to share great ideas for vital ministry among leaders

Submissions: Email query first; email manuscripts as attached file. Responds in eight weeks. Practical and relevant articles on innovative ways to do mission and ministry, 1,750 words. Bible: TNIV. Takes reprints from noncompetitive periodicals with letter of release from original publication.

Types of manuscripts: how-to, teaching

Topics: evangelism, service, planning, trust-building, leadership and organizational development, worship, preaching, hospitality, Christian education, faith formation, mentoring, training, partnerships, property and technology development, fund-raising, financial planning, stewardship, communications, marketing

Rights: all print and electronic

Payment: on publication
Guidelines: *netresults.org/writers*
Theme list: *netresults.org/writers/upcoming-themes*
Sample: on the website
Tip: "We look for practical, hands-on ministry ideas that an individual can put into practice. The best ideas are those the author has actually used successfully."

NEW FRONTIER CHRONICLE

30840 Hawthorne Blvd., Rancho Palos Verde, CA 90275 | 562-491-8343
new.frontier@usw.salvationarmy.org | *www.newfrontierchronicle.org*
Christin Davis Thieme, editor-in-chief

Parent company: The Salvation Army Western Territory
Type: monthly print newspaper
Audience: denomination in the territory
Purpose: to empower Salvationists to communicate and engage with the Army's mission
Submissions: Query first. Shares information from across The Salvation Army world, reports that analyze effective programs to identify the unique features and trends for what works, tips to help local congregations better engage in the issues of today, and influential voices on relevant (and sometimes controversial) matters.
Types: articles, reviews
Guidelines: *www.newfrontierchronicle.org/submit*

NEW IDENTITY MAGAZINE

PO Box 1002, Mount Shasta, CA 96067 | 310-947-8707
submissions@newidentitymagazine.com | *www.newidentitymagazine.com*
Cailin Briody Henson, editor-in-chief

Type: quarterly print and digital magazine
Audience: new believers
Purpose: to provide diverse, Bible-centered content to help lead new believers and seekers to a fuller understanding of the Christian faith
Submissions: Query first; prefers by email. Email requested manuscript. Responds in two to four weeks. Length: 500-3,500 words. Departments: "Grow," teaching new believers and seekers about different Christian perspectives on topics, understanding Christian concepts, jargon, disciplines, practical application of Scripture, etc.; "Connect," encouraging new believers and seekers

with testimonies, articles about relationships, fellowship, church, community, discussions and expressions of faith; "Live," engaging new believers and seekers to live out their faith in the real world, with stories of people actively pursuing God and their passions, organizations and resources to apply one's gifts, talents and desires to serve God and others, sharing the love of Christ in everyday arenas.

Types of manuscripts: personal experience, teaching, testimonies, how-to, opinion

Topics: spiritual growth, applying Scripture, relationships, salvation, church, service, evangelism

Rights: first, electronic, sometimes reprint (tell when/where appeared)

Payment: none

Guidelines: *www.newidentitymagazine.com/WritersGuidelines.pdf*

Sample: on the website

Tip: "Articles need creative, well-thought-out ideas that offer new insight. We value well researched, factually and biblically supported content."

NOW WHAT?

PO Box 33677, Denver, CO 80233
nowwhat@cog7.org | nowwhat.cog7.org
Sherri Langton, associate editor

Denomination: Church of God (Seventh Day)

Type: monthly digital magazine

Audience: seekers

Purpose: to address felt needs of the unchurched

Submissions: Each issue is built around a personal experience, with articles related to the topic. Personal experiences show a person's struggle that either led him to faith in Christ or deepened his walk with God. Unsolicited freelance: 100%. Buys ten to twelve per year. Email manuscripts and queries; query not necessary. Responds in four to ten weeks. Length: 1,000-1,500 words. Bible: prefers NIV. Avoid unnecessary jargon or technical terms. No Christmas or Easter pieces or fiction.

Types of manuscripts: personal experience

Topics: salvation, issues

Rights: first, electronic, reprint (tell when/where appeared)

Payment: $25-65, on publication

Guidelines: *nowwhat.cog7.org/send_us_your_story*

Tip: "Think how you can explain your faith, or how you overcame a problem, to a non-Christian. Use storytelling techniques, like dialogue, scenes, etc., with the conflict clearly stated."

OMS OUTREACH

941 Fry Rd., Greenwood, IN 46142 | 317-881-3333
editor@onemissionsociety.org | onemissionsociety.org/give/outreach
Susan Griswold Loobie, editor, sloobie@onemissionsociety.org

Parent company: One Mission Society
Type: triannual print and digital magazine
Purpose: to equip Christians to make disciples of Jesus Christ through informative, inspiring, and involvement-driven articles, which leads to deeper mission participation by serving, giving, and praying
Submissions: Articles 500-600 words to inform the public of ministry opportunities and report on ministry of various mission teams. Email for current needs. Bible version: ESV.
Sample: click link on the website

ON MISSION

4200 N. Point Pkwy., Alpharetta, GA 30022-4176 | 770-410-6000
fmorgan@namb.net | www.namb.net/on-mission-magazine
K. Faith Morgan, editor

Denomination: Southern Baptist
Parent company: North American Mission Board
Type: quarterly magazine
Audience: Christians who are impacting their world for Christ
Purpose: to highlight the work of missionaries and help readers be on mission where they work and live
Submissions: Open to freelance articles and reviews. Email for current needs.
Topics: missions, evangelism
Sample: download from website

OUR SUNDAY VISITOR NEWSWEEKLY

200 Noll Plaza, Huntington, IN 46750 | 800-348-2440, 260-356-8400
oursunvis@osv.com | www.osvnews.com
Gretchen R. Crowe, editor in chief

Denomination: Catholic
Type: weekly print and digital newspaper
Audience: denomination
Purpose: to provide timely coverage of important national and international religious events reported from a Catholic perspective

Submissions: Query and send manuscript only through the online form. Responds in four to six weeks. Articles: news analysis, 950-1,100 words, including sidebars, but occasionally as short as 500 words or as long as 2,000 words; "In Focus," a package of articles totaling 3,000-4,000 words by one or more authors, query first; features linked to current events and trends of the day, 1,350 words; essays on relevant issues of the day, 500-750 words; profiles, 500-750 words; Q&A interviews, 1,200 words. Bible: RSV.

Types of manuscripts: news, essays, interviews, profiles

Topics: Catholic perspective on issues and news

Payment: unspecified, within four to six weeks of acceptance

Guidelines: *osv.submittable.com/submit*

Tip: "Our mission is to examine the news, culture, and trends of the day from a faithful and sound Catholic perspective—to see the world through the eyes of faith. Especially interested in writers able to do news analysis (with a minimum of three sources) or news features."

OUTREACH

Story Ideas, 5550 Tech Center, Colorado Springs, CO 80919
tellus@outreachmagazine.com | *www.outreachmagazine.com*
James P. Long, editor

Type: bimonthly magazine

Audience: senior pastors and church leadership, as well as laypeople who are passionate about outreach

Purpose: to be the gathering place of ideas, insights, and stories for churches focused on reaching out to their community—locally and globally—with the love of Christ

Submissions: Email or mail query or complete manuscript with cover letter and published clips. Seasonal six months ahead. Responds in eight weeks. Articles, 1,200-2,500 words; features, 1,500-2,500 words; "Pulse" stories of what churches and individuals are doing, 200-300 words; ideas for outreach events, 300 words; and "Soulfires" profiles of people who are passionate about reaching others for Christ, 600 words.

Types of manuscripts: profiles, how-to

Topics: what's new in ministry, evangelism training, focus on retention, small groups, keeping visitors engaged

Rights: first, reprint (tell when/where published)

Payment: $700-1,000 for feature articles

Guidelines: *www.outreachmagazine.com/magazine/3160-writers-guidelines.html*

Tip: "While most articles are assigned, we do accept queries and manuscripts on speculation. Please don't query us until you've studied at least one issue of *Outreach*."

PARENTING TEENS

1 Lifeway Plaza, Nashville, TN 37234-0172 | 615-251-2196
scott.latta@lifeway.com | *www.lifeway.com/en/product-family/*
parenting-teens?intcmp=srdr-parenting%20teens
Scott Latta, editor

> **Parent company:** LifeWay Christian Resources
> **Denomination:** Southern Baptist
> **Type:** monthly print magazine
> **Audience:** parents of teens
> **Purpose:** to give parents encouragement and challenge them in their relationship with Christ, so they, in turn, can guide their teens
> **Submissions:** Manuscripts by assignment. Email résumé, bio, and clips to get an assignment. Offers timely information, encouragement, expert insight, and practical advice to parents of teens. Bible: CSB.
> **Payment:** unspecified
> **Guidelines:** by email
> **Sample:** on the website

PARENTLIFE

1 Lifeway Plaza, Nashville, TN 37234-0172 | 615-251-2196
parentlife@lifeway.com |
www.lifeway.com/en/product-familiy/parentlife-magazine
Nancy Cornwell, content editor

> **Parent company:** LifeWay Christian Resources
> **Denomination:** Southern Baptist
> **Type:** monthly print magazine
> **Audience:** parents of children birth to preteen
> **Purpose:** to encourage and equip parents with biblical solutions that will transform families
> **Submissions:** Serves as a springboard for parents who may feel exasperated or overwhelmed with information by offering a biblical approach to raising healthy, productive children. Offers practical ideas and information for individual parents and couples. Query first by email. Email requested manuscript as an attachment. Include one to three sidebars. Responds in six to twelve months. Length: 500-1,500 words. Bible: CSB.

Types of manuscripts: how-to, teaching, family devotional, sidebars
Topics: parenting, health, development, education, discipline, spiritual growth
Payment: unspecified
Guidelines: by email

PARISH LITURGY

16565 S. State St., South Holland, IL 60473 | 708-331-5485
acp@acpress.org | *www.americancatholicpress.org/parLit.html*
Rev. Michael Gilligan, executive director

Denomination: Catholic
Parent company: American Catholic Press
Type: quarterly magazine, circulation 950
Audience: parish priests and musicians
Purpose: to support parish leaders in planning the liturgy, resources for Sunday Mass
Submissions: Query by email or mail. Responds in eight weeks. Unsolicited freelance: 10%. Articles 400 words. Bible: NAB. Email for current needs.
Types of manuscripts: teaching, how-to, profiles
Topics: liturgy, sermons, petitions, music suggestions
Rights: all
Payment: not specified, on publication
Tip: "We use articles on the liturgy only—period. Send us well-informed articles on the liturgy."

PENTECOSTAL MESSENGER

PO Box 211866, Bedford, TX 76095 | 817-554-5900
communications@pcg.org | *www.pcg.org/pentecostal-messenger*
Dr. Wayman Ming, Jr., editor in chief

Denomination: Pentecostal Church of God (PCG)
Type: quarterly print magazine
Audience: denomination
Purpose: to impart the message of Jesus Christ, strengthen believers, resource the church, and promote the essential values of the PCG
Submissions: Email for current needs.
Sample: *www.pcg.org/digital-pm*

THE PLAIN TRUTH

1710 Evergreen St., Duarte, CA 91010 | 800-309-4466
managing.editor@ptm.org | *www.ptm.org/pt-magazine*

Brad Versak, editor

Parent company: Plain Truth Ministries
Type: quarterly digital and print magazine
Audience: general
Purpose: to discover authentic Christianity without all the religious "stuff"
Submissions: Queries only.
Types of manuscripts: teaching
Guidelines: by email
Sample: on the website

POINT

11002 Lake Hart Dr., Orlando, FL 32832 | 407-563-6083
mickeyseward@converge.org | *www.converge.org/point-magazine*
Mickey Seward, editor

Denomination: Baptist General Conference
Type: quarterly print and digital magazine
Audience: denomination
Purpose: to increase movement awareness, ownership, and involvement by publishing captivating God-stories of Converge people and regional ministries
Submissions: Open to freelance submissions. Email query with clips. Articles 300-1,400 words.
Types: personal experiences, profiles, reports
Rights: first, reprint, electronic
Payment: $60-280, on publication
Sample: on the website

POWER FOR LIVING

4050 Lee Vance Dr., Colorado Springs, CO 80918 | 800-708-5550, 719-536-0100
Powerforliving@davidccook.com | *davidccook.org/power-for-living*
Karen Bouchard, managing editor

Parent company: David C. Cook
Type: weekly take-home paper
Audience: general, ages 50 and older
Purpose: to connect God's truth to real life
Submissions: Looking for inspiring stories and articles about famous and ordinary people whose experiences and insights show the power of Christ at work in their lives. Length: 1,200-1,500 words. Buys twenty per year. Poetry related to matters of faith and biblically based, twenty lines; buys six to twelve per year. Columns

750 words; buys five to eight per year. Accepts reprints but prefers original work. Bible: NIV, KJV.

Types of manuscripts: personal experiences, interviews, poetry, columns

Topics: diverse range of subjects, from world missions to simple, relatable experiences with family and life

Rights: first, onetime, reprint

Payment: $375 for articles, $50 for poems, $150 for columns, on acceptance

Guidelines: download from website

PRAYER CONNECT

PO Box 10667, Terre Haute, IN 47801 | 812 238-5504

editor@prayerconnect.net | prayerconnect.net

Carol Madison, editor

Parent company: Church Prayer Leaders Network

Type: quarterly print and digital magazine; circulation 3,000 print; 10,000+ web; ads

Audience: believers with an interest in prayer, prayer leaders in local churches

Purpose: to encourage and equip believers toward a deeper walk with Jesus Christ through prayer

Submissions: Email as an attachment or mail manuscript; or send a query letter. Unsolicited freelance: 20%. Buys eight to twelve manuscripts per year. Length: 800-1,200 words, idea 250-500 words. Responds in two to four weeks. Bible: NIV.

Types of manuscripts: prayer guide, how-to, real-life story

Topic: prayer

Rights: first, reprint, electronic

Payment: 10¢/edited word, on publication; sometimes pays kill fee

Guidelines: *www.prayerleader.com/about-us/write-for-us*

Sample: on website

Tip: "The easiest place to break in is with our Tips & Tools section, which has simple ideas explaining something that can enhance your prayer life or grow prayer in your church."

PRESBYTERIANS TODAY

100 Witherspoon St., Louisville, KY 40202-1396 | 800-728-7228

editor@pcusa.org | www.presbyterianmission.org/ministries/today

Donna Frischknecht Jackson, editor

Denomination: Presbyterian Church (USA)

Type: bimonthly print and digital magazine

Audience: denomination

Purpose: to explore practical issues of faith and life, tell stories of Presbyterians who are living their faith, and cover a wide range of church news and activities

Submissions: Query first. Responds in two weeks. Prefers to work with published writers. Length: 1,000-1,800 words. Seasonal three months in advance. Freelance: 25%. Bible: NRSV.

Topics: features about Presbyterians, theology, Bible study, devotional helps, church's role in society

Payment: $75-300, on acceptance

PSYCHOLOGY FOR LIVING

PO Box 661900, Arcadia, CA 91066-1900

chibma@ncfliving.org | *ncfliving.org/psychology-for-living-literature/psychology-for-living-magazine.html*

Cynthia Hibma, editor

Parent company: Narramore Christian Foundation

Type: annual print journal

Audience: general

Purpose: to apply sound biblical and psychological principles to everyday issues of life

Submissions: Publishes articles that cover a wide range of personal and relational needs. Submit complete manuscript. Length: 1,200-1,700 words or fewer.

Types of manuscripts: how-to, teaching, personal experience

Topics: relationships, psychology, communication, emotions

Rights: first, reprint

Payment: $75-200

Guidelines: *ncfliving.org/psychology-for-living-literature/writers-guidelines.html*

Sample: download from the website

Tip: "Articles need to be written with laypeople in mind; technical terminology needs to be kept to a minimum. Also please avoid 'Christianeze' and suggestions that have a 'preachy' tone. Instead, give insight and understanding with practical applications that are well illustrated."

PURPOSE

PO Box 866, Harrisonburg, VA 22803 | 540-574-4874

PurposeEditor@mennomedia.org |

www.faithandliferesources.org/periodicals/purpose
April Yamasaki, editor

Denomination: Mennonite
Type: monthly take-home paper
Audience: denomination
Purpose: to encourage discipleship living
Submissions: Buys short, personal, true stories, 450-700 words, and poems/verse, 12 lines maximum. Both should illustrate practical ways Christians apply their faith in daily life; illustrate biblical understandings that support discipleship; and stress loyalty to the church and its peacemaking, missional, and related ministries. Prefers email submissions.
Types of manuscripts: personal experience, poetry
Topics: theme-related
Rights: onetime
Payment: $25-$50, $10-$20 for poetry
Guidelines: click from the website
Theme list: click from the website

REACH OUT, COLUMBIA

1051 Key Rd., Unit 57, Columbia, SC 29201
Lori@ReachOutColumbia.com | *www.ReachOutColumbia.com*
Lori Hatcher, editor

Type: monthly (9x) print magazine, circulation 20,000, takes ads
Audience: Christians
Purpose: to celebrate the life and work of Jesus Christ by sharing stories of how He is working through the lives of everyday people
Submissions: Email complete manuscript as attachment with a cover letter. Unsolicited freelance: 80%. Buys sixty manuscripts per year. Length: 500-1,250 words. Seasonal four to six months in advance. Responds in two weeks. Bible: NIV. Simultaneous OK.
Types of manuscripts: profile, teaching, devotional, testimony, feature
Topics: Christian life, profiles of national or South Carolina ministries or ministry leaders, parenting, Bible teaching, salvation testimonies, reflection pieces, missions, seasonal
Rights: onetime
Payment: none
Guidelines: *www.reachoutcolumbia.com/roc-info/article-submissions*
Sample: by mail with $3.00 for postage
Tip: "We are always looking for Christian living, devotional, and personal-testimony pieces. A fresh take on a familiar subject gets our attention."

RELEVANT

55 W. Church St., Ste. 211, Orlando, FL 32801 | 407-660-1411
editorial@relevantmagazine.com | *relevantmagazine.com*
Tyler Huckabee, senior editor

Type: bimonthly print and digital magazine
Audience: millennials
Purpose: to challenge people to go further in their spiritual journey;
live selflessly and intentionally; care about positively impacting
the world around them; and find the unexpected places God is
speaking in life, music, and culture
Submissions: Email query and complete manuscript as attachment.
Responds in one to two weeks or not interested. Length: 750-
1,000 words.
Topics: faith, culture, and intentional living
Payment: $100-400
Guidelines: *www.relevantmagazine.com/write*
Sample: on the website

RELIEF: A JOURNAL OF ART & FAITH

Reade Center 122, Taylor University, 236 W. Reade Ave., Upland, IN
46989
daniel@reliefjournal.com | *www.reliefjournal.com*
Daniel Bowman, Jr., editor in chief

Type: biannual print literary journal
Audience: general
Purpose: to promote full human flourishing in faith and art
Submissions: Looking for poetry and stories that reflect reality as
honestly as Scripture reflects reality. Submit manuscript through
the website only during October 1 to March 31. Costs $2 to
submit a manuscript. Length: stories, 8,000 words maximum;
poetry, 1,000 words maximum; creative nonfiction, exploratory
essays with an emotional arc that may or may not be narrative,
5,000 words maximum
Types of manuscripts: short stories, creative nonfiction, poetry
Rights: first, electronic
Payment: none
Guidelines: *www.reliefjournal.com/print-submit*

SACONNECTS

440 W. Nyack Rd., West Nyack, NY 10994-1739 | 845-620-7200
saconnects.org

Robert Mitchell, managing editor

Denomination: Salvation Army
Type: monthly print and digital magazine
Audience: denomination in the eastern territory
Submissions: Manuscripts only from people who live in the eastern territory. Email manuscripts as attachments through the website.
Types of manuscripts: news, how-to, personal experience
Guidelines: *saconnects.org/submission-guidelines-magazine*
Sample: on the website

ST. ANTHONY MESSENGER

28 W. Liberty St., Cincinnati, OH 45202-6498 | 513-241-5615
*MagazineEditors@Franciscanmedia.org |
info.FranciscanMedia.org/st-anthony-messenger*
Christopher Heffron, Susan Hines-Biggs, executive editors

Denomination: Catholic
Type: monthly print and digital magazine
Audience: family-oriented, majority are women ages 40-70
Purpose: to offer readers inspiration from the heart of Catholicism—the Gospels and the experience of God's people
Submissions: Query only by email. Responds in eight weeks. Email manuscripts as attachments. Seasonal one year in advance. Length: about 2,000 words or shorter pieces. Fiction 2,000-2,500 words; buys twelve per year. Stories should be about family relationships and about people struggling and coping with problems, triumphing in adversity, persevering in faith, overcoming doubt, or coming to spiritual insights. Poetry 20 lines maximum. Bible: NAB.
Types of manuscripts: profiles, biblical teaching, short stories, poetry
Topics: church, sacraments, education, spiritual growth, family, marriage, social issues
Rights: first, electronic
Payment: 20¢/word, $2/line for poetry with minimum of $20, on acceptance
Guidelines: *www.franciscanmedia.org/writers-guide*
Sample: *info.franciscanmedia.org/st-anthony-issues-2019*

SCP JOURNAL

PO Box 40015, Pasadena, CA 91114 | 510-540-0300
scp@scp-inc.org | www.scp-inc.org
Tal Brooke, editor

Parent company: Spiritual Counterfeits Project
Type: quarterly print journal
Audience: general
Purpose: to provide a biblical perspective on new religions and spiritual trends
Submissions: Query only. No unsolicited manuscripts. Articles analyze and discern the inside workings of new spiritual trends.
Guidelines: click Information tab

SHARING

PO Box 780909, San Antonio, TX 78278-0909 | 877-992-5222
sharing@OSLToday.org | *osltoday.org/sharing-magazine*
Jamie Henry, editor

Parent company: International Order of St. Luke the Physician
Type: bimonthly print magazine
Audience: general
Purpose: to inspire, educate, and inform about Christian healing of body, soul, and spirit
Submissions: Share your stories, experiences, thoughts, insights, inspirational poems, and testimonies of God's amazing power to heal. Length: articles 200-1,500 words, poetry 30-50 words. Prefers emailed submissions as attachments but will take them by mail.
Types of manuscripts: personal experience, testimonies, teaching, essays, poetry
Topics: theme-related
Rights: onetime
Payment: none

SHATTERED MAGAZINE

600 Boulevard South S.W., Ste. 104, Huntsville, AL 35802
256-783-8350
laurie@shattered.biz | *shatteredmagazine.net*
Laurie Rafferty Pallota, editor-in-chief

Type: quarterly print and digital magazine, takes ads
Audience: general
Purpose: to celebrate our unique, God-given stories
Submission: Looking for testimonies of encountering Jesus to use in the features, life, community, and mission sections. "Where did He meet you? Where does He continue to meet you? How has He used what others intended for evil in your life for good? How has He taken what you have screwed up and redeemed for His glory?

How has He used community to be a part of your story? Or, how has your community been a part of a larger story? Has God moved you to share Him with others? What has that looked like?" Query through the website.

Types of manuscripts: personal experience
Guidelines: *shatteredmagazine.net/want-to-write-for-shattered*

SOJOURNERS

408 C St. N.E., Washington, DC 20002 | 202-328-8842
submissions@sojo.net, reviews@sojo.net | www.sojo.net
Jim Rice, editor

> **Type:** monthly print and digital magazine
> **Audience:** community influencers
> **Purpose:** to explore the intersections of faith, politics, and culture; uncover in depth the hidden injustices in the world around us; and tell the stories of hope that keep us grounded, inspired, and moving forward
> **Submissions:** Query only with no attachments. Responds in six to eight weeks. Feature articles are typically 1,800-2,000 words. Mail poetry. Length: 25-40 lines. Often tries to use poetry geared toward particular seasons.
> **Types of manuscripts:** feature articles, reviews, poetry
> **Topics:** social justice, popular culture, spirituality
> **Rights:** all
> **Payment:** unspecified, $25 per poem, on publication
> **Guidelines:** *sojo.net/magazine/write*

SOUTHWEST KANSAS FAITH AND FAMILY

PO Box 1454, Dodge City, KS 67801 | 620-225-4677
info@swkfaithandfamily.org | www.swkfaithandfamily.org
Stan Wilson, publisher

> **Type:** monthly print newspaper
> **Audience:** residents of the area
> **Purpose:** to share the Word of God and news and information that honors Christian beliefs, family traditions, and values that are the cornerstone of our nation
> **Submissions:** Email query or complete manuscript.
> **Topics:** any Christian or family issue
> **Guidelines:** *www.swkfaithandfamily.org/submitarticle.html*

SPORTS SPECTRUM MAGAZINE

640 Plaza Dr., Ste. 110, Highlands Ranch, CO 80129 | 866-821-2971
jon@sportsspectrum.com | sportsspectrum.com/magazine
Jon Ackerman, managing editor

Parent company: Pro Athletes Outreach

Type: quarterly print and digital magazine

Audience: sports fans, predominantly male, ages 20-55

Purpose: to reach non-Christians with the gospel through the testimonies and experiences of sports figures

Submissions: If you are an experienced sports writer, send information about yourself with clips to get an assignment. Query only for article ideas. Articles generally run 1,500-2,000 words plus one or two sidebars of 150 words. Works five months in advance. Bible: NIV.

Rights: all

Payment: at least 21¢/word plus reasonable expenses

Tip: "It is essential that the athletes featured in *Sports Spectrum* demonstrate a strong Christian testimony. The fact that they occasionally talk about God or attend chapel is not enough to go on."

STANDARD

PO Box 843336, Kansas City, MO 64184-3336 | 816-931-1900
standard.foundry@gmail.com | www.thefoundrypublishing.com
Jeanette Gardner Littleton, editor

Denomination: Nazarene

Parent company: The Foundry Publishing

Type: weekly take-home paper, circulation 40,000

Audience: denomination

Purpose: to encourage and inspire our audience and to reinforce curriculum

Submissions: Email query letter or complete manuscript with cover letter as attachment. Accepts simultaneous submissions. Makes assignments. Unsolicited freelance: 20%. Buys 104 manuscripts per year. Length: 400 and 800-900 words. Seasonal one year in advance. Response time varies. Bible: NIV.

Types of manuscripts: personal experience, short stories, open to other styles

Topics: theme-related

Rights: first, reprint, all

Payment: $35 and $50, on acceptance

Guidelines and theme list: by email

Sample: email for PDF

Tip: "Writers should know basics of Wesleyan-Arminian theological perspective. Write to the theme list; please indicate which theme you're proposing it for. Nonfiction cannot be preachy; fiction cannot be trite. Put full contact information in the body of the manuscript, not only in the email. It helps to know if you're Nazarene or another Wesleyan/holiness denomination."

TEACHERS OF VISION

PO Box 45610, Westlake, OH 44145 | 888-798-1124

tov@ceai.org | ceai.org/teachers-of-vision-magazine

Dawn Molnar, managing editor

Parent organization: Christian Educators Association International

Type: print and digital magazine (3x), circulation 7,000, takes ads

Audience: Christian educators serving in public and private schools

Purpose: to provide biblically principled resources that encourage, equip, and empower Christian educators

Submissions: Email submission or query as attached file. Minifeatures, 400-800 words; theme-based features, 800-1,200 words; personal interest, 400-1,000 words; methodology and inspirational, 400-800 words. Unsolicited freelance: 5%. Buys fifteen manuscripts per year. Seasonal nine months in advance. Responds in one to two weeks during the school year. Bible: NIV.

Types of manuscripts: personal experience, how-to, poetry, inspirational, features, short stories

Topics: theme-based, educational success story, teaching techniques, news

Rights: first (includes digital copy and social-media sharing)

Payment: varies by article type, on publication, always pays kill fee

Guidelines: *ceai.org/tov-writers-guidelines*

Sample: download from website

Tip: "Readers look for educational articles that inspire and provide practical ideas they can use in their profession. Our writers integrate spiritual insights into their articles; use premises faithful to the teachings of Scripture in their writing; remain up-to-date on trends in education; present original ideas; provide material for practical classroom application; and submit clear, concise, and creative articles."

TESTIMONY/ENRICH

2450 Milltower Ct., Mississauga, ON L5N 5Z6, Canada | 905-542-7400
testimony@paoc.org | *www.testimony.paoc.ca*
Stacey McKenzie, editor

Parent company: Pentecostal Assemblies of Canada
Type: bimonthly print magazine
Audience: general
Purpose: to celebrate what God is doing in and through the
Fellowship, while offering encouragement to believers by providing
a window into the struggles that everyday Christians often
encounter
Submissions: Query first by email. Length: 800-1,000 words. Responds
in six to eight weeks. Seasonal four months ahead. Bible: NIV.
Types of manuscripts: personal experience, interviews, sidebars
Rights: first
Payment: unspecified
Guidelines: *testimony.paoc.org/submit*
Tip: "Our readership is 98% Canadian. We prefer Canadian writers or
at least writers who understand that Canadians are not Americans
in long underwear. We also give preference to members of this
denomination, since this is related to issues concerning our
fellowship."

THRIVE CONNECTION

PO Box 151297, Lakewood, CO 80215 | 303-985-2148
thriveconnection.com
Megan Lenhausen, communications director

Parent company: Thrive Ministry
Type: digital magazine, circulation 10,000
Audience: women in cross-cultural work overseas
Purpose: to empower and encourage women in cross-cultural work
Submissions: Articles 500-1,000 words. All submissions must be sent
through the website. Writers must be women who are or have been
in cross-cultural missions.
Types of manuscripts: personal experience, recipes
Topics: cross-cultural experiences, singleness, marriage, family,
spiritual formation, relationships; see subtopics on the website
Rights: first, onetime (with permission to archive permanently)
Payment: none
Sample: on the website

TIME OF SINGING: A JOURNAL OF CHRISTIAN POETRY

PO Box 5276, Conneaut Lake, PA 16316
timesing@zoominternet.net | www.timeofsinging.com
Lora Homan Zill, editor

Parent organization: Wind & Water Press

Type: quarterly print journal, circulation 250

Audience: general

Purpose: to reflect on our walk with God through the art and craft of poetry, to create a community of creative people who loves both the written and living Word and shares a Christian worldview

Submissions: Prefers poems without religious jargon, that show and don't tell and take creative chances with faith and our walk with God. Unsolicited freelance: 95%. Length: 40 lines maximum. Send complete manuscript by mail or email. Responds in three months. Seasonal six months ahead. Accepts simultaneous submissions. Buys 150 per year.

Types of manuscripts: poetry, assigned reviews of poetry books published by *Time Of Singing* poets

Topics: our walk with God, nature, the human condition, any topic

Rights: first, reprint (tell when/where published)

Payment: none

Guidelines: *www.timeofsinging.com/guidelines.html*

Sample: $4 each or 2/$7 (checks, money orders payable to Wind & Water Press)

Tip: "Study the craft of poetry. If you don't read poetry, you can't write it. I don't publish sermons that rhyme or greeting-card type poetry. *Time Of Singing* is a literary poetry journal. I love poets who think outside the theological box and challenge my assumptions. We don't write or read poetry to find answers but to wrestle with the questions."

TODAY'S CHRISTIAN LIVING

PO Box 5000, Iola, WI 54945 | 800-223-3161, 715-445-5000
dan@cross-life.us | www.todayschristianliving.org
Dan Brownell, editor

Type: bimonthly print and digital magazine

Audience: general

Purpose: to challenge Christians in their faith, so they may be strengthened to fulfill the call of God in their lives

Submissions: Prefers complete manuscripts; discourages queries. Personality and ministry profiles, 1,400-1,600 words plus sidebar of 150-250 words. Personal story/anecdote 670-700 words.

"Grace Notes," how important biblical principles and attributes are illustrated in everyday life, 650-700 words. Hospitality, inspirational story plus recipe, 700-1,500 words. Humorous anecdotes, 50-200 words.

Types of manuscripts: personal experience, profiles, recipes, humor
Rights: all
Payment: $25-150, after publication
Guidelines: *todayschristianliving.org/writers-guidelines*
Sample: on the website

TRUTH ALIVE

truthalive@sathyam.org | sathyam.org/truth-alive
Vimala Grace, director/editor

Parent company: Truth Ministries/Sathyam Publications in India
Type: monthly print and online magazine; circulation 6,000 print, 22,000 online
Submissions: Open to a series.
Types of manuscripts: feature, news, teaching with national and international perspective
Sample: online

U.S. CATHOLIC

205 W. Monroe St., Chicago, IL 60606 | 312-544-8169
submissions@clairetians.org | www.uscatholic.org
Meghan Murphy-Gill, managing editor

Denomination: Catholic
Type: monthly print magazine
Audience: denomination
Submissions: Email manuscripts. Responds in six to eight weeks. Seasonal six months in advance. Features that go beyond basic reporting by offering analysis and interpretation of the issues, 2,500-3,500 words. Essays, 800 to 1,600 words, present thoughtful reflections or opinions on concerns Catholics face in everyday life. "Practicing Catholic," 1,100 words with short sidebar, reflects on the meaning of a particular prayer practice. "Sounding Board" opinion piece, 1,400 words. Profiles, 800 words; reviews, 315 words; fiction, 1,500 words.
Types of manuscripts: essays, profiles, features, short stories, poetry, reviews
Payment: $75-500
Guidelines: *www.uscatholic.org/writers-guide*

VIBRANT LIFE

PO Box 5353, Nampa, ID 83653-5353 | 208-465-2584
email through website | www.vibrantlife.com
Heather Quintana, editor

Parent company: Pacific Press Publishing Association
Denomination: Seventh-day Adventist
Type: bimonthly print magazine
Audience: general
Purpose: to promote physical health, mental clarity, and spiritual balance from a practical, Christian perspective
Submissions: Send complete manuscript by email as attachment or by mail. Short articles, 450-650 words; feature articles, to 1,000 words plus a sidebar if informational.
Types of manuscripts: teaching, interviews, profiles, personal experiences, how-to, sidebar
Topics: health, exercise, nutrition
Rights: first, reprint
Payment: $100-300, on acceptance
Guidelines: *www.vibrantlife.com/writers-guidelines-2*
Tip: "Information must be reliable—no faddism. Articles should represent the latest findings on the subject, and if scientific in nature, should be properly documented. (References to other lay journals are generally not acceptable.)"

VICTORIOUS WOMEN IN CHRIST MAGAZINE

2310 S. Green Bay Rd., Ste. C #503, Racine, WI 53406
contactvwmag@ gmail.com | www.victoriouswomenmag.org
Semone Love, executive director

Type: quarterly print and digital magazine
Submissions: Length: maximum 500 words. Email as attachment in Microsoft Word.
Types of manuscripts: short stories, articles, poetry, personal experience
Topics: looking for women who have a faith-based story of victory
Rights: onetime
Payment: none

WAR CRY

615 Slaters Ln., PO Box 269, Alexandria, VA 22314 | 703-684-5500
thewarcry.org
Lt. Colonel Tim Foley, editor-in-chief

Denomination: Salvation Army

Type: monthly print and digital magazine plus special Christmas and Easter issues; circulation 185,000 in general, 1.7 million at Christmas, 1 million at Easter; takes ads

Audience: denomination plus general

Purpose: to represent the Army's mission of preaching the gospel of Jesus Christ and meeting human needs in His name without discrimination

Submissions: Length: 500-1,500 words. Seasonal six months in advance. Unsolicited freelance: 25%. Buys eighty per year. Email complete manuscript through online form. Responds in one month. Simultaneous OK. Seasonal six months ahead. Bible: NLT.

Types of manuscripts: features, short stories, fillers, sidebars, testimony

Topics: parenting, Christian life, evangelism, profiles, Christ and culture, contemporary issues, apologetics from Wesleyan perspective

Rights: first, reprint (tell when/where published), electronic

Payment: 35¢/word, 15¢/word for reprints, on acceptance

Guidelines and theme list: *thewarcry.org/contribute*

Sample: on the website

Tip: Needs Thanksgiving and other seasonal articles.

WORD&WAY

PO Box 1771, Jefferson City, MO 65102-1771 | 573-635-5939
bkaylor@wordandway.org | *wordandway.org*
Brian Kaylor, editor

Denomination: Baptist

Type: monthly magazine

Audience: denomination, general

Purpose: to accurately inform Baptists and others of relevant news, promote the work of Christ, and encourage inspirational living

Submissions: Email for needs.

Sample: click link on *www.wordandway.org/advertise*

YOUTHMINISTRY.COM

1515 Cascade Ave., Loveland, CO 80538 | 970-669-3836
puorgbus@group.com | *youthministry.com*

Parent company: Group

Type: website

Audience: youth workers and leaders

Purpose: to help leaders encourage teens to grow spiritually

Submissions: Email full manuscript. Length: 300-1,000 words.

Types of manuscripts: how-to, lesson plans, fillers, Bible studies

Topics: successful youth ministry strategies, including youth-led ministry ideas; understanding kids and youth culture; recruiting/training/keeping adult leaders; family ministry; staff issues; serving and training parents; professionalism; self-nurture; how-to articles on personal spiritual growth, time management, issues vital to working with young people, leadership skills (listening, discussion-leading), worship ideas, handling specific group problems, fun and experiential programming ideas, and active-learning meeting plans and retreats

Rights: all

Payment: $80, on acceptance

Guidelines: *grouppublishingps.zendesk.com/hc/en-us/articles/211878258-Submissions*

7

TEEN/YOUNG ADULT MARKETS

BOUNDLESS

8605 Explorer Dr., Colorado Springs, CO 80920 | 719-531-3400
editor@boundless.org | *www.boundless.org*
Lisa Anderson, director

Parent company: Focus on the Family
Type: website and articles; circulation 300,000 visitors per month
Audience: single young adults in 20s and 30s
Purpose: to help Christian young adults grow up, own their faith, date with purpose, and prepare for marriage and family
Submissions: Rarely accepts unsolicited articles but open to considering new writers. To get an assignment, send a sample or two of your writing, a link to your blog, and a proposal of what you're interested in writing about. Length: 1,200 words. Accepts unsolicited blog posts 500-800 words; email manuscript.
Bible: prefers ESV
Types of manuscripts: articles and blog posts
Topics: fit in these three categories: (1) adulthood: being single, career, family, money; (2) faith: spiritual growth, ministry; (3) relationships: dating, marriage, sexuality, community
Rights: all
Guidelines: *www.boundless.org/write-for-us*
Tip: "Aim to engage our readers' hearts, as we're primarily in the business of affecting lives, not changing society. Use personal stories as illustrations and to spark our readers' imaginations."

THE BRINK

See entry in "**Daily Devotional Booklets and Websites**."

BRIO

8605 Explorer Dr., Colorado Springs, CO 80920 | 719-531-3400
submissions@briomagazine.com | *www.briomagazine.com*
Pam Woody, editorial director, editor@briomagazine.com

Parent company: Focus on the Family
Type: bimonthly magazine, circulation 60,000
Audience: teen girls
Purpose: to provide inspiring stories, fashion insights, fun profiles, and practical tips, all from a biblical worldview
Submissions: Email as Word attachment. Fiction must be complete mansuscript. Length: 200-1,400 words.
Types of manuscripts: fiction, articles, profiles
Topics: seasonal, girl-like-me profile (1,200-1,400 words), character trait (650-750 words), entertainment/social media (800-900 words), prayer (200-300 words), relationships (800-900 words)
Rights: first
Payment: minimum 30¢/word, on acceptance
Guidelines: *media.focusonthefamily.com/brio/pdf/brio-writers-guidelines-2019.pdf*
Sample: *www.focusonthefamily.com/parenting/brio-magazine*
Tip: "We are looking for unique and interesting nonfiction articles, especially stories about real-life teen girls. Every article should have a Christian emphasis, though it shouldn't be preachy or overbearing. The topics, concepts, and vocabulary should be appropriate for our teen audience."

DEVOZINE

See entry in "**Daily Devotional Booklets and Websites**."

GIRLZ 4 CHRIST

Medford, OR
G4Csubmissions@gmail.com | *Girlz4Christ.org*
Jessica Lippe, editor/publisher, Girlz4christ@yahoo.com

Type: quarterly print and digital magazine, circulation 2,000, takes ads
Audience: teen girls
Purpose: to provide uplifting, quality media options to girls around the world
Submissions: Email complete manuscript as attachment. Accepts submissions from teens. Freelance: 100%. Accepts fifty manuscripts per year. Length: 100-1,000 words. Seasonal: two to three months in advance.

Types of manuscripts: devotions, interviews, games, how-to, short stories, sidebars, columns, fillers, reviews

Topics: fit one of these sections: "Godly Girlz," "Girlz in Action," "Beautiful Girlz," "Fun 4 Girlz"; beauty, health, fashion

Rights: all

Payment: free product

Guidelines: *girlz4christ.org/submissions*

Theme list: "Girlz 4 Christ Contributors" Facebook group

Sample: Join "Girlz 4 Christ Contributors" on Facebook, or order from *girlz4christ.org/print-copies*

Tip: "Read our magazines and books."

LOVE IS MOVING

Box 5885, West Beaver Creek PO, Richmond Hill, ON L4B 0B8, Canada | 905-479-5885

info@loveismoving.ca | *www.loveismoving.ca*

Ilana Reimer, editor

Parent company: The Evangelical Fellowship of Canada

Type: bimonthly print and digital magazine; circulation 5,000 print, 3,000 online; takes ads

Audience: teens and young adults

Purpose: to challenge youth to grow deeper in knowing God's love for them and to live out their faith with passion for Jesus and compassion for people

Submissions: Email query letter. Unsolicited freelance: 30%. Buys 120 manuscripts per year. Length: 400-1,000 words. Seasonal four months in advance. Responds in two weeks. Bible: NIV.

Types of manuscripts: personal experience, profile, column, review

Topic: Christian living

Rights: first, reprint (tell when/where published), electronic

Payment: none

Guidelines: *loveismoving.ca/about/submit-an-article*

Tip: "Best to have a Canadian angle or Canadian content."

PEER

615 Sisters Ln., Alexandria, VA 22314 | 703-684-5500

peermag.org

Captain Pamela Maynor, editor

Denomination: The Salvation Army

Type: monthly print and digital magazine

Audience: 16-22 years old

Purpose: to help young people develop a mature faith, a personal ministry, and a Christian perspective on everyday life

Submissions: Email complete manuscript through the website. Length: 800 words. Responds in four to six weeks or isn't interested. Submit at least two months in advance of theme issue. Bible: NLT.

Types of manuscripts: articles, profile

Topics: faith, current events, Christian living, culture

Rights: first, onetime, reprint

Payment: 35¢/word, 15¢/word for reprints

Guidelines and theme list: *peermag.org/contribute*

TAKE 5 PLUS
See entry in "**Daily Devotional Booklets and Websites**."

UNLOCKED
See entry in "**Daily Devotional Booklets and Websites**."

8

CHILDREN'S MARKETS

CADET QUEST

1333 Alger St. S.E., Grand Rapids, MI 49507 | 616-241-5616
submissions@CalvinistCadets.org | www.CalvinistCadets.org
Steve Bootsma, editor

Parent company: Calvinist Cadet Corps

Type: print magazine, 7x/year; 24 pages; circulation 6,000

Audience: boys ages 9-11

Purpose: to help boys grow more Christlike in all areas of life

Submissions: Unsolicited freelance: 5-10%. Buys 20 manuscripts per year. Mail complete manuscript, or email it in body of message. Selections made in May for the following September—May; responds in June. Accepts simultaneous submissions. Accepts manuscripts from kids and teens. Length: 1,000-1,500 words. Bible: NIV. Responds four months before publication.

Types of manuscripts: short stories, projects, puzzles, profiles

Topics: theme-related, profiles of Christian athletes, sports, camping, nature

Rights: first, reprint, all

Payment: at least 5¢/word

Guidelines and theme list: *counselors.calvinistcadets.org/ submissionshelp/quest-authors-info*

Sample: 9x12 SASE with $1.47 postage

Tip: "Looking for fun fiction, without being preachy, for preteen boys. It needs to have some action, and don't be cliché with a Jesus-always-wins type of ending."

DEVOKIDS

See entry in "**Daily Devotional Booklets and Websites**."

FOCUS ON THE FAMILY CLUBHOUSE

8605 Explorer Dr., Colorado Springs, CO 80920 | 719-531-3400
Rachel.Pfeiffer@fotf.org | www.clubhousemagazine.com
Rachel Pfeiffer, assistant editor

Parent company: Focus on the Family
Type: monthly print magazine with online extras, 32 pages,
circulation 80,000, takes ads
Audience: children ages 8-12
Purpose: to inspire, entertain, and teach Christian values to children
Submissions: Unsolicited freelance: 15%. Length: 500-2,000 words.
Buys eighty manuscripts per year. Mail complete manuscript, or
email it as attachment; cover letter required. Responds in three
months. Seasonal eight months ahead. Accepts submissions from
children and teens. Bible: HCSB. Once an author publishes with
us three or more times, we often begin to give assignments. We also
give assignments to writers whom we meet at Christian writers
conferences.
Types of manuscripts: nonfiction, short stories, crafts, recipes,
quizzes, interviews
Topics: personality stories of ordinary kids doing something
extraordinary, Christian living, apologetics
Rights: first
Payment: 15-25¢ per word, on acceptance, kill fee sometimes
Guidelines: *www.clubhousemagazine.com/en/submission-guidelines.aspx*
Sample: 9x12 SASE with check for $2.50 made out to Focus on the
Family
Tip: "Study the magazine to learn the voice and style. Best way to
break in is through nonfiction, especially 'Truth Pursuer' and kid-
profile articles."

FOCUS ON THE FAMILY CLUBHOUSE JR.

8605 Explorer Dr., Colorado Springs, CO 80920 | 719-531-3400
Kate.Jameson@fotf.org | www.clubhousejr.com
Kate Jameson, assistant editor

Parent company: Focus on the Family
Type: monthly print magazine with online extras, 32 pages,
circulation 50,000, ads
Audience: children ages 3-7
Purpose: to inspire, entertain, and teach Christian values to children
Submissions: Unsolicited freelance: 15%. Buys fifty manuscripts per

year. Length: 400-1,000 words. Mail complete manuscript; cover letter required. Responds in three months. Seasonal eight months ahead. Bible: NIrV. Accepts submissions from children and teens. Once an author publishes with us three or more times, we often begin to give assignments. We also give assignments to writers whom we meet at Christian writers conferences.

Types of manuscripts: Bible stories, kid profiles, nature/animal stories, recipes, crafts, short stories, poetry, activities, rebus, interviews, biographies

Topics: ordinary kids doing something extraordinary, Christian life

Rights: first

Payment: 15-25¢ per word, on acceptance

Guidelines: *www.clubhousejr.com/en/submission-guidelines.aspx*

Theme list: by email

Sample: 9x12 SASE with check for $2.50 made out to Focus on the Family

Tip: "Read the magazine to learn our style and reading level. Aim at early and beginning readers. Rebus and Bible stories are a great way to break in."

GUIDE

PO Box 5353, Nampa, ID 83653-5353
guide.magazine@pacificpress.com | *www.guidemagazine.org*
Lori Futcher, editor

Denomination: Seventh-day Adventist

Parent company: Pacific Press Publishing

Type: weekly take-home paper, circulation 26,000

Audience: ages 10-14

Purpose: to show readers, through stories that illustrate Bible truth, how to walk with God now and forever

Submissions: Prefers complete manuscript. Submit online or by mail with SASE. Responds in four to six weeks. Seasonal eight months in advance. Accepts submissions from teens 14 and older. Bible: NKJV.

Types of manuscripts: true stories 1,000-1,200 words (some shorter pieces 450 words and up), sometimes accepts quizzes and other unique nonstory formats; must include a clear spiritual element

Topics: adventure, personal growth, humor, inspiration (answers to prayer, biblical narratives, mission stories, and examples of young people living out their Christian beliefs), biography, nature

Rights: first, reprint (tell when and where published)

Payment: 7-10¢ per word, $25-40 for games and puzzles, on acceptance
Guidelines: *www.guidemagazine.org/writersguidelines*
Theme list: *guidemagazine.org/stories/4890-2016-theme-list-for-writers*
Sample: download from guidelines page
Tip: "Use your best short-story techniques (dialogue, scenes, a sense of plot) to tell a true story starring a kid age 10-14. Bring out a clear spiritual/biblical message. We publish multipart true stories regularly, two to twelve parts, 1,200 words each. All topics indicated need to be addressed within the context of a true story."

KEYS FOR KIDS
See entry in "**Daily Devotional Booklets and Websites.**"

KIDS ANSWERS
PO Box 510, Hebron, KY 41048 | 859-727-2222
editor@answersingenesis.com | *answersingenesis.org/kids/answers/magazine*
Mike Matthews, editor in chief

Parent company: Answers in Genesis
Type: bimonthly mini print magazine in *Answers* magazine, 8 pages
Audience: children
Purpose: to highlight the wonders of God's creation with kid-friendly information and images
Submissions: Only accepts one-paragraph article proposals with author's qualifications (300 words) via email. Once accepted, email article as an attachment. Responds in one month.
Types of manuscripts: nonfiction
Topics: theme-related
Rights: all
Payment: $75-125
Sample: on the website

THE KIDS' ARK
PO Box 3160, Victoria, TX 77903 | 800-455-1770
thekidsarksubmissions@yahoo.com | *thekidsark.com*
Beth Haynes, senior editor, editor@thekidsark.com

Type: quarterly print magazine, 36 pages
Audience: ages 6-12
Purpose: to enlighten children with the love and power of God

through Jesus Christ and to provide children with a solid biblical foundation on which to base their choices in life

Submissions: Email complete manuscript as a Word attachment. Responds in eight to ten weeks. Freelance: 100%. Length: 650 words maximum. Buys sixteen per year. Also accepts submissions from children and teens. Bible: NIV.

Types of manuscripts: nonfiction, short stories, games, puzzles

Topics: theme-related

Rights: first, electronic, reprint

Payment: $100 for first plus electronic, $25 for reprints, on publication

Guidelines and theme list: *thekidsark.com/guidelines.pdf*

Sample: *www.thekidsark.com/images/sample.pdf*

Tip: "Write for the 6- to 10-year-old reading level."

NATURE FRIEND

4253 Woodcock Ln., Dayton, VA 22821 | 540-867-0764
editor@naturefriendmagazine.com | *www.naturefriendmagazine.com*
Kevin Shank, editor

Parent company: Dogwood Ridge Outdoors

Type: monthly print magazine, 28 pages, circulation 10,000

Audience: ages 8-16

Purpose: to increase awareness of God and appreciation for God's works and gifts, to teach accountability toward God's works, and to teach natural truths and facts

Submissions: Freelance: 55%. Mail complete manuscript with SASE, or email as attachment. Length: 500-800 words. Buys forty to fifty per year. Seasonal four months in advance. Accepts simultaneous submissions. Bible: KJV only

Rights: first, reprint

Payment: 5¢/edited word, 3¢/word for reprints, on publication

Types: crafts, projects, experiments, fiction, articles, photo features

Topics: nature-related, science experiments, stories about people interacting with nature or about an animal, nature-friendly gardening, nature photography lessons, survival/wilderness first-aid, weather, astronomy, flowers, marine life

Guidelines: *naturefriendmagazine.com/index.pl?linkid=12;class=gen*

Sample: *www.naturefriendmagazine.com/index.pl?linkid=4;class=gen*

Tip: "While talking animals can be interesting and teach worthwhile lessons, we have chosen to not use them in *Nature Friend*. Excluded are puzzle-type submissions such as 'Who Am I?'"

OUR LITTLE FRIEND

PO Box 5353, Nampa, ID 83653
anita.seymour@pacificpress.com | primarytreasure.com
Anita Seymour, managing editor

> **Denomination:** Seventh-day Adventist
> **Parent company:** Pacific Press Publishing
> **Type:** weekly take-home paper, circulation 16,000
> **Audience:** ages 1-5
> **Purpose:** to teach about Jesus and the Christian life
> **Submissions:** Length: one to two double-spaced pages. Email complete manuscript as attached file. Seasonal eight to nine months ahead. Responds in four weeks. Buys fifty-two per year. Bible: ICB or NIrV.
> **Payment:** $25-50, on acceptance
> **Rights:** onetime, electronic
> **Type of manuscripts:** true stories
> **Topics:** Christian life, God's love, seasonal, nature, see list in guidelines
> **Guidelines:** *primarytreasure.com/for-writers*
> **Theme list:** by mail with SASE
> **Sample:** for 9x12 SAE
> **Tip:** "We need true, age-appropriate stories that teach about the Christian life."

POCKETS

See entry in "**Daily Devotional Booklets and Websites**."

PRIMARY TREASURE

PO Box 5353, Nampa, ID 83653
anita.seymour@pacificpress.com | www.primarytreasure.com
Anita Seymour, managing editor

> **Denomination:** Seventh-day Adventist
> **Parent company:** Pacific Press Publishing
> **Type:** weekly take-home paper, circulation 14,000
> **Audience:** ages 6-9
> **Purpose:** to teach children about the love of God and the Christian life through true stories
> **Submissions:** Freelance: 80%. Buys 104 per year. Email complete manuscript as attached file. Length: three to five double-spaced pages. Seasonal eight months ahead. Responds in four weeks.
> **Type of manuscripts:** true stories

Topics: Christian life, seasonal, nature, see list in guidelines
Rights: onetime, electronic
Payment: $25-50, on acceptance
Guidelines: *primarytreasure.com/for-writers*
Theme list: by mail with SASE
Sample: for 9x12 SAE
Tip: "We need age-appropriate stories that teach about Jesus and the Christian life."

ST. MARY'S MESSENGER

310 Birch St., Green River, WY 82935 | 270-325-3061
submissions@stmarysmessenger.com | stmarysmessenger.com
Kris Weipert, senior editor

Denomination: Catholic
Type: quarterly print magazine, 32 pages
Audience: ages 7-12
Purpose: to enlighten, entertain, and educate children about their Catholic faith
Submissions: Email or mail query for nonfiction, complete manuscript for fiction. Responds to queries in one to two weeks, to manuscripts in two to four weeks. Length: 300-900 words. Seasonal four months in advance. Accepts simultaneous submissions.
Types of manuscripts: nonfiction articles, short stories, poems, puzzles, games, activities, crafts, projects, recipes
Topics: biographies of saints, historical figures, or Catholic leaders in today's world; personal stories from kids, their families, or teachers, especially about works of mercy or helping other kids live their faith; articles about individuals who exemplify humility, Christ's love, and other virtues; articles about fun, interesting things that kids are doing; Catholic traditions in different cultures, rites, and countries; interviews or profiles of Catholics who are famous or well-known but also live their faith
Rights: first, reprint
Payment: $25-100 for article or story
Guidelines and theme list: *stmarysmessenger.com/submission-guidelines*
Tip: "We don't want every article to be explicitly religious, of course, nor do you have to be a Catholic to share your work."

Christian Writers Institute
Featured Course

Writing Children's Short Stories by Lurlene McDaniel

Normal price: $4
Savings: 100%
Market Guide price FREE

https://cwmg.link/children2020

How to Scan QR Codes
Use the camera on your smartphone to focus on the above QR code to activate the discount. It will give you the option to visit the site, which you will want to accept. If you are using an older smartphone, you may need to download a QR code scanning app. You can also visit the URL below the code to activate the discount on your computer.

9

WRITERS MARKETS

CHRISTIAN COMMUNICATOR

9118 W. Elmwood Dr., Ste. 1G, Niles, IL 60714-5820 | 847-296-3964
submissions@wordprocommunications.com | *www.ACWriters.com*
Lin Johnson, managing editor
samples, advertising, and subscriptions, ACWriters@aol.com

Parent company: American Christian Writers

Type: quarterly PDF magazine; circulation 600; subscription $29.95; ads

Audience: beginning to advanced writers, beginning to intermediate speakers

Purpose: to help Christian communicators improve their writing craft and speaking ability; provide practical information about the business, publishing, and freelance side of writing; keep them informed about markets; and encourage them in their ministries

Submissions: Unsolicited freelance: 50%. Queries or complete manuscript (prefers attachment) by email only. Pays $5-10 on publication for first or reprint (tell when/where appeared) rights. Responds in eight weeks. Seasonal four months ahead. No simultaneous submissions.

Types of manuscripts: How-to articles, 750-1,000 words, sixteen per year. Reviews of recent books on writing, publishing, and speaking, 250-350 words; query title first. Some sidebars. Prefers NIV. Poems to twenty lines on writing, publishing, and speaking only, six per year; send maximum of two poems. Interviews with Christian editors, 750-1,000 words, four per year, query first. Anecdotes for "A Funny Thing Happened on the Way to Becoming a Communicator" humor column, 75-300 words, sixteen per year.

Guidelines: *regaforder.wordpress.com/articles/guidelines-ad-rates*

Sample: *regaforder.wordpress.com/articles*

Tip: Greatest needs are anecdotes for the "Funny Thing Happened" column and articles on writing craft.

FELLOWSCRIPT

PO Box 99509, Edmonton, AB T5B 0E1, Canada
fellowscripteditor@gmail.com | *www.inscribe.org/fellowscript*
Nina Morey, editor-in-chief

Parent company: InScribe Christian Writers' Fellowship

Type: quarterly PDF and print magazine; circulation 200; subscription free with InScribe membership; ads

Audience: members of InScribe Christian Writers' Fellowship

Purpose: to provide support, inspiration, and instruction and provide members with an opportunity to submit work

Submissions: Submit complete manuscript by email. Pays 2.5¢ per word (Canadian funds) for onetime rights, 1.5¢ per word for reprint rights, extra .5¢ for publication with author's permission on the website for no more than three months. Pays by PayPal on publication. Themes listed on website.

Types of manuscripts: Feature articles, 750 words; columns, 300-600 words; reviews, 150-300 words; fillers/tips, 25-500 words; general articles, 700 words. Responds in four weeks. Submission deadlines are January 1, April 1, July 1, and October 1. Plans six months ahead.

Guidelines: *inscribe.org/fellowscript*

Tip: "We always prefer material specifically slanted toward the needs and interests of Canadian Christian writers. We give preference to members and to Canadian writers."

FREELANCE WRITER'S REPORT

PO Box A, North Stratford, NH 03590 | 603-922-8338
submissions@writers-editors.com | *www.writers-editors.com*
Dana K. Cassell, editor

Parent company: Writers-Editor Network

Type: monthly online and print newsletter; subscription $39-49

Audience: established writers

Purpose: to help serious, professional freelance writers—whether full-time or part-time—improve their earnings and profits from their editorial businesses

Submissions: Freelance: 25%. Complete manuscript by email as attachment or copied into message. Pays 10¢ per edited word on publication for onetime rights. Responds within one week.

Seasonal two months ahead. Accepts simultaneous submissions and reprints (tell when/where appeared).

Types of manuscripts: The bulk of the content is market news and marketing information—how to build a writing/editing business, how to maximize income. Articles to 900 words, fifty per year. Prose fillers to 400 words. Likes bulleted lists.

Guidelines: *www.writers-editors.com/Writers/Membership/Writer_ Guidelines/ writer_guidelines.htm*

Sample: *freelancekeys.com/samplecopy*

Tip: "No articles on the basics of freelancing since readers are established freelancers. Looking for marketing and business-building for freelance writers, editors, and book authors."

POETS & WRITERS MAGAZINE

90 Broad St., Ste. 2100, New York, NY 10004-2272 | 212-226-3586

editor@pw.org | *www.pw.org*

Melissa Faliveno, senior editor

Parent company: Poets & Writers, Inc.

Type: bimonthly print magazine; circulation 100,000; subscription $15.95; ads

Audience: emerging to established literary writers

Purpose: to provide practical guidance for getting published and pursuing writing careers

Submissions: Query with clips via email or mail. Pays $150-500 for exclusive worldwide, periodical publication and syndication rights in all languages and nonexclusive reprint rights shared 50/50 thereafter. Pays when scheduled for production. Responds in four to six weeks.

Types of manuscripts: "News & Trends," 500-1,200 words; "The Literary Life," essays, 1,500-2,500 words; "The Practical Writer," how-to and advice, 1,500-2,500 words; profiles and interviews, 2,000-3,000 words (35 per year)

Guidelines: *www.pw.org/about-us/about_poets_&_writers_ magazine*

Sample: sold at large bookstores and online

Tip: Most open to "News & Trends," "The Literary Life," and "The Practical Writer."

STORY EMBERS

140 Churchill Ln., Mount Airy, NC 27030

submissions@storyembers.org | *storyembers.org*

Josiah DeGraaf, editor-in-chief, josiah@storyembers.org
Brianna Storm Hilvety, managing editor, brianna@storyembers.org

Type: digital magazine updated three times a week, 50,000 page views per month

Audience: Christian writers

Purpose: to guide and inspire Christian storytellers to glorify God with excellent craftsmanship

Submissions: Email as attachment. Rights: first. No payment. Unsolicited freelance: 50%. Buys 150 manuscripts per year. Length: 750-3,000 words. Responds in two weeks.

Types of manuscripts: how-to on writing, especially fiction; also takes fiction and poetry

Guidelines: *storyembers.org/submissions*

Sample: see the website

Tip: "In our fiction, we're looking for stories that honestly depict the human experience as it is and that grapple with Christian themes without being simplistic or heavy-handed. In our nonfiction, we're looking for articles that delve into specific writing subjects in-depth in a practical way."

WORDS FOR THE WAY

5042 E. Cherry Hills Blvd., Springfield, MO 65809 | 417-812-5232
OzarksACW@yahoo.com | *www.ozarksacw.org*
Renee Srch, managing editor
Jeanetta Chrystie, acquisitions editor

Parent company: Ozarks Chapter of American Christian Writers

Type: bimonthly (5x) print and digital newsletter; circulation 60; subscription $10; ads

Audience: writers at all levels

Purpose: to encourage and educate Christians to follow their call to write and learn to write well

Submissions: Freelance: 95%. Buys forty-five manuscripts per year. Seasonal two months in advance. Responds in one month. Email query or complete manuscript as attachment with brief bio and photo. No payment for reprint and electronic rights. Responds in three weeks. Seasonal two months ahead.

Types of manuscripts: Length: 500-1,000 words. All submissions must speak to writing, the writing life, how to write better, etc., including any poetry or fillers. Personal experience: writing stories that teach something about the writing life. Encouragement to follow God's call to write. Poetry, sidebars, columns, fillers. Stories only from spring contest. Any Bible version.

Guidelines: *www.OzarksACW.org/guidelines.php*

Sample: request by email

Tip: "Write clearly about writing. Focus on a single topic per submission. Think 'What would help or encourage Christian writers and want-to-be writers?' and write your piece to help them."

THE WRITER

Editorial, Madavor Media, 25 Braintree Hill Office Park, Ste. 404, Braintree, MA 02184

tweditorial@madavor.com | *www.writermag.com*

Nicki Porter, senior editor

Parent company: Madavor Media

Type: monthly print and digital magazine; circulation 30,000; subscription $28.95; ads

Audience: writers at all levels

Purpose: to expand and support the work of professional and aspiring writers with a straightforward presentation of industry information, writing instruction, and professional and personal motivation

Submissions: Unsolicited freelance: 80%. Query first with short bio. Query for features six months ahead. No reprints. Pay varies by type and department on acceptance for first rights. If no response in two weeks, probably not interested.

Types of manuscripts: Primarily looking for how-to articles on the craft of writing. Also has a variety of columns and departments: "Breakthrough," first-person articles about a writer's experience in breaking through to publication, 1,000 words; "Writing Essentials," basics of the craft of writing, 1,000 words plus a short sidebar of resources; "Market Focus," reports on specific market areas, 1,000 words; "Off the Cuff," essays on a particular aspect of writing or the writing life, 1,000 words; "Poet to Poet," how-to on writing poetry, 500-750 words; "Take Note," topical items of literary interest, 200-500 words; "Writer at Work," specific writing problem and how it was successfully overcome on the way to publication, 750-1,500 words. Uses some sidebars.

Guidelines: *www.writermag.com/the-magazine/submission-guidelines*

Sample: sold at large bookstores

Tips: "Personal essays must provide takeaway advice and benefits for writers. Include plenty of how-to, advice, and tips on techniques. Be specific. All topics must relate to writing."

THE WRITER'S CHRONICLE

5245 Greenbelt Rd, Box #246, College Park, MD 20740 | 301-226-9710
chronicle@awpwriter.org | *www.awpwriter.org/magazine_media/writers_chronicle_overview*
Supriya Bhatnagar, editor

Parent company: Association of Writers & Writing Programs
Type: bimonthly print and digital magazine during academic year; circulation 35,000; subscription $20; ads
Audience: serious writers, writing students and teachers
Purpose: to provide diverse insights into the art of writing that are accessible, pragmatic, and idealistic for serious writers
Submissions: Unsolicited freelance: 90%. Submit via website portal. Pays $18 per 100 words for first and electronic rights on publication. Responds in three months. No simultaneous submissions.
Types of manuscripts: Interviews, 3,000-5,000 words; profiles and appreciations of contemporary writers, 2,000-5,000 words; essays on the craft of writing, 2,500-5,000 words; news features, 500-2,000 words. Uses some sidebars. Also buys blog posts year round for *The Writer's Notebook*, 500-1,500 words, $100 per post.
Guidelines: *www.awpwriter.org/magazine_media/submission_guidelines*
Tip: "Keep in mind that 18,000 of our 35,000 readers are students or just-emerging writers."

WRITER'S DIGEST

4445 Lake Forest Dr., Ste. 407, Blue Ash, OH 45242
wdsubmissions@aimmedia.com | *www.writersdigest.com*
Ericka McIntyre, editor-in-chief

Parent company: Active Interest Media
Type: print and digital magazine, eight issues/year; circulation 77,000; print subscription $19.96, digital $9.96; ads
Audience: aspiring and professional writers
Purpose: to celebrate the writing life and what it means to be a writer in today's publishing environment
Submissions: Unsolicited freelance, 20%; assigned, 60%. Email query or manuscript in the message or as a Microsoft Word attachment. Responds in two to four months. Pays 30-50¢ per word on

acceptance for first and electronic rights. No reprints.

Types of manuscripts: "Inkwell," opinion pieces, 800-900 words and short how-to pieces, trends, humor, 300-600 words; "5-Minute Memoir," 600-word essay reflections on the writing life; author profiles, 800-2,000 words; articles on writing techniques, 1,000-2,400 words; market reports. Seasonal eight months ahead. Requires requested manuscript by email, copied into message. Kill fee 25%. Regularly uses sidebars.

Guidelines: *www.writersdigest.com/submission-guidelines*; theme list: *www.writersdigest.com/advertise/editorialcalendar*

Sample: available at newsstands and through *www.writersdigestshop.com*

Tip: "Although we welcome the work of new writers, we believe the established writer can better instruct our readers. Please include your publishing credentials related to your topic with your submission."

WRITERSWEEKLY.COM

200 2nd Avenue S. #526, St. Petersburg, FL 33710 | 305-768-0261
Brian@booklocker.com | www.writersweekly.com
Brian Whiddon, managing editor
Angela Hoy, publisher

Parent company: BookLocker.com, Inc.

Type: weekly digital newsletter; circulation 30,000; free

Audience: writers seeking to make more money from their writing

Purpose: to feature paying markets (making more money through writing), as well as give publishing advice

Submissions: Freelance: 75%. Buys 200 per year. Length: 600 words. Email query letter in body of the message; don't send manuscript until requested. Seasonal two months in advance. Responds in one week. Simultaneous OK. Pays $60 on acceptance and only via PayPal for first or reprint nonexclusive rights. Pays kill fee.

Types of manuscripts: feature articles on how to make more money writing, articles on paying Christian markets for writers, features that teach book-marketing techniques, book and author backstories

Guidelines: *writersweekly.com/writersweekly-com-writers-guidelines*

Sample: on website

Tip: "Please review our guidelines and website before querying us. We require specific queries targeting our readership. Please do not send a message simply asking if you can write for us. Send an idea for an article."

WRITING CORNER

410-536-4610

editor@writingcorner.com | writingcorner.com

Type: website

Audience: writers at all levels

Purpose: to provide concrete, useful advice from those who have been in the trenches and made a successful journey with their writing

Submissions: Responds in two weeks; feel free to nudge after that. Send queries and manuscripts via email only. Accepts reprints. No payment for nonexclusive rights; regular contributors get free sidebar ads on the site. Length: 600-900 words.

Types of manuscripts: Open to how-to articles on writing fiction and nonfiction, writing life, tips and tricks, basic and advance writing techniques.

Guidelines: *writingcorner.com/main-pages/submission-guidelines*

Tip: "Our site visitors are from all areas of writing, so keep that audience in mind when writing for us."

PART 4

SPECIALTY MARKETS

10

DAILY DEVOTIONAL BOOKLETS AND WEBSITES

Note that most of these markets assign all manuscripts. If there is no information listed on getting an assignment, request a sample copy and writers guidelines if they are not on the website. Then write two or three sample devotions to fit that particular format, and send them to the editor with a request for an assignment.

THE BRINK

114 Bush Rd., Nashville, TN 37217 | 800-877-7030, 615-361-1221
thebrink@randallhouse.com | *www.thebrinkonline.com*
David Jones, young adult editor

> **Denomination:** Free Will Baptist
> **Parent company:** Randall House
> **Audience:** college students and young adults
> **Type:** quarterly print
> **Details:** Devotions are by assignment only to coordinate with the curriculum. For feature articles, such as interviews, stories, and opinion pieces, email query with 100-200-word excerpt if available. Does not respond unless interested. Rights: all.
> **Guidelines:** *thebrinkonline.com/contact*

CHRIST IN OUR HOME

PO Box 1209, Minneapolis, MN 55440-1209 | 800-328-4648
afsubmissions@augsburgfortress.org | *www.augsburgfortress.org*

> **Denomination:** Evangelical Lutheran Church in America

Audience: adults
Type: quarterly print and CD
Details: Assignment only. Submit sample devotions as explained in the guidelines. Length: 1210 characters, including spaces, maximum. Rights: all. Bible version: NRSV.
Guidelines: download from *ms.augsburgfortress.org/downloads/ Submission%20Guidelines.pdf?redirected=true*
Tip: "*Christ in Our Home* is read by people in many nations, so avoid thinking only in terms of those who live in the U.S."

CHRISTIANDEVOTIONS.US

PO Box 6494, Kingsport, TN 37663 | 423-384-4821
christiandevotionsministries@gmail.com | *www.ChristianDevotions.us*
Martin Wiles, managing editor; Cindy Sproles, executive editor

Parent company: Christian Devotions Ministries
Audience: adults, teens
Type: daily website
Details: Accepts freelance submissions. Length: 400 words. Payment: none. Rights: onetime. Bible version: author's choice, must be referenced.
Guidelines: *www.christiandevotions.us/writeforus*
Tip: "Follow our guidelines."

DEVOKIDS

renee@devokids.com | *devokids.com*
Renee McCausey, executive editor

Parent company: Christian Devotions Ministries
Audience: kids ages 7-10
Type: website
Details: Takes freelance submissions. Length: 75-250 words. Email as an attached Word document. Payment: none. Rights: onetime.
Also accepts: submissions from kids
Guidelines: *devokids.com/write-for-us*

DEVOTIONS

www.standardlesson.com/standard-lesson-resources
See *The Quiet Hour* for details.

DEVOZINE

1908 Grand Ave., Nashville, TN 37212 | 615-340-7252
devozine@upperroom.org | *devozine.org*

Sandy Miller, editor

Parent company: Upper Room Ministries
Audience: teens, ages 14-19
Type: bimonthly print
Details: Accepts freelance submissions. Themes and deadlines are posted on the website. Length: 150-250 words. Payment: $25 ($10-15 if part of a group). Weekend feature articles: 500-600 words; pays $100; query for an assignment.
Also accepts: poetry to 20 lines, submissions from teens
Guidelines: on website, Write for Us tab

FORWARD DAY BY DAY

412 Sycamore St., Cincinnati, OH 45202-4110 | 800-543-1813
editorial@forwardmovement.org | *www.forwardmovement.org*
Richelle Thompson, managing editor

Denomination: Episcopal
Audience: adults
Type: quarterly print, online, phone app, daily podcast and email
Details: Devotions are written on assignment. To get an assignment, send three sample meditations based on three of the following Bible verses: Psalm 139:21; Mark 8:31; Acts 4:12; Revelation 1:10. Likes author to complete an entire month's worth of devotions. Length: 210 words, including Scripture. Pays $300 for a month of devotions.
Guidelines: *www.forwardmovement.org/Pages/About/Writers-Guidelines.aspx*
Tip: "We ask writers to submit devotional readings for seven days, starting with Sunday. Writers have the freedom to choose their own themes and Bible readings. It helps to follow a general theme throughout the week. Indicate references for Bible quotations in parentheses in the body of the devotional. If you use a translation other than the New International Version, please indicate the translation for each quotation."

FRUIT OF THE VINE

211 N. Meridian St., Ste. 101, Newberg, OR 97132 | 503-538-9775
admin@barclaypress.com | *www.barclaypress.com*
Cleta Crisman, editor

Denomination: Quakers
Parent company: Barclay Press
Audience: adults

Type: quarterly print

Details: Accepts freelance submissions, one week at a time. Length: 250 words. Payment: contributor copies and subscription. Rights: onetime. Bible version: NIV.

Guidelines: *tinyurl.com/y8vwx5gj*

Tip: "We ask writers to submit devotional readings for seven days, starting with Sunday. Writers have the freedom to choose their own themes and Bible readings. It helps to follow a general theme throughout the week. Indicate references for Bible quotations in parentheses in the body of the devotional. If you use a translation other than the New International Version, please indicate the translation for each quotation."

GOD'S WORD FOR TODAY

1445 N. Boonville Ave., Springfield, MO 65802 | 417-862-2781
DDawson@ag.org | *ag.org/Resources/Devotionals/Gods-Word-for-Today*
Dilla Dawson, editor

Denomination: Assemblies of God

Audience: adults

Type: quarterly print, online

Details: Request writers guidelines and sample assignment (unpaid). After samples are approved, writers will be added to the list for assignments. Length: 210 words. Payment: $25/devotion. Rights: all. Bible version: NIV.

Tip: "Writers will receive detailed guidelines upon inquiry."

KEYS FOR KIDS

PO Box 1001, Grand Rapids, MI 49501-1001 | 616-647-4500
editorial@keysforkids.org | *www.keysforkids.org*
Courtney Lasater, editor

Parent company: Keys for Kids Ministries

Audience: children ages 8-12, often used for family devotions

Type: quarterly print, daily online, phone app

Details: Takes only freelance submissions. Payment: $30 on acceptance. Rights: all. Length: 375 words. Seasonal four to five months ahead. Bible version: NKJV.

Guidelines: *www.keysforkids.org/writersguidelines*

Tip: "Most of our stories use real-world illustrations to help kids understand spiritual truth."

LIGHT FROM THE WORD

PO Box 50434, Indianapolis, IN 46250-0434 | 317-774-7900
submissions@wesleyan.org | *www.wesleyan.org/wph*
Susan LeBaron, project communications manager

Denomination: Wesleyan
Audience: adults
Type: quarterly print, daily online
Details: Must be affiliated with The Wesleyan Church. Email three
sample devotions to fit the format and request an assignment.
Write "Devotion Samples" in the subject line. Length: 200-240
words. Payment: $200 for seven devotions. Rights: all. Bible
version: NIV.
Guidelines: *wesleyan.org/wph/writers-guidelines*
Tip: Wesleyan-Armenian doctrine.

LOVE LINES FROM GOD

128 Leyland Ct., Greenwood, SC 29649 | 864-554-3204
martinwileseditor@gmail.com | *www.lovelinesfromgod.com*
Martin Wiles, managing editor

Denomination: Baptist
Audience: adults
Type: daily website
Details: Accepts freelance submissions. Length: 400 words. Payment:
none. Rights: first. Bible version: NIV.
Guidelines: *lovelinesfromgod.blogspot.com/p/write-for-us_3.html*
Tip: "We are looking for devotions that uplift and encourage."

MUSTARD SEED MINISTRIES DEVOTIONALS

4854 W 350S, Berne, IN 46711 | 260-849-0549
email through website | *mustardseedministries.org*
Jan, editor

Audience: adults, teens
Type: weekly website
Details: Accepts freelance submissions through the website. See
samples there. Length: 225-275 words. Payment: none.
Accepts reprints.
Guidelines: *www.mustardseedministries.org/guidelines*
Tip: "We accept all types of devotions. Each should relate to a
personal story."

PATHWAYS—MOMENTS WITH GOD

2902 Enterprise Dr., Anderson, IN 46013 | 800-741-7721
krhodes@warnerpress.org | *www.warnerpress.org*
Karen Rhodes, editorial director of church and ministry resources

Denomination: Church of God
Audience: adults
Type: quarterly print
Details: Written on assignment only. To be considered as a writer, submit a sample devotional. Length: 140-150 words. Should give readers living examples of what the Bible passage is about and how it can apply to life.
Guidelines: *www.warnerpress.org/submission-guidelines*

POCKETS

1908 Grand Ave., Nashville, TN 37212 | 615-340-7252
pockets@upperroom.org | *pockets.upperroom.org*
Lynn W. Gilliam, editor

Parent company: Upper Room Ministries
Audience: children ages 6-12
Type: monthly print (except February)
Details: Primarily accepts unsolicited freelance manuscripts, only via mail. See the theme list and deadlines on the website. Payment on acceptance. Bible version: NRSV.
Types of manuscripts: Fiction and Scripture stories that can help children deal with real-life situations, 600-1,000 words, pays 14¢/word. Poems, 16 lines maximum, pays $25 and up. Articles about children involved in environmental, community, and peace/justice issues, 400-1,000 words, pays 14¢/word. Activities, puzzles, games, recipes: pays $25 and up.
Also accepts: submissions from children through age 12
Guidelines: *pockets.upperroom.org/write-for-us*
Tip: "We do not accept stories about talking animals or inanimate objects. Fictional characters and some elaboration may be included in Scripture stories, but the writer must remain faithful to the story."

THE QUIET HOUR

4050 Lee Vance Dr., Colorado Springs, CO 80918
thequiethour@davidccook.com | *www.davidccook.org*
Scott Stewart, editor

Parent company: David C. Cook

Audience: adults

Type: quarterly print

Details: By assignment only. North America postal address is necessary to receive contract and payment. Length: 200 words. Payment: $140 for seven devotions. Rights: all. Bible version: NIV, KJV.

Guidelines: *davidccook.org/wp-content/uploads/2018/02/Devotion-Quiet-Hour-Spec-Devotional-Guidelines.pdf*

Tip: "Submit spec devotional on a key verse you select in a Scripture passage of your choice. Begin with anecdotal opening then transition to relevant biblical insight and encouragement for a life of faith rooted in the key verse."

REFLECTING GOD

PO Box 419527, Kansas City, MO 64141 | 816-931-1900
dcbrush@wordaction.com | *reflectinggod.com*
Duane Brush, editor

Denomination: Nazarene

Audience: adults

Type: daily, online

Details: Send a couple of sample devotions to fit the format and request an assignment. Length: 180-200 words. Pays $115 for seven devotions.

Tip: "Our purpose is the pursuit to embrace holy living. We want to foster discussion about what it means to live a holy life in the 21st century."

THE SECRET PLACE

1075 First Ave., King of Prussia, PA 19406 | 610-768-2434
thesecretplace@judsonpress.com | *www.judsonpress.com*
Ingrid Dvirnak, editor

Denomination: American Baptist

Audience: adults

Type: quarterly print

Details: Accepts freelance submissions; does not give assignments. Length: 150-200 words. Payment: $20 per devotion. Rights: first. Bible version: no preference.

Guidelines: *www.judsonpress.com/Content/Site189/BasicBlocks/10258GUIDELINES_00000128358.pdf*

Tip: "Use less-familiar Bible verses."

TAKE 5 PLUS

1445 N. Boonville Ave., Springfield, MO 65802 | 417-862-2781
rl-take5plus@ag.org | *myhealthychurch.com*
Wade Quick, wquick@ag.org

Denomination: Assemblies of God

Audience: teens

Type: quarterly print

Details: Assignment only. Request via email writers guidelines and sample assignment (unpaid). After samples are approved, writers will be added to the list for assignments. Length: 210-235 words. Payment: $25 per devotion on acceptance. Rights: all. Bible version: NIV.

Tip: "Study the publication before attempting the sample assignment."

THESE DAYS: DAILY DEVOTIONS FOR LIVING BY FAITH

100 Witherspoon St., Louisville, KY 40202 | 800-624-2412
mlindberg@presbypub.com | *www.ppcbooks.com/thesedays.asp*
Mary Lindberg, editor

Denomination: Presbyterian Church (USA)

Audience: adults

Type: quarterly print

Details: Accepts freelance submissions. Length: 190 words. Payment: $100 or $150 worth of books for seven devotions. Rights: first. Bible version: NRSV.

Tip: "Write thoughtful entries based on a Scripture passage, use gender-inclusive language for God and humanity, and include a brief closing prayer."

UNLOCKED

PO Box 1001, Grand Rapids, MI 49501-1001 | 888-224-2324
Kandi@keysforkids.org | *www.unlocked.org*
Kandi Zeller, editor

Parent company: Keys for Kids Ministries

Audience: teens

Type: quarterly print, online

Details: Accepts only freelance submissions. Payment: $30 on acceptance. Rights: all. Length: 115-350 words. Takes teen writers. Bible version: CSB, NIV, NKJV, NLT, WEB.

Guidelines: *unlocked.org/writers-guidelines*

Tip: "*Unlocked* is a teen devotional that features daily, Scripture-rooted devotions from all different genres, including essay, poetry, sci-fi/fantasy, and more. We want our devotional pieces to challenge teens and help them wrestle with things they're dealing with, not talk down to them or shy away from deep topics. Successful submissions connect Jesus' life, death, and resurrection to the topic being addressed."

THE UPPER ROOM

1908 Grand Ave., Nashville, TN 37212 | 615-340-7252
ureditorial@upperroom.org | upperroom.org
Lindsay L. Gray, editorial director

Denomination: United Methodist
Audience: adults
Type: bimonthly print, daily online
Details: Accepts freelance submissions. Length: 300 words, which include everything on the printed page. Payment: $30 on publication. Rights: first, exclusive for one year. Bible versions: NIV, NRSV, CEB, KJV. Prefers submissions through the website.
Guidelines: *submissions.upperroom.org/guidelines?locale=en*
Tip: "A strong devotional will include three main elements: 1. A personal story or experience. 2. A connection to Scripture. 3. A way for the reader to apply the message to his or her own life."

THE WORD IN SEASON

PO Box 1209, Minneapolis, MN 55440-1209 | 414-963-1222
rochelle@writenowcoach.com | www.augsburgfortress.org
Rochelle Melander, managing editor

Denomination: Evangelical Lutheran Church in America
Audience: adults
Type: quarterly print
Details: Assignment only. Submit three sample devotions from an ECLA perspective as explained in the guidelines. Length: 1190 characters. Payment: $30 per devotion. Rights: all. Bible version: NRSV. Also takes prayers by assignment only; payment: $100 for nine.
Guidelines: download from *ms.augsburgfortress.org/downloads/Submission%20Guidelines.pdf?redirected=true*
Tip: "Use concrete language, use the historical-critical tools to understand the biblical passage, and tell us how this passage applies to our daily lives."

Christian Writers Institute Courses 2020 Devotional Bundle

Courses in this bundle:

- Prepare Your Heart to Be a Writer
- Deeper: Spiritual Formation for the Writer
- How to Write Devotionals
- The Four Cs of a Godly Writer
- The God Factor
- Five Marks of a Christian Writer

Normal price: $96
Savings: 50%
Market Guide price $48

https://cwmg.link/devo2020

How to Scan QR Codes

Use the camera on your smartphone to focus on the above QR code to activate the discount. It will give you the option to visit the site, which you will want to accept. If you are using an older smartphone, you may need to download a QR code scanning app. You can also visit the URL below the code to activate the discount on your computer.

11

DRAMA

CHRISTIAN PUBLISHERS, LLC

425 2nd St. NE, Cedar Rapids, Iowa 52401 | 319-368-8009
editor@christianpub.com | *www.christianpub.com*
Rhonda Wray, editor

Parent company: Brooklyn Publishers

Audiences: children, teens, adults

Submissions: Submit complete script, preferably through the website form or as an email attachment. Simultaneous submission is OK. Replies in at least three months. Publishes fifteen to thirty scripts per year; receives 250 submissions. Length: prefers 10-30 minutes, occasionally up to an hour.

Types: one-act plays, musicals, compilation of skits, monologues, readers theater, scripts for children and teens; most scripts are for Advent/Christmas or Lent/Easter

Also publishes: banners

Payment: 10% royalty, often to a fixed amount. No advance.

Guidelines: *www.christianpub.com/default.aspx?pg=ag*

Tip: "We like drama that is so enthralling it doesn't need elaborate productions with complicated sets and hard-to-obtain costumes and props. Scripts that meet a need in the life of a church are also welcome, such as mother-daughter event scripts. We embrace all styles, from humorous to solemn and worshipful. It would be most helpful to go to our website and familiarize yourself with the types of works we carry. Please include a cast list and production notes that share with would-be directors anything they need to know in order to stage your drama effectively."

CSS PUBLISHING GROUP, INC.

See entry in "**Book Publishers**."

DOVE CHRISTIAN PUBLISHERS

See entry in "**Book Publishers.**"

DRAMA MINISTRY

2814 Azalea Pl., Nashville, TN 37204 | 866-859-7622
service@dramaministry.com | www.dramaministry.com
Vince Wilcox, general manager

> **Audiences:** children, teens, adults
> **Submissions:** Open to all topics, including seasonal/holidays. Email or mail script. Buys all rights.
> **Types:** only short skits of 2-10 minutes, comedy, drama, monologue, readers theater

ELDRIDGE PUBLISHING CO., INC.

PO Box 4904, Lancaster, PA 17604 | 850-385-2463
newworks@histage.com | www.95church.com
Susan Shore, editor

> **Audiences:** children, teens, adults
> **Submissions:** Publishes twelve to fifteen scripts per year; receives fifty to seventy-five submissions annually. Length: minimum 20 minutes. Submit complete script via email. Simultaneous OK. Responds in three months.
> **Types:** full-length plays, one-act plays, compilations of skits, musicals, readers theater, monologues, children, teens
> **Payment:** 50% royalty, no advance
> **Guidelines:** *www.95church.com/submission-guidelines*
> **Tip:** "Please submit plays and musicals suitable for performance by all kinds and sizes of churches. We are an independent publisher not supported by any specific religious denomination. We welcome shows on all subjects; however, Christmas plays are very popular."

GROUP PUBLISHING

See entry in "**Book Publishers.**"

12

GREETING CARDS
AND **GIFTS**

BLUE MOUNTAIN ARTS, INC.
Editorial Dept., PO Box 1007, Boulder, CO 80306 | 303-449-0536
editorial@sps.com | www.sps.com

Audience: adults, teens

Products: general publisher with some inspirational greeting cards, calendars, gift books, bookmarks, magnets, wallet cards, miniature prints

Submissions: Looking for contemporary prose or poetry written from personal experience that reflects the thoughts and feelings people today want to communicate to one another but don't always know how to put into words. Have a loved one in mind as you write. Considers writings on special occasions (birthday, anniversary, congratulations, etc.), as well as the challenges and aspirations of life. Not looking for rhymed poetry, religious verse, humor, or one-liners. Length: 50 to 300 words. Buys all rights. Accepts freelance submissions by email or mail. Responds in four months or not interested. Holiday deadlines: Christmas and general holidays, July 15; Valentine's Day, September 12; Easter, November 8; Mother's Day, December 13; Father's Day, February 7.

Guidelines: *www.sps.com/help/writers_guidelines.html*

Payment: $300 per poem for worldwide, exclusive rights to publish it on a greeting card and other products; $50 per poem for one-time use in a book

DICKSONS, INC.
709 B Ave E, Seymour, IN 47274 | 812-522-1308
submissions@dicksonsgifts.com | www.dicksonsgifts.com

Audience: adults

Products: figurines, crosses, wall decor, mugs, flags

Submissions: Two to eight lines, maximum sixteen, suitable for plaques, bookmarks, etc. Email submission. Responds in three months. Subjects can cover any gift-giving occasion and Christian, inspirational, and everyday social-expression topics. Phrases or acrostics of one or two lines for bumper stickers are also considered. Buys reprint rights.

Guidelines: *www.dicksonsgifts.com/t-contact.aspx*

Payment: royalty, negotiable

Tip: Looking for religious verses.

ELLIE CLAIRE

6100 Tower Cir., Ste. 210, Franklin, TN 37013 | 615-932-7600
marilynj@worthypublishing.com | *www.worthypublishing.com*
Marilyn Jansen, editorial director

Parent company: Hachette Book Group

Audience: adults

Products: gifts, journals, devotionals, gift books

Submissions: Email submissions. Also makes assignments. To be considered for an assignment, email letter, résumé, three full samples of devotional writing. Buys all rights.

Guidelines: by email

Payment: flat fee, royalty; $30-40 per devotion

Tips: "Please do not send unsolicited manuscripts or samples. Contact us first with an introduction and elevator pitch. If we are interested, we will ask for more. We operate in the gift market, and the writing will need to reflect that. We are not interested in Bible studies but in inspirational and encouraging devotions, funny stories with a spiritual component, and compilations from a Christian worldview."

WARNER PRESS

2902 Enterprise Dr., Anderson, IN 46013 | 800-741-7721
editors@warnerpress.org | *www.warnerpress.org*
Karen Rhodes, editorial director of church and ministry resources

Denomination: Church of God

Audience: children, adults

Products: boxed everyday and Christmas cards

Submissions: Most accepted verses average four lines in length. Themes include birthday, anniversary, baby congratulations, sympathy, get well, kid's birthday and get well, thinking of you, friendship, Christmas, praying for you, encouragement. Use a conversational tone with no lofty poetic language, such as *thee, thou, art*. Responds in six to eight weeks. Email or mail with SASE. Buys all rights. Deadines: everyday, July 31; Christmas, October 1. **Guidelines:** *www.warnerpress.org/submission-guidelines*

13

TRACTS

The following companies publish gospel tracts but do not have writers guidelines. If you are interested in writing for them, email or phone to find out if they currently are looking for submissions. Also check your denominational publishing house to see if it publishes tracts.

CHRISTIAN LIGHT PUBLICATIONS
PO Box 1212, Harrisonburg, VA 22803-1212 | 800-776-0478
info@clp.org | *www.clp.org*

FELLOWSHIP TRACT LEAGUE
PO Box 164, Lebanon, OH 45036 | 513-494-1075
mail@fellowshiptractleague.org | *www.fellowshiptractleague.org*

GOOD NEWS PUBLISHERS
1300 Crescent St., Wheaton, IL 60187 | 630-682-4300
info@crossway.org | *www.crossway.org*

GOSPEL PUBLISHING HOUSE
1445 N. Boonville Ave., Springfield, MO 65802 | 800-641-4310
newproducts@gph.org | *gospelpublishing.com*

GOSPEL TRACT SOCIETY
PO Box 1118, Independence, MO 64051 | 816-461-6086
gospeltractsociety@gmail.com | *gospeltractsociety.org*

GRACE VISION PUBLISHERS
321-745-9966 (text only)
email through the website | *www.gracevision.com/en*

MOMENTS WITH THE BOOK
PO Box 322, Bedford, PA 15522 | 814-623-8737
email through the website | *mwtb.org*

TRACT ASSOCIATION OF FRIENDS
1501 Cherry St., Philadelphia, PA 19102
info@tractassociation.org | *www.tractassociation.org*

14

BIBLE CURRICULUM

This list includes only the major, nondenominational curriculum publishers. If you are in a denominational church, also check its publishing house for curriculum products. Plus some organizations, like Awana Clubs International and Pioneer Clubs, also produce curriculum for their programs.

Since Bible curriculum is written on assignment only, you'll need to get samples for age groups you want to write for (from the company's website, large Christian bookstores, or your church) and study the formats and pieces. Look for editors' names on the copyright pages of teachers manuals, or call the publishing house for this information.

Then write query letters to specific editors. Tell why you're qualified to write curriculum for them, include a sample of curriculum you've written or other sample of your writing, and ask for a trial assignment. Since the need for writers varies widely, you may not get an assignment for a year or more.

Some of these companies also publish undated, elective curriculum books that are used in a variety of ministries. Plus some book publishers publish lines of Bible-study guides. (See "**Book Publishers.**") These are contracted like other books with a proposal and sample chapters.

A BEKA BOOKS

PO Box 17900, Pensacola, FL 32522-7900 | 877-356-9385
www.joyfullifesundayschool.com
   Type: Sunday school
   Imprint: Joyful Life

DAVID C . COOK

4050 Lee Vance Dr., Colorado Springs, CO 80918 | 800-708-5550
shop.davidccook.org

Types: Sunday school
Imprints: Accent, The Action Bible, Bible-in-Life, Echoes, Encounter, Gospel Light, HeartShaper, Scripture Press, Standard Lesson, TruStory, and some denominational imprints

GROUP PUBLISHING

1515 Cascade Ave., Loveland, CO 80538 | 970-669-3836
PuorgBus@group.com | *www.group.com*
Types: Sunday school, vacation Bible school, children's worship
Imprints: Be Bold, Buzz, Dig In, FaithWeaver NOW, FaithWeaver Friends, Fearless Conversation, Grapple, Hands-On Bible, LIVE, Play-n-Worship, Kids Own Worship
Guidelines: *grouppublishingps.zendesk.com/hc/en-us/articles/211878258-Submissions*

UNION GOSPEL PRESS

2000 Brookpark Rd., Cleveland, OH 44109 | 800-638-9988
editorial@uniongospelpress.com | *uniongospelpress.com*
Type: Sunday school
Guidelines: *uniongospelpress.com/index.php/prospective-writers*

URBAN MINISTRIES, INC.

1551 Regency Ct., Calumet City, IL 60409-5448 | 800-860-8642
urbanministries.com
Types: Sunday school, vacation Bible school

15

MISCELLANEOUS

These companies publish a variety of books and other products that fall into the specialty-markets category, such as puzzle books, game books, children's activity books, craft books, charts, church bulletins, and coloring books.

BARBOUR PUBLISHING
See entry in "**Book Publishers**."

BROADSTREET PUBLISHING
See entry in "**Book Publishers**."

CHRISTIAN FOCUS PUBLICATIONS
See entry in "**Book Publishers**."

DAVID C . COOK
shop.davidccook.org
See entry in "**Book Publishers**."

GROUP PUBLISHING
See entry in "**Book Publishers**."

ROSE PUBLISHING
See entry in "**Book Publishers**."

WARNER PRESS
2902 Enterprise Dr., Anderson, IN 46013 | 800-741-7721
editors@warnerpress.org | www.warnerpress.org
Karen Rhodes, editorial director of church and ministry resources
   Denomination: Church of God

Church bulletins: Short devotions that tie into a visual image and incorporate a Bible verse. Especially interested in material for holidays and special Sundays, such as Christmas, New Year's Day, Palm Sunday, Easter, Pentecost, and Communion. General themes are also welcome. Length: 250 words maximum. Deadline: April 30. Buys all rights. Payment varies.

Children's coloring and activity books: Most activity books focus on a Bible story or biblical theme, such as love and forgiveness. Ages range from preschool (ages 2-5) to upper elementary (ages 8-10). Include activities and puzzles in every upper-elementary book. Coloring-book manuscripts should present a picture idea and a portion of the story for each page. Deadlines: May 1 and October 1. Payment varies.

Guidelines: *www.warnerpress.org/submission-guidelines*

PART 5

SUPPORT
FOR
WRITERS

16

LITERARY AGENTS

Asking editors and other writers is a great way to find a reliable agent. You may also want to visit *www.sfwa.org/other-resources/for-authors/writer-beware/agents* for tips on avoiding questionable agents and choosing reputable ones.

The general market has an Association of Authors' Representatives (*www.aaronline.org*), also known as *AAR*. To be a member, the agent must agree to a code of ethics. The website has a searchable list of agents. Some listings below indicate agents who belong to the AAR. Lack of such a designation, however, does not indicate the agent is unethical; most Christian agents are not members.

ALIVE LITERARY AGENCY

7680 Goddard St., Ste. 200, Colorado Springs, CO 80920 | 719-260-7080
submissions@aliveliterary.com | *www.aliveliterary.com*

Agents: Bryan Norman (president), Lisa Jackson (vice president), Andrea Heinecke

Agency: Established in 1989 by Rick Christian. Represents more than 125 clients. Member of Association of Authors' Representatives.

Types of books: adult novels, nonfiction, crossover, juvenile

New clients: Only taking proposals from authors who are personally referred by clients or close contacts of Alive. Contact by email. Responds in six to eight weeks to referrals only; may not respond to unsolicited submissions.

Commission: 15%

AMBASSADOR LITERARY AGENCY

PO Box 50358, Nashville, TN 37205 | 615-370-4700
info@AmbassadorAgency.com | *www.AmbassadorAgency.com*

Agent: Wes Yoder, *wes@AmbassadorSpeakers.com*

Agency: Established in 1973. Represents twenty-five to thirty clients.

New clients: Open to unpublished book authors. Contact by email with a short description of the manuscript and a request to submit it for review. Responds in four to six weeks.

Types of books: adult nonfiction and fiction, crossover books, no sci-fi or medical

Commission: 15%

Fees: none

APOKEDAK LITERARY AGENCY

113 Winn Ct., Waleska, GA 30183 | 678-744-7745
submissions@sally-apokedak.com | *sally-apokedak.com*

Agent: Sally Apokedak

Agency: Established in 2017. Represents ten clients.

Also does: online courses, editing, consulting, critiquing, websites

Types of books: children's, adult, fiction, nonfiction

Specialty: children's fiction

New clients: Open to writers met at conferences. Initial contact: email with full proposal, referral from current client. Accepts simultaneous submissions. Responds in three months.

Commission: 15%

Fees: none

Tip: "Visit my blog, come to a retreat I'm doing, or meet me at a conference. And most importantly, write a book I can't put down."

BANNER LITERARY

PO Box 1828, Winter Park, CO 80482
mike@mikeloomis.co | *www.mikeloomis.co*

Agent: Mike Loomis

Agency: Established in 2004. Represents forty-eight clients.

Types of books: nonfiction, self-help, business, inspiration, politics

New clients: Open to writers who have not published a book and self-published writers. Contact through email or website form. Responds in two weeks.

Commission: 15%

Fees: none

Other services: See listing in "⟨...⟩

Tip: "Send your web address wi⟨...⟩

THE BINDERY

128 E. Las Animas St., Colorado Spri⟨...⟩
Info@thebinderyagency.com | www.TheB⟨...⟩

Agent: Alexander Field (principle a⟨...⟩
(managing director)

Agency: Established in 2017. Repre⟨...⟩

Types of books: fiction, Christianit⟨...⟩
formation, memoir, biography, s⟨...⟩
relationships, and more

New clients: We represent authors at all levels: well-established
authors who have published dozens of books and first-time
authors. We're incredibly selective; but if we love the concept, the
author's influence, and, ultimately, the read itself, we'll make an
offer of representation. Initial contact: email, website form, mail,
referral from current client. Query first or send full proposal.
Accepts simultaneous submissions. Responds in eight to ten weeks.

Commission: 15%

Fees: none

Tip: "Our number one piece of advice is this: Take your time. Writing
a book takes a long time; requires investment from your future
publishing team; and once you put a book out into the world, we
all hope it will be out there for years, decades. So don't rush. Shape
your content and book concept with care. Build your platform and
influence in the world, not to make yourself famous, but in order
to reach people with the content you're creating and, eventually,
the book you're writing."

THE BLYTHE DANIEL AGENCY, INC.

PO Box 64197, Colorado Springs, CO 80962-4197 | 719-213-3427
submissions@theblythedanielagency.com | www.theblythedanielagency.com

Agents: Blythe Daniel; Stephanie Alton, literary and marketing agent

Agency: Established in 2005. Represents eighty-five clients. Sells to
general market too.

Also does: publicity and blog campaigns; see listing in "Publicity and
Marketing Services" chapter

Types of books: Christian life, spiritual growth, current events,
inspirational/narrative nonfiction, business/leadership, church

, parenting, social issues, women's issues, ___, devotionals, children's, Bible study. Voices: ___ers, business leaders, moms, pastors, bloggers/ ___rs, and others who have an established organization or ___stry or are a part of one

cialty: Christian living

ew clients: Open to writers who have not published a book, well-established book writers, writers met at conferences, references from current clients. Contact: email with full proposal, referral from current client. Accepts simultaneous submissions. Responds in four weeks if interested, longer if you submit during their conference season

Other services: See listing in "Publicity and Marketing Services."

Commission: 15% of standard book royalties, other formats vary

Fees: none

Tip: "Writers need to see if their book category fits what we're acquiring. Tell us in an elevator pitch what your book is about, who the book is for, and how you are connected to the audience. We want to see you know how to build your audience even if it is not large. We look at unique visitors per month, email subscribers, podcast subscribers, YouTube presence, online outlets the writer contributes to, social-media presence, speaking schedule, and how you are networked with other writers.

"Even if you don't have all of these things but have some of them, show us what you have done, rather than what you are planning to do.

"Give us what you are saying in your book that no one else is saying. You need a distinguishable book hook that stands out from similar books. Conduct searches to compare the content of your book to others already published (not just the format or who it's for). We want to see a paragraph description of how your book compares. We need to see how you have developed your concept in a way that makes us say, 'I haven't thought about that before' or 'I haven't heard anyone say it like this.'

"Make sure you include a marketing plan with your submission, as this helps us see how you will market your book, including endorsements."

BOOKS & SUCH LITERARY MANAGEMENT

52 Mission Cir., Ste. 122, PMB 170, Santa Rosa, CA 95409-5370
representation@booksandsuch.com | www.booksandsuch.com

Agents: Janet Kobobel Grant (president), Wendy
president), Rachelle Gardner, Rachel Kent, C
Agency: Established in 1996. Represents 250 cl
Types of books: adult fiction and nonfiction; s
no poetry, academic books, or speculative a
New clients: Open to writers who have not published
established book writers, and self-published writers. Contact
by email with query first. Accepts simultaneous submissions.
Responds in six to eight weeks if interested.
Commission: 15%
Fees: none
Tip: "Provide clear and compelling details about your project in your
query. We read each query we receive and forward to the agent
most likely to be interested in your project if it seems to be a good
fit for our agency."

CHRISTIAN LITERARY AGENT

PO Box 428, Newburg, PA 17240 | 717-423-6621
keith@christianliteraryagent.com | www.christianliteraryagent.com

Agent: Keith Carroll
Agency: Established in 2010. Represents sixty-three clients.
Also does: writer coaching
Types of books: Christian, inspirational
Specialty: nonfiction
New clients: Open to new book authors, self-published writers, and
writers who have a strong desire to break into the larger market.
Initial contact: email, phone, website form, referral from current
client. Responds in three to four weeks. Accepts simultaneous
submissions.
Commission: 10%
Fees: $90 for admin costs

CURTIS BROWN, LTD.

10 Astor Pl., New York, NY 10003-6935 | 212-473-5400
info@cbltd.com | www.curtisbrown.com

Agent: Laura Blake Peterson, *lbp@cbltd.com*
Agency: Member of Association of Authors' Representatives. General
agency that handles some religious/inspirational books.
Types of books: fiction, nonfiction, children's
New clients: Email query, and attach the first fifty pages of your

manuscript. Include "lbpquery" in the subject line of your email. Responds in three to four weeks only if interested in your book.

YLE YOUNG LITERARY ELITE, LLC
PO Box 1, Clarklake, MI 49230 | 330-651-1604
submissions@cyleyoung.com | *www.cyleyoung.com*

> **Agents:** Cyle Young, Tessa Emily Hall, Bethany Morehead, Caroline George, Hope Bolinger
> **Agency:** Established in 2018. Represents eighty clients.
> **Types of books:** children's, middle grade, YA, and adult; fiction, and nonfiction
> **Specialty:** children's and nonfiction
> **New clients:** Open to well-established book authors, writers met at conferences, prospective authors with large platforms or social-media followings. Contact by email with full proposal. Responds in three months or longer.
> **Commission:** 15%
> **Tip:** "We look for projects with great writing, big ideas, and great platform."

D. C. JACOBSON & ASSOCIATES
PO Box 80945, Portland, OR 97280 | 503-850-4800
submissions@dcjacobson.com | *www.dcjacobson.com*

> **Agents:** Jenni Burke (president), Tawny Johnson, Joy Eggerichs Reed
> **Agency:** Established in 2006. Represents more than 100 clients.
> **Types of books:** adult fiction and nonfiction
> **New clients:** Open to unpublished and self-published book authors. Email submissions and queries; no mail submissions. Fiction proposals must include complete manuscript. Responds in two months. Accepts simultaneous submissions.
> **Commission:** 15%
> **Fees:** none
> **Tip:** "Please review our submission guidelines at *dcjacobson.com/submissions*."

DANIEL LITERARY GROUP
601 Old Hickory Blvd. #56, Brentwood, TN 37027 | 615-730-8207
submissions@danielliterarygroup.com | *www.danielliterarygroup.com*

> **Agent:** Greg Daniel, *greg@danielliterarygroup.com*
> **Agency:** Established in 2007. Represents forty clients.

Types of books: nonfiction of all types

New clients: Open to new clients who have not published books. Contact by email; no attachments. Query first. Accepts simultaneous submissions. Responds in three to four weeks. No new fiction clients.

Commission: 15%

Fees: none

Tip: "Research the agency first before submitting to be sure your project is appropriate for us."

FINE PRINT LITERARY MANAGEMENT

115 W. 29th St., 3rd Fl., New York, NY 10001 | 212-279-1282
peter@fineprintlit.com | www.fineprintlit.com

Agent: Peter Rubie

Agency: General agency that handles some spirituality books.

Types: adult fiction and nonfiction, some middle grade and YA fiction

New clients: Open to unpublished authors. Email query.

Commission: 15%

GARY D. FOSTER CONSULTING

733 Virginia Ave., Van Wert, OH 45891 | 419-238-4082
gary@garydfoster.com | www.garydfoster.com

Agent: Gary Foster

Agency: Established in 1989. Represents more than fifty clients.

Types of books: biographies, inspirational, gift, crossover, YA nonfiction

New clients: Open to unpublished, well-established, and self-published authors. Email query or referral from current client. Accepts simultaneous submissions. Responds in one to three weeks.

Commission: 15%

Fees: nominal initial fee

Tip: "Review my website prior to contacting me."

HARTLINE LITERARY AGENCY

123 Queenston Dr., Pittsburgh, PA 15235 | 412-829-2483
jim@hartlineliterary.com | www.hartlineagency.com

Agents: Jim Hart, *jim@hartlineliterary.com*; Joyce A. Hart, *joyce@hartlineliterary.com*; Cyle Young, *cyle@hartlineliterary.com*; Linda Glaz, *linda@hartlineliterary.com*; Patricia Riddle-Gaddis, *patricia@hartlineliterary.com*

Agency: Established in 1992. Represents 260 clients.

Types of books: Jim Hart: nonfiction: Christian living, church growth, leadership, business, social issues, ministry, parenting, self-help; fiction: suspense/thrillers, romance (contemporary, historical, suspense, Amish), women's fiction, literary, fantasy, sci-fi, and speculative; not looking at children's or middle-grade fiction at this time

Linda Glaz: fiction: romance, either contemporary, suspense, or historic; no children's books

Cyle Young: YA, middle grade, chapter books, easy readers, picture books, and board books; genre fiction, especially romance, speculative (sci-fi and fantasy); nonfiction: parenting, leadership, ministry, and self-help; screenplays

Patricia Riddle-Gaddis: fiction: sweet romance, cozy mysteries, and young-adult categories (think *The Princess Diaries* and a modern Nancy Drew); a range of nonfiction

New clients: Open to writers who have not published a book, well-established book writers, self-published writers, writers met at conferences. Initial contact: email with full proposal. Accepts simultaneous submissions. Responds in six to eight weeks.

Commission: 15%, foreign 20%, films 20-25%

Fees: none

Tips: "Please look at our website before submitting. Guidelines are listed, along with detailed information about each agent. Be sure to include your bio and publishing history with your proposal. The author-agent relationship is a team effort. Working together we can make sure your manuscript gets the exposure and attention it deserves."

HIDDEN VALUE GROUP, LLC

27758 Santa Margarita Pkwy. #361, Mission Viejo, CA 92691
bookquery@hiddenvaluegroup.com | *www.HiddenValueGroup.com*

Agent: Nancy Jernigan, *njerigan@hiddenvaluegroup.com*

Agency: Established in 2001.

Also does: coaching

Types of books: family, marriage, parenting, fiction, inspirational, self-help, business, women's and men's issues

New clients: Open to previously published authors only, not including self-publishing. Mail or email proposal with two or three chapters. Responds in four to six weeks.

Commission: 15%

Fees: none

Tip: "Include how you will help support the marketing of your project. Include all social-media numbers; social-media platforms; radio, print, and TV marketing."

K J LITERARY SERVICES, LLC

1540 Margaret Ave., Grand Rapids, MI 49507 | 616-551-9797
kim@kjliteraryservices.com | *www.kjliteraryservices.com*

Agent: Kim Zeilstra
Agency: Established in 2006.
Also does: editing, proofreading, project management, permissions
New clients: Only taking new authors by referral at this time. Initial contact by email or phone.
Commission: 15%

KIRKLAND MEDIA MANAGEMENT

PO Box 1539, Liberty, TX 77575 | 936-581-3944
admin@kirklandmediamanagment.com |
www.KirklandMediaManagement.com

Agent: Jessica Kirkland
Types of books: fiction, nonfiction, film contracts in the inspirational market; no children's, short stories, or poetry
New clients: Email query only. Guidelines on the website.
Commission: 15%

THE KNIGHT AGENCY

232 W. Washington St., Madison, GA 30650 | 706 473-0994
pamela.harty@knightagency.net | *knightagency.net*

Agent: Pamela Harty
Agency: Established in 1996. Member of Association of Authors' Representatives. Agency represents 330 authors.
Types of books: Christian living
New clients: Open to writers who have not published a book, well-established book writers, and self-published writers. Initial contact by query via Query Manager on the website. All other queries will not be reviewed or returned. Responds in six weeks.
Commission: 15%
Fees: none
Tip: "Please visit our website for submission guidelines."

LITERARY MANAGEMENT GROUP, LLC

PO Box 41004, Nashville, TN 37204 | 615-812-4445

brucebarbour@literarymanagementgroup.com |
www.literarymanagementgroup.com

Agent: Bruce R. Barbour
Agency: Established in 1996. Represents more than 100 clients.
Also does: book packaging, publishing consulting
Type of books: adult nonfiction; no gift books, memoir, text/
academic
New clients: No unpublished authors. Email proposal. Accepts
simultaneous submissions. Responds in three to four weeks.
Commission: 15%
Fees: none

MACGREGOR AND LUEDEKE

PO Box 1316, Manzanita, OR 97130 | 503-389-4803
chip@macgregorliterary.com | *www.macgregorandluedeke.com*

Agents: Chip MacGregor (president), Amanda Luedeke (vice
president)
Agency: Established in 2006. Member of Association of Authors'
Representatives. Represents sixty clients.
Types of books: wide variety of nonfiction and select list of novelists
Specialty: memoir, Christian living
New clients: Open to writers with an established platform and a solid
book idea. Initial contact: website form, referral from current
client; query first. Not accepting unsolicited fiction manuscripts.
Accepts simultaneous submissions. Responds in one month.
Commission: 15%
Fees: none
Tip: "A well-written proposal and sample chapters is the best way to
gain our attention. We're always looking for fresh ideas expressed
through great writing, from authors with a proven platform."

MARK SWEENEY & ASSOCIATES

302 Sherwood Dr., Carol Stream, IL 60188 | 630-580-9745
sweeney2@comcast.net

Agents: Mark Sweeney, Janet Sweeney
Agency: Established in 2003. Represents 105 clients.
Types of books: memoir, narrative nonfiction, Christian living,
apologetics
Specialty: popular apologetics
New clients: Looking for authors with a great book idea who have

both the skill to communicate in writing and a platform from which to write. Initial contact: email, referral from current client. Query first. Responds in one week.

Commission: 15%

Fees: none

Tip: "Be as precise as possible in describing your book project and platform."

MARTIN LITERARY & MEDIA MANAGEMENT

914 164th St. S.E., Ste. B12, #307, Mill Creek, WA 98102 | 206- 466-1773

adria@martinliterarymanagment.com | *www.martinlit.com*

Agent: Adria Goetz

Agency: General agency established in 2003. Adria has more than twenty-five clients.

Types of books: picture books, middle grade, young adult, adult fiction/nonfiction, devotionals, Christian living, lifestyle

Specialty: "I look for books that delight readers, that help inspire wonder and imagination, that foster deep empathy and compassion for our fellow human beings, that provide rich character representation of marginalized people groups, that take the reader on an adventure, that uncover fascinating stories from history's footnotes, that explore issues of faith and how to apply Christ's teachings to our own life, that celebrate women and the female experience, that ask nitty gritty questions and don't settle for easy answers, that make people disappointed when they have to close the book and go to bed, and books that add a touch of magic to readers' lives."

New clients: Open to writers who have not published a book, self-published writers, writers met at conferences. Contact by email. Accepts simultaneous submissions. Responds in two weeks. Be sure to read *www.martinlit.com/submission-policy*.

Commission: 15%, foreign 25%

Other services: film and TV adaptation

Tip: "Check out my full wish list, which is updated frequently, at *adriagoetz.com*."

METAMORPHOSIS LITERARY AGENCY

646-397-1640

info@metamorphosisliteraryagency.com | *www.metamorphosisliteraryagency.com*

Agents: Stephanie Hansen, *info@metamorphosisliteraryagency.com*; Amy Brewer, *abrewer@metamorphosisliteraryagency.com*; Lauren Miller, *lmiller@metamorphosisliteraryagency.com*

Agency: General agency established in 2016. Represents ninety Christian clients.

Types of books: picture books, adult fiction, some nonfiction

New clients: Open to writers who have not published a book, well-established book writers, writers met at conferences. Initial contact: website form. Responds in three months.

Commission: 15%

Fees: none

Tip: "Our mission is to help authors become traditionally published. We represent well-crafted commercial fiction and nonfiction. Metamorphosis Literary Agency works with authors to ensure that every book is in the best presentable form. Our publishing connections come from numerous conferences, hard work, and genuine care. We do not charge reading fees as we adhere to the Association of Authors' Representatives' Canon of Ethics."

NATASHA KERN LITERARY AGENCY, INC.

PO Box 1069, White Salmon, WA 98672
agent@natashakern.com | *www.natashakernliterary.com*

Agent: Natasha Kern

Agency: Established in 1987. Represents thirty-six religious clients.

Types of books: adult fiction

New clients: Closed to queries from unpublished writers. Open to meeting with writers at conferences and accepting referrals from current clients and editors. Cannot read unsolicited queries or proposals.

THE SEYMOUR AGENCY

475 Miner Street Rd., Canton, NY 13617 | 239-398-8209
nicole@theseymouragency.com | *www.theseymouragency.com*

Agents: Nichole Resciniti; Julie Gwinn, *julie@theseymouragency.com*; Lizzie Poteet, *lizzie@theseymouragency.com*

Agency: Established in 1992. Member of Association of Authors' Representatives.

Types of books: inspirational, YA, middle grade, picture books, mysteries, thrillers, romance, science fiction, fantasy, women's fiction, literary fiction, historical fiction, speculative fiction, assorted nonfiction

New clients: Open to writers who have not published a book, well-established book writers, self-published writers, and writers met at conferences. Contact by email with one-page query first or referral from current client. Responds in two weeks to queries, three months to proposals.

Commission: 15%

Fees: none

Tip: "Hone your craft. Take advantage of writers groups, critique partners, etc., to polish your manuscript into the best shape it can be."

SPENCERHILL ASSOCIATES

8126 Lakewood Main St. #204, Lakewood Ranch, FL 34202 | 941-907-3700

submissions@spencerhillassociates.com | *www.spencerhillassociates.com*

Agent: Karen Solem

Agency: Member of Association of Authors' Representatives. Established in 2001. General agent who represents fifteen to twenty-five clients with religious books.

Types of books: adult fiction and nonfiction

New clients: Initial contact by querying through website form or email. Responds in three months.

Commission: 15%

STANLEY O. WILLIFORD LITERARY AGENCY

9013 Buckles St., Downey, CA 90241 | 562-382-3516

query@thewillifordagency.com

Agent: Stanley O. Williford

Agency: Established in 2016. Represents fifteen clients.

Types of books: any Christian

Specialty: Charismatic authors

New clients: Open to writers who have not published a book, well-established book writers, self-published writers, writers met at conferences. Initial contact: email with query, phone. Responds in two weeks.

Commission: 15%

Fees: none

Tip: "I will represent any Christian writer as long as he or she adheres to Christian precepts."

THE STEVE LAUBE AGENCY

24 W. Camelback Rd. A-635, Phoenix, AZ 85013 | 602-336-8910

info@stevelaube.com | www.stevelaube.com

Agents: Steve Laube, *krichards@stevelaube.com*; Tamela Hancock Murray, *ewilson@stevelaube.com*; Bob Hostetler, *rgwright@ stevelaube.com*

Agency: Established in 2004. Represents more than 330 clients.

Types of books: adult fiction in all subgenres and nonfiction of all types; see website blog post by each agent for what he or she is looking for

New clients: Open to unpublished and published authors. Email proposal as attachment according to the guidelines on the website. Steve Laube also will take proposals by mail. Accepts simultaneous submissions. Responds in eight weeks.

Commission: 15%

Fees: none

Tip: "Please follow the guidelines! Since your book proposal is like a job application, you want to present yourself in the most professional manner possible. Your proposal will be a simple vehicle to convey your idea to us and, ultimately, to a publisher."

SUSAN SCHULMAN LITERARY AGENCY LLC

454 W. 44, New York, NY 10036 | 917-488-0906
www.schulmanagency.com

Agents: Susan Schulman, *Susan@schulmanagency.com*; Christine LeBlond, *Cleblond@Schulmanagency.com*

Agency: General agency established in 1990. Represents 150 clients. Member of Association of Authors' Representatives.

Types of books: fiction, nonfiction

Specialty: books for, by, and about women and women's issues and interests

New clients: Open to writers at all levels, including self-published. Contact with email query or referral from current client. Accepts simultaneous submissions. Responds in two weeks.

Commission: 15%

Fees: none

Tip: "Know your market for your project. Please do not submit first drafts or unedited or unfinished projects."

VAN DIEST LITERARY AGENCY

34947 S.E. Brooks Rd., Boring, OR 97009 | 503-676-8009
david@christianliteraryagency.com | www.ChristianLiteraryAgency.com

Agent: David Van Diest

Agency: Established in 2003. Represents twenty-five clients.
Types of books: nonfiction, select fiction, children's
New clients: Open to unpublished authors. Contact by email through the website. Responds in one month or not interested.
Commission: 15%
Fees: none
Tip: "We believe the best books are yet to be written! We're not talking about 'new truth' revealed, but God's timeless truth delivered to a new audience, in a way that is fresh, understandable, and applicable to them and their lives."

WENDY SHERMAN ASSOCIATES, INC.

27 W. 24th St., Ste. 700B, New York, NY 10110 | 212-279-9027
submissions@wsherman.com | *www.wsherman.com*

Agents: Wendy Sherman, Cherise Fisher
Agency: General agency that handles some religious books. Established in 1999.
Types of books: adult spirituality and Christianity
New clients: Open to unpublished authors. Contact by email query only. Guidelines on the website.
Commission: 15%
Tip: "We have infinite respect for those writers who craft compelling query letters and follow our guidelines. Remember, there is an art to creating a truly sensational query letter!"

WHEELHOUSE LITERARY GROUP

Nashville, TN
info@wheelhouseliterary.com | *www.wheelhouseliterarygroup.com*

Agent: Jonathan Clements
Agency: Established in 2010 after Jonathan worked for five years with authors and brands for another agency.
Types of books: inspirational, historical, contemporary, military fiction; biography/memoir, sports, current events, pop culture
New clients: Email or send through the website form, following the requirements on the site. Responds in two months if interested in more information.

WILLIAM K. JENSEN LITERARY AGENCY

119 Bampton Ct., Eugene, OR 97404 | 541-688-1612
queries@wkjagency.com | *www.wkjagency.com*

Agents: William K. Jensen, Rachel MacMillan, Teresa Evenson

Agency: Established in 2005. Represents more than fifty clients.

Types of books: most types of Christian books, including Christian living, devotional, marriage, family life, apologetics, biography, gift books, cookbooks, prophecy, humor, health, inspirational, political, social issues, women's and men's issues, adult fiction; no science fiction, fantasy, or youth

New clients: Open to unpublished authors. Contact by email only; no attachments. See the website for complete query details. Accepts simultaneous submissions. Responds in one month or not interested.

Commission: 15%

Fees: none

WINTERS & KING, INC.

2448 E. 81st St., Ste. 5900, Tulsa, OK 74137-4259 | 918-494-6868
dboyd@wintersking.com |
wintersking.com/practice-areas/publishing-agent-services

Agent: Thomas J. Winters

Agency: Established in 1983. Represents 150 clients. Part of a law firm.

Types of books: fiction, nonfiction

New clients: Open to well-established book writers only. Contact by email. Responds in two weeks.

Commission: 15%

Fees: none

Other services: Legal review of publishing contracts, drafting of work-for-hire agreements to contract writer/editor services, copyright/trademark filing

Tip: "Submissions should be carefully edited and free of typos. Accompanying manuscripts or sample chapters for presentation to publishers should be edited, typo-free, and basically print-ready."

WOLGEMUTH & ASSOCIATES

Aurora, CO | 407-909-9445
info@wolgemuthandassociates.com | *www.wolgemuthandassociates.com*

Agents: Robert Wolgemuth, Andrew Wolgemuth, Erik Wolgemuth, Austin Wilson

Agency: Established in 1992. Member of Association of Authors' Representatives.

Types of books: teen/YA and adult nonfiction

New clients: Only authors
book or by referral fron
email. Accepts simulta
Commission: 15%
Fees: none

WORDSERVE LITER/

7500 E. Arapahoe Rd., St
303-471-6675
admin@wordserveliterar

Agents: Greg Johns
Freese, *sarah@u*
wordserveliterary.com;

Agency: Established in 2003. Represe..

Types of books: Any and all Christian books in no...
fiction, as well as children's, gift books, and specialty. In the general
market, we are successfully placing books in business, health,
military, history, memoir, and YA fiction and are open to other
select genres.

New clients: Open to writers who have not published a book, self-
published writers, and writers met at conferences. Launches ten to
fifteen new authors every year. Has an active presence with general-
market houses for authors with strong and growing platforms.
Email query first. Accepts simultaneous submissions. Responds in
one to two months.

Commission: 15%

Fees: none

Other services: For agency clients, we can help with publishing via
FaithHappenings Publishers, an arm of the agency for books authors
need right away, those that aren't sold to traditional publishers, and
out-of-print books the author needs back in circulation.

Tip: "Follow instructions on how to query our agency on our website.
If you send your query to one of the agents' direct emails, it will
still be considered; but you will not receive an automatic response.
After sixty days, you may assume your project isn't right for us."

WORDWISE MEDIA SERVICES

4083 Avenue L, Ste. 255, Lancaster, CA 93536 | 661-382-8083
get.wisewords@gmail.com | *www.wordwisemedia.com*

Agents: Steven Hutson (owner), *steve@wordwisemedia.com*; David
Fessenden; Michelle S. Lazurek

11. Represents sixty clients, half
. Member of Association of Authors'

vels and nonfiction for adults and children, picture

pen to unpublished book authors. Prefers referrals or
e meets. For all submissions, use the query form on the
. For other inquiries, phone or email is OK; no postal mail.
pts simultaneous submissions. Responds in one month; OK
nudge after then.

mission: 15%

ees: maybe for printing and postage at cost for a manuscript mailed
to a publisher

Tip: "For all submissions, please follow the instructions on the website
carefully. Specify the agent's name in the email subject line if you
have a preference."

YATES & YATES

1551 N. Tustin Ave., Ste. 710, Santa Ana, CA 92705 | 714-480-4000
email@yates2.com | www.yates2.com

Agents: Sealy Yates, Matt Yates, Curtis Yates, Mike Salisbury
Agency: Established in 1989.
Types of books: adult nonfiction
New clients: No unpublished authors. Contact by email.
Commission: negotiable
Tip: "Our holistic approach combines agency representation, expert
legal advice, marketing guidance, career coaching, creative
counseling, and business-management consulting. We work with
clients to focus their efforts, hone and sharpen their messages,
obtain broad distribution, increase their influence, and build a
lasting and successful career. In short, we help our clients make
their ideas matter."

Christian Writers Institute Courses
2020 Literary Agent Bundle

Courses in this bundle:

- The Elements of an Effective Book Proposal
- The 10 Ks of a Good Book
- Do I Need an Agent?
- Mistakes New Writers Make
- How to Use *The Christian Writers Market Guide*
- How to Sell Everything You Write
- Redeeming Rejection
- The Publishing Process
- The Power Book Proposal
- The Ten Enemies of Good Writing

Normal price: $85
Savings: 53%
Market Guide price $39.95

https://cwmg.link/agents2020

How to Scan QR Codes

Use the camera on your smartphone to focus on the above QR code to activate the discount. It will give you the option to visit the site, which you will want to accept. If you are using an older smartphone, you may need to download a QR code scanning app. You can also visit the URL below the code to activate the discount on your computer.

17

WRITERS CONFERENCES AND SEMINARS

SOUTHERN CHRISTIAN WRITERS CONFERENCE

Tuscaloosa, Al | June | *www.southernchristianwriters.com*

> **Director:** Cheryl Wray, *scwritersconference@gmail.com*
> **Description:** The SCWC is a two-day conference for beginners or experienced writers that focuses on several genres: nonfiction books, magazines, fiction, grammar, business aspects, legal aspects, etc.
> **Faculty includes:** editors, agents, and publishers
> **Attendance:** 160-200

ARIZONA

AMERICAN CHRISTIAN WRITERS MENTORING RETREAT

Phoenix, AZ | September 11-12 | *acwriters.com*

> **Director:** Reg A. Forder, PO Box 110390, Nashville, TN 37222; 800-21-WRITE; *ACWriters@aol.com*
> **Description:** Two-day intensive, hands-on work on a manuscript submitted in advance. Teachers include Lin Johnson and Jim Watkins.
> **Attendance:** 6-30

CALIFORNIA

MOUNT HERMON CHRISTIAN WRITERS CONFERENCE

Mount Hermon, CA (near Santa Cruz) | April 3-7 (preconference clinics April 1-3) | *writers.mounthermon.org*

Director: Kathy Ide, 37 Conference Dr., Felton, CA 95018; 831-335-4466; *Kathy.Ide@MountHermon.org*

Description: For more than fifty years, the Mount Hermon Christian Writers Conference has helped writers learn, connect, network, and achieve the publishing goals God has for them, all at an inspirational retreat center nestled in the beautiful California redwoods. Whether you desire to publish the traditional way with a royalty publisher or you intend to go the indie-publishing route, you'll find agents, editors, and fellow writers who can instruct, direct, and encourage you.

Faculty includes: editors, agents, and publishers

Speaker: Charles Martin

Special tracks: advanced writers, teens

Scholarships: partial, full

Attendance: 300

Contest: First-Timers Contest awards ten full scholarships, including meals and lodging, for people who have never attended a Mount Hermon Christian Writers Conference

PENCON

CA | July 8-11 | *penconeditors.com*

Director: Cristel Phelps, *admin@penconeditors.com*

Description: PENCON is the only conference for editors in the Christian market. Note: This conference changes location every year.

Faculty includes: editors and publishers

Scholarships: full and partial

Attendance: 75

SoCAL CHRISTIAN WRITERS' CONFERENCE

Azusa, CA | July 8-11 | *www.SoCalCWC.com*

Director: Kathy Ide, *KathyIde@SoCalCWC.com*

Description: With agents, acquisitions editors, and multipublished authors, we offer excellent opportunities to meet with and learn from top-name professionals in the Christian publishing industry.

Faculty includes: editors, agents, publishers

Scholarships: full and partial

Attendance: 150

Contest: Promising Beginnings contest offers one full scholarship, including meals, lodging, and travel stipend.

WEST COAST CHRISTIAN WRITERS LIT MASTERCLASS

Livermore, CA | February 28-29 | *www.westcoastchristianwriters.com*

Director: Susy Flory, *westcoastchristianwriters@gmail.com*

Description: The LIT Masterclass is aimed at intermediate to advanced writers, giving them the opportunity to get individualized help with their work-in-progress. This year, the conference will include both small mastermind groups (circles) and workshops.

Faculty includes: editors, agents,

Speakers: Sharon Elliott, Bob Hostetler

Scholarships: partial

Attendance: 75

Contest: Awards for fiction and nonfiction. Check our website for details.

COLORADO

COLORADO CHRISTIAN WRITERS CONFERENCE

Estes Park, CO | May 13-16 | *colorado.writehisanswer.com*

Director: Marlene Bagnull, 951 Anders Rd., Lansdale, PA 19446; 484-991-8581; *mbagnull@aol.com*

Description: To encourage and equip you to write about a God who is real, is reachable, and changes lives. Sharpen your writing and marketing skills from your choice of eight continuing sessions and more than fifty workshops. Seven keynotes, four or more one-on-one 15-minute appointments.

Special track: teens

Faculty includes: editors, agents, and publishers

Scholarships: partial

Attendance: 220

Contest: For registered conferees. Entries based on the conference theme of "Write/Live His Answer" from Habakkuk 2:2. Prose (maximum 500 words) or poetry by published and not-yet-published authors. The winner in each of the four categories receives 50% off the registration fee for the following year. Entry fee $10.

EVANGELICAL PRESS ASSOCIATION ANNUAL CHRISTIAN MEDIA CONVENTION

Colorado Springs, CO | April 15-17 | *epaconvention.com*

> **Director:** Lamar Keener, Executive Director, PO Box 1787, Queen Creek, AZ 85142; 888-311-1732; *director@evangelicalpress.com*
>
> **Description:** A convention for everyone involved in Christian periodicals and content-based websites. Preconference intensive on content strategy with Lou Ann Sabatier. Note: This conference changes locations every year.
>
> **Faculty includes:** editors, publishers
>
> **Attendance:** 200
>
> **Contest:** for members of the Evangelical Press Association, including freelance writers who enter articles or blog posts

WRITE IN THE SPRINGS CONFERENCE

Colorado Springs, CO | April 3-4 | *www.acfwcosprings.com/WITS2020*

> **Director:** Erin Kohler, *erin730kohler@gmail.com*
>
> **Description:** Annual conference for Christian writers of all genres in the breathtaking Rocky Mountains. Dubbed "one of the best small conferences consistently year after year."
>
> **Faculty includes:** editors
>
> **Speaker:** Susan May Warren
>
> **Scholarships:** full
>
> **Attendance:** 65

WRITERS ON THE ROCK

Denver, CO | February 29 | *www.writersontherock.com*

> **Director:** David Rupert, 14473 W. 3rd, Golden, CO 80401; 720-237-7487; *conference@writersontherock.com*
>
> **Description:** A yearly gathering of Christian writers in our community who come from a variety of experience levels in order to write the words that will help change the world.
>
> **Attendance:** 300

CONNECTICUT

reNEW RETREAT FOR NEW ENGLAND WRITING & SPEAKING

West Hartford, CT | October 9-11 | *www.reNEWwriting.com*

Director: Lucinda Secrest McDowell, reNEW Writing, PO Box 290707, Wethersfield, CT 06129; 860-402-9551; *info@ reNEWwriting.com*

Description: reNEW is a spiritual retreat for writers and speakers— "Renewed in knowledge after the image of Him" (Colossians 3:10). Our creative community focuses on honing our craft (teaching and workshops), writing time, worship, an encouraging community, and growing in faith.

Faculty includes: editors, agents, publishers

Special track: speaking

Scholarships: partial

Attendance: 70

DELAWARE

DELMARVA CHRISTIAN WRITERS CONFERENCE

Georgetown, DE | October 17 | *delmarvawriters.com/conference*

Director: Candy Abbott, Crossroad Community Church, 20864 State Forest Rd., Georgetown, DE 19947; 302-542-8510; *info@ delmarvawriters.com*

Description: Sponsored by Delmarva Christian Writers Association, the conference features a keynote speaker, morning and afternoon workshops, continental breakfast and lunch, plus other activities.

Faculty includes: editors

Scholarships: full

Attendance: 60

FLORIDA

AMERICAN CHRISTIAN WRITERS MENTORING RETREAT

Orlando, FL | November 13-14 | *acwriters.com*

Director: Reg A. Forder, PO Box 110390, Nashville, TN 37222; 800-21-WRITE; *ACWriters@aol.com*

Description: Two-day intensive, hands-on work on a manuscript submitted in advance. Teachers include Lin Johnson and Jim Watkins.

Attendance: 6-30

FLORIDA CHRISTIAN WRITERS CONFERENCE

Leesburg, FL | October 21-25 | *word-weavers.com/floridaevents*

Director: Eva Marie Everson, PO Box 520224, Longwood, FL 32752; 407-615-4112; *FloridaCWC@aol.com*

Description: We have moved from spring to autumn! As always, we bring in the best in Christian publishing, from agents to editors, publishers to freelance writers and speakers. We offer eight to ten continuing sessions and nearly 60 workshops over the course of our four-day conference. A not-to-be-missed conference for writers of all genres and levels.

Special tracks: teens, advanced writers, speaking

Faculty includes: editors, agents, and publishers

Speaker: Bill Myers

Scholarships: full, partial

Attendance: 250

Contest: See the website for details.

GEORGIA

AMERICAN CHRISTIAN WRITERS MENTORING RETREAT

Atlanta, GA | July 10-11 | *acwriters.com*

Director: Reg A. Forder, PO Box 110390, Nashville, TN 37222; 800-21-WRITE; *ACWriters@aol.com*

Description: Two-day intensive, hands-on work on a manuscript submitted in advance. Teachers include Lin Johnson and Jim Watkins.

Attendance: 6-30

WORD WEAVERS INTERNATIONAL KID'S LIT CONFERENCE

Toccoa, GA | March 19-22 | *word-weavers.com/georgiaevents*

Director: Eva Marie Everson, PO Box 520224, Longwood, FL 32752; 407-615-4112; *wordweaversinternational@aol.com*

Description: Our spring conference is genre specific. This year we will focus on Kid's Lit, bringing in the top agents, editors, and freelancers to encourage, meet with, instruct, and excite children's book writers. We will span from board books to young adult.

Faculty includes: editors, agents, and publishers

Speaker: Dandi Daley Mackall

Scholarships: partial, full

Attendance: 50
Contest: See website for details.

ILLINOIS

WRITE-TO-PUBLISH CONFERENCE

Wheaton, IL (Chicago area) | June 17-20 | *www.writetopublish.com*

Director: Lin Johnson, 9118 W. Elmwood Dr., Ste. 1G, Niles, IL 60714-5820; 847-296-3964; *lin@writetopublish.com*

Description: For more than 40 years, Write-to-Publish has been training writers and connecting them with editors who want to publish their work and with literary agents who want to represent them. You will hear what editors, publishers, and agents in the Christian market are looking for and meet with them one-on-one to discuss your ideas and manuscripts. You also will learn how to write a variety of publishable manuscripts, improve your writing skills, find appropriate markets for your ideas, and deal with the business side of writing. Plus you will have multiple opportunities to get feedback on your manuscripts.

Faculty includes: editors, agents, and publishers

Plenary speaker: Allie Pleiter

Attendance: 150-175

Contest: Best New Writer and Writer of the Year awards, both for alumni who attend this year. Serious Writer contests in multiple genres for unpublished and published writers.

INDIANA

TAYLOR UNIVERSITY'S PROFESSIONAL WRITERS' CONFERENCE

Upland, IN | July 24-25 | *taylorprofessionalwritersconferences.weebly.com*

Director: Linda K. Taylor, 236 W. Reade Ave., Upland, IN 46989; 765-998-5591; *TaylorPRWConference@gmail.com*

Description: Hear from agents, editors, and authors who will inspire and encourage you. The new one-extra-day track on Thursday, July 23, will include an advanced track for writers ready for more and a teen track for those looking to discover more about the publishing world.

Faculty includes: editors, agents, publishers

Speakers: Lissa Halls Johnson, James Watkins

Special track: teens, advanced writers
Attendance: 120

KANSAS

CALLED TO WRITE
Pittsburg, KS | April 3-4 | *calledtowriteconference.wordpress.com*
> **Director:** Barbara Gordon, PO Box 33, Moundville, MO 64771;
> *calledtowriteconference@gmail.com*
> **Description:** The Called to Write Conference is an annual conference
> sponsored by Christian Writers Fellowship, Girard, KS. Main
> sessions and workshops are designed for both beginning and
> seasoned writers.
> **Faculty includes:** editors
> **Scholarships:** partial
> **Attendance:** 50
> **Contest:** for fiction, nonfiction, poetry, devotionals, children's fiction,
> and children's nonfiction

KENTUCKY

KENTUCKY CHRISTIAN WRITERS CONFERENCE
Elizabethtown, KY | June 18-20 | *www.kychristianwriters.com*
> **Director:** Hallee Bridgman, PO Box 2719, Elizabethtown, KY 42702;
> *info@kychristianwriters.com*
> **Description:** The KCWC is an annual conference designed to
> encourage and equip Christian writers in their quest for
> publication. The 2020 theme is Write the Vision.
> **Faculty includes:** editors, agents, publishers
> **Special track:** teens
> **Speaker:** Bob Hostetler
> **Scholarships:** partial
> **Attendance:** 100

MICHIGAN

AMERICAN CHRISTIAN WRITERS MENTORING RETREAT
Grand Rapids, MI | June 5-6 | *acwriters.com*

Director: Reg A. Forder, PO Box 110390, Nashville, TN 37222; 800-21-WRITE; *ACWriters@aol.com*
Description: Two-day intensive, hands-on work on a manuscript submitted in advance. Teachers include Jim Watkins.
Attendance: 6-30

BREATHE CHRISTIAN WRITERS CONFERENCE

Grand Rapids, MI | October 18-19 | *www.breatheconference.com*

Director: Ann Byle, 1765 3 Mile Rd. N.E., Grand Rapids, MI 49515; 616-389-4436; *register@breatheconference.com*
Description: Breathe offers thirty-six breakouts, two plenary breakouts, and two keynote addresses, with sessions for both advanced and beginning writers. We have a strong community feel and welcome all writers.
Faculty includes: editors, agents, and publishers
Scholarships: full
Attendance: 160
Contest: See website.

MARANATHA CHRISTIAN WRITERS' CONFERENCE

Norton Shores, MI | October 1-3 | *www.maranathachristianwriters.com*

Director: Sherry Hoppen, 4759 Lake Harbor Rd., Norton Shores, MI 49441; 231-798-2161; *info@maranathachristianwriters.com*
Description: A broad variety of publishers, agents, and editors. Up to five one-to-one appointments with the experts at no additional charge.
Faculty includes: agents, editors, and publishers
Scholarships: partial
Attendance: 80

SPEAKUP CONFERENCE

Grand Rapids, MI | July 9-11 | *www.speakupconference.com*

Director: *bonnie@speakupconference.com*
Description: Offers two tracks: writing and speaking. In the speakers track, you have an opportunity to try out what you are learning in small, interactive groups with a trained professional leading the feedback. In the writers track, you may preselect up to four 15-minute appointments with writing professionals.
Faculty includes: editors, agents, publishers
Scholarships: partial

MINNESOTA

AMERICAN CHRISTIAN WRITERS MENTORING RETREAT

Minneapolis, MN | August 7-8 | *acwriters.com*

Director: Reg A. Forder, PO Box 110390, Nashville, TN 37222; 800-21-WRITE; *ACWriters@aol.com*

Description: Two-day intensive, hands-on work on a manuscript submitted in advance. Teachers include Lin Johnson and Jim Watkins.

Attendance: 6-30

THE BUSINESS OF BEING A SPIRITUAL WRITER

Minneapolis, MN | April 29 | *writingforyourlife.com/conferences*

Director: Brian Allain, *brian@writingforyourlife.com*

Description: Not only do authors need a platform, they must enter the market strategically in order to make that platform, and that book, happen. They must operate like an entrepreneur—agile, flexible, and creative in their business. This seminar is a step-by-step roadmap of best practices for figuring it all out.

Attendance: 30

NORTHWESTERN CHRISTIAN WRITERS CONFERENCE

St. Paul, MN | July 24-25 | *www.northwesternchristianwritersconference.com*

Contact: *ncwc@unwsp.edu*, 866-821-5151

Description: Northwestern Christian Writers Conference is your opportunity to learn from successful authors, acquisitions editors, and literary agents. Gather with writers from around the country to be encouraged, equipped, and inspired. Learn from and ask questions of other industry experts during the breakout sessions.

Faculty includes: editors, agents

Scholarships: partial

WRITING FOR YOUR LIFE

Minneapolis, MN | April 27-28 | *writingforyourlife.com/conferences*

Director: Brian Allain, *brian@writingforyourlife.com*

Description: The conference is open to all who are interested in spiritual writing, as well as those interested in reading spiritual books.

Speaker: Barbara Brown Taylor

Attendance: 100

MISSOURI

AMERICAN CHRISTIAN FICTION WRITERS (ACFW) CONFERENCE

St. Louis, MO | September 17-20 | *www.ACFW.com/conference*

Director: Robin Miller, PO Box 101066, Palm Bay, FL 32910-1066; *director@ACFW.com*

Description: Continuing education sessions and workshop electives specifically geared for five levels of fiction-writing experience from beginner to advanced. New: Track for readers, ACFW Storyfest.

Special track: advanced writers

Faculty includes: editors and agents

Scholarships: full

Attendance: 500

Contest: The Genesis Contest is for unpublished writers whose Christian fiction manuscript is completed. The Carol Awards honor the best of Christian fiction from the previous calendar year.

HEART OF AMERICA CHRISTIAN WRITERS NETWORK

Kansas City, MO | October | *www.hacwn.org*

Director: Jeanette Littleton, 3706 N.E. Shady Lane Dr., Gladstone, MO 64119; 816-459-8016; *jeanettedl@earthlink.net*

Description: We specialize in having faculty who are looking for new writers.

Faculty includes: editors, agents, and publishers

Attendance: 100

Contests: In eight categories. Prizes include critiques and consultations.

NEW JERSEY

REALM MAKERS

Atlantic City, NJ | July 16-18| *www.realmmakers.com*

Director: Becky Minor, 939 N. Washington St., Pottstown, PA 19464; *info@faithandfantasyalliance.com*

Description: Realm Makers is for writers of faith who create science fiction, fantasy, and related subgenres. Note: This conference changes location every year.

Scholarships: full and partial, based on merit and needs

Faculty includes: agents and editors from both CBA and general markets

Attendance: 200+
Contest: for published books and book covers with cash awards

NEW YORK

THE BUSINESS OF BEING A SPIRITUAL WRITER

New York City, NY | June 29 | *writingforyourlife.com/conferences*

> **Director:** Brian Allain, *brian@writingforyourlife.com*
> **Description:** Not only do authors need a platform, they must enter the market strategically in order to make that platform, and that book, happen. They must operate like an entrepreneur—agile, flexible, and creative in their business. This seminar is a step-by-step roadmap of best practices for figuring it all out.
> **Attendance:** 30

NORTH CAROLINA

ASHEVILLE CHRISTIAN WRITERS CONFERENCE

Asheville, NC | February 21-23 |
www.ashevillechristianwritersconference.com

> **Director:** Cindy Sproles, PO Box 6494, Kingsport, TN 37663; *cindybootcamp@gmail.com*
> **Description:** Held at the Cove, the Billy Graham Training Center, ACWC caters to conferees by giving personal, one-on-one attention and helping guide writers to their calling within the writing world.
> **Faculty includes:** editors, agents, publishers
> **Speakers:** Bob Hostetler, Eva Marie Everson, Larry Leech
> **Scholarships:** partial
> **Attendance:** 120
> **Contest:** Sparrow Book Award for a new manuscript and the opportunity for the winning book to be seen by a publishing board

BLUE RIDGE MOUNTAINS CHRISTIAN WRITERS CONFERENCE

Black Mountain, NC | May 24-28 | www.*BlueRidgeConference.com*

> **Director:** Edie Melson, 604 S. Almond Dr., Simpsonville, SC 29681; 864-373-4232; *Edie@ediemelson.com*
> **Description:** We are a multidiscipline conference equipping writers of all levels and changing the world one writer at a time.

Special tracks: advanced writers, teens, speaking
Faculty includes: editors, agents
Scholarships: partial
Attendance: 550
Contests: Selah, open to published writers (traditional and self-published); Director's Choice, open to former conferees who have a published book (traditional or self-published); Foundation Awards, open to unpublished attendees

THE BUSINESS OF BEING A SPIRITUAL WRITER

Charlotte, NC | March 26 | *writingforyourlife.com/the-business-of-being-a-spiritual-writer-charlotte-2020*

Director: Brian Allain, *brian@writingforyourlife.com*
Description: Not only do authors need a platform, they must enter the market strategically in order to make that platform, and that book, happen. They must operate like an entrepreneur—agile, flexible, and creative in their business. This seminar is a step-by-step roadmap of best practices for figuring it all out.
Attendance: 30

MOUNTAINSIDE MARKETING CONFERENCE

Black Mountain, NC | January 17-20 | *www.MountainsideMarketingConference.com/event/mountainsidemarketing*

Director: Edie Melson, 604 S. Almond Dr., Simpsonville, SC 29681; 864-373-4232; *Edie@ediemelson.com*
Description: A blogging, branding, and social media conference.
Speakers: Edie Melson, DiAnn Mills
Attendance: 50

MOUNTAINSIDE NOVELIST RETREAT

Black Mountain, NC | October 4-7 | *ridgecrestconferencecenter.org/event/mountainsidenovelist*

Directors: Edie Melson, DiAnn Mills, *edie@ediemelson.com*
Description: Writing craft and creativity. Professional faculty. Small, intimate group, critiques, contests, workshops, private appointments, writing time, and fun.
Faculty includes: editors, agents, publishers
Special track: advanced writers
Attendance: 25-35
Contest: For unpublished writers: Best Title, First Sentence, First Paragraph, First Page, Proposal, Golden Leaf Award

SHE SPEAKS CONFERENCE

Concord, NC | July 31—August 1 | *shespeaksconference.com*

> **Director:** Lisa Allen, 630 Team Rd. #100, Matthews, NC 28105; 704-849-2270; *shespeaks@Proverbs31.org*
> **Description:** Speaking and writing tracks.
> **Faculty includes:** editors and agents
> **Attendance:** 700

WRITING FOR YOUR LIFE

Charlotte, NC | March 24-25 | *writingforyourlife.com/charlotte-2020*

> **Director:** Brian Allain, *brian@writingforyourlife.com*
> **Description:** The conference is open to all who are interested in spiritual writing, as well as those interested in reading spiritual books.
> **Faculty includes:** agents
> **Speaker:** Barbara Brown Taylor
> **Attendance:** 100

OHIO

OHIO CHRISTIAN WRITERS CONFERENCE

Ashville, OH | November | *ohiochristianwriters.com*

> **Director:** Cody Morehead, 735 Reading Rd., Mason, OH 45040; 937-207-3152; *cody@realpubzoo.com*
> **Description:** Engaging and relevant.
> **Special track:** advanced writers
> **Faculty includes:** editors, agents, publishers
> **Attendance:** 100+
> **Contest:** Almost an Author and Blue Seal Awards

OREGON

OREGON CHRISTIAN WRITERS FALL CONFERENCE

Tualatin (Portland), OR | October | *www.oregonchristianwriters.org*

> **Contact:** Tracie Heskett, 1075 Willow Lake Rd. N., Keizer, OR 97303; 503-393-3356; *contact@oregonchristianwriters.org*
> **Description:** Two morning keynote addresses and two workshops with four choices each.
> **Speaker:** Roseanna White
> **Attendance:** 125

OREGON CHRISTIAN WRITERS SPRING CONFERENCE

Eugene, OR | May 6 | *www.oregonchristianwriters.org*

Contact: Tracie Heskett, 1075 Willow Lake Rd. N., Keizer, OR 97303; 503-393-3356; *contact@oregonchristianwriters.org*

Speaker: Matt Mikalatos

Description: Two morning keynote addresses and two workshops with four choices each.

Attendance: 100

OREGON CHRISTIAN WRITERS SUMMER COACHING CONFERENCE

Portland, OR | August 17-20 | *www.oregonchristianwriters.org*

Director: Lindy Jacobs, 1075 Willow Lake Rd. N., Kelzer, OR 97303; 503-393-3356; *summerconf@oregonchristianwriters.org*

Description: Annual four-day conference offers one-on-one meetings with editors and agents, manuscript reviews, mentoring, intensive coaching classes in the craft of writing for beginning writers as well as published authors. Highlights include daily worship, inspiring keynotes, professional panels, and early-morning devotions.

Special tracks: preconference seminar with Christopher Vogler, advanced writers, teens, speaking

Faculty includes: editors, agents

Speakers: Rachel Hauck, Brett Lott

Scholarships: partial

Attendance: 275

Contest: Cascade Writing Contest (see Chapter 23 "Contests") winners are announced during this conference

OREGON CHRISTIAN WRITERS WINTER CONFERENCE

Salem, OR | February 22 | *www.oregonchristianwriters.org*

Contact: Tracie Heskett, 1075 Willow Lake Rd. N., Keizer, OR 97303; 503-393-3356; *contact@oregonchristianwriters.org*

Description: Two morning keynote addresses and two workshops with four choices each.

Speaker: Sarah Sundin

Attendance: 125

PENNSYLVANIA

GREATER PHILADELPHIA CHRISTIAN WRITERS CONFERENCE

Lansdale, PA | end of July/early August | *philadelphia.writehisanswer.com*

Director: Marlene Bagnull, 951 Anders Rd., Lansdale, PA 19446; 484-991-8581; *mbagnull@aol.com*

Description: To encourage and equip you to write about a God who is real, who is reachable, and who changes lives. Seven continuing sessions, forty-two workshops, six keynotes, authors night, and book signing.

Special track: teens

Faculty includes: editors, agents, and publishers

Scholarships: partial

Attendance: 200

Contest: For registered conferees. Entries based on the conference theme of "Write/Live His Answer" from Habakkuk 2:2. Prose (maximum 500 words) or poetry by published and not-yet-published authors. The winner in each of the four categories receives 50% off the registration fee for the following year. Entry fee $10.

LANCASTER CHRISTIAN WRITERS ANNUAL ONE-DAY CONFERENCE

Lancaster, PA | April 4 | *lancasterchristianwriterstoday.blogspot.com*

Director: Jeanette Windle, *jeanette@jeanettewindle.com*

Description: One-day conference with fiction and nonfiction tracks, keynote, bookstore, and individual consultations with faculty.

Attendance: 80

MONTROSE CHRISTIAN WRITERS CONFERENCE

Montrose, PA | July 12-17 | *www.montrosebible.org/OurEvents.aspx*

Director: Marsha Hubler, 1833 Dock Hill Rd., Middleburg, PA 17842; 570-837-0002; *marshahubler@outlook.com*

Description: The Montrose Christian Writers Conference offers classes and workshops not only for published authors but also for beginners. The classes focus on all genres, social media, marketing, and music composition. Every year, conferees say the highlight of their week was the praise and worship time every morning before classes begin.

Faculty includes: editors and agents

Special tracks: advanced writers and teens
Scholarships: partial, including Shirley Brinkerhoff Memorial Scholarship, a $200 grant toward tuition, given to a writer who has not yet secured a book contract but is actively striving to hone the craft of writing
Attendance: 75

ST. DAVIDS CHRISTIAN WRITERS' CONFERENCE

Grove City, PA | June 24-28 | *www.stdavidswriters.com/conference*

> **Director:** Sue Boltz, *treasurer@stdavidswriters.com*
> **Description:** Small Christian writers conference to learn, grow, and connect in your writing journey.
> **Faculty includes:** editors and agents
> **Speakers:** Eva Marie Everson, Sally Apokedak, Bob Hostetler
> **Scholarships:** full and partial
> **Attendance:** 45
> **Contests:** See detailed list on the website.

SOUTH CAROLINA

CAROLINA CHRISTIAN WRITERS CONFERENCE

Spartanburg, SC | March 27-28 | *www.fbs.org/writers*

> **Director:** Linda Gilden, 250 E. Main St., Spartanburg, SC 29360; 864-583-7245; *linda@lindagilden.com*
> **Description:** This conference focuses on encouraging writers to take their writing to the next level and to write with excellence.
> **Faculty includes:** editors, agents, publishers
> **Scholarships:** full
> **Attendance:** 100
> **Contest:** in several genres for all levels of writers

WRITE2IGNITE CONFERENCE FOR CHRISTIAN WRITERS OF CHILDREN AND YOUNG ADULT LITERATURE

Tigerville, SC | September | *write2ignite.com*

> **Director:** Deborah S. DeCiantis, PO Box 41, Tigerville, SC 29688; 803-517-4143; *info.write2ignite@gmail.com*
> **Description:** Write2Ignite seeks to: (1) inspire and challenge novice to experienced writers, middle school through adult, to serve God and young readers through their writing; (2) facilitate Christian writers' development by providing instruction on writing craft and

professional publishing, especially of children's and young-adult literature; and (3) connect authors with one another and with published authors, editors and literary agents, illustrators, and other writing and publishing professionals.

Faculty inludes: editors, agents, and publishers
Special tracks: teens, advanced writers
Scholarships: full, partial
Attendance: 55-80
Contest: Unpublished Picture Book manuscript

TENNESSEE

AMERICAN CHRISTIAN WRITERS MENTORING RETREAT

Nashville, TN | April 17-18 and October 2-3 | *acwriters.com*

Director: Reg A. Forder, PO Box 110390, Nashville, TN 37222; 800-21-WRITE; *ACWriters@aol.com*
Description: Two-day intensive, hands-on work on a manuscript submitted in advance. Teachers include Lin Johnson and Jim Watkins.
Attendance: 6-30

THE ART OF WRITING

Nashville, TN | November 7 | *www.christyawards.com*

Director: Cindy Carter, ECPA, *info@christyawards.com*
Description: A focused conference for writers, storytellers, and publishing curators. Held in conjunction with the Christy Awards.
Faculty includes: editors, publishers
Attendance: 150

MID-SOUTH CHRISTIAN WRITERS CONFERENCE

Collierville, TN | March 20-21 | *MidSouthChristianWriters.com*

Director: April Carpenter, PO Box 236, Nesbit, MS 38651; 901-378-0504; *registration@midsouthchristianwriters.com*
Description: The MSCWC encourages beginning and experienced communicators to develop their writing talents for God's glory. All who enjoy writing are welcome.
Faculty includes: editors, agents, publishers
Speaker: Rachel Hauck
Attendance: 125

TEXAS

BAYOU CITY CHRISTIAN WRITERS CONFERENCE

Houston, TX | October | *wotsACFW.blogspot.com*

> **Director:** Kathrese McKee, 8715 Green Hollow Ln., Spring, TX 77379; 281-787-6938; *wots.ACFW@gmail.com*
>
> **Description:** Bayou City Christian Writers Conference was created to support and educate Christian authors, particularly fiction authors, on matters of craft, networking, and marketing. Writers ages 13 and up are welcome.
>
> **Special track:** advanced writers
>
> **Attendance:** 35
>
> **Contest:** This contest is held in conjunction with the Storming the Short Story Contest. Information will be published on the website.

COLLAB CONFERENCE

Waco, TX | April 15-17 | *www.collab-conference.com*

> **Director:** Elizabeth Oates, 712 Austin Ave., Waco, TX 76712; 254-855-9429; *info@collab-conference.com*
>
> **Description:** Collab Conference is a distinct Christian women's conference for those longing to live out their God-given calling through writing, blogging, speaking, teaching, and leading.
>
> **Faculty includes:** agents
>
> **Scholarships:** full
>
> **Attendance:** 50

TEXAS CHRISTIAN WRITERS CONFERENCE

Houston, TX | August | *www.centralhoustoniwa.com*

> **Director:** Martha Rogers, 6038 Greenmont, Houston, TX 77092; 713-686-7209; *marthalrogers@sbcglobal.net*
>
> **Faculty includes:** editors
>
> **Attendance:** 60
>
> **Contests:** Inspirational Writers Alive! Open Writing Competition

WASHINGTON

NORTHWEST CHRISTIAN WRITERS RENEWAL

Bellevue, WA | May 15-16 | *www.nwchristianwriters.org/2020Renewal*

> **Directors:** Charles and Perry Harris, PO Box 2706, Woodinville, WA 98072; 206-250-6885; *renewal@nwchristianwriters.org*

Description: This conference is where writers, editors, and publishers can connect, network, and collaborate. Conferees will sharpen their skills, learn strategies, and form connections to boost their success on the writing journey.
Faculty includes: editors, agents, publishers
Speaker: Mary Demuth
Scholarships: full
Attendance: 130

WISCONSON

KARITOS ART AND WORSHIP CONFERENCE
Milwaukee, WI | July 23-25 | *karitos.org*
    Director: Bob Hay, PO Box 17218, Indianapolis, IN 46217; 847-925-8018; *info@karitos.com*
    Description: The mission of Karitos is to provide biblically based artistic and technical growth experiences to Christian artists, including writers.
    Attendance: 150

THE BUSINESS OF BEING A SPIRITUAL WRITER
Milwaukee, WI | April 24 | *writingforyourlife.com/the-business-of-being-a-spiritual-writer-milwaukee-2020*
    Director: Brian Allain, *brian@writingforyourlife.com*
    Description: Not only do authors need a platform, they must enter the market strategically in order to make that platform, and that book, happen. They must operate like an entrepreneur—agile, flexible, and creative in their business. This seminar is a step-by-step roadmap of best practices for figuring it all out.
    Attendance: 30

PUBLISHING IN COLOR
Milwaukee, WI | April 25 | *publishingincolor.com/conferences*
    Director: Brian Allain, *brian@writingforyourlife.com*
    Description: Publishing in Color conferences are intended to help overcome the fact that in today's spiritual publishing industry writers of color are under-represented. These conferences feature publishing industry representatives and are focused on how to get published with a little how to market and how to write thrown in.

Faculty includes: editors, agents, publishers
Attendance: 100

AUSTRALIA

OMEGA WRITERS CONFERENCE

Kingscliff, NSW | October 23-25 | *www.omegawriters.org*

Director: Raewyn Elsegood, *conference@omegawriters.org*
Description: Educational workshops, supportive genre groups, inspiring awards night, and keen publishers and editors ready to equip you for your next steps in your writing journey.
Faculty includes: publishers, editors
Keynote speaker: Susan May Warren
Scholarships: full and partial
Attendance: 80-150
Contest: Caleb Awards with $400 prize vouchers to assist your writing; scholarship contest with full costs of conference, including meals, lodging, and fee

CANADA

InSCRIBE CHRISTIAN WRITERS' FELLOWSHIP FALL CONFERENCE

Edmonton, AB | September 24-26 | *inscribe.org/events/fall-conference*

Director: *president@inscribe.org*
Description: Encouragement and inspiration for new and seasoned writers.
Scholarships: full, partial
Special track: advanced writers
Faculty includes: editors, publishers
Attendance: 50

NEW ZEALAND

NZ CHRISTIAN WRITERS RETREAT

Whitianga, New Zealand | April 30—May 3 |
www.nzchristianwriters.org/retreat-2020

Director: Justin St. Vincent, 179B St. Johns Road, St. Johns, Auckland, North Island 1072; *editor@xtrememusic.org*

Description: Our seminar speakers will inspire, refresh, and upskill each of us on our writing journey.
Faculty includes: editors, publishers
Attendance: 40

CONFERENCES THAT CHANGE LOCATIONS

The following conferences change locations every year but are listed with their 2020 locations:

AMERICAN CHRISTIAN FICTION WRITERS CONFERENCE

EVANGELICAL PRESS ASSOCIATION ANNUAL CONVENTION

PENCON

REALM MAKERS

Christian Publishing Show
Featured Episode

Podcast episode: How to Pitch Your Book at a Writers' Conference with Bob Hostetler
Market Guide price FREE

https://cwmg.link/pitch2020

How to Scan QR Codes
Use the camera on your smartphone to focus on the above QR code to activate the discount. It will give you the option to visit the site, which you will want to accept. If you are using an older smartphone, you may need to download a QR code scanning app. You can also visit the URL below the code to activate the discount on your computer.

18

WRITERS GROUPS

In addition to the groups listed here, check these websites for other groups in your area:

American Christian Writers chapters: *www.acwriters.com*
American Christian Fiction Writers chapters: *www.ACFW.com*
Word Weavers International chapters: *www.Word-Weavers.com*

NATIONAL AND ONLINE

ACFW BEYOND THE BORDERS

www.facebook.com/groups/ACFWBeyondtheBorders

> **Contact:** Iola Goulton, *iola@iolagoulton.com*
> **Members:** 100
> **Affiliation:** American Christian Fiction Writers

AMERICAN CHRISTIAN FICTION WRITERS

ACFW.com

> **Contact:** Robin Miller, executive director, PO Box 101066, Palm Bay, FL 32910; *director@ACFW.com*
> **Services:** Email loop, genre Facebook pages, online courses, critique groups, and local and regional chapters. Sponsors contests for published and unpublished writers and conducts the largest fiction writers conference annually.
> **Members:** 2600+

CHRISTIAN AUTHORS NETWORK

ChristianAuthorsNetwork.com

> **Meetings:** Online and at major writing-industry events, daily via private loop
> **Contact:** Angela Breidenbach, *contact@christianauthorsnetwork.com*
> **Members:** 115
> **Membership fee:** $50/year plus $50 one-time fee

CHRISTIAN INDIE AUTHOR NETWORK
www.christianindieauthors.com
> **Meetings:** 24/7 on Facebook and website
> **Contact:** Mary C. Findley, 918-805-0669, *mjmcfindley@gmail.com*
> **Members:** 400+

CHRISTIAN WOMEN WRITER'S GROUP
cwwriters.com
> **Meetings:** weekly and monthly communications
> **Contact:** Jen Gentry, 918-724-3996, *jennyokiern37@gmail.com*
> **Members:** 100+
> **Affiliation:** Christian Indie Author Network

INSPIRE CHRISTIAN WRITERS
www.inspirewriters.com
> **Meetings:** regional and online critique groups
> **Contact:** Robynne Miller, 530-217-8233, *inspiredirectors@gmail.com*
> **Members:** 150
> **Affiliation:** West Coast Christian Writers

INTERNATIONAL CHRISTIAN FICTION WRITERS
icfw.com
> **Meetings:** private Facebook group
> **Contact:** Iola Goulton, *iolaschristianreads@gmail.com*
> **Members:** 1,100
> **Affiliation:** American Christian Fiction Writers

PEN-SOULS
> **Meetings:** online and email; monthly reminders are emailed to members to pray for one another and share urgent, personal prayer requests and publishing announcements
> **Contact:** Janet Ann Collins, 530-272-4905, *jan@janetanncollins.com*
> **Members:** 10-12

REALM MAKERS
www.realmmakers.com
> **Meetings:** quarterly online
> **Contact:** Rebecca Minor, *members@realmmakers.com*
> **Membership:** 100
> **Membership fee:** $40-100/year

WORD WEAVERS INTERNATIONAL, INC.
www.Word-Weavers.com

Contact: Eva Marie Everson, president, PO Box 520224, Longwood, FL 32708; 407-615-4112; *WordWeaversInternational@aol.com*

Services: Local chapters and Google Hangouts for manuscript critiquing. Sponsors Florida Christian Writers Conference and North Georgia Christian Writers Conference.

Members: 750

Membership fee: $45/year, adults; $35/year, students

WORD WEAVERS INTERNATIONAL ONLINE CRITIQUE GROUPS
www.Word-Weavers.com

Meetings: via Google Hangouts and Zoom; times vary, two hours

Contact: *wordweaversinternational@aol.com*

Members: 6 per group

Membership fee: $60

Affiliation: Word Weavers International

ALABAMA

WORD WEAVERS NORTH ALABAMA

Meetings: Hartsell; third Thursday of the month, 10:00 a.m.-noon

Contact: Lisa Worthey Smith, *LisaWSmith75@gmail.com*

Members: 10

Membership fee: $45/year

Affiliation: Word Weavers International

ARIZONA

CHANDLER WRITERS' GROUP
chandlerwriters.wordpress.com

Meetings: member's home, near Gilbert and Ocotillo Roads; first Friday of the month, 9:00-11:30 a.m.

Contact: Jenne Acevedo, 480-510-0419, *editor@jenneacevedo.com*

Members: 10

Membership fee: none

CHRISTIAN WRITERS OF THE WEST

www.christianwritersofthewest.com

> **Meetings:** Denny's, 4400 N. Scottsdale Rd., Scottsdale; last Saturday of the month, 1:00-3:00 p.m.
> **Contact:** Brenda Poulos, 480-628-6728, *mtnst14@gmail.com*
> **Members:** 30
> **Membership fee:** $10/year
> **Affiliation:** American Christian Fiction Writers

FOUNTAIN HILLS CHRISTIAN WRITERS' GROUP

> **Meetings:** Fountain Hills Presbyterian Church, 13001 N. Fountain Hills Blvd., Fountain Hills; second Friday of the month, 9:00 a.m. to noon
> **Contact:** Jewell Johnson, 480-836-8968, *tykeJ@juno.com*
> **Members:** 12
> **Membership fee:** $10/year
> **Affiliation:** American Christian Writers

ARKANSAS

ACFW ARKANSAS

acfwarkansas.com

> **Meetings:** Searcy Public Library, 113 E. Pleasure Ave., Searcy; second Saturday of the month, 1:00 p.m.
> **Contact:** Linda Fulkerson, *ACFWarinfo@gmail.com*
> **Members:** 20
> **Affiliation:** American Christian Fiction Writers

ACFW NORTHWEST ARKANSAS CHAPTER

www.facebook.com/groups/127662834752320/?ref=bookmarks

> **Meetings:** Robinson Avenue Church of Christ, 1506 W. Robinson Ave., Springdale; first Saturday of the month, 3:30 p.m.
> **Contact:** Robyn Hook, *contact@robynhook.com*
> **Members:** 12
> **Membership fee:** $10 plus ACFW fee
> **Affiliation:** American Christian Fiction Writers, American Christian Writers

CALIFORNIA

ACFW ORANGE COUNTY
acfwoc.com
> **Meetings:** Marie Callendar's, 307 E. Katella Ave., Orange; second
> Thursday of the month, 6:30 p.m.
> **Contact:** Susan K. Beatty, *susan@susankbeatty.com*
> **Members:** 15
> **Membership fee:** $10
> **Affiliation:** American Christian Fiction Writers

ACFW SAN FRANCISCO BAY AREA CHAPTER
facebook.com/ACFWSFBayArea
> **Meetings:** Crosswalk Community Church, 445 S. Mary Ave.,
> Sunnyvale; third Saturday of odd months, 10 a.m. to noon
> **Contact:** Beth Worcester, *bworcester@gmail.com*
> **Members:** 15
> **Membership fee:** $17/year plus national dues
> **Affiliation:** American Christian Fiction Writers, American Christian
> Writers

WORD WARRIORS
www.facebook.com/wordwarriorswriters
> **Meetings:** 3 Crosses Church, 20600 John Dr., Castro Valley; first
> Monday of the month September—June, 7:00 p.m.
> **Contact:** Debbie Jones Warren, 510-329-4141, *debbiencj@aim.com*
> **Members:** 15
> **Membership fee:** none

COLORADO

ACFW COLORADO SPRINGS
acfwcosprings.com
> **Meetings:** First Evangelical Free Church, 3022 W. Fontanero St.,
> Colorado Springs; first Saturday of the month, 10:00 a.m.-noon
> **Contact:** Erin Kohler, *erin730kohler@gmail.com*
> **Members:** 45
> **Affiliation:** American Christian Fiction Writers

ACFW COLORADO WESTERN SLOPE
www.westernslopeACFW.blogspot.com
> **Meetings:** The Artful Cup, 3090 N. 12th St., Grand Junction; fourth Saturday of the month, 10:00 a.m.
> **Contact:** Templa Melnick, *temple.melnick@gmail.com*
> **Members:** 9
> **Membership fee:** $10/year
> **Affiliation:** American Christian Fiction Writers

ACFW SOUTH DENVER
www.facebook.com/milehighscribes
> **Meetings:** Highlands Ranch Library, 9292 S. Ridgeline Blvd., Highlands Ranch; see website for day and time
> **Contact:** through Facebook
> **Members:** 10
> **Affiliation:** American Christian Fiction Writers

SPRINGS WRITERS
springswriters.wordpress.com
> **Meetings:** Woodmen Valley Chapel, 250 E. Woodmen Rd., Colorado Springs; second Tuesday of each month except July, August, and December, 6:00-8:00 p.m.
> **Contact:** Scoti Springfield Domeij, 719-209-9066, *springswriters@gmail.com*
> **Members:** 350
> **Membership fee:** none

WORD WEAVERS PIKES PEAK
www.facebook.com/groups/415291469231448
> **Meetings:** Mountain Springs Church, 7345 Adventure Way, Colorado Springs; third Saturday of each month
> **Contact:** Tez Brooks, *tezwrites@gmail.com*, 407-797-4408
> **Members:** 10
> **Membership fee:** $45 per year
> **Affiliation:** Word Weavers International

WRITERS ON THE ROCK
www.writersontherock.com/groups
> **Meetings:** twelve locations in Colorado, various meeting times; see the website for locations
> **Contact:** David Rupert, 720-237-7487, *david@writersontherock.com*

Members: 580
Membership fee: none

CONNECTICUT

WORD WEAVERS BERKSHIRES
wordweaversberkshires.org
> **Meetings:** Sherman Church, 6 Church Rd., Sherman; third Saturday
> of the month, 9:00 a.m. to noon
> **Contact:** Tara Alemany, *info@wordweaversberkshires.org*
> **Members:** 15
> **Membership fee:** $45/year
> **Affiliation:** Word Weavers International

DELAWARE

DELMARVA CHRISTIAN WRITERS' FELLOWSHIP
www.delmarvawriters.com
> **Meetings:** Georgetown Presbyterian Church, Tunnell Hall, 203 N.
> Bedford St., Georgetown; third Saturday of the month, 9:00 a.m.
> to noon
> **Contact:** Candy Abbott, 302-856-6649, *cfa@candyabbot.com*
> **Members:** 20
> **Membership fee:** none
> **Affiliation:** Vine and Vessels

KINGDOM WRITERS FELLOWSHIP
> **Meetings:** Atlanta Road Alliance Church, 22625 Atlanta Rd.,
> Seaford; second Tuesday of the month, 6:00-8:30 p.m.
> **Contact:** Eva Maddox, 302-628-4594, *evacmaddox@outlook.com*
> **Members:** 8

FLORIDA

SONSHINE SCRIBES
www.cfACFW.org
> **Meetings:** Grace Covenant Presbyterian Church, 1655 Peel Ave., Orlando;
> third Saturday of the month, January—October, noon to 2 p.m.
> **Contact:** Kristen Stieffel, 407-928-7801, *treasurer@cfACFW.com*

Members: 15
Affiliation: American Christian Fiction Writers

SOUTH FLORIDA WORD WEAVERS

Meetings: Gracepoint Church, 5590 N.E. 6th Ave., Fort Lauderdale;
second Saturday of the month, 9:30 a.m.-12:30 p.m.
Contact: Patricia Hartman, *patricia@patriciahartman.com*
Members: 15
Membership fee: $45/year
Affiliation: Word Weavers International

SPACE COAST WORD WEAVERS

Meetings: Central Brevard Library, 308 Forrest Ave., Cocoa; second
Sunday of the month, 2:00-4:30 p.m.
Contact: Evelyn Miracle, *eveymiracle@gmail.com*
Members: 12
Membership fee: $45/year
Affiliation: Word Weavers International

SUNCOAST CHRISTIAN WRITERS GROUP

Meetings: Panera Bread, Largo Mall, 10500 Ulmerton Rd., Largo;
third Thursday of the month, 10 a.m.
Contact: Elaine Creasman, 727-251-3756, *emcreasman@aol.com*
Members: 15
Membership fee: none

WORD WEAVERS DESTIN

Meetings: Village Baptist Church, 101 Matthew Dr.; second Saturday
of the month, 9:30 a.m.-12:30 p.m.
Contact: Susan Neal, *susanneal@bellsouth.net*
Members: 18
Membership fee: $45/year
Affiliation: Word Weavers International

WORD WEAVERS GAINESVILLE

www.facebook.com/groups/277156498961942
Meetings: various locations; fourth Sunday of the month, 2:00-4:30 p.m.
Contact: Lorilyn Roberts, *authorLorilynRoberts@gmail.com*,
352-359-6941 (text)
Members: 5
Membership fee: $45/year
Affiliation: Word Weavers International

WORD WEAVERS LAKE COUNTY

Meetings: Leesburg Public Library, 100 E. Main St.., Leesburg; second Saturday of the month, 10:00 a.m.-12:30 p.m.
Contact: Frank Stanfield, *FrankEStanfield@gmail.com*
Members: 7
Membership fee: $45/year
Affiliation: Word Weavers International

WORD WEAVERS MARIANNA

Meetings: Eastside Baptist Church, 4785 Highway 90; third Saturday of the month, 9:30 a.m.-noon
Contact: Sherri Stone, *sherristone62@hotmail.com*, 850-718-7247
Members: 5
Membership fee: $45
Affiliation: Word Weavers International

WORD WEAVERS NAPLES

Meetings: North Naples Baptist Church, 1811 Oakes Blvd.; third Tuesday of the month, 6:30-9:00 p.m.
Contact: Julie Christian, *ugabuggy3@gmail.com*
Members: 8
Membership fee: $45
Affiliation: Word Weavers International

WORD WEAVERS OCALA CHAPTER

Meetings: Belleview Public Library, 13145 S.E. County Hwy. 484, Belleview; second Friday of the month, 10:00 a.m.-12:30 p.m.
Contact: Jennifer Odom, *odomj@live.co*
Members: 10+
Membership fee: $45/year
Affiliation: Word Weavers International

WORD WEAVERS OF CLAY COUNTY

Meetings: Panera Bread, 1510 County Rd. 220, Fleming Island; third Saturday of the month, 10:00 a.m.-12:30 p.m.
Members: 7
Membership fee: $45/year
Affiliation: Word Weavers International

WORD WEAVERS OF SARASOTA
Meetings: First United Methodist Church, 104 S. Pineapple Ave.; fourth Sunday of the month, 2:00 p.m.
Contact: Sam Wright, *drsamwright@comcast.net*, 941-900-8231
Members: 5
Membershiip fee: $45
Affiliation: Word Weavers International

WORD WEAVERS OF THE TREASURE COAST
Meetings: First Church of God, 1105 58th Ave., Vero Beach; first Saturday of the month or second Saturday if the first falls on a major holiday, 9:30 a.m.-noon
Contact: Del Bates, *handstoblessu_@hotmail.com*
Members: 17
Membership fee: $45/year
Affiliation: Word Weavers International

WORD WEAVERS ORLANDO
Meetings: Calvary Chapel, 5015 Goddard Ave.; second Saturday of the month, 10:00 a.m.-12:30 p.m.
Contact: Dona Yohe, *dona.Yohe@gmail.com*
Members: 40-45
Membership fee: $45/year
Affiliation: Word Weavers International

WORD WEAVERS PENSACOLA
Meetings: Hillcrest Baptist Church, 800 E. 9 Mile Rd.; second Tuesday of the month, 5:30-8:00 p.m.
Contact: Ginny Cruz, *gincru@gmail.com*
Affiliation: Word Weavers International

WORD WEAVERS TAMPA
www.facebook.com/search/top/?q=word%20weavers%20tampa&epa=SEARCH_BOX
Meetings: Jan Powell, 1901 S. Village Ave.; first Saturday of the month, 9:30 a.m. to noon
Contact: Sharron Cosby, *sharroncosby@gmail.com*
Members: 22
Membership fee: $45/year
Affiliation: Word Weavers International

WORD WEAVERS VOLUSIA COUNTY

Meetings: Faith Church of United Brethren in Christ, 4700 S. Clyde Morris Blvd., Port Orange; first Monday of the month, 7:00 p.m.
Contact: Renee Hanson, *rlhhh2@gmail.com*, 386-341-7576
Members: 25
Membership fee: $45/year
Affiliation: Word Weavers International

GEORGIA

ACFW NORTHWEST GEORGIA

acfwnorthwestga.blogspot.com

Meetings: Marietta; second Tuesday of each month, 630-8:30 p.m.
Contact: Cindy Stewart, *cindy@cindykstewart.com*
Members: 14
Membership fee: $15
Affiliation: American Christian Fiction Writers

CHRISTIAN AUTHORS GUILD

www.christianauthorsguild.org

Meetings: Prayer & Praise Christian Fellowship, 6409 Bells Ferry Rd., Woodstock; first Monday of the month, except holidays, 7:00 p.m.
Contact: Diana Baker, 404-536-3887, *dianabaker215@gmail.com*
Members: 45-50
Membership fee: $30/year

WORD WEAVERS GREATER ATLANTA

Meetings: 4541 Vendome Pl. N.E., Roswell; first Saturday of the month, 9:00-noon
Contact: Barbara Fox, *barb@barbjfox.com*
Membership fee: $45/year
Affiliation: Word Weavers International

WORD WEAVERS WOODSTOCK

Meetings: Prayer & Praise Christian Fellowship, 6409 Bells Ferry Rd.; third Monday of the month, 6:30-9:00 p.m.
Contact: Frieda Dixon, *friedasdixon@gmail.com*
Members: 20
Membership fee: $45/year
Affiliation: Word Weavers International, Christian Authors Guild

ILLINOIS

ACFW CHICAGO CHAPTER
www.ACFWchicago.com
> **Meetings:** Schaumburg Public Library, 130 S. Roselle Rd.,
> Schaumburg; second Friday of every month, 6:30-8:30 p.m.
> **Contact:** Susan Miura, 847-714-4755 *susan.miura@yahoo.com*
> **Members:** 25
> **Membership fee:** $25/month
> **Affiliation:** American Christian Fiction Writers

WORD WEAVERS AURORA CHAPTER
> **Meetings:** Colonial Cafe, 1961 W. Galena Blvd.; second Saturday of
> each month, 1:00-3:00 p.m.
> **Contact:** JoDee Starrick, *JoDee.Starrick@gmail.com*
> **Members:** 18
> **Membership fee:** $45/year
> **Affiliation:** Word Weavers International

WORD WEAVERS LAND OF LINCOLN
> **Meetings:** Lincoln Christian University, 100 Campus View Dr.,
> Lincoln; second Saturday of every month, 10:00 a.m.
> **Contact:** April Godsil, *godsil@springnet1.com*
> **Members:** 9
> **Membership fee:** $45/year
> **Affiliation:** Word Weavers International

WORD WEAVERS ON THE BORDER
> **Meetings:** fourth Wednesday of the month, 7:00-8:00 p.m.
> **Contact:** Fred Von Kamecke, *FVonKamecke@comcast.net*
> **Members:** 8
> **Membership fee:** $45/year
> **Affiliation:** Word Weavers International

INDIANA

ACFW INDIANA CHAPTER
www.hoosierink.blogspot.com
> **Meetings:** various places in Indiana, quarterly
> **Contact:** Linda Samaritoni, *lindasamaritoni@gmail.com*

Members: 50
Affiliation: American Christian Fiction Writers

BLUFFTON CHRISTIAN WRITING CLUB

Facebook group: Bluffton IN Christian Writing Group

Meetings: River Terrace Retirement Community, 400 Caylor Blvd.;
third Monday of the month, 6:30-8:30 p.m.
Contact: Kayleen Reusser, *kjreusser@adamswell.com*
Members: 12
Membership fee: none

FORT WAYNE CHRISTIAN WRITING CLUB

Meetings: Waynedale Public Library, 2200 Lower Huntington Rd.;
fourth Tuesday of the month, 6:00-8:00 p.m.
Contact: Kayleen Reusser, *kjreusser@adamswells.com*
Members: 10

HEARTLAND CHRISTIAN WRITERS

www.HeartlandChristianWriters.com

Meetings: Mount Pleasant Christian Church, 381 N. Bluff Rd.,
Greenwood; third Monday of every month, 10:00 a.m. and
6:30 p.m.
Contact: John Walker, *johnmatthewwalkerauthor@gmail.com*
Members: 20
Membership fee: none

IOWA

WORD WEAVERS DES MOINES

Meetings: Union Park Baptist Church, 821 Arthur Ave.; last Monday
of the month except holidays, 6:30-8:30 p.m.
Contact: Alex Long, *alexdavidlong@gmail.com*
Members: 10
Membership fee: $45
Affiliation: Word Weavers International

KANSAS

ACFW KANSAS CITY WEST
www.facebook.com/ACFWKansasCityWestChapter
> **Meetings:** Bonner Springs City Library, 201 N. Nettleton Ave.,
> Bonner Springs; second Saturday of every month, 1:00-3:00 p.m.;
> optional critique group, 3:30-5:00 p.m.
> **Contact:** Sue Hollaway, *shollaway2008@gmail.com*
> **Members:** 10-15
> **Affiliation:** American Christian Fiction Writers

KENTUCKY

WORD WEAVERS BOONE COUNTY
www.facebook.com/groups/349709925923088
> **Meetings:** Boone County Public Library Scheben Branch, 8899 US
> 42, Union; first Saturday of the month, 10:30-12:30 p.m.
> **Contact:** Karisa Moore, *karisam660@gmail.com*
> **Members:** 10
> **Membership fee:** $10
> **Affiliation:** Word Weavers International

LOUISIANA

SOUTHERN CHRISTIAN WRITERS
scwguild.com
> **Meetings:** Gospel Bookstore, Westside Shopping Center,
> 91 Westbank Expy., Gretna; third Saturday of the month,
> January— October, 10:00 a.m.
> **Contact:** Teena Myers, *scwg@cox.net*
> **Members:** 30
> **Membership fee:** $50/year (optional, other benefits)
> **Affiliation:** Southern Christian Writers Guild—Northshore

MARYLAND

MOUNTAIN CHRISTIAN WRITER'S GROUP
portionofgrace.blogspot.com

Meetings: New Life Center, Room 26, 1824 Mountain Rd., Bel Air; Sundays, 2:30-4:30 p.m.
Contact: Christy Struben, 410-259-3673, *cstruben711@gmail.com*
Members: 20-30
Membership fee: none

MICHIGAN

WORD WEAVERS WEST MICHIGAN—GRAND RAPIDS NORTH

Meetings: Russ' Restaurant, 3531 Alpine Ave. N.W., Walker; first and third Tuesday of the month, 6:00-8:00 p.m.
Contact: Terry DeBoer, *terryjdb@gmail.com*, 616-340-4459
Members: 6-8
Membership fee: $45/year
Affiliation: Word Weavers International

WORD WEAVERS WEST MICHIGAN—GRANDVILLE

Meetings: Russ' Restaurant, 4440 Chicago Dr., S.W., Grandville; first and third Tuesdays, 6:30-8:30 p.m.
Contact: Kathy Bruins, *KBruins77@gmail.com*
Members: 5
Membership fee: $45/year
Affiliation: Word Weavers International

WORD WEAVERS WEST MICHIGAN—HOLLAND ZEELAND

Meetings: City on a Hill, 100 Pine St., Zeeland; first and third Tuesdays of the month, 12:30-2:30 p.m.
Contact: Denise Vredevoogd, 616-745-4461, *djoy757@hotmail.com*
Members: 10
Affiliation: Word Weavers International

WORD WEAVERS WEST MICHIGAN—MUSKEGON/ NORTON SHORES

Meetings: Norton Shores Public Library, 705 Seminole Rd., Norton Shores; first and third Tuesdays, 5:45-7:45 p.m.
Contact: Kathy Bruins, *KBruins77@gmail.com*
Members: 10
Membership fee: $45/year
Affiliation: Word Weavers International

MINNESOTA

ACFW MINNESOTA NICE
www.ACFWminnesotanice.com
> **Meetings:** Trinity Baptist Church, 2220 Edgerton St., Maplewood;
> usually fourth Sunday of the month, 6:00-8:00 p.m.
> **Contact:** Gabrielle Meyer, *ACFW.mn_nice@yahoo.com*
> **Members:** 25
> **Affiliation:** American Christian Fiction Writers

MINNESOTA CHRISTIAN WRITERS GUILD
www.mnchristianwriters.com
> **Meetings:** Oak Knoll Lutheran Church, 600 Hopkins Crossroad,
> Minnetonka; second Monday of the month, September—May,
> 7:00-8:30 p.m.
> **Contact:** Pat vanderMerwe, *pdvdm@comcast.net*
> **Membership fee:** $50/year

MISSISSIPPI

BYHALIA CHRISTIAN WRITERS GROUP
> **Meetings:** First United Methodist Church, 2511 Churst St.; first
> Saturday of the month, 9:00-11:00 a.m.
> **Contact:** April Carpenter, 901-378-0504, *april.carpenter@comcast.net*
> **Members:** 18
> **Affiliation:** American Chrstian Writers

MISSOURI

HEART OF AMERICA CHRISTIAN WRITERS NETWORK
www.hacwn.org
> **Meetings:** Greater Kansas City area; monthly informational meetings,
> biweekly critique groups
> **Contact:** Jeanette Littleton, 816-459-8016, *HACWN@earthlink.net*
> **Members:** 150

HEARTLAND CHRISTIAN COLLEGE WRITERS GUILD
www.facebook.com/groups/663817230321189

Meetings: Solid Rock Café, 6512 Shelby Rd., Bethel; first Monday of
the month, 6:30 p.m.
Contact: Kathy Nickerson, *Kathy@kathynick.com*
Members: 20
Membership fee: none

OZARKS CHAPTER OF AMERICAN CHRISTIAN WRITERS
www.OzarksACW.org
Meetings: University Heights Baptist Church, 1010 S. National,
Springfield; second Saturday, September—May, 10:00 a.m.-2:00
p.m.
Contact: Dr. Jeanetta Chrystie, 417-832-8409,
OzarksACW@yahoo.com
Members: 50
Membership fee: $20/year, $30 family, $10 newsletter
subscription only
Affiliation: American Christian Writers

NEBRASKA

MY THOUGHTS EXACTLY
mythoughtsexactlywriters.wordpress.com
Meetings: Keene Memorial Library, 1030 N. Broad St., Fremont;
third Monday of the month
Contact: Cheryl Paden, 402-727-6508,
cheryl@seekingbalancebycheryl.com
Members: 9
Membership fee: none

NEW JERSEY

ACFW NY/NJ CHAPTER
www.journeywithwords.com
Meetings: South Ridge Community Church, 7 Pittstown Rd.,
Clinton, NJ; first Saturday of the month, 10:00 a.m.-noon
Contact: Cher Gatto, *cherlyngatto@gmail.com*, 315-926-9277
Members: 20
Membership fee: $20/year
Affiliation: American Christian Fiction Writers

NORTHERN NJ CHRISTIAN WRITERS GROUP

www.njcwg.blogspot.com

> **Meetings:** Cornerstone Christian Church, 495 Wyckoff Ave.,
>   Wyckoff; first Saturday of each month, 10:00 a.m. to noon
> **Contact:** Barbara Higby, 551-804-1014, *bhigby9323@gmail.com*
> **Members:** 12
> **Membership fee:** none

NEW YORK

SOUTHERN TIER CHRISTIAN WRITERS

> **Meetings:** Olean First Baptist Church, 133 S. Union St., Olean;
>   monthly
> **Contact:** Deb Wuethrich, 716-379-8702, *deborahmarcein@gmail.com*
> **Members:** 8
> **Membership fee:** none
> **Affiliation:** American Christian Writers

WORD WEAVERS WESTERN NEW YORK

> **Meetings:** 2458 Rush Mendon Rd., Honeoye Falls; third Tuesday of the
>   month, 6:30-9:00 p.m.
> **Contact:** Karen Rode, *karen.a.rode@gmail.com*
> **Members:** 2
> **Membership fee:** $45/year
> **Affiliation:** Word Weavers International

NORTH AND SOUTH DAKOTA

ACFW DAKOTAS

www.facebook.com/groups/ACFWDakotas

> **Meetings:** location, day of week, and frequency varies by region
> **Contact:** Shannon McNear, 843-327-0583, *sdmcnear@gmail.com*
> **Members:** 15
> **Affiliation:** American Christian Fiction Writers

NORTH CAROLINA

WILMINGTON WORD WEAVERS

> **Meetings:** Impact Church, 3131 Randall Pkwy. #1; second Monday of
>   the month, 6:30-8:30 p.m.

Contact: Andy Lee, *WordsByAndyLee@gmail.com*
Affiliation: Word Weavers International

WORD WEAVERS CHARLOTTE BRANCH
charlottewordweavers.com
> **Meetings:** Waverly Whole Foods, Community Room, 7221 Waverly
> Walk; first Saturday of the month, 10:00 a.m.-noon
> **Contact:** Kim Dent, 330-904-5130, *kimberlyjamesdent@gmail.com*
> **Members:** 20
> **Membership fee:** $45
> **Affiliation:** Word Weavers International

WORD WEAVERS PIEDMONT TRIAD
> **Meetings:** Wellspring Community Church, 600 May Rd.,
> Thomasville; third Saturday of the month, 9.30 a.m.-noon
> **Contact:** Renee Leonard Kennedy, *ReneeLK3588@icloud.com*, 336-
> 491-2040
> **Members:** 10
> **Membership fee:** $45
> **Affiliation:** Word Weavers International

OHIO

ACFW OHIO
www.facebook.com/groups/220166801456380
> **Meetings:** Etna United Methodist Church, 500 Pike St., Etna; first
> Saturday of the month, noon to 3:00 p.m.
> **Contact:** Rebecca Waters, *rwaters.author@gmail.com*
> **Membership:** 20
> **Affiliation:** American Christian Fiction Writers

BEING A HAPPY HEALTHY HOLY WOMAN
www.facebook.com/HappyHealthyHolyWoman
> **Meetings:** Abundant Season Anointed Ministries International, 643
> Troy St., Dayton; conference call monthly, annual meeting
> **Contact:** Dr. J. Robinson, 937-275-3770, *happyhealthyholy@live.com*
> **Members:** 1,100
> **Membership fee:** none

COLUMBUS CHRISTIAN WRITERS ASSOCIATION (CCWA)/POTTERS HOUSE SCRIBES

Meetings: Potters House Church of God, 3220 Lowell Dr.,
Columbus; second Saturday of every month
Contact: Mina R. Raulston, 614-507-7893, *m_raulston@hotmail.com*
Members: 20
Membership fee: none

DAYTON CHRISTIAN SCRIBES

facebook.com/DaytonChristianScribes

Meetings: Kettering Seventh-Day Adventist Church, 3939
Stonebridge Rd., Kettering; second Thursday of the month, 7:00-
9:00 p.m.
Contact: Lois Pecce, 937-433-6470
Members: 35
Affiliations: Dayton Christian Writers Guild, Middletown Area
Christian Writers

DAYTON CHRISTIAN WRITERS GUILD

www.facebook.com/ChristianAuthorToles

Meetings: Corinthian Baptist Church, 700 S. James McGhee Blvd.;
second Saturday of the month, 2:00 p.m.
Contact: Tina Tole, through Facebook page

MAC WRITERS (MIDDLETOWN AREA CHRISTIAN WRITERS)

www.facebook.com/MACwriters

Meetings: Healing Word Assembly of God, 5303 S. Dixie Hwy.,
Middletown; second Tuesday of each month, 7:00-8:30 p.m.
Contact: Donna Shepherd, 513-423-1627, *donna.shepherd@gmail.com*
Members: 20
Membership fee: $30/year, $5/meeting

WORD WEAVERS NORTHEAST OHIO

Meetings: Ashland Church of the Brethren, 122 E. 3rd St., Ashland;
first Thursday of each month, 6:30-8:30 p.m.
Contact: Tina Hunt, *tmh4957@gmail.com*
Members: 8
Membership fee: $45/year
Affiliation: Word Weavers International

OKLAHOMA

FELLOWSHIP OF CHRISTIAN WRITERS

fellowshipofchristianwriters.org

> **Meetings:** Kirk of the Hills Presbyterian Church, 4102 E. 61st, Tulsa; second Tuesday of month, 7:00 p.m.
> **Contact:** Elece Hollis, *elecehollis@gmail.com*
> **Members:** 50
> **Membership fee:** $35/year

OKLAHOMA CHRISTIAN FICTION WRITERS

okchristianfictionwriters.com

> **Meetings:** Henderson Hills Baptist Church, 1200 E. I-35 Frontage Rd., Edmond; third Saturday of each month, 1:00-3:00 p.m.
> **Contact:** Chris Tarpley, *ocfwchapter@gmail.com*
> **Members:** 35
> **Affiliation:** American Christian Fiction Writers

WORDWRIGHTS

www.wordwrights-okc.com

> **Meetings:** Catholic Pastoral Center, Room B13, 7501 N.W. Expressway, Oklahoma City; second Saturday of the month, 10:00 a.m. to noon
> **Contact:** Milton Smith, *hiswordmatters@yahoo.com*
> **Members:** 30

OREGON

OREGON CHRISTIAN WRITERS

www.oregonchristianwriters.org

> **Meetings:** Portland metro area, three all-day Saturday conferences, summer coaching conference
> **Contact:** *president@oregonchristianwriters.com,* 503-927-5701
> **Membership fee:** $60/year, $75 couples, $35 students and seniors

WORD WEAVERS PORTLAND EAST

> **Meetings:** Panera Bread, 1017 N.W. Civic Dr., Gresham; second Saturday of every month, 9:30-11:00 a.m.
> **Contact:** Tere Belcher, *223penandcamera@gmail.com*
> **Members:** 7

Membership fee: $45/year adults; $35/year teens
Affiliation: Word Weavers International

WORDWRIGHTS

Meetings: Gresham/east Multnomah County; two times a month, Thursday afternoons
Contact: Susan Thogerson Maas, 503-663-7834, *susan.maas@frontiercom*
Members: 5
Membership fee: none
Affiliation: Oregon Christian Writers

PENNSYLVANIA

CHRISTIAN WRITERS GUILD

Meetings: Perkins Restaurant, 505 Galleria Dr., Johnstown; last Tuesday of each month, 1:00 p.m.
Contact: Betty Rosian, 814-255-4351, *wordsforall@hotmail.com*
Members: 12
Membership fee: $1/meeting

GREATER PHILLY CHRISTIAN WRITERS FELLOWSHIP

www.writehisanswer.com/cwfsmorningcritiquegroup

Meetings: 951 Anders Rd., Lansdale; monthly, usually the third Thursday, 10 a.m.-12:30 p.m.
Contact: Marlene Bagnull, 484-991-8581, *mbagnull@aol.com*
Members: 10
Membershiip fee: none

JOHNSTOWN AREA CHRISTIAN WRITERS GUILD

Meetings: Perkins Restaurant, 505 Galleria Dr., Richland; last Tuesday of each month except December, 1:00 p.m.
Contact: Betty Rosian, 814-255-4351, *louiserosian@gmail.com*
Members: 12
Membership fee: $10/year

LANCASTER CHRISTIAN WRITERS

lancasterchristianwriterstoday.blogspot.com

Meetings: Lancaster Alliance Church, 210 Pitney Rd.; third Saturday of the month, 9:30 a.m. to noon
Contact: Jeanette Windle, *jeanette@jeanettewindle.com*

Affiliation: American Christian Writers

LANSDALE, PA WOMEN'S CRITIQUE GROUP
www.writehisanswer.com/cwfseveningcritiquegroup
> **Meetings:** 951 Anders Rd., Lansdale; every other Thursday, 7:30-
> 10:00 p.m.
> **Contact:** Marlene Bagnull, 484-991-8581, *mbagnull@aol.com*
> **Members:** 12
> **Membership fee:** none

WORD WEAVERS PITTSBURGH
> **Meetings:** St. Matthew AME Zion Church, 345 Thorn St., Sewickley;
> first Thursday of the month, 6:00-8:00 p.m.
> **Contact:** Christina Leeman, *Christina@shewhohonors.com*
> **Affiliation:** Word Weavers International

SOUTH CAROLINA

ACFW SC
scwritersACFW.blogspot.com
> **Meetings:** North Anderson Baptist Church, 2308 N. Main St.,
> Anderson; fourth Saturday of the month except July and
> December, 2:00-5:00 p.m.
> **Contact:** Elva Cobb Martin, 864-226-7024, *elvacmartin@gmail.com*
> **Members:** 20+
> **Membership fee:** $21/year
> **Affiliation:** American Christian Fiction Writers

AIKEN WORD WEAVERS
aikenwordweavers.com
> **Meetings:** Trinity United Methodist Church, 2724 Whiskey Rd.;
> second Tuesday of the month, 7:00 p.m.
> **Contact:** Lee Russ, *LeeAllenRuss@gmail.com*, 864-608-5530
> **Members:** 10
> **Membership fee:** $45
> **Affiliation:** Word Weavers International

WORD WEAVERS CHARLESTON
www.facebook.com/groups/2112701302307131
> **Meetings:** Walton Hall, St. John's Parish Church, 3673 Maybank

Hwy., John's Island; third Saturday of the month, 10:00 a.m.-noon
Contact: Bonnie Anderson, *bonnieanderson0706@gmail.com*
Members: 10
Membership fee: $45/year
Affiliation: Word Weavers International

WORD WEAVERS LEXINGTON CHAPTER
www.LexingtonWordWeavers.com
Meetings: Trinity Baptist Church, 2003 Charleston Hwy., Cayce;
second Monday of every month, 6:45-9:00 p.m.
Contact: Jean Wilund, *info@lexingtonwordweavers.com*
Members: 33
Membership fee: $45/year
Affiliation: Word Weavers International

WORD WEAVERS SUMMERVILLE
Meetings: Summerville Presbyterian Church, 407 S. Laurel St.,
Summerville; first Monday of each month, 7:00 p.m.
Contact: Jeannine Brummett, *Summerville.lady@yahoo.com*
Members: 9
Membership fee: $45/year
Affiliation: Word Weavers International

WORD WEAVERS UPSTATE SC
Meetings: Fountain Inn First Baptist Church, 206 N. Weston St.,
Fountain Inn; second Thursday of the month, 9:30 a.m.-12:30 p.m.
Contact: Tammy Karasek, *wwupstatesc@yahoo.com*
Members: 34
Membership fee: $45/year
Affiliation: Word Weavers International

WRITING FOR HIM
Meetings: Spartanburg County Library Headquarters, 151 Church
St., Spartanburg; second Thursday of the month, 9:45 a.m.
Contact: Linda Gilden, *linda@lindagilden.com*
Members: 30
Membership fee: none

TENNESSEE

ACFW MEMPHIS

Meetings: Compassion Church, 3505 S. Houston Levee, Germantown; third Saturday of the month except December, 10 a.m. to noon
Contact: Loretta Eidson, *Loretta@LorettaEidson.com*
Members: 15
Affiliation: American Christian Fiction Writers

ACFW MIDDLE TENNESSEE CHAPTER

www.acfwmidtn.org

Meetings: Woodmont Baptist Church, 2100 Woodmont Blvd., Nashville; every other month, 10 a.m. to noon
Contact: *acfwmidtn.org/contact-us*
Members: 30
Membership fee: $24
Affiliation: American Christian Fiction Writers

WORD WEAVERS NASHVILLE

Meetings: Goodletsville Public Library, 205 Rivergate Pkwy., Goodlettsville; second Saturday of the month, 10:00 a.m.-noon
Contact: Angelene Woodard, *theunqualifiedmom@gmail.com*
Membership fee: $45/year
Affiliation: Word Weavers International

TEXAS

ACFW CENTRAL TEXAS CHAPTER

www.centexACFW.com

Meetings: Georgetown Public Library, 402 W. 8th St., Georgetown; second Saturday of the month, 9:30-11:30 a.m.
Contact: Vanetta Chapman, *vanettachapman@gmail.com*
Members: 20
Membership fee: $20 plus national dues
Affiliation: American Christian Fiction Writers

ACFW DFW CHAPTER (AKA READY WRITERS)

www.dfwreadywriters.blogspot.com

Meetings: Arlington Community Church, 1715 W. Randol Mill Rd., Arlington; second Saturday of every month, 10:00 a.m.
Contact: Stacy Simmons, *stacy.t.simmons@gmail.com*
Members: 25-30
Affiliation: American Christian Fiction Writers

ACFW, THE WOODLANDS
wotsACFW.blogspot.com

Meetings: Lupe Tortilla, 19437 Interstate 45, Shenandoah; third Saturday of every month except October and December, 11:00 a.m.-1:00 p.m.
Contact: Annette O'Hare, *wots.ACFW@gmail.com*
Members: 30
Membership fee: $30/year
Affiliation: American Christian Fiction Writers

ALAMO CITY CHRISTIAN FICTION WRITERS

Meetings: La Madeleine, 722 N.W. Loop 410, San Antonio; second Saturday of the month, 10 a.m. to noon
Contact: Kristi Holl, *kristi.holl@gmail.com*
Members: 15
Affiliation: American Christian Fiction Writers

CENTRAL HOUSTON INSPIRATIONAL WRITERS ALIVE!
www.centralhoustoniwa.com

Meetings: Houston's First Baptist Church, 7474 Katy Fwy. (I-10); second Thursday of each month except July, August, and December, 7:00 p.m.
Contact: Dana Battista, 832-315-8430, *loveeternal@comcast.net*
Members: 22

CHRISTIAN WRITERS WORKSHOP (CWW)

Meetings: Woodway First Baptist Church, 101 Ritchie Rd., Waco; beginning in January each year, we meet for eleven consecutive Wednesday evenings; four critique groups meet year round once a month
Contact: Reita Hawthorne, *reitahawthorne2@gmail.com*, 254-339-3060
Members: 50
Membership fee: none

ROARING WRITERS

roaringwriters.org
> **Meetings:** various locations in Dallas/Fort Worth area; check the
> website
> **Contact:** Jan Johnson, email through website
> **Members:** 250

ROCKWALL CHRISTIAN WRITERS GROUP

rcwg.blogspot.com
> **Meetings:** Lake Pointe Church, 701 E. I-30; second Monday of each
> month, 7:00 p.m.
> **Contact:** Darren Sapp, 214-477-4039, *darrenlsapp@gmail.com*
> **Members:** 40

VIRGINIA

CAPITAL CHRISTIAN WRITERS

ccwritersfellowship.org
> **Meetings:** Truro Episcopal Church, Gunnell House, 10520 Main St.,
> Fairfax; second Monday of odd months
> **Contact:** Betsy Dill, 703-803-9447, *ccwriters@gmail.com*
> **Members:** 25
> **Membership fee:** $40

WASHINGTON

VANCOUVER CHRISTIAN WRITERS

> **Meetings:** Vancouver; first Monday of each month, 9:00 a.m.
> **Contact:** Jon Drury, 510-909-0848, *jondrury2@yahoo.com*
> **Members:** 14
> **Affiliation:** Oregon Christian Writers

WALLA WALLA CHRISTIAN WRITERS

> **Meetings:** SonBridge, 1200 S.E. 12th St., College Place; first and third
> Tuesday of each month, 3:00 p.m.
> **Contact:** Helen Heavirland, 541-938-3838, *hlh@bmi.net*
> **Members:** 5

WISCONSIN

ACFW WISE
www.facebook.com/wiseacfw
> **Meetings:** Brookfield Public Library, Rotary Club room, 1900 N. Calhoun Rd., Brookfield; first Tuesday of the month, 6:30 p.m.
> **Contact:** Nancy Radosevich, *nancyr@wi.rr.com*, 262-442-7736
> **Members:** 12
> **Membership fee:** $25/year
> **Affiliation:** American Christian Fiction Writers

PENS OF PRAISE CHRISTIAN WRITERS
> **Meetings:** Faith Church, 2201 42nd St., Manitowoc; third Monday of every month, 6:30-8:30 p.m.
> **Contact:** Becky McLafferty, 920-758-9196, *rebeccamclafferty@gmail. com* or Sue Kinney, 920-242-3631, *susanmarlenekinney@gmail. com*
> **Members:** 8-12

WESTERN WISCONSIN CHRISTIAN WRITERS GUILD
www.wwcwg.com
> **Meetings:** Bethesda Lutheran Church, 123 W. Hamilton, Eau Claire; second Tuesday of each month, September—May, 7:00 p.m.
> **Contact:** Sheila Wilkinson, 715-839-1207, *wwcwg.info@gmail.com*
> **Members:** 15
> **Membership fee:** $30

WORD AND PEN CHRISTIAN WRITERS
wordandpenchristianwriters.wordpress.com
> **Meetings:** St. Thomas Episcopal Church, 226 Washington St., Menasha; second Monday of the month except December, 6:30 p.m.
> **Contact:** Chris Stratton, 920-739-0752, *gcefsi@new.rr.com*
> **Members:** 14
> **Membership fee:** $10/year

AUSTRALIA AND NEW ZEALAND

AUSTRALASIAN CHRISTIAN WRITERS (ACW)

australasianchristianwriters.com,
www.facebook.com/groups/AustralasianChristianWriters

> **Meetings:** Tuesday book chats on website and in Facebook group
> **Contacts:** Narelle Atkins, Jenny Blake, and Iola Goulton,
> *australasianchristianwriters.com/contact*
> **Members:** 700
> **Affiliation:** Omega Writers

CHRISTIAN WRITERS DOWNUNDER (CWD)

christianwritersdownunder.blogspot.com,
www.facebook.com/groups/121373687949378

> **Meetings:** Facebook discussions, occasional physical meetings
> **Contact:** Jeanette O'Hagan, *cwdbloggers@gmail.com*
> **Members:** 1,100
> **Affiliation:** Omega Writers

NEW ZEALAND CHRISTIAN WRITERS

www.nzchristianwriters.org

> **Meetings:** for locations and leaders: *www.nzchristianwriters.org/groups*
> **Contact:** Justin St. Vincent, *president@nzchristianwriters.org*
> **Members:** 210+

CANADA

InSCRIBE CHRISTIAN WRITERS' FELLOWSHIP

inscribe.org

> **Contact:** Tracy Krauss, *tracy.krauss@gmail.com*
> **Service:** Canadian group with chapters across the country. See the
> website for locations. Also sponsors workshops, a fall conference,
> and contests and produces the quarterly magazine *FellowScript* that
> is included with membership.
> **Membership:** 175
> **Membership fee:** $50-70/year, $100 family

MANITOBA CHRISTIAN WRITERS ASSOCIATION

> **Meetings:** Bleak House, 1637 Main St., Winnipeg; Saturdays once a
> month, 1:30-4:00 p.m.

Contact: Frieda Martens, 204-256-3642, *friedamartens1910@gmail.com*
Membership: 16
Membership fee: $25/year, $3 visitors
Affiliation: InScribe Christian Writers' Fellowship

THE WORD GUILD
www.thewordguild.com

Contact: Ruth Thorogood, executive director, Box 77001, Markham, ON L3P OC8, Canada; 800-969-9010; *info@thewordguild.com*
Services: Regional writers chapters across Canada. Sponsors contests and awards for Canadian Christian writers.
Members: 325

19

EDITORIAL SERVICES

Entries in this chapter are for information only, not an endorsement of editing skills. Before hiring a freelance editor, ask for references if they are not posted on the website; and contact two or three to help determine if this editor is a good fit for you. You may also want to pay for an edit of a few pages or one chapter before hiring someone to edit your complete manuscript.

A LITTLE RED INK | BETHANY KACZMAREK
Jarrettsville, MD | 443-608-4013
editor@bethanykaczmarek.com | *www.bethanykaczmarek.com*
> **Contact:** email
> **Services:** manuscript evaluation, substantive editing/rewriting, copyediting, proofreading
> **Types of manuscripts:** short stories, novels, adult, teen/YA
> **Charges:** hourly rate
> **Credentials/experience:** "An ACFW Editor of the Year finalist (2015), Bethany enjoys working with both traditional and indie authors. Several of her clients are award-winning and best-selling authors, though she does work with aspiring authors as well. She has edited for speculative fiction publishing houses Enclave Publishing and Brimstone Fiction."

A LITTLE RED INK | ERYNNE NEWMAN
Travelers Rest, SC | 919-229-1357
ALittleRedInk@gmail.com | *www.ALittleRedInk.com*
> **Contact:** email, website form
> **Services:** manuscript evaluation, substantive editing/rewriting, copyediting, proofreading
> **Types of manuscripts:** short stories, novels, book proposals, adult, teen/YA

Charges: hourly rate

Credentials/experience: Rita Award-winning editor with five years of experience.

A WAY WITH WORDS WRITING AND EDITORIAL SERVICES | RENEE GRAY-WILBURN

Colorado Springs, CO | 719-271-7076

waywords@earthlink.net | awaywithwordswriting.wordpress.com

Contact: email

Services: substantive editing/rewriting, copyediting, proofreading, ghostwriting, coauthoring, write website text, create small group/ Bible study guides, write curriculum lesson plans, write discussion questions for books, write from transcriptions, write children's books and other material, résumé design and writing

Types of manuscripts: articles, nonfiction books, devotionals, short stories, novels, curriculum, gift books, technical material, adult, teen/YA, picture books, easy readers, middle grade

Charges: hourly rate, project fee

Credentials/experience: "More than twenty years of freelance writing and editing. Wrote five children's books for Capstone Press; extensive curriculum writing for David C. Cook and Group Publishing; wrote children's articles/activities and parenting articles for Focus on the Family; developed online study guides for Wallbuilders; extensive copyediting and proofreading for NavPress (including the Remix Message Bible), David C. Cook, WaterBrook, and major international ministries, as well as numerous independent authors. Writing and editing experience for both fiction and nonfiction manuscripts in children, YA, and adult markets."

AB WRITING SERVICES LLC | ANN BYLE

Grand Rapids, MI

annbyle@gmail.com | www.annbylewriter.com

Contact: email

Services: manuscript evaluation, copyediting, proofreading, ghostwriting, coauthoring, book-contract evaluation, brochures, newsletters, website text, discussion questions for books, back-cover copy, writing coach, substantive editing/rewriting

Types of manuscripts: articles, nonfiction books, devotionals, novels, press releases, query letters, book proposals, adult, picture books

Charges: flat fee, hourly rate

Credentials/experience: "Years of experience as a freelance journalist, coauthor and ghostwriter, copyeditor, and press-release writer. Her work experience includes Moody Publishing, *The Grand Rapids Press*, and Our Daily Bread Ministries. She writes for *Publishers Weekly* and *Grand Rapids Magazine* and has cowritten several books. She is the author of *Christian Publishing 101*."

ABOVE THE PAGES | PAM LAGOMARSINO

Coulterville, CA | 209-878-0245
abovethepages@gmail.com | *www.abovethepages.com*

Contact: email

Services: manuscript evaluation, substantive editing/rewriting, copyediting, proofreading, create small group/Bible study guides, write discussion questions for books

Types of manuscripts: articles, nonfiction books, devotionals, short stories, curriculum, gift books, adult, teen/YA, picture books, easy readers, middle grade, homeschool and children's ministry materials

Charges: flat fee, word rate

Credentials/experience: "AA in English communication; two years of editing experience for Christian nonfiction books, devotionals, sermons, workbooks, homeschool curriculum, and children's materials; certificates in Essential Skills for Editing nonfiction and editing children's books from The Christian PEN; certificate for Keys to Effective Editing from Sandhills Community College."

ACEVEDO WORD SOLUTIONS LLC | JENNE ACEVEDO

480-510-0419
editor@jenneacevedo.com | *www.jenneacevedo.com*

Contact: email

Services: substantive editing/rewriting, copyediting, proofreading, create newsletters, write website text, create small group/Bible study guides, write discussion questions for books, writing coach, manuscript evaluation, book-contract evaluation, brochures, curriculum, back-cover copy

Types of manuscripts: articles, nonfiction books, devotionals, query letters, book proposals, curriculum, gift books, adult, teen/YA, picture books, easy readers, middle grade, short stories, novels, Bible studies, academic

Charges: hourly rate, word rate

Credentials/experience: "Editor, managing editor, and consultant for private and corporate clients. Works with a variety of editors and freelancers. Proofreader for publishers. Cofounder of Christian Editor Network LLC, former director of The Christian PEN: Proofreaders and Editors Network, former director of PENCON (for five years), member of Christian Editor Connection, editing/proofreading instructor for The PEN Institute, founder and director of the Chandler Writers' Group (AZ) since 2011."

ACW CRITIQUE SERVICE | REG A. FORDER

PO Box 110390, Nashville, TN 37222 | 800-21-WRITE
ACWriters@aol.com | *www.ACWriters.com*

Contact: email

Services: manuscript evaluation, substantive editing/rewriting, copyediting, proofreading

Types of manuscripts: articles, nonfiction books, devotionals, poetry, short stories, novels, query letters, book proposals, curriculum, scripts, gift books, technical material, adult, teen/YA, picture books, easy readers, middle grade

Charges: flat fee, hourly rate, page rate, word rate

Credentials/experience: Established for 35 years. Staff of experienced editors.

ADIRONDACK EDITING | SUSAN UTTENDORFSKY

adirondackediting@gmail.com | *www.adirondackediting.com*

Contact: email

Services: manuscript evaluation, substantive editing/rewriting, copyediting, proofreading, ghostwriting, writing coach, coauthoring, small group/Bible study guides, discussion questions for books, writing coach

Types of manuscripts: technical material, nonfiction books, short stories, novels, book proposals, articles, devotionals, Bible studies, gift books, adult, teen/YA, picture books, easy readers, middle grade, technical material

Charges: word rate

Credentials/experience: "Let your creativity run wild! . . . And let us worry about the little things. Along with me, several well-qualified editors work under Adirondack Editing's umbrella. I maintain full editorial control over all manuscripts submitted and review any work performed for me, so you gain two sets of eyes on your material! Our experience is varied in terms of materials edited and length of time freelancing. We provide typical copyediting services, along with a specialized Full-Package Edit not found anywhere else! It includes unlimited resubmissions covering everything: substantive/developmental, copy/line edit, and final proofread."

AM EDITING AND FREELANCE WRITING |
ANGELA MCCLAIN
amediting35@gmail.com | *www.amediting.webs.com*
Contact: email
Services: manuscript evaluation, copyediting, proofreading, ghostwriting, coauthoring, create brochures, create newsletters, website text, small group/Bible study guides, writing coach, discussion questions for books, back-cover copy
Types of manuscripts: nonfiction books, devotionals, poetry, short stories, novels, gift books, articles, Bible studies, teen/YA, adult, picture books, easy readers, middle grade
Charges: page rate
Credentials/experience: "As an editor, Angela is a communications professional who assists writers with writing tasks. Angela is an experienced editor and writer with thorough knowledge of grammar, composition, and other fields relating to the written word. Angela works as a freelance contractor who assists writers with the creation and presentation of written material. Angela works on written material in various capacities, from simple proofreading of internal documents to the creation, presentation, and sometimes even publication of mass-printed material. In addition to the general requirements of written language, she ensures the material conforms to the needs of the author. Angela pays close attention to detail. Angela possesses these traits as well as an overall talent for written communication."

AMBASSADOR COMMUNICATIONS |
CLAIRE GRACE HUTCHINSON
13733 W. Gunsight Dr., Sun City West, AZ 85375 | 812-390-7907
claire@clairehutchinson.net | *www.clairehutchinson.net*
Contact: email
Services: manuscript evaluation, substantive editing/rewriting, copyediting, proofreading, write website text, create small group/ Bible study guides, write discussion questions for books, writing coach, newsletters, academic, script analysis, books into scripts
Types of manuscripts: articles, nonfiction books, devotionals, poetry, short stories, novels, query letters, scripts, gift books,

curriculum, Bible studies, adult, teen/YA, picture books, easy readers, middle grade

Charges: based on type of project

Credentials/experience: "M.A. English, Cert. Professional Program in Screenwriting, UCLA. Writer of the film *Lucky's Treasure*, distributed by Pureflix and Universal. 11 years copyediting an academic journal. 17 years as a script analyst and screenwriter."

AMI EDITING | ANNETTE IRBY

Tacoma, WA

editor@AMIediting.com | www.AMIediting.com

Contact: email

Services: manuscript evaluation, substantive editing/rewriting, copyediting, proofreading, critiquing

Types of manuscripts: short stories, novels

Charges: hourly rate

Credentials/experience: "Annette spent five years working in acquisitions with a CBA publisher. She has fifteen years of experience editing in the CBA marketplace and has worked with several well-known authors and publishers. She's an author and book reviewer. See her website for testimonials."

AMY BOEKE'S EDITING SERVICE | AMY BOEKE

3149 Sandy Hollow Rd., Rockford, IL 61109

abboeke@gmail.com

Contact: email

Services: substantive editing/rewriting, copyediting, proofreading, ghostwriting, create brochures, create newsletters, write website text, create small group/Bible study guides, write curriculum lesson plans, write discussion questions for books, writing coach, back-cover copy

Types of manuscripts: articles, nonfiction books, devotionals, short stories, novels, query letters, book proposals, curriculum, Bible studies, gift books, adult, teen/YA

Charges: hourly rate

Credentials/experience: "BA English studies, Taylor University; MAT secondary English education, Rockford College. Eight years of experience freelance editing/writing."

AMY DROWN
Kalispell, MT | 719-244-1743
editing@amydrown.com | www.amydrown.com/editing
   Contact: email
   Services: manuscript evaluation, substantive editing/rewriting, copyediting, proofreading
   Types of manuscripts: novels, adult, teen/YA, back-cover copy, pitch sheets
   Charges: flat fee, word rate
   Credentials/experience: "Internationally recognized freelance editor specializing in inspirational fiction writing and editing since 2009. I contract with publishers, as well as directly with authors, both published and prepublished, and offer highly competitive rates."

ANDREA MERRELL
60 McKinney Rd., Travelers Rest, SC 29690 | 864-616-5889
*AndreaMerrell7@gmail.com | www.AndreaMerrell.com,
www.TheWriteEditing.blogspot.com*
   Contact: email, website form
   Services: manuscript evaluation, substantive editing/rewriting, copyediting, proofreading, writing coach, website coach, back-cover copy
   Types of manuscripts: articles, nonfiction books, devotionals, short stories, novels, adult, teen/YA
   Charges: hourly rate
   Credentials/experience: "Professional freelance editor. Associate editor with LPC Books and Christian Devotions Ministries. Member of The Christian PEN: Proofreaders and Editors Network."

ANDY SCHEER EDITORIAL SERVICES
5074 Plumstead Dr., Colorado Springs, CO 80920 | 719-282-3729
Andy@AndyScheer.com | AndyScheer.com
   Contact: email
   Services: manuscript evaluations and critiques, copyediting, substantive editing/rewriting, back-cover copy and makeovers
   Types of manuscripts: novels, nonfiction books, short stories, book proposals, one-sheets, adult, teen/YA
   Charges: page rate; per project for critiques, back-cover copy, and one-sheets

Credentials/experience: "More than thirty years of experience in Christian writing, editing, and publishing. Former editor-in-chief of Jerry B. Jenkins Christian Writers Guild. Has served as a judge for national fiction and nonfiction contests and edited fiction and nonfiction for *New York Times* best-selling authors."

ANN KROEKER

Westfield, IN | 317-763-0002
ann@annkroeker.com | *annkroeker.com*

Contact: email
Service: writing coach
Types of manuscripts: articles, nonfiction books, devotionals, poetry, short stories, query letters, book proposals, gift books, adult
Charges: flat fee, hourly rate
Credentials/experience: "Coaching offered as a package of services at a monthly rate; for occasional, one-time coaching needs I charge an hourly rate. When a client requests extensive editorial services that exceed the scope of the coaching package, I quote a flat rate per project."

ANNE RAUTH

3120 Karnes Blvd., Kansas City, MO 64111 | 913-710-8484
anne@annerauth.com

Contact: email
Services: newsletters, marketing and blog posts to promote your book and writing
Types of manuscripts: blog posts, websites
Charges: hourly rate
Credentials/experience: "Anne Rauth has been working in the marketing field for over twenty years at Fortune 500 Companies, nonprofit organizations as well as assisting individuals promote their books."

ARMOR OF HOPE WRITING AND PUBLISHING SERVICES, LLC | DENISE WALKER

Covington, GA | 678-656-8930
dwalker@armorofhopewritingservices.com |
www.armorofhopewritingservices.com

Contact: email
Services: copyediting, proofreading, ghostwriting, coauthoring, write curriculum lesson plans, write discussion questions for books

Types of manuscripts: nonfiction books, devotionals, short stories, novels, curriculum, teen/YA, picture books, easy readers, middle grade

Charges: fees are on the website

Credentials/experience: Freelance proofreader (children's books and Christian manuscripts), middle-school language arts teacher for twelve years.

AUTHOR SUPPORT SERVICES | RUSSELL SHERRAD

Carmichael, CA | 916-967-7251

russellsherrard@reagan.com | www.sherrardsebookresellers.com/WordPress/author-support-services-the-authors-place-to-get-help

Contact: email

Services: manuscript evaluation, substantive editing/rewriting, copyediting, proofreading, blog administration

Types of manuscripts: articles, nonfiction books, devotionals, short stories, novels, teen/YA, picture books, easy readers, middle grade

Charges: flat fee

Credentials/experience: "Writing and editing ebooks since 2009, freelance services for multiple number of clients."

AVODAH EDITORIAL SERVICES | CHRISTY DISTLER

Warminster, PA | 267-231-6723

email through website | www.avodaheditorialservices.com

Contact: email

Services: manuscript evaluation, substantive editing/rewriting, copyediting, proofreading

Types of manuscripts: nonfiction books, devotionals, poetry, short stories, novels, adult, picture books, easy readers

Charges: word rate

Credentials/experience: "Educated at Temple University and University of California–Berkeley. Thirteen years of editorial experience, both as an employee and a freelancer. Currently works mostly for publishing houses but accepts freelance work as scheduling allows."

BA WRITING SOLUTIONS LLC | BLAKE ATWOOD

Richardson, TX

blake@blakeatwood.com | www.blakeatwood.com

Contact: website form, email

Services: manuscript evaluation, substantive editing/rewriting, copyediting, proofreading, ghostwriting, coauthoring, book-contract evaluation, write discussion questions for books, back-cover copy, book project management

Types of manuscripts: nonfiction books, devotionals, query letters, book proposals, short stories, novels, adult

Charges: word rate, hourly rate, flat fee

Credentials/experience: "Since 2014, Blake Atwood has worked with dozens of Christian nonfiction authors to hone their manuscripts and book proposals through developmental editing, copyediting, coauthoring, and ghostwriting. He is traditionally published as a coauthor of *The Father Effect* and has self-published multiple titles, including *The Gospel According to Breaking Bad*. Blake has ghostwritten five books and has coauthored two. He is a certified editor with the Christian Editor Connection and an instructor for their PEN Institute. He teaches writing and editing seminars for Writing Workshops Dallas, and he's a member of the Editorial Freelancers Association and the Nonfiction Authors Association."

BANNER LITERARY | MIKE LOOMIS
Mike@MikeLoomis.co | www.MikeLoomis.co

Contact: email, website form

Services: manuscript evaluation, substantive editing/rewriting, copyediting, proofreading, ghostwriting, coauthoring, book-contract evaluation, newsletters, small group/Bible study guides, curriculum lesson plans, discussion questions for books, writing coach, back-cover copy

Types of manuscripts: articles, nonfiction books, devotionals, query letters, book proposals, curriculum, Bible studies

Charges: flat fee, custom

Credentials/experience: "I'm a book developer, ghostwriter, and editor. I also coach authors on planning the best book for their goals. Because of my twenty years of experience in publishing, I help authors refine their idea, polish their work, and reach their audience. I've worked with *New York Times* bestselling authors, publishers (Simon & Schuster, Multnomah, Zondervan, Random House, Nelson, NavPress, and Penguin) but am most energized by helping first-time authors."

BARBARA KOIS
1007 Cherry St., Wheaton, IL 60187 | 630-532-2941
barbara.kois@gmail.com | www.barbarakois.com

Contact: email

Services: manuscript evaluation, substantive editing/rewriting, copyediting, proofreading, ghostwriting, coauthoring, write website text, newsletters, write discussion questions for books, writing coach, back-cover copy

Types of manuscripts: articles, nonfiction books, devotionals, poetry, short stories, novels, Bible studies, gift books, adult, teen/YA

Charges: custom

Credentials/experience: "Barbara is a writer, editor, author coach, and speaker for writers conferences. She has written or cowritten eight books. She has published more than six hundred articles in the *Chicago Tribune,* as well as articles in a variety of magazines. She has edited hundreds of books for authors, spanning many topics. She is a regular contributor to technology and other corporate websites and serves as a corporate communications consultant."

BOOKOX | THOMAS WOMACK

165 S. Timber Creek Dr., Sisters, OR 97759 | 541-788-6503
Thomas@BookOx.com | www.BookOx.com

Contact: email

Services: manuscript evaluation, substantive editing/rewriting, copyediting, create small group/Bible study guides, writing coach

Types of manuscripts: nonfiction books, devotionals, novels, Bible studies, adult, short stories, book proposals, gift books, academic

Charges: flat fee, word rate

Credentials/experience: "Four decades of full-time book editing experience."

BREAKOUT EDITING | DORI HARRELL

Yakima, WA | 509-910-2220
doriharrell@gmail.com | www.doriharrell.wixsite.com/breakoutediting

Contact: email

Services: substantive editing/rewriting, copyediting, proofreading, write website text

Types of manuscripts: articles, nonfiction books, devotionals, short stories, novels, query letters, adult, teen/YA, picture books, middle grade

Charges: word rate

Credentials/experience: "Dori is a multiple award-winning writer. She freelance edits full-time and has edited more than a hundred novels and nonfiction books. As an editor, she releases more than twenty-five books annually."

BRENDA WILBEE

4631 Quinn Ct. #202, Bellingham, WA 98226
Brenda@BrendaWilbee.com | *www.BrendaWilbee.com*

Contact: email, website form

Services: manuscript evaluation, substantive editing/rewriting, indexing

Types of manuscripts: nonfiction books, devotionals, novels, memoirs, middle grade, adult

Charges: hourly rate, flat fee, page rate, custom

Credentials/experience: "I've been helping writers find their voice for more than 20 years. I hold an MA in Professional Writing, a BA in Creative Writing, and an AA in Visual Communications. I've written ten books, with over 700,000 books sold, written dozens of articles, and for 18 years wrote for *Guideposts Daily Devotionals*. I contributed to Zondervan's *Women's Devotional Bible #2*, wrote the chapter on fiction for *Inside Religious Publishing*, and appear in other anthologies. I taught college and university composition for 7 years. I've presented workshops on all aspects of commercial writing at writers conferences and press conventions. For many years I served on the board for the Pacific NW Writers Association. My goal is to help all writers realize their potential as a unique force for good in a troubled world."

BRIANNA STORM HILVETY

brianna@theliterarycrusader.com | *www.theliterarycrusader.com*

Contact: email, website form

Services: copyediting, proofreading

Types of manuscripts: articles, nonfiction books, short stories, novels, devotionals, Bible studies, adult, teen/YA, middle grade

Charges: word rate, custom

Credentials/experience: "Brianna has five years of experience working on a variety of projects for individual clients, publishers, and writers organizations, including Gilead Publishing, Castle Gate Press, and KingdomPen.org. She cofounded, co-owns, and codirects StoryEmbers.org, a website dedicated to guiding and inspiring Christian novelists. As managing editor, she oversees the entire publishing department and its personnel, ensuring that content is processed, scheduled, and posted on the site weekly. Currently, she personally handles the copyediting of all submissions, in addition to serving as a judge for the yearly story contests. Her professional affiliations include Gold membership at The Christian PEN, editing certifications from The PEN Institute, and copyediting and proofreading expertise at the Christian Editor Connection."

BROOKSTONE CREATIVE GROUP | SUZANNE KUHN

PO Box 211, Evington, VA 24550 | 302-514-7899
www.brookstonecreativegroup.com
  Contact: website form
  Services: substantive editing, copyediting, proofreading, coaching, one-sheets, book proposals, ghostwriting
  Types of manuscripts: books
  Charges: flat fee
  Credentials/experience: Suzanne has more than thirty years of book-specific experience. Brookstone is an expansion of her business, SuzyQ, with a team of almost two dozen professionals who bring a wide range of knowledge and experience to help you get published.

BUTTERFIELD EDITORIAL SERVICES |
DEBRA L. BUTTERFIELD

4810 Gene Field Rd. #2, St. Joseph, MO 64506 | 816-752-2171
deb@debralbutterfield.com | *TheMotivationalEditor.com*
  Contact: email
  Services: manuscript evaluation, substantive editing/rewriting, copyediting, writing coach
  Types of manuscripts: articles, novels, book proposals, adult, query letters
  Charges: word rate
  Credentials/experience: "Nine years experience as a freelance editor and five years experience as a traditional publishing house editor."

C. S. LAKIN

cslakin@gmail.com | *www.livewritethrive.com*
  Contact: email, website form
  Services: manuscript evaluation, substantive editing/rewriting, copyediting, proofreading, website text, small group/Bible study guides, curriculum lesson plans, writing coach, newsletters
  Types of manuscripts: articles, nonfiction books, devotionals, poetry, short stories, novels, query letters, book proposals, gift books,

scripts, curriculum, Bible studies, gift books, adult, teen/YA, picture books, easy readers, middle grade, scene or chapter outlines

Charges: hourly rate, page rate

Credentials/experience: "With more than fifteen years' experience as a copyeditor, and having authored and published twenty novels and ten nonfiction books, I bring a wealth of experience and expertise to my critiques and editing. I critique more than two hundred manuscripts a year and have more than a million words of instruction for writers at my blog *Live Write Thrive*. More than a thousand writers have benefited from my online video courses at *cslakin.teachable.com*. Fast turnaround time, encouraging support, and dependability are the things I strive for with all my clients."

CARLA ROSSI EDITORIAL SERVICES | CARLA ROSSI

The Woodlands, TX

carla@carlarossi.com | www.carlarossi.com

Contact: email

Services: manuscript evaluation, substantive editing/rewriting, copyediting, writing coach, specializing in content editing of romance fiction

Types of manuscripts: short stories, novels, adult

Charges: word rate

Credentials/experience: "Freelance editor for two years. Traditionally published since 2008. Independently published since 2014. Silver member of The Christian PEN. Member of Romance Writers of America and serve on the board of my local chapter."

CHRISTIAN COMMUNICATOR MANUSCRIPT CRITIQUE SERVICE | SUSAN TITUS OSBORN

3133 Puente St., Fullerton, CA 92835 | 714-313-8651

susanosb@aol.com | www.christiancommunicator.com

Contact: email, phone

Services: manuscript evaluation, substantive editing/rewriting, copyediting, proofreading, ghostwriting, book-contract evaluation, write website text, create small group/Bible study guides, write curriculum lesson plans, write discussion questions for books, writing coach

Types of manuscripts: articles, nonfiction books, devotionals, poetry, short stories, novels, query letters, book proposals, curriculum, scripts, gift books, technical material, adult, teen/YA, picture books, easy readers, middle grade

Charges: flat fee, hourly rate, page rate, word rate

Credentials/experience: "Have a staff of fourteen editors with more than thirty years of experience. Recommended by Evangelical Christian Publishers Association and a number of publishing houses and agents."

CHRISTIAN EDITOR CONNECTION | KATHY IDE

Coordinator@ChristianEditor.com | www.ChristianEditor.com

Contact: email

Services: manuscript evaluation, substantive editing/rewriting, copyediting, proofreading, ghostwriting, coauthoring, writing coach

Types of manuscripts: articles, nonfiction books, devotionals, poetry, short stories, novels, query letters, book proposals, curriculum, scripts, gift books, technical material, adult, teen/YA, picture books, easy readers, middle grade

Charges: flat fee, hourly rate, page rate, word rate

Description: "The Christian Editor Connection began in 2007 as a matchmaking service to connect authors, publishers, and agents with qualified, established, professional editorial freelancers who meet their specific needs."

THE CHRISTIAN PEN: PROOFREADERS AND EDITORS NETWORK | KATHY IDE

director@TheChristianPEN.com | www.thechristianpen.com

Contact: website form

Service: membership network for Christian editors

Charges: annual membership fee

Description: "The Christian PEN is dedicated to equipping aspiring and established freelance editors with education, networking, and community. We offer three levels of membership: bronze, silver, and gold. Our members range from no experience to highly experienced professionals."

CHRISTIANBOOKPROPOSALS.COM | CINDY CARTER

408-966-3998

ccarter@ecpa.org | www.ChristianBookProposals.com

Contact: website form

Service: online proposal-submission service

Types of manuscripts: book proposals for all kinds of books and all ages

Charges: $98 for six months

Description: Managed by the Evangelical Christian Publishers Association (ECPA).

CM CREATIVE CONSULTING, LLC | CHRISTI MCGUIRE

Lakewood Ranch, FL | 941-201-8964
Christi@ChristiMcGuire.com | www.ChristiMcGuire.com

Contact: email

Services: manuscript evaluation, substantive editing/rewriting, copyediting, proofreading

Types of manuscripts: nonfiction books, devotionals, query letters, book proposals, curriculum, adult

Charges: hourly rate, word rate

Credentials/experience: "Christi, freelance editor, writer, and consultant, has been in the Christian publishing industry for 17 years. Currently, her primary focus is partnering with authors in the creative process to polish their nonfiction book manuscripts and help them navigate the path to publishing. She is on the teaching faculty for PENCON, as well as a member of the Editorial Freelance Association."

COLLABORATIVE EDITORIAL SOLUTIONS | ANDREW BUSS

info@collaborativeeditorial.com | collaborativeeditorial.com

Contact: email

Services: copyediting, proofreading

Types of manuscripts: articles, nonfiction books, devotionals, Bible studies, technical material, adult, academic

Charges: hourly rate, page rate

Credentials/experience: "I'm a professional editor with more than five years of full-time experience working with authors and scholarly publishers such as InterVarsity Press, Reformation Heritage, P&R Publishing, Georgetown University Press, and Baylor University Press. Although I primarily work in the genre of scholarly nonfiction, I'm always keen to work with creative and thoughtful authors, whatever the topic or genre. I'm a member of the Editorial Freelancers Association and the Society of Biblical Literature."

CORNERSTONE-INK EDITING | VIE HERLOCKER

PO Box 342, Fancy Gap, VA 24328
vherlock@yahoo.com | www.cornerstone-ink.com

Contact: email

Services: manuscript evaluation, substantive editing/rewriting, copyediting

Types of manuscripts: articles, nonfiction books, devotionals, short stories, novels, query letters, book proposals, adult, teen/YA, middle grade

Charges: custom

Credentials/experience: "Member of the Christian PEN, Christian Editor Connection, Word Weavers, and ACFW. Ten years of experience as executive editor for a small traditional publisher. Associate editor for a regional magazine."

THE CORPORATE PEN | CATHY STREINER

Orange Park, FL | 480-419-0356
Cathy@thecorporatepen.com | *www.thecorporatepen.com*

Contact: email

Services: substantive editing/rewriting, copyediting, proofreading, coauthoring, create brochures, create newsletters, write website text, create small group/Bible study guides, write discussion questions for books, writing coach, back-cover copy

Types of manuscripts: articles, nonfiction books, devotionals, short stories, novels, scripts, gift books, technical material, poetry, curriculum, Bible studies, academic, picture books, easy readers, middle grade, adult, teen/YA

Charges: flat fee, page rate, word rate, hourly rate with a maximum amount, custom

Credentials/experience: "Extensive experience with the written word. Cathy began making her living as a writer prior to 1990, and in 2001 established her own company. She self-published a Christian novel in 2009 under a pseudonym and enjoys using her writing and editing skills to help other Christians."

CREATIVE EDITORIAL SOLUTIONS | CLAUDIA VOLKMAN

13128 Silver Thorn Loop, North Fort Myers, FL 33903 | 203-645-5600
cvolkman@mac.com

Contact: email

Service: substantive editing/rewriting, copyediting, proofreading, ghostwriting, coauthoring, newsletters, website text, small group/Bible study guides, discussion questions for books, writing coach, back-cover copy, indexing

Types of manuscripts: articles, nonfiction books, devotionals, novels, Bible studies, gift books, adult

Charges: word rate

Description: "I have been a publishing professional for over thirty-five years and have worked for several well-known trade publishers. I also have had a thriving freelance business since 2007."

CREATIVE ENTERPRISES STUDIO |
MARY HOLLINGSWORTH

Bedford, TX | 817-312-7393

ACreativeShop@aol.com | CreativeEnterprisesStudio.com

Contact: email

Services: manuscript evaluation, substantive editing/rewriting, copyediting, proofreading, ghostwriting, coauthoring, write website text, write discussion questions for books

Types of manuscripts: nonfiction books, devotionals, short stories, novels, book proposals, curriculum, gift books, adult, teen/YA, picture books, easy readers, middle grade

Charges: rates vary according to the work required, estimates provided

Description: "CES is a publishing services company, hosting more than 150 top Christian publishing freelancers. We work with large, traditional Christian publishers on books by best-selling authors. We also produce custom, first-class books on a turnkey basis for independent authors, ministries, churches, and companies."

CREWS AND COULTER EDITORIAL SERVICES |
KAY COULTER

806 Hopi Trl., Temple, TX 76504 | 254-778-6490

bkcoulter@sbcglobal.net | www.crewscoultereditingservices.com

Contact: email

Services: manuscript evaluation, substantive editing/rewriting, copyediting, proofreading, ghostwriting, coauthoring, create brochures, create newsletters, small group/Bible study guides, curriculum, back-cover copy

Types of manuscripts: nonfiction books, devotionals, short stories, novels, book proposals, curriculum, gift books, adult, teen/YA, Bible studies

Charges: hourly rate

Credentials/experience: "I have 17 years in editing experience, working with several publishers and many individuals in over 300 projects. I'm the author of three published books. I have much experience with non-native English speakers. I am a member of The Christian PEN and Christian Editing Connection."

CROSS & DOT EDITORIAL SERVICES | KATIE VORREITER

San Jose, CA | 408-812-3562
Katie@CrossAndDot.net | www.CrossAndDot.net

Contact: email

Services: copyediting, proofreading

Types of manuscripts: articles, nonfiction books, devotionals, short stories, novels, curriculum, gift books, technical material, adult, teen/YA, middle grade

Charges: flat rate

Credentials/experience: Certificate in professional sequence in editing, U.C. Berkeley; MA in international management; BA in English and Spanish.

CYPRESS WIND | RACHEL HILLS

Mooresville, IN | 317-443-0019
www.CypressWind.com

Contact: website form

Services: substantive editing/rewriting, copyediting, proofreading, writing coach, web page and blog copyediting

Types of manuscripts: articles, nonfiction books, short stories, novels, adult, teen/YA

Charges: rates based on the project

Credentials/experience: "I have sixteen years of experience editing for academics and various certifications and training in editing and writing."

DONE WRITE EDITORIAL SERVICES |
MARILYN A. ANDERSON

127 Sycamore Dr., Louisville, KY 40223 | 502-244-0751
shelle12@aol.com | www.TheChristianPEN.com

Contact: email

Services: copyediting, proofreading, brochures, newsletters, website text, small group/Bible study guides, curriculum lesson plans, discussion questions for books

Types of manuscripts: articles, nonfiction books, devotionals, poetry, short stories, novels, curriculum, technical material, adult, picture books, book proposals, Bible studies, gift books, academic

Charges: hourly rate

Credentials/experience: "I am qualified by an MA in English and a BA in English and the humanities from the University of Louisville. I taught English grammar and literature for four years and have tutored ESL students since 2004. I worked as a writer, editor, and proofreader of educational curriculum, as well as in the energy, utility, and benefits industries for about eighteen years. To date, I have edited seventy-eight books, forty-eight doctoral dissertations, a master's thesis, a handbook, workbook, and leader's guide, as well as innumerable business projects. I have written a company history in three different formats and a glossary of utility terms. I conduct editing and proofreading services for both publishing houses, independent authors, and several ministries. I am a charter and gold member of The Christian PEN: Proofreaders and Editors Network and a tested member of the Christian Editor Connection."

ECHO CREATIVE MEDIA | BRENDA NOEL

Smyrna, TN | 615-223-0754
bnoel@thewordeditor.com | *echocreativemedia.weebly.com*

Contact: email

Services: substantive editing/rewriting, copyediting, proofreading, ghostwriting, write website text, create small group/Bible study guides, write curriculum lesson plans, write discussion questions for books

Types of manuscripts: articles, nonfiction books, devotionals, short stories, book proposals, curriculum, gift books, adult, teen/YA, picture books, easy readers

Charges: flat fee, hourly rate

Credentials/experience: Sixteen years of experience in the Christian publishing industry.

EDIT RESOURCE, LLC | ERIC AND ELISA STANDFORD

19265 Lincoln Green Ln., Monument, CO 80132 | 719-290-0757
info@editresource.com | *www.editresource.com*

Contact: website form

Services: manuscript evaluation, substantive editing/rewriting, copyediting, proofreading, ghostwriting, coauthoring, create small group/Bible study guides, curriculum lesson plans, write discussion questions for books, writing coach, back-cover copy

Types of manuscripts: nonfiction books, devotionals, novels, query letters, book proposals, curriculum, Bible studies, adult, teen/YA

Charges: flat fee, hourly rate

Credentials/experience: "Eric and Elisa have a combined forty plus years of editorial experience, both as in-house employees and as independent service providers, and are well-recognized members of the Christian publishing community. They also represent other top indie editors; see the Team page on the website."

EDITING BY LUCY | LUCY CRABTREE

Lawrence, KS | 913-543-1782

editingbylucy@gmail.com | editingbylucy.com

Contact: email

Services: copyediting, proofreading

Types of manuscripts: articles, nonfiction books, short stories, novels, query letters, book proposals, adult

Charges: word rate

Credentials/experience: "Polished writer and editor with nine years of professional experience in the publishing industry (seven years) and educational settings (two years). Well-versed in Microsoft Office and Adobe Creative Suite. Familiarity with Associated Press, American Psychological Association, and *Chicago Manual* style books. Experience with Drupal, WordPress, and Blogger."

EDITING GALLERY LLC | CAROL CRAIG

2622 Willona Dr., Eugene, OR 97408 | 541-735-1834

kf7orchid@gmail.com | www.editinggallery.com

Contact: email

Services: manuscript evaluation, substantive editing/rewriting, writing coach, copyediting, proofreading

Types of manuscripts: novels, query letters, book proposals, adult, teen/YA, picture books, easy readers, middle grade, nonfiction books

Charges: hourly rate

Credentials/experience: "I have been a developmental editor for over 20 years. Plus I have edited dozens of books that have been picked up by traditional publishers. You can see a small sampling of them on my website. I work with both published authors and newer writers hoping to get a jump start on their writing."

eDITMORE EDITORIAL SERVICES | TAMMY DITMORE

501-I S. Reino Rd. #194, Newbury Park, CA 91320 | 805-630-6809

tammy@editmore.com | www.editmore.com

Contact: email

Services: manuscript evaluation, substantive editing/rewriting, copyediting, proofreading, website text, small group/Bible study guides, write discussion questions for books

Types of manuscripts: articles, nonfiction books, devotionals, curriculum, Bible studies, gift books, adult, teen/YA, academic

Charges: custom

Credentials/experience: "A specialist in nonfiction, I offer consultations, critiques, developmental editing, copyediting, and proofreading services. I work closely with authors, publishers, editors, organizations, and businesses. My specialties include Christian and spiritual material, academic authors and publishers, personal histories and current events, and publications on aging and Alzheimer's disease. I am familiar with Chicago, APA, MLA, SBL, and AP styles."

EDITOR FOR YOU | MELANIE RIGNEY

4201 Wilson Blvd., Arlington, VA 22203-4417 | 703-863-3940
editor@editorforyou.com | *www.editorforyou.com*

Contact: email

Service: manuscript evaluation

Types of manuscripts: nonfiction books, devotionals, novels, query letters, book proposals

Charges: flat fee, hourly rate

Credentials/experience: "Melanie Rigney has decades of experience as a writer and editor, including time at *Writer's Digest* and *Advertising Age*. In the past 15 years, Editor for You has helped hundreds of authors, agents, and publishers. Melanie is also the author of numerous books for Franciscan Media and Bayard, and contributes to *Living Faith*, *Catholic Digest*, Catholic Mom, Women in the New Evangelization, and other sites and publications."

EDITOR WORLD, LLC | PATTI FISHER

119 Blue Grass Trl., Newport, VA 24128 | 614-500-3348
info@editorworld.com | *www.editorworld.com*

Contact: email

Services: copyediting, proofreading

Types of manuscripts: articles, nonfiction books, devotionals, poetry, short stories, novels, query letters, book proposals, curriculum, Bible studies, scripts, gift books, technical material, adult, teen/YA, easy readers, middle grade

Charges: word rate

Credentials/experience: "Clients can choose a professional editor based on the editor's profile, such as qualifications, skills, number of pages edited, and previous client ratings. Our editing panel includes university faculty, professional editors, published authors, and retired professionals who love words more than anything else. Our editors are tested on their editing skills before being accepted to provide editing services through Editor World. Choose your own personal editor to improve your work based on his or her qualifications, expertise, skills, and ratings/reviews, benefiting from our strict deadlines and affordable fees."

ELAINA RAMSEY

Alexandria, VA | 703-403-3424
elainabueno@gmail.com

Contact: email

Services: substantive editing/rewriting, copyediting, proofreading, write website text, create small group/Bible study guides, write curriculum lesson plans, write discussion questions for books

Types of manuscripts: articles, devotionals, curriculum, scripts

Charges: hourly rate

Credentials/experience: "As a former editor of *Sojourners* magazine, I am experienced in editing religious and social-justice content from across the theological and political spectrum. Trained in Associated Press style. I am adept at developing discussion guides, toolkits, and preaching resources. MTS degree and solid experience leading campaigns. I specialize in faith-based media, messaging, and advocacy for racial justice and women's empowerment."

ELISABETH WARNER

Long Island, NY
editor@elisabethwarner.com | *www.elisabethwarner.com/services*

Contact: website form

Services: substantive editing/rewriting, copyediting, proofreading, small group/Bible study guides, discussion questions for books, indexing

Types of manuscripts: nonfiction books, devotionals, novels, Bible studies, academic, adult, teens/YA, middle grade

Charges: page rate

Credentials/experience: "Years of editing experience in academic, faith-based fiction, and faith-based nonfiction writing. Gives personalized, encouraging feedback and fully edits your manuscript with meticulous attention to detail."

ELOQUENT EDITS, LLC | DENISE ROEPER
Port Orange, FL | 386-299-8814
denise.eloquentedits@gmail.com | www.eloquentedits.com
> **Contact:** email
> **Services:** copyediting, proofreading
> **Types of manuscripts:** nonfiction books, short stories, novels, teen/YA, middle grade
> **Charges:** word rate, also review a document and provide an estimate
> **Credentials/experience:** "I have edited and proofread print matter ranging from brochures, business print, website content to fiction manuscripts. Specialties are editing fiction, motivational, and spiritual print. Accepting projects that require a short turnaround time."

EMH INDEXING SERVICES | ELISE HESS
314 Mountain View Dr., Lead, SD 57754 | 605-641-3014
emhess5@gmail.com
> **Contact:** email
> **Services:** indexing
> **Charges:** page rate
> **Credentials/experience:** "I have experience in subject, Scripture, and name indexes, as well as index updates. I have written indexes for Moody Publishers, Wiley Publishers, and many more. My husband and I are pastors, and I have a Biblical Studies degree so I am very familiar with Christian materials."

FACETS EDITORIAL SERVICES | DEBORAH CHRISTENSEN
PO Box 354, Addison, IL 60107 | 630-830-5787
dcfacets@earthlink.net | www.Plowingthefields.wordpress.com
> **Contact:** email
> **Services:** substantive editing/rewriting, copyediting, proofreading, write website text
> **Types of manuscripts:** articles, nonfiction books, devotionals, novels, adult, teen/YA
> **Charges:** hourly rate
> **Credentials/experience:** "I have over 30 years experience with editing and proofreading. I served as an editor for Christian Service

Brigade and a mentor for the Christian Writer's Guild. I'm proficient with *The Associated Press Stylebook*, *The Chicago Manual of Style*, and *The Christian Writer's Manual of Style*."

FAITH EDITORIAL SERVICES | REBECCA FAITH

PO Box 184, Novelty, OH 44072 | 216-906-0205
rebecca@faitheditorial.com | *www.faitheditorial.com*

Contact: email, website form, mail

Services: substantive editing/rewriting, copyediting, proofreading, create small group/Bible study guides

Types of manuscripts: articles, nonfiction books, technical material, adult, teen/YA, sermons, devotionals, curriculum, Bible studies, academic

Charges: hourly rate

Credentials/experience: "My experience editing in the Christian market includes six years as managing editor for a Christian nonprofit; another six years editing and writing content for a global Christian ministry, including sermons and sermon transcripts; and copyediting nonfiction Christian books and devotionals. In addition, I edit technical, engineering, medical, and educational material for various independent and publishing clients. I hold membership in the EFA and Christian PEN."

FAITHFULLY WRITE EDITING | DAWN KINZER

dawnkinzer@comcast.net | *www.faithfullywriteediting.com*

Contact: email

Services: manuscript evaluation, substantive editing/rewriting, copyediting, proofreading

Types of manuscripts: short stories, novels

Charges: flat fee, page rate

Credentials/experience: "Dawn Kinzer launched Faithfully Write Editing in 2010. She is currently focusing on editing fiction: full-length novels, novellas, and short stories. She is a member of the Northwest Christian Writers Association, American Christian Fiction Writers, The Christian PEN, and the Christian Editor Connection. Four of her own novels have been published, and her work has also been included in devotionals and magazines. Dawn co-hosts and writes for the Seriously Write blog, which is dedicated to encouraging and equipping Christian writers."

FAITHFUL-WORDS | ELIZABETH BELASCO

500 Skyline Ridge Lookout, Wimberley, TX 78676 | 512-705-1584
elizabethbelasco@faithful-words.com | Faithful-Words.com

> **Contact:** email, website form
>
> **Services:** substantive editing/rewriting, copyediting, proofreading, small group/Bible study guides, curriculum lesson plans, discussion questions for books
>
> **Types of manuscripts:** articles, nonfiction books, devotionals, curriculum, Bible studies, academic
>
> **Charges:** flat fee, hourly rate, page rate, word rate, custom
>
> **Credentials/experience:** "Ten years experience as an academic editor and Christian writer of brief commentaries, Bible study guides, and devotionals. If you need editorial help or original writing, please contact me. I am happy to discuss your project and collaborate to finish the work."

FAITHWORKS EDITORIAL & WRITING, INC. | NANETTE THORSEN SNIPES

PO Box 1596, Buford, GA 30518 | 770-945-3093
nsnipes@bellsouth.net | www.faithworkseditorial.com

> **Contact:** email, website form
>
> **Services:** manuscript evaluation, copyediting, proofreading, brochures, create newsletters, website text, work-for-hire projects
>
> **Types of manuscripts:** articles, nonfiction books, devotionals, poetry, short stories, query letters, gift books, adult, picture books, easy readers, middle grade, memoirs, business
>
> **Charges:** hourly rate, page rate
>
> **Credentials/experience:** "Member: The Christian PEN (Proofreaders & Editors Network), Christian Editor Connection, Christian Editor Network. Proofreader for corporate newsletters, thirteen years. Published writer for more than twenty-five years. Published hundreds of articles in magazines and stories in more than sixty compilation books, including Guideposts, B&H, Regal, and Integrity. Twelve years of editorial experience in both adult and children's short fiction and books, memoirs, short stories, devotions, articles, business. Rates are generally by page but, under specific circumstances, by the hour. Editorial clients have published with such houses as Zondervan, Tyndale, and Revell."

FICTION LAB | DAN LARSEN

55150 Airlane Dr., 6C, Yucca Valley, CA 92284 | 951-313-5426
bookmdnl@gmail.com

Contact: email
Services: manuscript evaluation, substantive editing/rewriting, copyediting, proofreading
Types of manuscripts: nonfiction books, novels, adult, teen/YA, middle grade
Charges: word rate
Credentials/experience: "Career freelance editor, fiction, over 20 years, more than 1,500 titles so far, employed by top NYC publishers, endorsed by bestselling authors, member of Christian Editor Connection and Christian Proofreaders and Editors Network."

FINAL TOUCH PROOFREADING & EDITING |
HEIDI MANN

Ely, MN | 701-866-4299
mann.heidi@gmail.com | www.FinalTouchProofreadingAndEditing.com

Contact: email
Services: copyediting, proofreading
Types of manuscripts: articles, nonfiction books, devotionals, novels, curriculum, adult, teen/YA, picture books, easy readers, middle grade, Bible studies
Charges: flat rate, hourly rate
Credentials/experience: "Fourteen years of experience as a seminary-trained Lutheran pastor; excellent understanding of writing mechanics and style, honed through years of higher education and professional use; freelance editor since 2007 serving authors, publishers, and other entities; have completed multiple educational courses to enhance my knowledge and skills; passionate about writing that intersects with Christian faith. Member of The Christian PEN."

FISTBUMP MEDIA, LLC | DAN KING

Sarasota, FL | 941-780-4179
dan@fistbumpmedia.com | fistbumpmedia.com

Contact: email
Services: manuscript evaluation, proofreading, write website text
Types of manuscripts: nonfiction books, devotionals, short stories, novels, teen/YA, adult

Charges: flat rate, word rate

Credentials/experience: "Fistbump Media provides self-publishing support services in addition to blog/website hosting and design, email subscriber management, and social-media services. We support experienced and first-time writers and leverage the power of self-publishing. References and portfolio are on the website."

THE FOREWORD COLLECTIVE, LLC |
MOLLY KEMPF HODGIN, NICOLE CORSE LEVINE

1726 Charity Dr., Brentwood, TN 37027

info@theforewordcollective.com | *www.theforewordcollective.com*

Contact: email, website form

Services: manuscript evaluation, substantive editing/rewriting, copyediting, proofreading, ghostwriting, coauthoring, brochures, newsletters, website text, writing coach, back-cover copy

Types of manuscripts: articles, nonfiction books, devotionals, novels, query letters, book proposals, gift books, adult, teens/YA, picture books, easy readers, middle grade

Charges: custom rate

Credentials/experience: "We employ a wide variety of creative professionals on a per-project basis, including editors, copyeditors, designers, writers, photographers, marketers, and public-relations pros. We have more than thirty years of publishing experience between us, and we want to put that experience to work for you. Molly was most recently the associate publisher for the specialty division of HarperCollins Christian Publishing, handling gift and children's books. Nicole was most recently the editorial director at InSight Publishing."

FREELANCE WRITING & EDITING SERVICES |
ROBIN SCHMITT

Rockford, MI | 616-350-0576

schmitt.freelancer@sbcglobal.net | *robinschmitt.com*

Contact: email, phone

Services: manuscript evaluation, substantive editing/rewriting, copyediting, ghostwriting, coauthoring, brochures, newsletters, website text, small group/Bible study guides, curriculum lesson plans, discussion questions for books, writing coach, back-cover copy

Types of manuscripts: articles, nonfiction books, devotionals, short stories, novels, curriculum, Bible studies, scripts, gift books, adult, teens/YA, picture books, easy readers, middle grade

Charges: flat fee, hourly rate, page rate, word rate

Credentials/experience: "More than 20 years of experience as a writer and editor in Christian publishing. I've edited many books, both fiction and nonfiction, for adults, teens, and children. In every project I take on, I always strive for the highest standard of excellence."

FRENCH AND ENGLISH COMMUNICATION SERVICES |
DIANE GOULLARD

3104 E. Camelback Rd. #124, Phoenix, AZ 85016-4502 | 602-870-1000
RequestFAECS2008@cox.net | *www.FrenchAndEnglish.com*

Contact: email, phone, website form, mail

Services: copyediting, proofreading, coauthoring, brochures, website text, small group/Bible studies, discussion questions for books; French to English and English to French proofreading, translating

Types of manuscripts: articles, nonfiction books, devotionals, poetry, short stories, novels, query letters, book proposals, curriculum, Bible studies, scripts, gift books, technical material, adult, teens/YA, picture books, easy readers, middle grade, scientific, lyrics

Charges: flat fee, hourly rate, page rate, word rate, custom

Credentials/experience: "Visit my website for bio, references, and experience."

GALADRIEL GRACE

galadriel@galadrielgrace.com | *galadrielgrace.com*

Contact: email, website form

Services: substantive editing/rewriting, copyediting, proofreading, create brochures, create newsletters, write website text, create small group/Bible study guides, write curriculum lesson plans, ghostwriting, back-cover copy

Types of manuscripts: articles, nonfiction books, devotionals, poetry, short stories, novels, query letters, book proposals, curriculum, Bible studies, adult, teens/YA, picture books, easy readers, middle grade

Charges: flat rate, page rate, word rate

Credentials/experience: "PEN certified editor, several years working with authors to help them present their best work and market themselves better."

GINGER KOLBABA

Elgin, IL | 847-366-6547

ginger@gingerkolbaba.com | *www.gingerkolbaba.com*

  Contact: email

  Services: manuscript evaluation, substantive editing/rewriting, copyediting, proofreading, ghostwriting, coauthoring, create small group/Bible study guides, write discussion questions for books, writing coach

  Types of manuscripts: articles, nonfiction books, devotionals, novels, query letters, book proposals, adult, teen/YA

  Charges: hourly rate for editing, flat rate for writing

  Credentials/experience: "More than twenty years in the industry. Former editor of *Today's Christian Woman* and *Marriage Partnership* magazines and *Kyria.com*, all national, award-winning publications of Christianity Today International. Written or contributed to more than thirty books and five hundred articles, both in print and online. Clients include many publishing houses and best-selling authors."

HANEMAN EDITORIAL | NATALIE HANEMAN

Franklin, TN | 615-712-4430

nathanemann@gmail.com | *www.nataliehanemannediting.com*

  Contact: email

  Services: manuscript evaluation, substantive editing/rewriting, copyediting

  Types of manuscripts: nonfiction books, novels, book proposals, adult, teen/YA, middle grade

  Charges: flat fee

  Credentials/experience: "Eleven years in-house at publishing houses, eight of those at Thomas Nelson in the fiction division under the tutelage of Allen Arnold. Since 2012, I've been freelance editing fiction and nonfiction (substantive and line), as well as helping authors get their synopses ready to submit to agents. I've edited more than three hundred manuscripts and particularly love working with newer authors or authors who are unsure if they should publish traditionally or indie. Certified by the Christian Editors Connection."

HAYHURST EDITORIAL LLC | SARAH HAYHURST

1441 Haynescrest Ct., Grayson, GA 30017 | 470-825-2905

sarah@sarahhayhurst.com | *www.sarahhayhurst.com*

Contact: email

Services: substantive editing/rewriting, copyediting, proofreading, website text

Types of manuscripts: articles, nonfiction books, devotionals, Bible studies, adult

Charges: word rate

Credentials/experience: "Sarah graduated as the valedictorian of her class in high school, earned an associate degree in Secretarial Science in 1991, and pursued a bachelor's degree in Communication Arts in 2014, graduating cum laude. Sarah has enjoyed a variety of positions, such as editor/online teacher for a publishing company, managing editor for a university, computer/ESL teacher for a school, marketing manager for a law firm and an engineering firm, and communications director for a school. Sarah is a gold-level member of The Christian PEN and Christian Editor Network with whom she passed extensive testing and demonstrated expertise in the substantive editing, copyediting and proofreading of both fiction and nonfiction manuscripts as well as other nonfiction content. Sarah has over ten years of experience in editing and started her own editorial company in 2014."

HENRY MCLAUGHLIN

817-703-9875

henry@henrymclaughlin.org | www.henrymclaughlin.org

Contact: email, phone

Services: manuscript evaluation, substantive editing/rewriting, ghostwriting, writing coach

Types of manuscripts: nonfiction books, short stories, novels, adult

Charges: custom rate

Credentials/experience: "For the past several years I have served as a coach and editor to many writers in both fiction and nonfiction. I have also ghostwritten. My work is in both Christian and general markets. For me, building a relationship with the author is key to any editing. It's important for me to know the author's heart and desire for their work. As an editor, my goal is to help them achieve their dream by providing editing and coaching geared to helping them develop and grow as writers."

HESTERMAN CREATIVE | DR. VICKI HESTERMAN

PO Box 333, Napoleon, OH 43545

vhes@mac.com

Contact: email

Services: manuscript evaluation, substantive editing/rewriting, copyediting, proofreading, coauthoring, create newsletters, write website text, create small group/Bible study guides, writing coach, back-cover copy

Types of manuscripts: articles, nonfiction books, devotionals, novels, query letters, book proposals, Bible studies, gift books, adult

Charges: hourly rate, firm estimate with sample

Credentials/experience: "Writer, editor, photographer, college professor with 30 years experience in newspapers, magazines, books."

HONEST EDITING SERVICES | BILL LELAND

Bend, OR

bill@writersedgeservice.com | www.honestediting.com

Contact: email, website form

Services: "Honest Editing offers three specific editorial services for Christian manuscripts. (1) We can create professional proposals for enhancing your presentation to publishers; (2) We can do a full evaluation of a manuscript that identifies both strengths and weaknesses in a manuscript and points the author in the right direction to improve the manuscript/writing style; (3) We can perform a full edit, page by page, of an entire manuscript. All these are done by professional editors for a flat fee as outlined at our website."

Types of manuscripts: nonfiction books, devotionals, novels, book proposals, Bible studies, gift books, adult, teen/YA

Charges: flat fee

HONEYCOMB HOUSE PUBLISHING LLC |
DAVID E . FESSENDEN

dave@fessendens.net | www.davefessenden.com,
www.fromconcepttocontract.com

Contact: email

Services: manuscript evaluation, substantive editing/rewriting, copyediting, brochures, newsletters, book-contract evaluation, write website text, create small group/Bible study guides, write discussion questions for books, writing coach, back-cover copy, coauthoring

Types of manuscripts: nonfiction books, devotionals, academic, novels, book proposals, Bible studies, gift books, adult, teen/YA , middle grade

Charges: flat fee

Credentials/experience: "David E. Fessenden, publisher for Honeycomb House Publishing LLC, has degrees in journalism and theology, and over 30 years of experience in writing, editing, and editorial management for Christian book publishers."

INKSMITH EDITORIAL SERVICES | LIZ SMITH

1002 Scotch Pine Way, Mebane, NC 27302 | 336-514-2331

liz@inksmithediting.com | *www.inksmithediting.com*

Contact: email, phone, website form

Services: substantive editing/rewriting, copyediting, proofreading, indexing

Types of manuscripts: articles, nonfiction books, devotionals, Bible studies

Charges: word rate

Credentials/experience: "Liz Smith is a freelance editor and indexer who specializes in Christian nonfiction. She has a passion to help others publish works that edify the body of Christ. Liz has edited dozens of published books and articles, working with Christian publishers and both new and experienced authors. She also helps writers self-publish. In addition, Liz has over twenty years of experience as a homeschool mom of nine. In that time, she's had much practice teaching and reviewing persuasive and technical writing as well as correcting numerous essays and reports."

INKSNATCHER | SALLY HANAN

Austin, TX | 512-351-5869

inkmeister@inksnatcher.com | *www.inksnatcher.com*

Contact: email, text

Services: substantive editing/rewriting, copyediting, proofreading, ghostwriting, coauthoring, write website text, write discussion questions for books

Types of manuscripts: articles, nonfiction books, short stories, novels, curriculum, gift books, adult, teen/YA, easy readers, middle grade

Charges: flat rate, hourly rate, word rate

Credentials/experience: "Established in 2007, Inksnatcher has edited books and written copy for Bobby Conner, Shawn Bolz, Jon Hamill, and Dennis Cramer, among many others."

INSPIRATION FOR WRITERS, INC. | SANDY TRITT

1527 18th St., Parkersburg, WV 26101 | 304-428-1218
IFWeditors@gmail.com | www.InspirationForWriters.com

> **Contact:** email, phone
> **Services:** manuscript evaluation, substantive editing/rewriting, copyediting, proofreading, ghostwriting, write curriculum lesson plans, write discussion questions for books, writing coach, consulting
> **Types of manuscripts:** nonfiction books, devotionals, short stories, novels, query letters, book proposals, curriculum, scripts, gift books, adult, teen/YA, middle grade
> **Charges:** flat fee, word rate
> **Credentials/experience:** "We are one of the oldest and most respected editing/writing companies on the Internet today. All our editors-writers are published authors with years of editing experience who've been specially trained to edit according to our high standards."

JAMES WATKINS

jim@jameswatkins.com | jameswatkins.com

> **Contact:** email
> **Services:** manuscript evaluation, substantive editing/rewriting, copyediting, ghostwriting, coauthoring, write website text, write discussion questions for books, writing coach
> **Types of manuscripts:** articles, nonfiction books, devotionals, book proposals, adult
> **Charges:** page rate
> **Credentials/experience:** "Award-winning editor (four Evangelical Press Awards), developed the editing course at Taylor University, served as an editor and editorial director at Wesleyan Publishing House for more than twenty years, and is the author of twenty books and more than 2,000 articles."

JAMIE CHAVEZ

jamie.chavez@gmail.com | www.jamiechavez.com

> **Contact:** email
> **Services:** manuscript evaluation, substantive editing/rewriting, copyediting
> **Types of manuscripts:** articles, nonfiction books, novels, adult, teen/YA, picture books, easy readers, middle grade, devotionals
> **Charges:** flat fee

Credentials/experience: "Jamie Chavez worked for more than ten years in the Christian publishing industry and twenty as a professional copywriter before becoming a freelance editor in 2004. Books she's edited have become *New York Times* best sellers, won Christy and Carol Awards, and been finalists for many other awards and honors. She enjoys the collaborative nature of editing and finds long-term relationships especially rewarding—bring on the second, third, fourth book in the series! Jamie counts many national publishing houses as clients, many authors as friends, and spends her days making good books better."

JANIS WHIPPLE

9608 Regiment Ct., Land O Lakes, FL 34638 | 954-579-8545
janiswhipple@gmail.com

Contact: email

Services: manuscript evaluation, substantive editing/rewriting, copyediting, proofreading, coauthoring, create brochures, create small group/Bible study guides, write discussion questions for books, writing coach

Types of manuscripts: articles, nonfiction books, devotionals, query letters, book proposals, curriculum, gift books, adult, teen/YA

Charges: hourly rate, sometimes does fee projects

Credentials/experience: "Thirty years of editing, ten years as an in-house editor with B&H Publishers in acquisitions and managing editing, fifteen years as a freelance editor and writing coach."

JAY PAYLEITNER

629 N. Tyler Rd., Saint Charles, IL 60174 | 630-377-7899
jaypayleitner@gmail.com | *www.jaypayleitner.com*

Contact: email

Services: ghostwriting, coauthoring, brochures, back-cover copy

Types of manuscripts: nonfiction books, devotionals, scripts, gift books, picture books

Charges: flat fee

Credentials/experience: "Jay Payleitner spent a decade on Michigan Avenue in Chicago writing and producing ads and commercials for Corona, Kroger, and Midway Airlines (with Mike Ditka). He also led the creative team that named SunChips. Following God's clear call, Jay spent two decades as a freelance radio producer working with Josh McDowell, Chuck Colson, Toby Mac, Voice of the Martyrs, The Salvation Army, Bible League, National Center for

Fathering, and others. He has written literally thousands of PSAs and spots for dozens of ministries. Most notably, Jay has written more than 25 books including *52 Things Kids Need from a Dad*, *52 Things Wives Need from Their Husbands*, and *What If God Wrote Your Bucket List*? selling more than a half-million copies. Jay has been a guest multiple times on The Harvest Show, Moody Radio, and Focus on the Family."

JEANETTE GARDNER LITTLETON, PUBLICATION SERVICES

3706 N.E. Shady Lane Dr., Gladstone, MO 64119-1958 | 816-459-8016
jeanettedl@earthlink.net | *www.linkedin.com/in/jeanette-littleton-b1b790101*

Contact: email

Services: manuscript evaluation, substantive editing/rewriting, copyediting, proofreading, book-contract evaluation, create brochures, create newsletters, write website text, create small group/Bible study guides, write curriculum lesson plans, write discussion questions for books, back-cover copy, indexing

Types of manuscripts: articles, nonfiction books, devotionals, short stories, novels, query letters, book proposals, curriculum, Bible studies, gift books, technical material, adult, teen/YA

Charges: flat fee, hourly rate, page rate

Credentials/experience: "I've been a full-time editor and writer for thirty years for a variety of publishers. I've written five thousand articles and edited thousands of articles and dozens of books. Please see my profile at LinkedIn."

JEANETTE HANSCOME

San Ramon, CA
jeanettehanscome@gmail.com | *jeanettehanscome.com*

Contact: email, website form

Services: manuscript evaluation, substantive editing/rewriting, copyediting, ghostwriting, coauthoring, write website text, write discussion questions for books, writing coach, back-cover copy, brochures, newsletters

Types of manuscripts: articles, nonfiction books, devotionals, short stories, novels, query letters, book proposals, gift books, adult, teen/YA, middle grade, blog posts

Charges: hourly rate

Credentials/experience: "I am the author of five books and hundreds of published articles, devotions, and stories. My experience includes twenty-two years as a writer and fifteen years as a freelance editor."

JEFF PEPPLE

15317 Laurel Ridge, Leo, IN 46765 | 260-627-7347
jhpepple@hotmail.com

Contact: email, phone
Services: manuscript evaluation, substantive editing/rewriting, copyediting, proofreading, write website text
Types of manuscripts: articles, nonfiction books, devotionals, short stories, novels, curriculum, scripts, gift books, technical material, adult, teen/YA, easy readers, middle grade
Charges: flat fee, hourly rate, page rate, word rate
Credentials/experience: BA in professional writing, Taylor University.

JENNIFER EDWARDS COMMUNICATIONS | JENNIFER EDWARDS

4130 Miners Trl., Loomis, CA 95650 | 916-768-4207
mail.jennifer.edwards@gmail.com | www.jedwardsediting.net

Contact: email
Services: manuscript evaluation, substantive editing/rewriting, copyediting, proofreading, write website text, create small group/ Bible study guides, write discussion questions for books, back-cover copy
Types of manuscripts: articles, nonfiction books, devotionals, curriculum, academic, technical material, book proposals, Bible studies, adult
Charges: flat fee, hourly rate
Credentials/experience: "Jennifer is an established professional editor and writer serving Christian authors and publishers. She edits primarily non-fiction works, specializing in developmental, content, and line editing. She is thorough, fast, and flexible, with fair rates. Jennifer earned an MA in Biblical/Theological Studies from Western Seminary. Her seminary training has proven invaluable to clients by providing a critical eye for content, a thorough understanding of Scripture, and insightful theological thinking. She manages publishing & marketing for Principles to Live By, a non-profit that publishes discipleship materials for Christians worldwide (*www.ptlb.com*). She freelances for Lexham

Press and BMH Publishing working with talented authors and editorial teams on numerous titles."

JHWRITING+ | NICOLE HAYES

Randleman, NC | 410-709-8549
jhwritingplus@yahoo.com | www.jhwritingplus.com

Contact: email

Services: manuscript evaluation, substantive editing/rewriting, copyediting, proofreading, ghostwriting, coauthoring, write website text, create small group/Bible study guides, write curriculum lesson plans, write discussion questions for books, writing coach

Types of manuscripts: articles, nonfiction books, devotionals, poetry, short stories, novels, curriculum, gift books, technical material, adult, teen/YA

Charges: flat rate, word rate

Credentials/experience: "Bachelor's degree in English; PhD in education. Although I do most writing, editing, and proofreading projects, my niche is creative nonfiction (engaging, dramatic, factual prose). I have been writing and editing for more than twenty-five years."

JLC SERVICES | JODY COLLINS

1403 Newport Ct. S.E., Renton, WA 98058 | 425-260-0948
heyjode70@yahoo.com | www.jodyleecollins.com

Contact: email

Services: copyediting, proofreading, writing coach, back-cover copy, book-project consultant

Types of manuscripts: articles, nonfiction books, devotionals, poetry, book proposals, Bible studies, picture books

Charges: flat fee

Credentials/experience: "BA in liberal studies, English major. Teaching credential, 1991. More than twenty-five years of experience writing online and in print. Author of *Living the Season Well: Reclaiming Christmas*. Ten plus projects completed since 2012."

JOHN SLOAN LLC | JOHN SLOAN

830 Grey Eagle Cir. N., Colorado Springs, CO 80919 | 719-888-0365
jsjohnsloan@gmail.com

Contact: email

Services: substantive editing/rewriting, ghostwriting, coauthoring, writing coach, consulting, teaching seminars to companies and conferences

Types of manuscripts: articles, nonfiction books, short stories, adult

Charges: flat fee, hourly rate

Credentials/experience: "John Sloan was executive editorial specialist with Zondervan for 35 years. As an executive editor, he used his experience and creativity to advocate nonfiction narrative with authors and agents. He guides authors in finalizing book organization for proposals and final writings. And he gives different approaches to structure and unity, suggesting rearrangements of material in new frameworks; helps authors discover the voice they've struggled to find in writing their works; and edits projects in line with these editorial approaches. He is available as a mentor and editorial advocate."

JOT OR TITTLE EDITORIAL SERVICES |
SAMUEL RYAN KELLY
sam@jotortittle.com | jotortittle.com

Contact: email

Services: manuscript evaluation, substantive editing/rewriting, copyediting, proofreading, writing coach, academic

Types of manuscripts: manuscript evaluation, substantive editing/ rewriting, copyediting, proofreading, writing coach, academic

Charges: hourly rate

Credentials/experience: "Sam has a double BA in English and biblical and religious studies and an MA in theology. He specializes in academic writing and has a background in biblical languages, but he likes to bring his expertise to a variety of projects. In addition to his freelance work, Sam does research for pastors and churches at Docent Research Group and serves as an associate editor with Wordsmith Writing Coaches."

JOY MEDIA | JULIE-ALLYSON IERON
Park Ridge, IL
joy@joymediaservices.com | www.joymediaservices.com

Contact: email

Services: manuscript evaluation, substantive editing/rewriting, copyediting, ghostwriting, coauthoring, write website text, create small group/Bible study guides, write discussion questions for books, writing coach

Types of manuscripts: articles, nonfiction books, devotionals, book proposals, gift books, adult

Charges: hourly rate

Credentials/experience: "Master's degree in journalism and more than twenty-five years of experience in Christian publishing, writing, editing, and public relations. Specializes in Christian living, Bible study, and business/ministry promotions. Coaches first-time authors."

KACI LANE CREATIONS, LLC | KACI LANE HINDMAN

15900 Jackson Trace Rd., Coker, AL 35452 | 205-210-1130
kacilane@gmail.com

Contact: email

Services: proofreading, coauthoring, website text, back-cover copy

Types of manuscripts: articles, nonfiction books, devotionals, novels

Charges: hourly rate

Credentials/experience: "I have a degree in communications, majoring in journalism and minoring in both English and creative writing. After college, I started out as a copy editor for a Christian company and then worked as the production editor for The University of Alabama Press. In this role, I edited both manuscripts and design elements for books on different academic subjects. I now design magazines and write for various clients. Over the past decade, I have had hundreds of articles published about all kinds of subjects, both online and in traditional print."

KAREN APPOLD

Macungie, PA | 610-351-5400
kappold@msn.com

Contact: email

Services: copyediting, proofreading, brochures, newsletters, website text

Types of manuscripts: articles, curriculum, academic

Charges: flat fee, hourly rate, word rate

Credentials/experience: "I am an award-winning journalist with a BA from Penn State University in English (Writing). I have more than 25 years of professional editorial experience. I mainly write on healthcare/medical and retail, but welcome Christian-themed work."

KATHY IDE BOOK SERVICES | KATHY IDE

Kathy@KathyIde.com | *www.KathyIde.com*

Contact: email, website form

Services: manuscript evaluation, copyediting, proofreading, ghostwriting, coauthoring, create small group/Bible study guides, writing coach, substantive editing/rewriting, brochures, newsletters, small group/Bible studies, discussion questions for books

Types of manuscripts: articles, nonfiction books, devotionals, short stories, novels, query letters, book proposals, Bible studies, scripts, gift books, curriculum, adult, teen/YA

Charges: hourly rate

Credentials/experience: "Kathy Ide is the author of *Proofreading Secrets of Best-Selling Authors* and the *Capitalization Dictionary* and editor/compiler of the Fiction Lover's Devotional series. She's been a professional freelance editor and writing mentor since 1998, working with Christian authors of all genres at all levels. She directs the SoCal Christian Writers' Conference and Mount Hermon Christian Writers Conference. Having founded The Christian PEN: Proofreaders and Editors Network, Christian Editor Connection, and PENCON, she is now owner of the Christian Editor Network LLC, parent company to those organizations as well as The PEN Institute."

KATHY TYERS GILLIN

Bozeman, MT
kathytyers@yahoo.com | www.kathytyers.com

Contact: email

Services: substantive editing/rewriting, copyediting, proofreading, writing coach

Types of manuscripts: articles, nonfiction books, novels, adult, teen/YA

Charges: hourly rate

Credentials/experience: "*New York Times* best-selling author of ten science-fiction novels and three nonfiction books, including *Writing Deep Viewpoint: Invite Your Readers Into the Story*. Experience editing multiple fiction genres and nonfiction from scholarly theological works to family history. Thirty years writing experience. MA in Christianity and the arts, Regent College, Canada."

KATIE PHILLIPS CREATIVE SERVICES | KATIE PHILLIPS

2727 N. Amidon, Wichita, KS 67204 | 316-293-9202
katie@katiephillipscreative.com | www.katiephillipscreative.com

Contact: email

Services: manuscript evaluation, substantive editing/rewriting, writing coach, author branding, marketing courses

Types of manuscripts: novels, adult, teen/YA

Charges: word rate

Credentials/experience: "Katie has been writing and editing professionally for over 10 years. She has a BA in Journalism and Mass Communications and earned a Journeyman certificate through the Christian Writers Guild with mentors DiAnn Mills and Les Stobbe. She has worked for multiple newspapers and oversaw communications for the European region of a global nonprofit, before helping found an indie press. Her clients have gone on to win or final in multiple industry awards, sign agents and publishing deals, and receive a *Publishers Weekly* starred review."

KEELY BOEVING EDITORIAL | KEELY BOEVING

Denver, CO | 303-916-7498

keely.boeving@gmail.com | *www.keelyboeving.com*

Contact: email

Services: manuscript evaluation, substantive editing/rewriting, copyediting, ghostwriting, coauthoring

Types of manuscripts: nonfiction books, novels, query letters, book proposals, adult, teen/YA, middle grade

Charges: hourly rate

Credentials/experience: "Experienced editor and copy editor, formerly worked in editorial for Oxford University Press. Have worked with independent clients, literary agencies, and publishers as a freelancer for the past several years."

KELLY KAGAMAS TOMKIES

Bexley, OH | 614-270-0185

kellytomkies@gmail.com

Contact: email

Services: substantive editing/rewriting, copyediting, proofreading, ghostwriting, writing coach

Types of manuscripts: articles, nonfiction books, devotionals, short stories, novels, query letters, book proposals, adult, teen/YA, picture books, easy readers, middle grade

Charges: flat fee

Credentials/experience: "I have nearly twenty years of editorial experience, including authoring seven books for different publishers, contributing chapters to two National Geographic books, serving as editor of three major business magazines, and years of experience writing and editing for publishers and individual authors. My client list includes HarperCollins, John Wiley & Sons, McGraw-Hill, Kirkus Editorial, Fountainhead Press, Barbour Books, Vantage Press, and Gadfly, LLC, as well as individual authors who wish to find publishers or self-publish."

KEN WALKER

729 Ninth Ave. #331, Huntington, WV 25701 | 304-525-3343
kenwalker33@gmail.com | *www.KenWalkerWriter.com*

Contact: email
Services: manuscript evaluation, substantive editing/rewriting, ghostwriting, coauthoring, write discussion questions for books
Types of manuscripts: articles, nonfiction books, devotionals, Bible studies, adult
Charges: hourly rate
Credentials/experience: "Longtime freelance writer and book editor, ghostwriter, written or edited more than 70 books. Certified with Christian Editor Connection."

KIM PETERSON

1114 Buxton Dr., Knoxville, TN 37922
petersk.ktp@gmail.com

Contact: email
Services: manuscript evaluation, substantive editing/rewriting, copyediting, proofreading, create brochures, create newsletters, write website text, create small group/Bible study guides, write curriculum lesson plans, write discussion questions for books, writing coach, back-cover copy, coauthoring
Types of manuscripts: articles, nonfiction books, devotionals, poetry, short stories, novels, query letters, book proposals, curriculum, academic, Bible studies, gift books, technical material, adult, teen/YA, picture books, easy readers, middle grade
Charges: hourly rate
Credentials/experience: "College writing instructor (27+ years), freelance writer (30+ years), freelance editor (10+ years), conference speaker (13 years), book award judge (8 years), and former agent's fiction reader (9 years). MA in print communication."

KRISTEN STIEFFEL

kristen@kristenstieffel.com | *www.kristenstieffel.com*

Contact: email

Services: manuscript evaluation, substantive editing/rewriting, copyediting, proofreading, ghostwriting, coauthoring, writing coach

Types of manuscripts: short stories, novels

Charges: custom

Credentials/experience: "Fantasy and Science Fiction specialist. Trained in developmental editing and copyediting by the Editorial Freelancers Association and in substantive editing by the Christian Proofreader and Editor Network. Edited dozens of books, including more than 20 sci-fi and fantasy titles. Also an editor with Havok Publishing. Author of *Alara's Call* (fantasy) and *Tales of the Phoenix* (science fiction)."

LEE WARREN COMMUNICATIONS | LEE WARREN

Omaha, NE | 402-740-5795

leewarrenjr@outlook.com | *www.leewarren.info/editing*

Contact: email

Services: copyediting, proofreading

Types of manuscripts: nonfiction books, devotionals, novels

Charges: word rate

Credentials/experience: "Lee Warren has copyedited for three publishing houses, one manuscript critique service, and a Christian newspaper. He's also copyedited and proofread dozens of manuscripts through his own service; testimonials available on the website."

LES STOBBE

201 E. Howard St., Apt. E-46, Tryon, NC 28782 | 828-808-7127

lhstobbe123@gmail.com | *www.stobbeliterary.com*

Contact: email

Services: substantive editing/rewriting, ghostwriting, coauthoring, book-contract evaluation, writing coach, back-cover copy

Types of manuscripts: nonfiction books, devotionals, book proposals, curriculum, Bible studies, adult

Charges: flat fee, custom

Credentials/experience: "Magazine editor, book editor, curriculum editor, writer of small-group studies, title-creation specialist, ghostwriter for national clients, writer coach and agent, international lecturer on writing, journalist in residence at Gordon College. I deliver assignments on time."

LESLIE L. MCKEE EDITING | LESLIE L. MCKEE
lmckeeediting@gmail.com | lmckeeediting.wixsite.com/lmckeeediting

Contact: email

Services: substantive editing/rewriting, copyediting, proofreading, write discussion questions for books, back-cover copy

Types of manuscripts: nonfiction books, devotionals, poetry, short stories, novels, adult, teen/YA, picture books, easy readers, middle grade, articles

Charges: page rate, word rate, per-project rate

Credentials/experience: "Freelance editor and proofreader with various publishing houses (large and small) since 2012, working with traditionally published and self-published authors. Member of The Christian PEN and American Christian Fiction Writers. See website for details on services offered, as well as testimonials and a portfolio."

LESLIE SANTAMARIA
leslie@lesliesantamaria.com | www.lesliesantamaria.com

Contact: email

Services: manuscript evaluation, copyediting, proofreading, writing coach, back-cover copy

Types of manuscripts: nonfiction books, query letters, book proposals, picture books, easy readers, middle grade

Charges: page rate, flat fee

Credentials/experience: "Published author, freelance editor, and writing coach, with more than 200 pieces published in periodicals, specializing in children's literature."

LIBBY GONTARZ WORD SERVICES | LIBBY GONTARZ
480-278-4848
libbygontarz@gmail.com | www.libbygontarz.com

Contact: email, phone

Services: substantive editing/rewriting, copyediting, curriculum lesson plans, discussion questions for books, back-cover copy, proofreading, website text, small group/Bible studies

Types of manuscripts: articles, nonfiction books, curriculum, Bible studies, adult, middle grade, devotionals

Charges: page rate, sample edit and quote available

Credentials/experience: "Libby has helped multiple Christian nonfiction and personal memoir writers to bring their own dreams into focus and reality. She continues to contract with book publishers and corporate clients as well as individuals. Libby has written and edited educational materials for instruction and assessment of student learning at the elementary, junior high, and high school levels. These print and online materials are currently in international use in public classrooms as well as private Christian schools and homeschools."

LIFE LAUNCH ME | JANE RUBIETTA
418 W. Touhy Ave., Park Ridge, IL 60068 | 847-363-6364
jane@lifelaunchme.com | www.LifeLaunchMe.com

Contact: email

Services: manuscript evaluation, substantive editing/rewriting, proofreading, ghostwriting, coauthoring, book-contract evaluation, brochures, newsletters, small group/Bible study guides, writing coach

Types of manuscripts: articles, nonfiction books, devotionals, novels, query letters, book proposals, adult

Charges: flat fee, hourly rate, custom fee

Credentials/experience: "Jane Rubietta has written 20 books, 100s of articles, helped train countless writers and speakers for more than 20 years. She's co-authored three books, and is the Assistant Director of the Write-to-Publish Conference. Jane speaks internationally and also trains writers and speakers at conferences around the globe."

LIGHTHOUSE EDITING | DR. LON ACKELSON
13326 Community Rd. #11, Poway, CA 92064 | 858-748-9258
Isaiah68la@sbcglobal.net | lighthouseedit.com

Contact: website form

Services: manuscript evaluation, substantive editing/rewriting, copyediting, proofreading, ghostwriting, coauthoring, back-cover copy

Types of manuscripts: articles, nonfiction books, devotionals, query letters, book proposals, curriculum, Bible studies, adult

Charges: flat fee, hourly rate, page rate

Credentials/experience: A professional editor for thirty-three years and a published writer for forty years.

LIGHTNING EDITING SERVICES | DENISE LOOCK
699 Golf Course Rd., Waynesville, NC 28786 | 908-868-5854
denise@lightningeditingservices.com | www.lightningeditingservices.com

Contact: email

Services: manuscript evaluation, substantive editing/rewriting, copyediting, proofreading, create newsletters, create small group/ Bible study guides, write discussion questions for books, coauthoring, brochures, website text, back-cover copy

Types of manuscripts: articles, nonfiction books, devotionals, gift books, novels, Bible studies, adult, teen/YA, middle grade

Charges: flat fee, hourly rate, custom

Credentials/experience: "Denise Loock is an editor, writer, and speaker. As a general editor, she helps Lighthouse Publishing of the Carolinas produce fiction and nonfiction books. As a freelance editor, she helps published and unpublished writers create clean, concise, and compelling manuscripts that will attract publishers and intrigue readers. Her twenty-nine years of experience as a high-school teacher and a college instructor enable her to work with both new and seasoned authors."

LINDSAY A. FRANKLIN

Escondido, CA | 858-243-8134
Lindsay@LindsayAFranklin.com | lindsayafranklin.com

Contact: email

Services: manuscript evaluation, substantive editing/rewriting, copyediting, proofreading, ghostwriting, coauthoring, writing coach

Types of manuscripts: nonfiction books, short stories, novels, adult, teen/YA, picture books, easy readers, middle grade

Charges: hourly rate, word rate

Credentials/experience: "Award-winning, published author; member of The Christian PEN."

LINE UPON LINE | LYNNE TAGAWA

San Antonio, TX | 210-544-4397
lbtagawa@gmail.com | www.lynnetagawa.com

Contact: email

Services: copyediting, proofreading

Types of manuscripts: articles, nonfiction books, short stories, novels, curriculum, scripts, adult, teen/YA, middle grade; specializing in theological, historical, and science/medicine

Charges: word rate

Credentials/experience: "Copy editor with Chapel Library of Pensacola; high-school writing instructor; silver member of The

Christian PEN; author of *Sam Houston's Republic*; member of American Christian Fiction Writers."

LINORE BURKARD EDITORIAL SERVICES |
LINORE ROSE BURKARD

PO Box 674, Waynesville, OH 45068 | 513-331-0143

Admin@LinoreBurkard.com | *www.LilliputPressllc.com*

Contact: email

Services: manuscript evaluation, substantive editing/rewriting, discussion questions for books, writing coach, back-cover copy

Types of manuscripts: novels, teens/YA, easy readers, middle grade

Charges: flat rate, hourly rate

Credentials/experience: "Linore Burkard is a multi-published author with a love of literature. Since earning a magna cum laude degree from CUNY in English Literature, Linore has written novels, articles, a screenplay, poetry, blog posts, writing workshop curricula, and edited newsletters and books for numerous clients. After a low cost initial evaluation of a potential client's work, she will provide either a flat fee or hourly rate. Page and/or word rates can be negotiated if desired."

LISA BARTELT
Lancaster, PA | 717-673-7236

lmbartelt@gmail.com | *lisabartelt.com*

Contact: email

Services: copyediting, proofreading, coauthoring, create newsletters, write website text

Types of manuscripts: articles, nonfiction books, devotionals, novels, query letters

Charges: hourly rate

Credentials/experience: "Eight years of writing and editing for daily newspapers; member of American Christian Fiction Writers and The Christian PEN; published articles in *Thriving Family*, *Prayer Connect*, and *The Upper Room*; wrote curriculum for Group Publishing."

LISSA HALLS JOHNSON EDITORIAL |
LISSA HALLS JOHNSON

13926 Double Girth Ct., Matthews, NC 28105 | 479-220-8662

lissahallsjohnson@gmail.com | *lissahallsjohnson.com*

Contact: email

Services: manuscript evaluation, substantive editing/rewriting, writing coach

Types of manuscripts: novels, memoir, teens/YA

Charges: hourly rate

Credentials/experience: "Editor for fiction, nonfiction narrative, memoir for 20+ years. Some writers have received Christy Award finalist awards or nominations, on bestselling lists, *Publishers Weekly* starred reviews."

LOGOS WORD DESIGNS, LLC | LINDA NATHAN

PO Box 735, Maple Falls, WA 98266-0735 | 360-599-3429
linda@logosword.com | www.logosword.com

Contact: email

Services: manuscript evaluation, substantive editing/rewriting, copyediting, ghostwriting, write website text, write discussion questions for books, brochures, newsletters, small group/Bible study guides, back-cover copy

Types of manuscripts: articles, nonfiction books, devotionals, short stories, novels, query letters, book proposals, Bible studies, academic, gift books, technical material, adult, teen/YA

Charges: word rate, page rate, hourly rate, flat fee, custom

Credentials/experience: "Linda Nathan has over 30 years of experience as a professional independent freelance writer, editor, and publishing consultant, working with authors and institutions on a wide range of projects. She is a published author with 10 years of experience in the legal field and has spoken on the radio and at conferences and seminars. Since 1992 she has run her own company, Logos Word Designs, LLC. Linda has a B.A. in Psychology from the University of Oregon and master's level work. She is a freelance staff editor with Redemption Press, a Gold member of the Christian Editor Connection, and a member of four other professional writers' and editors' associations."

LOUISE M. GOUGE, FICTION EDITOR

2529 Colony Ave., Kissimmee, FL 34744 | 407-694-5765
Louisemgouge@aol.com | louisemgougeauthor.blogspot.com

Contact: email

Services: copyediting, proofreading, substantive editing/rewriting

Types of manuscripts: short stories, novels, book proposals, query letters

Charges: word rate, hourly rate

Credentials/experience: "Louise M. Gouge is a retired college English professor and the author of twenty-five novels. For editing, she utilizes CMOS and MLA. Copyediting includes checking grammar, punctuation, spelling, and phrasing. Substantive editing includes making sure character arcs are balanced, the story is well-paced, and the conclusion is satisfying. Checking a client's research will raise the cost, the amount depending upon how much research is required. Novel editing $500-2000."

LUCIE WINBORNE

Longwood, FL | 321-439-7743
lwinborne704@gmail.com | *www.bluetypewriter.com*

Contact: email
Services: copyediting, proofreading
Types of manuscripts: articles, nonfiction books, devotionals, poetry, short stories, novels, query letters, book proposals, curriculum, scripts, gift books, adult, teen/YA, easy readers, middle grade, blog posts
Charges: hourly rate
Credentials/experience: "Member of The Christian PEN and Editorial Freelancers Association. Copy editor for Global Hope Network International and Ask God Today Ministries. Proofreader for Lighthouse Publishing of the Carolinas. Experience in proofreading and copyediting fiction, nonfiction, educational, and business documents. Demonstrated adherence to deadlines and excellent communication skills."

MANYESHA BATIST INC. | MANYESHA BATIST

4071 Orleans Ct., Denver, CO 80249 | 303-253-0424
mybatistinc@gmail.com | *mybatistinc.journoportfolio.com*

Contact: email
Services: substantive editing/rewriting, copyediting, proofreading, ghostwriting, coauthoring, brochures, newsletters, website text, discussion questions for books, back-cover copy
Types of manuscripts: articles, nonfiction books, devotionals
Charges: flat fee, hourly rate, page rate, word rate
Credentials/experience: "Manyesha Batist is a seasoned journalist with more than 17 years of experience as both an editor and writer."

MARCY WEYDEMULLER

San Francisco, CA | 925-876-4860
marcy@sowinglightseeds.com

> **Contact:** email
> **Services:** manuscript evaluation, substantive editing/rewriting, create small group/Bible study guides, write curriculum lesson plans, write discussion questions for books, writing coach
> **Types of manuscripts:** articles, nonfiction books, devotionals, short stories, novels, curriculum, adult, teen/YA, picture books, easy readers, middle grade
> **Charges:** hourly rate
> **Credentials/experience:** "I have worked on more than forty published novels, and four of the authors I work with have published three or more series. My current edits have included historical fiction, historical Christmas novella, YA contemporary, middle-readers both historical and contemporary, suspense-mystery, woman's romance, and memoir. I have more than twenty-five years of experience writing, mentoring, and teaching, both in fiction and nonfiction, including Bible studies and college composition. I have completed a BA in history and sociology and an MFA in writing, with a special focus on fantasy, poetry, and children's literature."

MARK MY WORD EDITORIAL SERVICES, LLC |
VICKI ADANG

Indianapolis, IN | 317-549-5176
vadang@outlook.com | www.mmwLLC.net

> **Contact:** email
> **Services:** manuscript evaluation, substantive editing/rewriting, copyediting, proofreading
> **Types of manuscripts:** articles, nonfiction books, adult, teen/YA, easy readers, middle grade
> **Charges:** hourly rate
> **Credentials/experience:** "I have more than twenty years of editorial experience, ranging from Christian fiction (*The Hungering Dark* by Stephen Clark) to reference works (*Comparative Religion For Dummies*) to creative nonfiction (*Busy and Blessed: 10 Simple Steps for Parents Seeking Peace*)."

MARTI PIEPER

Mount Dora, FL | 352-409-3136
marti@martipieper.com | www.martipieper.com

Contact: email

Services: manuscript evaluation, substantive editing/rewriting, copyediting, proofreading, ghostwriting, coauthoring, write website text, create small group/Bible study guides, write curriculum lesson plans, write discussion questions for books, writing coach

Types of manuscripts: articles, nonfiction books, devotionals, poetry, query letters, book proposals, curriculum, adult, teen/YA

Charges: flat fee, hourly rate

Credentials/experience: "BS in education, MDiv in communications. Fifteen years professional writing and editorial experience, including magazine editing and freelance editing for publishers. Have ghostwritten eight traditionally published nonfiction books, one a best-seller."

MEGHAN BIELINSKI PROFESSIONAL WRITING AND EDITING SERVICES | MEGHAN BIELINSKI STOLL

mbielinski34@gmail.com
the-efa.org/membershipinfo/meghan-bielinski-21154

Contact: website form

Services: copyediting, proofreading

Types of manuscripts: nonfiction books, short stories, novels, adult, teen/YA

Charges: word rate

Credentials/experience: "Writing and editing are my passions. Since graduating with a bachelor's in English literature, I have gained four years of experience offering professional editing services. I work with both fiction and nonfiction, most notably self-help, lifestyle, personal finance, YA novels, Christian, and historical fiction."

MENTOR ME CAREER NETWORK | CHERYL ROGERS

Tampa, FL | 863-288-0802
cheryl@mentormecareernetwork.com | www.mentormecareernetwork.com

Contact: email

Services: manuscript evaluation, substantive editing/rewriting, copyediting, proofreading, ghostwriting, coauthoring, create brochures, create newsletters, write website text, create small group/Bible study guides, writing coach

Types of manuscripts: articles, nonfiction books, adult, teen/YA, middle grade

Charges: flat rate, hourly rate, word rate

Credentials/experience: "BA in journalism and sociology; more than five years of book editing/freelancing; one year of newspaper copyediting; eleven years of newspaper reporting; four years of desktop design, including brochures, booklets, and flyers."

MISSION AND MEDIA | MICHELLE RAYBURN

715-382-6030

info@missionandmedia.com | www.missionandmedia.com

Contact: email

Services: substantive editing/rewriting, copyediting, proofreading, ghostwriting, brochures, newsletters, website text, small group/ Bible study guides, discussion questions for books

Types of manuscripts: nonfiction books, Bible studies

Charges: flat fee, hourly and word rates

Credentials/experience: "Michelle Rayburn has been a freelance writer for 17 years and has edited for Christian publishers as well as for indie authors. Has also worked in the marketing and public relations industry. Michelle has an MA in ministry leadership and has published hundreds of articles and Bible studies as well as three books. She specializes in Christian living, Bible study, humor, and self-help."

MONICA SHARMAN EDITING | MONICA SHARMAN

monicasharman@yahoo.com | www.monicasharman.wordpress.com/monica-sharman-editing

Contact: email

Services: copyediting, proofreading, website text, small group/Bible study guides, curriculum lesson plans

Types of manuscripts: articles, nonfiction books, devotionals, poetry, short stories, curriculum, Bible studies, technical material, adult, teen/YA, picture books, easy readers, middle grade

Charges: hourly fee

Credentials/experience: "Former clients include traditional publishers, Bible curriculum publishers, self-publishing authors, and websites. Characterized by a good eye for detail, preserving and improving the author's voice, and meeting or beating deadlines, Monica has edited devotionals, Bible studies, nonfiction, adult fiction, picture books, and poetry."

MWORDS | MARLENE MCCURLEY

Milcreek, WA | 425-243-4660
mwordsedit@gmail.com | www.mwords.net

Contact: email

Services: manuscript evaluation, substantive editing/rewriting, copyediting, proofreading

Types of manuscripts: articles, nonfiction books, devotionals, short stories, novels, gift books, adult, teen/YA, picture books, easy readers, middle grade

Charges: word rate

Credentials/experience: "Editing credential from the Graham School at the University of Chicago. Member of Northwest Independent Editors Guild, Editorial Freelancers Association, The Christian PEN, and Northwest Christian Writers Association (NCWA). Volunteer for the Alzheimer's Association and NCWA. Fifteen years of experience in multiple genres."

NATALIE NYQUIST

nyquist.n.m@gmail.com | natalienyquist.com

Contact: email

Services: copyediting, proofreading, bibliographies, citations

Types of manuscripts: nonfiction books, academic, adult

Charges: flat fee, hourly rate

Credentials/experience: "600+ projects for traditional publishers, including more than 35,000 pages proofread. Graduate Editing certificate from the University of Chicago, now instructor and course developer for UC Berkeley Extension's Professional Editing Sequence. Freelance copyeditor for HarperCollins Publishers, including work with *New York Times* bestselling authors and projects. Expert at *Chicago Manual of Style* and creating/formatting citations and bibliographies."

NEXT INDEX SERVICES | JESSICA MCCURDY CROOKS

6703 N.W. 7th Ave., KIN 2614, Miami, FL 33126-6007 | 876-354-4084
Jessica@JessicaCrooks.com | www.next-index.com

Contact: email

Services: copyediting, proofreading, website text, indexing

Types of manuscripts: articles, nonfiction books, devotionals, novels, adult, teen/YA, middle grade

Charges: flat fee, hourly rate, page rate, word rate

Credentials/experience: "My training as a librarian and records manager gives me an eye for detail and finding information. I also know how readers tend to search for information, a skill that helps me arrive at keywords and phrases for the indexes I write. I have more than twenty years of indexing experience."

NOBLE CREATIVE, LLC | SCOTT NOBLE

PO Box 131402, St. Paul, MN 55113 | 651-494-4169

snoble@noblecreative.com | *www.noblecreative.com*

Contact: email

Services: manuscript evaluation, substantive editing/rewriting, copyediting, proofreading, ghostwriting, write website text, create small group/Bible study guides, writing coach

Types of manuscripts: articles, nonfiction books, devotionals, query letters, book proposals, curriculum, adult

Charges: flat fee

Credentials/experience: "Nearly twenty years of experience as an award-winning journalist, writer, editor, and proofreader. More than 1,000 published articles, many of them prompting radio and television appearances. Won several awards from Evangelical Press Association. Worked with dozens of published authors and other public figures, as well as first-time authors and small businesses. Have a BA and MS from St. Cloud State University and an MA from Bethel Seminary."

NOVEL IMPROVEMENT EDITING SERVICES |
JEANNE MARIE LEACH

PO Box 552, Hudson, CO 80642

jlmntlady@colorado.net | *novelimprovement.com*

Contact: email, website form

Services: manuscript evaluation, substantive editing/rewriting, copyediting, writing coach, ghostwriting, back-cover copy

Types of manuscripts: short stories, novels, query letters, book proposals, poetry, adult, teen/YA

Charges: flat fee, page rate

Credentials/experience: "Multi-published author, past coordinator and current gold member of The Christian PEN: Proofreaders and Editors Network; member of Christian Editor Network; and member of the American Christian Fiction writers, where I received the 2012 Member Service Award. I teach online courses through my website on editing fiction to editors and authors. I've been editing, mentoring, and critiquing for thirteen years and over a dozen of my clients have gone on to win numerous writing awards and have made various bestsellers' lists."

OASHEIM EDITING SERVICES | CATHY OASHEIM
Chantilly, VA | 720-373-9486
admin@cathyoasheim.com | *www.cathyoasheim.wordpress.com*

Contact: email

Services: substantive editing/rewriting, copyediting, proofreading, create newsletters, write website text, create small group/Bible study guides, write curriculum lesson plans, write discussion questions for books

Types of manuscripts: articles, nonfiction books, devotionals, short stories, novels, query letters, gift books, technical material, adult, teen/YA, picture books, easy readers, middle grade

Charges: flat fee, hourly rate, page rate, word rate

Credentials/experience: "Copy editor providing substantial editing services for Christian fiction and nonfiction, military stories, oral history, and academia using American Psychological Association, MLA, Associated Press, and *The Christian Writer's Manual* style guides. More than twelve years of technical writing experience, more than four years working with a Christian independent publishing company. Constant Contact and Mail Chimp, devotionals, newsletters, book covers, e-book formatting, I can do. Christian, former telecom engineer (technical), degree in applied psychology (APA), mediator (contracts), and Navy veteran (oral history)."

ODD SOCK PROOFREADING & COPYEDITING | STEVE MATHISEN
807 Maple St., Hoquiam, WA 98550 | 206-660-8431
scmathisen98037@hotmail.com | *oddsock.me*

Contact: email, website form

Services: substantive editing/rewriting, copyediting, proofreading, manuscript evaluation, newsletters

Types of manuscripts: nonfiction books, short stories, novels, adult, teen/YA, middle grade

Charges: word rate

Credentials/experience: "I have been in the business for several years and have multiple repeat customers. I am also on the editorial staff of Lighthouse Publishing of the Carolinas and Redemption Press. I work on multiple genres including historical fiction, historical romance, speculative fiction, action thrillers, newsletters, and others. Check out my website to see covers and testimonials."

OUR WRITTEN LIVES | RACHAEL HARTMAN
Universal City, TX | 318-319-6893
publisher@owlofhope.com | *www.OurWrittenLives.com*
   Contact: email
   Services: manuscript evaluation, substantive editing/rewriting, copyediting, proofreading, ghostwriting, coauthoring, book-contract evaluation, create small group/Bible study guides, write curriculum lesson plans, write discussion questions for books, writing coach
   Types of manuscripts: articles, nonfiction books, devotionals, curriculum
   Charges: hourly rate
   Credentials/experience: "Member of Christian Indie Publishing Association. MS in human services, specialization in counseling; BA in liberal studies with a minor in writing; and certified life coach. Ten years in the writing and publishing industry; established Our Written Lives in 2013; author of three books."

PAMELA GOSSIAUX
734-846-0112
pam@pamelagossiaux.com | *www.PamelaGossiaux.com*
   Contact: email
   Services: manuscript evaluation, substantive editing/rewriting, copyediting, proofreading, write website text, write discussion questions for books, ghostwriting, coauthoring, small group/Bible study guides, writing coach, back-cover copy, book shepharding, author consultation
   Types of manuscripts: articles, nonfiction books, devotionals, short stories, novels, query letters, book proposals, gift books, adult, teen/YA, picture books, easy readers, middle grade, Bible studies, technical material
   Charges: custom fee
   Credentials/experience: "Pam is an editor, ghost-writer, business writer, and book marketing expert who works in a wide variety of fiction and nonfiction genres. Her clients are *USA TODAY*, *Wall Street Journal* and Amazon bestselling authors, as well as first-time writers. Pam has a dual BA degree from the University of Michigan in Creative Writing and English Language and Literature and is

an Associated Press award-winning journalist with over 20 years of news writing experience. She is also an international best-selling author, a keynote speaker, and teaches writing workshops. She's available to work with you on any size project, whether you're a first time writer or a seasoned author."

PEGGYSUE WELLS

3419 E. 1000 North, Roanoke, IN 46783 | 260-433-2817
peggysuewells@gmail.com | www.PeggySueWells.com

Contact: email, website form

Services: manuscript evaluation, substantive editing/rewriting, copyediting, ghostwriting, coauthoring, create small group/ Bible study guides, write curriculum lesson plans, write discussion questions for books, writing coach, back-cover copy

Types of manuscripts: articles, nonfiction books, devotionals, short stories, novels, query letters, book proposals, curriculum, Bible studies, scripts, gift books, technical material, adult, teen/YA, picture books, easy readers, middle grade

Charges: hourly rate

Credentials/experience: "The bestselling author of 29 books, PeggySue Wells is the go-to person to create, write, or polish, a project to be publish-ready. From idea to published manuscript, PeggySue provides coaching, writing, and finishing."

PERFECT WORD EDITING SERVICES | LINDA HARRIS

5785 Cedar Creek View #101, Colorado Springs, CO 80915 | 719-464-5189
lharris@perfectwordediting.com | www.perfectwordediting.com

Contact: email, website form

Services: substantive editing/rewriting, copyediting, proofreading, create brochures, newsletters, create small group/Bible study guides, write curriculum lesson plans, write discussion questions for books, back-cover copy

Types of manuscripts: articles, nonfiction books, devotionals, query letters, book proposals, curriculum, Bible studies, academic, adult, picture books, easy readers, middle grade

Charges: page rate, word rate

Credentials/experience: "More than thirty-five years of experience in editing and writing. Member of The Christian PEN and The Christian Editor Connection. Instructor of Editing Children's

Books class for The PEN Institute, speaker at PENCON conference. Specializing in children's book editing."

PICKY, PICKY INK | SUE R. MIHOLER

1075 Willow Lake Rd. N., Keizer, OR 97303 | 503-393-3356
suemihler@comcast.net

Contact: email
Services: copyediting, small group/Bible study guides, brochures, newsletters, website text, back-cover copy
Types of manuscripts: articles, nonfiction books, devotionals, Bible studies, gift books
Charges: hourly rate
Credentials/experience: "I follow *The Chicago Manual of Style* and have edited for both publishers and authors who plan to self-publish since 1998."

PLOT & PROSE | MARY KEANE

Park Ridge, IL | 773-691-7477
info@plotandprose.com | *www.plotandprose.com*

Contact: email
Services: substantive editing/rewriting, copyediting, proofreading
Types of manuscripts: short stories, novels, adult, teen/YA, easy readers, middle grade
Charges: word rate
Credentials/experience: "Completed Fiction Editing 1, 2, 3 from The Christian PEN. Writer and indie author. Specializing in independent authors, debut authors, e-book publishing."

PRATHER INK LITERARY SERVICES | VICKI PRATHER

Coldwater, MS | 601-573-4295
pratherINK@gmail.com | *pratherink.wordpress.com*

Contact: email
Services: copyediting, proofreading, coauthoring
Types of manuscripts: nonfiction books, devotionals, poetry, short stories, novels, gift books, adult, teen/YA, picture books, middle grade
Charges: hourly rate, word rate
Credentials/experience: The Christian PEN silver member.

PROFESSIONAL PUBLISHING SERVICES |
CHRISTY CALLAHAN

PO Box 461, Waycross, GA 31502 | 912-809-9062
professionalpublishingservices@gmail.com | professionalpublishingservices.us

Contact: email

Services: manuscript evaluation, substantive editing/rewriting, copyediting, proofreading, newsletters, website text, small group/ Bible study guides, curriculum lesson plans, discussion questions for books, writing coach

Types of manuscripts: nonfiction books, devotionals, short stories, novels, curriculum, Bible studies, gift books, technical material, academic, adult, teen/YA

Charges: flat fee, hourly rate, custom

Credentials/experience: "Christy graduated Phi Beta Kappa from Carnegie Mellon University and then earned her MA in Intercultural Studies from Fuller Seminary. A gold member of The Christian PEN: Proofreaders and Editors Network and certified by the Christian Editor Connection (CEC), she was selected as a judge for the 2016 CEC Excellence in Editing Award in the category of nonfiction. Christy has taken the following courses with The Christian PEN: Editing Fiction I & II and Advanced Fiction Editing. She also completed the 40-hour Foundational Course (Christian track) with the Institute for Life Coach Training."

PWC EDITING | PAUL W. CONANT
527 Bayshore Pl., Dallas, TX 75217-7755 | 214-289-3397
pwcediting@gmail.com | www.pwc-editing.com

Contact: email

Services: copyediting, proofreading, brochures, newsletters, website text

Types of manuscripts: articles, nonfiction books, devotionals, short stories, novels, query letters, book proposals, Bible studies, technical material, adult, teens/YA, middle grade, academic

Charges: hourly rates; prefers a 2,000-word sample in order to make the most appropriate estimate for a manuscript

Credentials/experience: "Member of Christian Editors Connection, The Christian PEN, and *Thumbtack.com*. Fifteen years of experience with dissertations, twenty-two years with magazines, twenty years with books. Has worked with new or ESL writers, as well as publishers."

REBECCA LUELLA MILLER

rluellam@yahoo.com | rewriterewordrework.wordpress.com

Contact: email

Services: manuscript evaluation, substantive editing/rewriting, copyediting, proofreading, writing coach

Types of manuscripts: articles, nonfiction books, devotionals, short stories, novels, query letters, book proposals, technical material, adult, teen/YA

Charges: flat fee, page rate, word rate

Credentials/experience: "Rebecca has worked as a freelance editor for fifteen years, editing books by such authors as Bryan Davis and Jill Williamson and working with AMG Publishers on other projects. Previously she taught English at the middle-school and high-school levels. She has a BA in English from Westmont College."

REBECCA LYLES

Boise, ID | 208-562-1592
beckylyles@beckylyles.com | www.beckylyles.com

Contact: email

Services: manuscript evaluation, substantive editing/rewriting, copyediting, proofreading, writing coach

Types of manuscripts: articles, nonfiction books, devotionals, short stories, novels, query letters, book proposals, adult, teen/YA

Charges: hourly rate, page rate

Credentials/experience: "Rebecca is a multipublished author who has edited fiction and nonfiction for more than fifteen years, including brochures, white papers, newsletters, educational material, and Bible studies on the nonfiction side and short stories, children's books, and award-winning novels on the fiction side."

RED QUILL EDITING | JUDITH ROBL

PO Box 802, Lyons, KS 67554
jrlight620@yahoo.com | www.judithrobl.com

Contact: email

Services: copyediting, proofreading, brochures, website text, writing coach, back-cover copy, newsletters, manuscript evaluation, substantive editing/rewriting

Types of manuscripts: articles, devotionals, short stories, novels, query letters, book proposals, Bible studies, gift books, adult

Charges: page rate, custom

Credentials/experience: "Editing with an eye to perfection and total respect for the author's vision and voice. Former English teacher, author, founder Central Kansas Christian Writers Critique Group, more than a decade of experience with private clients."

REFINE SERVICES | KATE MOTAUNG
kate@refineservices.com | www.refineservices.com

Contact: email

Services: copyediting, proofreading, writing coach, small group/Bible studies, discussion questions for books

Types of manuscripts: articles, nonfiction books, devotionals, Bible studies, poetry, short stories, novels, query letters, adult, teens/YA, picture books, easy readers, middle grade

Charges: word rate

Credentials/experience: "Kate Motaung is an experienced copyeditor who enjoys helping authors refine their work to create an exceptional finished product. Kate is also a traditionally published and self-published author who can relate to the writing and publishing process and give insight into the right next steps."

REVISIONS BY RACHEL, LLC | RACHEL E. NEWMAN
Owasso, OK | 918-207-2833
Editor@RevisionsbyRachel.com | www.RevisionsbyRachel.com

Contact: email

Services: manuscript evaluation, substantive editing/rewriting, copyediting, proofreading, indexing

Types of manuscripts: nonfiction books, novels, query letters, book proposals, curriculum, adult, teen/YA, picture books, easy readers, middle grade, speculative fiction

Charges: word rate

Credentials/experience: "Rachel holds a BS in paralegal studies from Northeastern State University in Oklahoma. She graduated summa cum laude in 2006 and was awarded the Certified Paralegal designation by the National Association of Legal Assistants. Certified with Christian Editor Connection. She is a gold member of The Christian PEN: Proofreaders and Editors Network, is an established freelance editor with Christian Editor Connection, is an instructor with The PEN Institute, serves as a judge for the Excellence in Editing Award, and has served as faculty for PENCON."

RICK STEELE EDITORIAL SERVICES | RICK STEELE
26 Dean Rd., Ringgold, GA 30736 | 706-937-8121

rsteelecam@gmail.com | steeleeditorialservices.myportfolio.com
Contact: email, website form
Services: manuscript evaluation, substantive editing/rewriting, copyediting, proofreading, coauthoring, book-contract evaluation. small group/Bible study guides, curriculum lesson plans, discussion questions for books, writing coach, back-cover copy
Types of manuscripts: nonfiction books, devotionals, poetry, short stories, novels, query letters, book proposals, curriculum, Bible studies, gift books, adult, teen/YA, middle grade
Charges: flat fee, page rate, critiques are charged by the page
Credentials/experience: "With more than twenty years of experience working for a traditional, royalty publisher in the religious market, Rick Steele provides an array of freelance editorial services ranging from fiction and nonfiction manuscript editing, proofreading, and critiquing to help with query letters and proposal drafting."

ROBIN'S RED PEN | ROBIN PATCHEN
1808 Thunderbird Blvd., Edmond, OK 73013 | 405-816-4867
robin@robinpatchen.com | robinpatchen.com/editing
Contact: email
Services: manuscript evaluation, substantive editing/rewriting, copyediting, writing coach
Types of manuscripts: nonfiction books, devotionals, short stories, novels, adult, teen/YA, middle grade
Charges: page rate
Credentials/experience: "Nominated for ACFW's 2018's Editor of the Year, Robin Patchen is a multi-published award-winning author and freelance editor specializing in Christian fiction. As a general editor with Lighthouse Publishing of the Carolina's Smitten line, she has the privilege of working with exceptionally talented romance authors. She is one of the authors of *5 Editors Tackle the 12 Fatal Flaws of Fiction Writing*, an in-depth guide to self-editing. Patchen loves mentoring new authors and helping established authors polish their books. She enjoys reading and editing almost every clean YA and adult genre."

SALISBURY ALEXANDER COMMUNICATIONS |
KIRT G. SALISBURY
153 Monticello Ave., Rio Linda, CA 45673 | 760-212-2872
kirtwrites81@icloud.com
Contact: email

Services: ghostwriting, brochures, newsletters, website text, back-cover copy

Types of manuscripts: technical material, articles, devotionals, query letters, response letters, nonfiction books

Charges: flat fee

Credentials/experience: "Has written advertising and promotional materials for high-tech scientific equipment, Christian and biomedical magazines, and biomedical newsletters. Ghostwritten for more than twenty-four major Christian ministries for their partner communications, premium books, fundraising appeals, and response letters."

SARAH HAMAKER

4207 Collier Rd., Fairfax, VA 22030 | 703-691-1676
shamaker@verizon.net | *sarahhamakerfiction.com*

Contact: email

Services: copyediting, proofreading, ghostwriting, write website text

Types of manuscripts: articles, nonfiction books, novels, query letters, book proposals, adult

Charges: flat fee, hourly rate

Credentials/experience: "I'm a professional freelance writer and editor with more than twenty years of editorial and book-editing experience. I've worked as a project manager/ghostwriter on numerous projects, including books and articles. I work to ensure we're a good fit before proceeding and love helping writers polish their work."

SCRIVEN COMMUNICATIONS | KATHIE SCRIVEN

22 Ridge Rd. #220, Greenbelt, MD 20770 | 240-542-4602
KathieScriven@yahoo.com | *www.linkedin.com/in/kathie-scriven-46981037*

Contact: email, phone

Services: manuscript evaluation, substantive editing/rewriting, copyediting, proofreading

Types of manuscripts: articles, short stories, nonfiction books, book proposals, query letters, website text, back-cover copy, adult

Charges: hourly rate

Credentials/experience: "I have edited more than eighty Christian nonfiction books and more than a hundred shorter projects, including booklets, biographical sketches, press releases, and grant applications. Former editor of four Christian publications and freelance writer for several Christian and general-market publications. Bachelor's degree in mass communication with a concentration in journalism from Towson University. I'm happy to email a document that describes my credentials and experience in more detail."

SHARMAN'S EDITS | SHARMAN J. MONROE

Washington, DC

myjourneytome@gmail.com | *www.sharmansedits.com*

Contact: website form

Services: substantive editing, proofreading

Types of manuscripts: nonfiction books, devotionals, novels, teen/ YA

Charges: custom

Credentials/experience: "Ms. Monroe has over 25 years of experience in the areas of writing, proofreading and editing. She has edited and proofed more than twenty books, nonfiction and fiction, and of different genres ranging from Christian to guides/handbooks to mystery to self-help to YA to urban, based on Christian principles over the past few years. The majority is by first-time authors, are self-published works and can be found on Amazon."

SHARON HINCK

Minneapolis, MN | 952-886-0040

s.hinck@comcast.net | *www.sharonhinck.com*

Contact: email

Services: substantive editing/rewriting, copyediting

Types of manuscripts: novels

Charges: word rate

Credentials/experience: "MA; more than ten years' experience of editing dozens of authors from beginners through *New York Times* best-selling writers; experienced novelist; thorough yet encouraging."

SHERRY CHAMBLEE

Sun Valley, CA | 818-767-8765

chambleeservices@gmail.com | *www.offscript.weebly.com*

Contact: email

Services: copyediting, proofreading

Types of manuscripts: articles, nonfiction books, devotionals, poetry, short stories, novels, gift books, technical material, adult, teen/YA, picture books, easy readers, middle grade

Charges: word rate

Credentials/experience: "I am a freelance editor, working directly with authors for the past five years. I have edited both fiction and nonfiction, including works ranging from illustrated children's picture books and middle-grade chapter books to young-adult and adult Christian fiction."

SHERYL MADDEN

Seattle, WA | 206-919-2203
madden58sheryl@gmail.com | www.editorsherylmadden.com

 Contact: email

 Services: copyediting, proofreading, brochures, newsletters, website text, small group/Bible study guides, discussion questions for books, back-cover copy

 Types of manuscripts: articles, nonfiction books, devotionals, short stories, novels, Bible studies, adult

 Charges: page rate

 Credentials/experience: Certificate in professional editing, freelancing since 2015.

SHIRL'S EDITING SERVICES | SHIRL THOMAS

9379 Tanager Ave., Fountain Valley, CA 92708 | 714-968-5726
shirlth@verizon.net

 Contact: email, phone

 Services: manuscript evaluation, substantive editing/rewriting, copyediting, proofreading, ghostwriting, coauthoring, writing coach

 Types of manuscripts: articles, nonfiction books, devotionals, poetry, short stories, novels, query letters, book proposals, scripts, gift books, technical material, adult

 Charges: hourly rate

 Credentials/experience: Professional writer since 1973 and editor since 1994. Complete résumé available.

SIGHTHOUND EDITORIAL SERVICES | MEGAN LEE

Herndon, VA | 703-229-2369
sighthoundeditorial@gmail.com | www.meganwhitsonlee.net/editing

 Contact: email

 Services: manuscript evaluation, substantive editing/rewriting, copyediting, proofreading, write discussion questions for books, writing coach

Types of manuscripts: novels, adult, teen/YA

Charges: flat fee, hourly rate, page rate, word rate

Credentials/experience: "I'm a published author with an MFA in creative writing from George Mason University. As an editor with Pelican Book Group, I evaluate manuscripts for acquisition and work closely with authors and other editors to ensure manuscripts meet their potential throughout the publication process. Additionally, I've taught English to high school and college students for the past fifteen years."

SO IT IS WRITTEN LLC | TENITA JOHNSON

Rochester, MI | 313-999-6942

info@soitiswritten.net | www.soitiswritten.net

Contact: emails

Services: copyediting, proofreading, ghostwriting, write website text, writing coach

Types of manuscripts: articles, nonfiction books, devotionals, poetry, short stories, novels, adult, teen/YA, picture books, easy readers, middle grade

Charges: page rate

Credentials/experience: "More than sixteen years of writing and editing experience in all forms of media, including newspapers, magazines, and manuscripts."

STARCHER DESIGNS | KARA STARCHER

Chloe, WV | 330-705-3399

info@starcherdesigns.com | www.starcherdesigns.com

Contact: email

Services: manuscript evaluation, substantive editing, copyediting, ghostwriting, coauthoring, writing coach, back-cover copy

Types of manuscripts: nonfiction books, novels, curriculum, Bible studies, adult, teen/YA

Charges: word rate

Credentials/experience: "BA in publishing with a minor in English; twenty years experience as a freelance editor working for small publishing houses and independent authors; ten years experience as managing editor for various nonprofit organizations; other experience in high school English education and journalism. Member of American Christian Fiction Writers."

STEEPLE VIEW COACHING | ANDREA BOESHAAR

PO Box 33, Newberg, WI 53060 | 414-708-8930
AuthorAndreaBoeshaar@gmail.com | www.AndreaBoeshaar.com

Contact: email

Services: manuscript evaluation, substantive editing/rewriting, writing coach

Types of manuscripts: short stories, novels, teen/YA

Charges: page rate

Credentials/experience: "Author of more than thirty books, certified Christian life coach."

STICKS AND STONES | JAMIE CALLOWAY-HANAUER

Annapolis, MD | 510-972-3285
snsedits@gmail.com | www.snsedits.com

Contact: email

Services: manuscript evaluation, substantive editing/rewriting, copyediting, proofreading, ghostwriting, coauthoring, book-contract evaluation, write website text, create small group/Bible study guides, write curriculum lesson plans, write discussion questions for books, writing coach

Types of manuscripts: articles, nonfiction books, devotionals, poetry, short stories, novels, query letters, book proposals, curriculum, adult, teen/YA, easy readers, middle grade

Charges: flat fee

Credentials/experience: "Jamie has eighteen years of experience in the editing field. Previously a full-time public interest attorney who also edited part-time, she is now the owner-operator of Sticks and Stones, where she specializes in academic, legal, and faith-based fiction and nonfiction for adults and teens; ghostwriting; and proposal and query review and development."

SUE A. FAIRCHILD, EDITOR

sueafairchild74@gmail.com | suessimplesnippets.wordpress.com

Contact: email, website form

Services: substantive editing/rewriting, copyediting, proofreading, website text, small group/Bible study guides, discussion questions for books, writing coach, back-cover copy

Types of manuscripts: nonfiction books, devotionals, short stories, novels, Bible studies, gift books, adult, teen/YA, middle grade, picture books, easy readers

Charges: word rate

Credentials/experience: "Proofreader for Iron Stream Media, editor/ coach for Redemption Press, editor for Elk Lake Publishing, Inc."

SUPERIOR EDITING SERVICE | JAN ACKERSON

611 S. Elm, Three Oaks, MI 49128 | 269-756-9912
jan_ackerson@yahoo.com | *www.superioreditingservice.com*

Contact: email
Services: substantive editing/rewriting, copyediting, writing coach
Types of manuscripts: poetry, short stories, novels, gift books, adult, teen/YA, picture books, easy readers, middle grade
Charges: word rate
Credentials/experience: "Seven years editing (both freelance and for Breath of Fresh Air Press), author of *Stolen Postcards*, short stories in multiple anthologies."

SUSAN KING EDITORIAL SERVICES | SUSAN KING

Franklin, TN | 615-202-6019
susan@susankingedits.com | *susankingedits.com*

Contact: email
Services: substantive editing/rewriting, copyediting, proofreading, ghostwriting, coauthoring
Types of manuscripts: articles, nonfiction books, devotionals, poetry, short stories, novels, query letters, gift books, adult
Charges: hourly rate
Credentials/experience: "Of my more than 27 years in the industry, I served over 20 years as an editor for *The Upper Room*. For the past 20 years, I have trained writers at over one hundred Christian writers' conferences in the U.S. and Canada. My professional life has also included teaching Freshman English, American literature, and feature-writing classes at Lipscomb University, Biola University, and Abilene Christian University for a total of 27 years. Currently, I am the compiler and editor of the Short and Sweet book series."

SUSAN R. EDITORIAL | SUSAN RESCIGNO

2927 Lexington Ave., Mohegan Lake, NY 10547 | 914-844-5217
SusanR.Edit@gmail.com | *srescigno7.wixsite.com/mysite*

Contact: website form
Services: copyediting, proofreading, academic, indexing
Types of manuscripts: nonfiction books

Charges: custom rate

Credentials/experience: "Why should you hire me? (1) Knowledge: I have 25+ years of publishing experience, managing the preproduction process from author manuscript to published file or bound book. I am familiar with Chicago and AP styles. (2) Skills: I am extremely focused and detail-oriented, proficient with electronic editing using Microsoft Word's track changes and able to create back-of book indices with Sky Index Pro Software. (3) Passion: I am passionate about books that educate and inspire. I am especially interested in books about business, holistic health, and spirituality."

TANDEM SERVICES | JENNIFER CROSSWHITE

PO Box 222, Yucaipa, CA 92399

jennifer@tandemservicesink.com | *www.tandemservicesink.com*

Contact: email, website form

Services: manuscript evaluation, substantive editing/rewriting, copyediting, ghostwriting, coauthoring, writing coach, book-contract evaluation, back-cover copy

Types of manuscripts: nonfiction books, devotionals, novels, query letters, book proposals, adult, teen/YA

Charges: custom

Credentials/experience: "I have over 15 years of experience in business, marketing, and publishing. Over this time, I have held the titles of marketing director, managing editor, graphic designer, and director of communication. My skills include complex project management, writing and editing, marketing, and graphic design. I am an agented author, having ghost-written nonfiction and written bestselling novels, curriculum, and award-winning articles and short stories. My clients include Our Daily Bread Ministries, Credo Communications, Zondervan, HarperCollins Christian Publishing, Barbour Publishing, and Concordia. I have degrees in Business Administration, History, and Comparative Literature from the University of California. I partner with other industry experts to create a team that will provide you with the best product possible. I look forward to partnering with you to bring your ideas to market."

THREE FATES EDITING | SARAH LIU

28 Close Hollow Dr., Hamlin, NY 14464 | 585-489-0862

sarah.grace@threefatesediting.com | *www.threefatesediting.com*

Contact: email

Services: manuscript evaluation, substantive editing/rewriting, copyediting, proofreading, ghostwriting, website text, small group/Bible study guides

Types of manuscripts: articles, nonfiction books, devotionals, poetry, short stories, novels, Bible studies, gift books, technical material, academic, adult, teen/YA, picture books, easy readers, middle grade; specializes in science fiction and fantasy

Charges: word rate

Credentials/experience: "I have an MA in creative writing and am the founder of a literary journal. I have been freelance editing since 2012."

TISHA MARTIN EDITORIAL | TISHA MARTIN

210 S. 66th Ave., Yakima, WA 98908

tisha@tishamartin.com | www.tishamartin.com/editing-services

Contact: email

Services: manuscript evaluation, substantive editing/rewriting, copyediting, proofreading, write curriculum lesson plans, write discussion questions for books, writing coach, back-cover copy, small group/Bible study guides, ghostwriting, website text

Types of manuscripts: nonfiction books, devotionals, short stories, novels, curriculum, adult, teen/YA, articles, book proposals, scripts

Charges: flat fee, word rate, hourly rate

Credentials/experience: "Although I have been immersed in the editing and writing world for over fifteen years, since 2017 I have worked on over 300 books and manuscripts in all levels of editing with new and published authors, publishers, and film producers. (Portfolio via website.) From contest judging and critiques to editing and proofreading to writing marketing copy and ghostwriting—it's my desire to work as a team and to deliver a professionally edited book you can be proud of. The top skills I bring to the table in each project are the ability to hear the author's message and cultivate context to the story because editing is a pure gift to the writer and ultimately to the reader. Contact me for an introductory chat and let's go from there!"

TRAILBLAZE WRITING & EDITING | SARAH BARNUM

sarah@trail-blazes.com | trail-blazes.com

Contact: email

Services: manuscript evaluation, substantive editing/rewriting, copyediting, proofreading, newsletters, website text, brochures

Types of manuscripts: articles, nonfiction books, devotionals, short stories, novels, gift books, adult, teen/YA

Charges: word rate

Credentials/experience: "Sarah Barnum is a published writer who brings an eye for both detail and story. She is a member of Inspire Christian Writers and The Christian PEN and serves on the leadership team for the West Coast Christian Writers Conference. If you want to make your writing clean and compelling, let's take this journey together!"

TUPPANCE ENTERPRISES | JAMES PENCE

PO Box 99, Greenville, TX 75403 | 469-730-6478
james@pence.com | jamespence.com

Contact: email, phone

Services: manuscript evaluation, substantive editing/rewriting, copyediting, proofreading, coauthoring, writing coach, ghostwriting

Types of manuscripts: articles, nonfiction books, devotionals, short stories, novels, query letters, book proposals, Bible studies, technical material, adult, teen/YA, middle grade

Charges: word rate, hourly rate, flat fee

Credentials/experience: "James has been writing and editing professionally since 2000, and is a traditionally published author of ten books. Publishers include Osborne/McGraw-Hill, Tyndale, Kregel, Baker (co-author), Thomas Nelson (ghostwriter), and Mountainview Books. Published works include textbooks, how-to, novels (adult and YA), Christian living, and memoir."

TURN THE PAGE WRITER CRITIQUES | CINDY THOMSON

Pataskala, OH | 614-354-3904
cindyswriting@gmail.com | cindyswriting.com/hire-me

Contact: email

Services: manuscript evaluation, proofreading, critiques

Types of manuscripts: articles, novels

Charges: page rate, word rate

Credentials/experience: "Traditionally published author of eight books, past mentor for the Jerry B. Jenkins Christian Writers Guild, mentor for local high-school students."

THE VERSATILE PEN | CHRISTY PHILLIPPE

8816 S. 73rd East Ave., Tulsa, OK 74133 | 918-284-7635

christy6871@aol.com | www.theversatilepen.com

Contact: email

Services: manuscript evaluation, substantive editing/rewriting, copyediting, proofreading, create brochures, create newsletters, write website text, create small group/Bible study guides, write curriculum lesson plans, write discussion questions for books

Types of manuscripts: articles, nonfiction books, devotionals, short stories, novels, curriculum, gift books, adult, teen/YA

Charges: hourly rate, word rate

Credentials/experience: "More than twenty years of experience as managing editor, senior editor, and editorial director of various publishing companies and as the owner of The Versatile Pen."

WHALIN & ASSOCIATES | W. TERRY WHALIN

Highlands Ranch, CO 80126 | 720-708-4953

terry@terrywhalin.com | terrywhalin.blogspot.com

Contact: email

Services: substantive editing/rewriting, ghostwriting, coauthoring, create small group/Bible study guides, write discussion questions for books

Types of manuscripts: nonfiction books, devotionals, book proposals, gift books, adult

Charges: flat fee

Credentials/experience: "Terry has written more than sixty books for traditional publishers, including one book that has sold more than 100,000 copies. He has written for more than fifty publications and worked in acquisitions at three publishing houses."

WHITE PENCIL PRODUCTIONS, INC. | KARLA DIAL

620 Dee Ct., Redding, CA 96002 | 719-930-3094

email through website | Karladial.com

Contact: email

Services: substantive editing/rewriting, copyediting, proofreading, ghostwriting, coauthoring, brochures

Types of manuscripts: articles, nonfiction books, short stories, novels, adult, teen/YA

Charges: $500 retainer, which sometimes covers the whole cost, then an hourly fee

Credentials/experience: "I am an award-winning journalist with more than 20 years of experience as a reporter, writer, managing editor, and editor in chief at both daily and monthly, local and national publications. You have something to say; I can help you say it the best way possible."

WILDCAT WRITING SERVICES | JEFF ADAMS

3675 N. Verdugo Rd., Kingman, AZ 86409 | 928-716-9673
jeffadams@frontiernet.net | *wildcatwritingservices.com*

Contact: email

Services: manuscript evaluation, substantive editing/rewriting, brochures, newsletters, website text, small group/Bible study guides, curriculum lesson plans, discussion questions for books, writing coach, back-cover copy, book proposals

Types of manuscripts: nonfiction books, devotionals, query letters, book proposals, curriculum, Bible studies, gift books, adult

Charges: custom

Credentials/experience: "I'm a substantive editor certified by Christian Editor Connection. I've contributed to more than 25 books. I create, evaluate, and prepare book proposals, including chapter-by-chapter synopsis and sample chapters, for presentation to editors, publishers, and agents. I help writers write better."

WORD MARKER EDITS | KATHRESE MCKEE

8765 Spring Cypress, Ste. L219, Spring, TX 77379 | 281-787-6938
kmckee@kathresemckee.com | *www.wordmarkeredits.com*

Contact: email

Services: manuscript evaluation, substantive editing/rewriting, copyediting, proofreading, ghostwriting

Types of manuscripts: short stories, novels, adult, teen/YA, middle grade

Charges: hourly rate, page rate, word rate

Credentials/experience: "Kathrese is an editor, fiction author, former middle-school reading and ESL teacher, speaker, and blogger. She specializes in editing speculative fiction written from a Christian worldview but is also available to edit other genres and fiction for the general market. She is a silver member of The Christian PEN: Proofreaders and Editors Network."

WORDMELON, INC. | MARGOT STARBUCK

308-A Northwood Cir., Durham, NC 27701 | 919-321-5440
wordmelon@gmail.com | *www.wordmelon.com*

Contact: website form

Services: manuscript evaluation, substantive editing/rewriting, ghostwriting, coauthoring

Types of manuscripts: nonfiction books, book proposals

Charges: flat fee

Credentials/experience: "Margot Starbuck, a graduate of Westmont College and Princeton Theological Seminary, is passionate about effective communication. A *New York Times* bestselling writer, Margot is the author or collaborator on more than twenty books. She is a popular presenter at writing conferences and has won awards including the nonfiction book of the year from the Advanced Writers and Speakers Association and several Selah Awards."

WORDPOLISH EDITORIAL SERVICES | YVONNE IJE KANU

yvonneikanu@gmail.com | www.wordpolish.net

Contact: email, website form

Services: manuscript evaluation, substantive editing/rewriting, copyediting, proofreading, website text, academic

Types of manuscripts: articles, nonfiction books, devotionals, poetry, short stories, novels, query letters, book proposals, curriculum, Bible studies, scripts, gift books, technical material, adult, teen/YA, easy reader

Charges: word rate

Credentials/experience: "Yvonne Ije Kanu is a professional editor with a BA in English and Political Science, certificates in Publishing and Technical Writing, and over eight years of experience in fields ranging from publishing to business communication, public relations, and technical communication."

WORDS FOR WRITERS | GINNY L. YTTRUP

Granite Bay, CA | 916-276-7359

email through website | www.wordsforwriters.net

Contact: email

Services: manuscript evaluation, substantive editing/rewriting, proofreading, writing coach

Types of manuscripts: articles, nonfiction books, devotionals, short stories, novels, query letters, book proposals, adult, teen/YA

Charges: hourly rate, page rate

Credentials/experience: "Ginny is an award-winning novelist and trained life coach who combines her skills when coaching writers and evaluating manuscripts. She works with beginning and published writers of both fiction and nonfiction."

WRITE BY LISA | LISA THOMPSON
Litchfield Park, AZ | 623-258-5258
writebylisa@gmail.com | *www.writebylisa.com*

Contact: email

Services: manuscript evaluation, substantive editing/rewriting, copyediting, proofreading, ghostwriting, coauthoring, create newsletters, write website text, create small group/Bible study guides, write curriculum lesson plans, write discussion questions for books, writing coach

Types of manuscripts: articles, nonfiction books, devotionals, short stories, novels, query letters, book proposals, curriculum, gift books, adult, teen/YA, middle grade

Charges: word rate

Credentials/experience: "I have a BA in elementary education with a minor in English. I have been writing and editing full-time since 2009 and have satisfied clients all over the world, many of whom return for additional business and refer other clients to me."

WRITE CONCEPTS, LLC | ALICE CRIDER
590 Highway 105 #107, Monument, CO 80132 | 719-651-0160
editoralicecrider@gmail.com | *www.alicecrider.com*

Contact: website form

Services: manuscript evaluation, substantive editing/rewriting, website text, writing coach, back-cover copy, book proposals

Types of manuscripts: nonfiction books, devotionals, query letters, book proposals, memoir, adult

Charges: custom rate

Credentials/experience: "Alice Crider has served in Christian publishing since 1998, focusing on reviewing, acquiring, developing, and editing manuscripts. She specializes in developmental, content, and line editing. She is skilled at analyzing a manuscript's strengths and weaknesses and at suggesting improvements and revisions. Having worked with dozens of bestselling authors, those who work with Alice produce better manuscripts than they could write alone."

THE WRITE EDITOR | ERIN K. BROWN
Corvallis, MT | 406-239-5590

thewriteeditor@gmail.com | www.writeeditor.net

    Contact: email

    Services: manuscript evaluation, substantive editing/rewriting, copyediting, proofreading, write discussion questions for books

    Types of manuscripts: articles, nonfiction books, devotionals, short stories, novels, query letters, book proposals, curriculum, gift books, adult, teen/YA, middle grade

    Charges: flat fee, hourly rate, word rate, page rate

    Credentials/experience: "Erin is a full-time, professional freelance editor, proofreader, and writer (since 2001). Her editing specialty is nonfiction works, including self-help, how-to, devotionals, Bible studies, biography, memoir, history, apologetics, leadership, ministry, family, health and wellness, inspiration, personal growth, relationships, success, and homeschool. Erin's formal training in editorial practices and procedures, ten years in Christian retailing, twenty-six years in education, and more than ten years as a judge for a national fiction award affords her a wide knowledge and experience base that she brings to her editing. She combines her love of editing and teaching through The Pen Institute, teaching nonfiction editing skills to other professional editors. She is also director of the PEN Institute."

WRITE HIS ANSWER MINISTRIES | MARLENE BAGNULL

951 Anders Rd., Lansdale, PA 19446 | 484-991-8581
mbagnull@aol.com | writehisanswer.com

    Contact: email, phone

    Services: manuscript evaluation, copyediting, proofreading

    Types of manuscripts: articles, nonfiction books, devotionals, short stories, novels, adult

    Charges: flat fee, hourly rate

    Credentials/experience: "More than thirty-five years of experience in publishing, leading critique groups, and directing writers conferences; author of nine books and more than a thousand sales to Christian periodicals; editor, typesetter, and publisher of ten Ampelos Press books."

WRITE NOW EDITING | KARIN BEERY

PO Box 31, Elk Rapids, MI 49629
karin@karinbeery.com | www.writenowedits.com

    Contact: email

    Services: manuscript evaluation, substantive editing/rewriting

    Types of manuscripts: novels, adult

Charges: page rate, word rate

Credentials/experience: "Karin Beery received her substantive fiction training through the Christian Proofreaders and Editors Network. She now teaches those classes through their sister organization, the PEN Institute. In addition to her freelance work, she has worked as a general editor with Lighthouse Publishing of the Carolinas' Smitten imprint, and currently serves as the managing editor for their women's fiction imprint, Guiding Light."

WRITE PATHWAY EDITORIAL SERVICES | ANN KNOWLES

Wilmington, NC | 910-231-9520
annknowles03@aol.com | write-pathway.blogspot.com

Contact: email

Services: copyediting, proofreading, ghostwriting, coauthoring, writing coach, transcription, Spanish translation

Types of manuscripts: articles, nonfiction books, devotionals, poetry, short stories, novels, query letters, book proposals, curriculum, gift books, adult, teen/YA, picture books, easy readers, middle grade

Charges: project cost

Credentials/experience: "Retired educator, MA in education, certified ESL and Spanish; ESL training consultant for public schools and community colleges. I joined The Christian PEN: Proofreaders and Editors Network in 2005 and started Write Pathway in 2007. I have taken numerous courses from The Christian PEN, American Christian Fiction Writers, Write Integrity Press, and Christian Writers International."

WRITE WAY COPYEDITING LLC | DIANA SCHRAMER

Sun Prairie, WI | 608-837-8091
diana@writewaycopyediting.com | www.writewaycopyediting.com

Contact: email

Services: manuscript evaluation, substantive editing/rewriting, copyediting, brochures, newsletters, website text, small group/ Bible study guides, back-cover copy

Types of manuscripts: articles, nonfiction books, devotionals, Bible studies, novels, gift books, adult, teen/YA, easy readers, middle grade

Charges: hourly rate

Credentials/experience: "I have edited 100+ book manuscripts freelance for the past 8 years. I also evaluate manuscripts and offer in-depth review. In addition, as a writer myself I relate well to writers as a fellow writer. The writing journey is not only technical, but also emotional and spiritual. As a writer and an editor I understand the full process and enjoy supporting other writers in developing their God-given talents and achieving their God-given dreams."

WRITER JUSTIFIED | JUDY HAGEY

Des Moines, Iowa

judy.hagey@gmail.com | judyhagey.com

> **Contact:** email
>
> **Services:** copyediting, proofreading, brochures, newsletters, website text
>
> **Types of manuscripts:** articles, nonfiction books, short stories, novels, academic, adult
>
> **Charges:** page rate
>
> **Credentials/experience:** "Gold member of Christian Professional Educators Network, member of Christian Editors Connection. Knowledgeable in *The Chicago Manual of Style*, Turabian, APA, and various institution-specific style guides. Ten years as communication coordinator for a discipleship ministry, responsible for compiling, editing/proofreading print and e-communication; managed production of a dozen small-group study books. A diligent, meticulous freelance copy editor/proofreader with an excellent record of client satisfaction."

WRITER'S EDGE SERVICE | BILL LELAND

Wheaton, IL

info@writersedgeservice.com | www.writersedgeservice.com

> **Contact:** email
>
> **Services:** Professional editors with many years of experience in working with major Christian publishers evaluate, screen, and expose potential books to traditional Christian publishing companies.
>
> **Types of manuscripts:** books, all kinds except poetry, and all ages
>
> **Charges:** $99
>
> **Description:** "For more than twenty years, it has been a method of effective communication between writers and major traditional Christian publishers. Because most traditional publishers no longer accept unsolicited manuscripts, new or relatively unknown writers have little chance to be seen by a traditional publisher unless they have a credible literary agent. Writer's Edge Service, in

full cooperation with more than seventy-five traditional, royalty-based Christian publishers, gives writers another option. The acquisition editors of these companies view relevant manuscripts that make the cut at Writer's Edge because they know they have been carefully screened and evaluated before being passed to them for consideration. Over the years, hundreds of authors have been successfully published because of Writer's Edge Service."

THE WRITER'S FRIEND | DONNA CLARK GOODRICH

Mesa, AZ | 480-962-6694
dgood648@aol.com | *www.thewritersfriend.net*

Contact: email
Services: copyediting, proofreading
Types of manuscripts: articles, nonfiction books, devotionals, short stories, novels, query letters, book proposals, gift books, adult, teen/YA, picture books, easy readers, middle grade
Charges: hourly rate, page rate
Credentials/experience: More than fifty years editing and proofreading for publishers and writers.

THE WRITER'S TABLET AGENCY | TERRI WHITMIRE

4371 Roswell Rd #315, Marietta, GA 30062 | 770-648-4101
Writerstablet@gmail.com | *www.Writerstablet.org,*
www.FunCreativeWriting.com

Contact: email, phone
Services: manuscript evaluation, substantive editing/rewriting, copyediting, proofreading, create brochures, create newsletters, write website text, create small group/Bible study guides, write curriculum lesson plans, write discussion questions for books, writing coach, back-cover copy
Types of manuscripts: articles, nonfiction books, devotionals, short stories, novels, curriculum, Bible studies, technical material, adult, teen/YA, picture books, easy readers, middle grade
Charges: flat fee, hourly rate, word rate
Credentials/experience: "Owner, Terri Whitmire, and her team of skilled writers, editors, and marketers are diverse and prepared to fulfill your content needs. At The Writer's Tablet Agency, we believe that words are critical in communicating your unique message. Together, we will develop or edit your content to tailor fit your individual objectives. Whether you need to write a novel, perfect a presentation, or build an e-commerce website,

Writer's Tablet will provide expertise and scrupulous attention to detail every step of the way. A seasoned author and successful writing consultant, Mrs. Whitmire earned a bachelor's degree in Information Technology from North Carolina's historic A&T State University. She pursued a writing certification from the Institute of Children's Literature. She is the author of five published books and passionately provides inspired written solutions to businesses and aspiring authors. Some of her clients have gone on to be best-selling authors, public speakers, and leaders in their industry."

WRITTEN BY A PRO | SHARLA TAYLOR

PO Box 223, Polk City, FL 33868 | 912-656-6857
writtenbyapro@msn.com | *www.writtenbyapro.com*

Contact: email
Services: manuscript evaluation, substantive editing/rewriting, copyediting, proofreading, ghostwriting, coauthoring, write website text, create small group/Bible study guides, write curriculum lesson plans, write discussion questions for books, writing coach, résumé/CV writer, LinkedIn profile writer
Types of manuscripts: articles, nonfiction books, devotionals, short stories, novels, query letters, book proposals, curriculum, scripts, gift books, adult, teen/YA, middle grade
Charges: flat fee, hourly rate, word rate
Credentials/experience: "Certified professional résumé writer; certified career enlightenment LinkedIn writer; experienced job-search strategist with more than twenty years in the careers industry; leads a free online Bible study for job seekers based on the Theology of Work project (*www.theologyofwork.org*). Sharla has developed thousands of résumés for business leaders, executives, career-changers, people reentering the workforce, and recent college graduates."

YO PRODUCTIONS, LLC | YOLONDA TONETTE SANDERS

PO Box 32329, Columbus, OH 43232 | 614-452-4920
info_4u@yoproductions.net | *www.yoproductions.net*

Contact: email, phone, website form
Services: manuscript evaluation, substantive editing/rewriting, copyediting, proofreading, ghostwriting, coauthoring, brochures, newsletters, create small group/Bible study guides, write

curriculum lesson plans, write discussion questions for books, writing coach, back-cover copy

Types of manuscripts: articles, nonfiction books, devotionals, poetry, short stories, novels, query letters, book proposals, curriculum, Bible studies, scripts, technical material, adult, teen/YA, academic

Charges: flat fee, hourly rate, word rate, custom

Credentials/experience: "More than thirteen years of professional editing and writing experience, editor and writer for a national publication."

YOUR TIME TO WRITE | MARY BUSHA

Ocala, FL | 517-416-0133
yourtimetowrite@gmail.com

Contact: email

Services: manuscript evaluation, copyediting, proofreading, writing coach

Types of manuscripts: nonfiction books, devotionals, book proposals, gift books

Charges: hourly rate, page rate

Credentials/experience: "More than thirty-five years in publishing, including newspapers, magazines, and books. Works with author from book idea to publication and all steps in between. Full résumé available on request. First one-hour consultation at no charge."

INTERNATIONAL

ANNE HAMILTON

QLD, Australia

Contact: message via *www.facebook.com/armourbooks.au*

Credentials/experience: Multi-award winning author and editor.

AOTEAROA EDITORIAL SERVICES | VENNESSA NG

PO Box 228, Oamaru, New Zealand 9444 | +6 422 434 6995
aotearoa.editorial@gmail.com | *www.aotearoaeditorial.com*

Contact: email

Services: manuscript evaluation, substantive editing/rewriting, copyediting, proofreading, writing coach

Types of manuscripts: short stories, novels, adult

Charges: page rate

Credentials/experience: "Fourteen years of experience working with Christian fiction authors. Member of The Christian PEN."

BOOK WHISPERS

Capalaba, QLD 4157, Australia | +617 3167 6513

info@bookwhispers.com.au | www.bookwhispers.com.au

Contact: email

Services: manuscript evaluation, structural editing, copyediting, proofing, back-cover copy, marketing copy, experienced, knowledgeable advice and recommendations on accessing the Australian educational and trade markets

Credentials/experience: The team has more than ten years of experience in traditional publishing.

CELTICFROG EDITING | ALEX MCGILVERY

Kamloops, BC, Canada | 250-819-4275

thecelticfrog@gmail.com | celticfrogediting.com

Contact: email, website form

Services: manuscript evaluation, writing coach

Types of manuscripts: articles, nonfiction books, devotionals, short stories, novels, adult, teen/YA, middle grade

Charges: based loosely on word count

Credentials/experience: "I have been reviewing and critiquing books for more than three decades, and editing since 2014. One client compared my work favourably with the editors at a traditional publisher."

CHRISTIAN EDITING SERVICES | IOLA GOULTON

78 Maungawhare Pl., Tauranga, Bay of Plenty 3110, New Zealand

igoulton@christianediting.co.nz | www.christianediting.co.nz

Contact: email, website form

Services: manuscript evaluation, substantive editing/rewriting, copyediting, newsletters, website text

Types of manuscripts: short stories, novels, teen/YA, middle grade

Charges: hourly rate

Credentials/experience: "Iola Goulton of Christian Editing Services is a New Zealand-based freelance editor specializing in Christian fiction. Iola holds a degree in marketing and has been editing since 2012. Iola has completed courses with Lawson Writer's Academy, Michael Hauge, and the Christian Proofreaders and Editors Network, and has taught for Omega Writers, New Zealand Christian Writers, and Romance Writers of New Zealand. She won the 2016 American Christian Fiction Writers Genesis Award

(Novella), and copyedited *Then There Was You* by Kara Isaac, which won the 2018 Romance Writers of America RITA Award (Romance with Religious or Spiritual Elements), and was a finalist in the Carol Awards."

EXTRA INK EDITS | MEGAN EASLEY-WALSH
Ireland but American editor
www.Megan@ExtraInkEdits.com | *meganeasleywalsh.com/editing-services*
> **Contact:** email
> **Services:** manuscript evaluation, copyediting, proofreading, writing coach, back-cover copy
> **Types of manuscripts:** nonfiction books, devotionals, short stories, novels, query letters, Bible studies, gift books, adult, teen/YA
> **Charges:** flat fee, page rate
> **Credentials/experience:** "More than ten years of experience as a writing consultant and editor, best-selling author, former college writing teacher."

GRACE BRIDGES
New Zealand
gracebridges1@gmail.com | *www.gracebridges.kiwi*
> **Contact:** email
> **Services:** manuscript evaluation, copyediting, proofreading
> **Types of manuscripts:** short stories, novels, adult, teen/YA, middle grade, speculative genre
> **Charges:** word rate
> **Credentials/experience:** "Multiple winner of the Sir Julius Vogel Award from the Science Fiction and Fantasy Association of New Zealand, founding member and mentor at Realm Makers, editor and mentor for Young NZ Writers, and has edited dozens of published books including many anthology projects. Author of the Earthcore series and more."

IMMORTALISE | BEN MORTON
Australia
info@immortalise.com.au | *www.immortalise.com.au*
> **Contact:** email
> **Services:** writing coaching, manuscript assessment, editing, proofreading
> **Charges:** page rate (where pages average 250 -300 words)

Credentials/experience: "Published author, creative writing teacher, experienced editor and publisher, MA fiction writing supervisor."

NEXT LEVEL EDITING AND TRANSCRIPTION |
DARLENE OAKLEY

St. Catharines, ON, Canada | 289-696-2382
nextleveleditingandt@gmail.com | nextleveleditingandtranscription.com

Contact: email

Services: manuscript evaluation, substantive editing/rewriting, copyediting, proofreading

Types of manuscripts: articles, nonfiction books, devotionals, poetry, gift books, short stories, novels, Bible studies, teen/YA

Charges: word rate

Credentials/experience: "Fifteen+ years of editing experience (independent & for publishing companies), many repeat and word-of-mouth clients; particular attention to punctuation, sentence structure, and syntax, character development (fiction) and argument development (nonfiction)."

NITPICKING WITH A PURPOSE | MARSHA MALCOLM

Savanna-la-mar, Westmoreland, Jamaica | 876-823-2092
purposefulnitpicker@gmail.com
www.linkedin.com/in/marsha-malcolm-4791549a

Contact: email

Services: copyediting, proofreading

Types of manuscripts: short stories, novels, picture books, easy readers, middle grade

Charges: word rate

Credentials/experience: Expert rating certification in Keys to Editing.

RED LOUNGE FOR WRITERS | CECILY PATERSON

NSW, Australia
cecilyapaterson@gmail.com | www.redloungeforwriters.com

Contact: website form

Services: editing, writing coach

Types of manuscripts: specializes in memoir

SUSAN J. BRUCE

Susan@susanjbruce.com | www.susanjbruce.com

Contact: email

Services: manuscript assessment, copyediting, proofreading

Types of manuscripts: short stories, novels, nonfiction, devotionals, teen/YA, adult

Charges: flat fee, hourly rate

Credentials/experience: "Master of Arts in Creative Writing. For more details see *www.susanjbruce.com/Editing*."

VINEMARC COMMUNICATIONS | MARCIA LAYCOCK

PO Box 637, Blackfalds, AB, Canada T0M 0J0 | 403-885-9828
vinemarc@telus.net | *www.marcialeelaycock.com*

Contact: email

Services: manuscript evaluation, copyediting, proofreading

Types of manuscripts: articles, nonfiction books, devotionals, poetry, short stories, novels, gift books, adult, teen/YA

Charges: flat fee

Credentials/experience: "Marcia has been publishing for almost thirty years. Her work has been endorsed by Janette Oke, Phil Callaway, and Sigmund Brouwer. She has won many awards for her writing and taught writing courses at conferences and online."

THE WRITE FLOURISH | TIM AND NOLA PASSMORE

Toowoomba, Australia

nola@thewriteflourish.com.au | *www.thewriteflourish.com.au*

Contact: email

Services: manuscript assessments, structural editing, copyediting, proofreading, mentoring

Types of manuscripts: adult and YA novels, poetry, memoirs, devotional books, creative nonfiction, academic, manuals, articles, short stories, book proposals

Charges: hourly rate

Credentials/experience: "Tim and Nola Passmore each have more than 20 years' experience as university academics. Nola also has a degree in creative writing. They founded The Write Flourish in 2014 and have edited a wide range of manuscripts across a variety of styles and genres. They have also had many of their own short pieces published including fiction, poetry, devotions, memoir, nonfiction and academic articles. They would love to help you add the right flourish to your manuscript."

412

Christian Writers Institute Courses
2020 Editor Bundle

Courses in this bundle:
- When to Break the Rules of Writing
- What Editors Won't Tell You
- Working with Your Editor
- 10 Easy But Essential Self-Editing Tips
- 12 Ways to Please an Editor

Normal price: $45
Savings: 40%
Market Guide price $27

https://cwmg.link/editor2020

How to Scan QR Codes

Use the camera on your smartphone to focus on the above QR code to activate the discount. It will give you the option to visit the site, which you will want to accept. If you are using an older smartphone, you may need to download a QR code scanning app. You can also visit the URL below the code to activate the discount on your computer.

20

PUBLICITY AND MARKETING SERVICES

THE ADAMS GROUP | GINA ADAMS

6688 Nolensville Rd., Ste. 108-149, Brentwood, TN 37027 |
615-776-1590

gina@adamsgroup.com | *www.adamsprgroup.com*

> **Contact:** email, phone, website form
>
> **Services:** publicity, social-media marketing, press kits, contributed content, media interviews, branding
>
> **Books:** all faith-based genres
>
> **Charges:** flat fee
>
> **Credentials/experience:** "Gina Adams has served in the Christian marketplace for over 30 years representing singers, bands, films, authors, speakers, and major conference events. In 1994, Gina formed The Adams Group, an independent PR and marketing firm dedicated to working with artists and authors who need assistance with promoting their products and increasing their national exposure. Her clients have appeared on a variety of Christian and mainstream media outlets, including Focus on the Family, TBN, *Fox News*, *60 Minutes*, American Family Radio, *The 700 Club*, *The New York Times*, CBN, Daystar, and *CBS This Morning*, among a myriad of other broadcast and print outlets.
>
> Gina holds a BS in business and marketing from Murray State University and a certificate of achievement in Christian apologetics from Biola University. She has also earned an Expert Rating Certification in Social Media Marketing. She is a member of the Evangelical Press Association, Media Entertainment & Technology Alliance, Gospel Music Association Hall of Fame Committee, and National Religious Broadcasters."

AUDRA JENNINGS PR

2609 Sandy Ln., Corsicana, TX 75110 | 903-874-8363
ajenningspr@gmail.com | www.audrajennings.com

Contact: email

Services: publicity, blog tours, author-assist services, social-media management, giveaways, graphics

Specialty: Christian titles to Christian media

Books: nonfiction, fiction, children's

Charges: flat fees for publicity and blog tours, hourly rates for author-assist and other services

Credentials/experience: "I have worked in Christian PR since 2002. For 16 years, I worked with two different agencies before branching out on my own. Over the years, I have worked with all of the well-known, traditional Christian publishers. I also work directly with authors. In addition to my freelance clients, I am on staff part-time with a publisher."

AUTHOR MEDIA | THOMAS UMSTATTD, JR.

PO Box 5690, Austin, TX 78763 | 512-582-7290
thomas@authormedia.com | www.authormedia.com

Contact: website form

Services: marketing consulting, web development, branding, web design

Books: fiction, nonfiction, children's

Charges: flat fee, hourly rate

Credentials/experience: More than ten years of experience, included in "101 Best Websites for Authors" by *Writer's Digest*.

AUTHOR SUPPORT SERVICES | RUSSELL SHERRARD

Carmichael, CA | 916-967-7251
russellsherrard@reagan.com | www.sherrardsebookresellers.com/WordPress/author-support-services-the-authors-place-to-get-help

Contact: email

Services: Twitter and Facebook marketing, submitting URL to search engines

Books: Christian ebooks, fiction, nonfiction

Charges: flat fee

Credentials/experience: Writing and editing since 2009; currently providing freelance services for multiple clients.

BANNER CONSULTING | MIKE LOOMIS

PO Box 1828, Winter Park, Co 80482

Mike@MikeLoomis.co | www.MikeLoomis.co

Contact: email, website form

Services: book-launch planning, branding, article curation and placement, web development, PR

Specialty: branding and marketing strategy

Books: nonfiction

Charges: custom fee

Credentials/experience: "I've worked with internationally known brands and *New York Times* bestsellers. I've helped clients get breakthrough PR, speaking engagements, and bestseller lists."

THE BLYTHE DANIEL AGENCY, INC . | BLYTHE DANIEL

email through website | www.theblythedanielagency.com

Blythe Daniel, publicist

Stephanie Alton, marketing manager

Contact: website form

Services: range of publicity campaigns utilizing broadcast and print media and the internet, including blogs, websites, online magazines, TV and radio interviews, book reviews, and book launches

Books: primarily adult and young-adult nonfiction

Charges: customized by campaign

Credentials/experience: "We have personal relationships with hundreds of media outlets that we have developed over the last 20 years in the business. Through our relationships, understanding of the changing media landscape, and careful selection of content we promote, we are able to provide our clients more opportunities to bring recognition to their book(s)." Blythe worked five years as the publicity director and two years as the marketing director for Thomas Nelson.

BROOKSTONE CREATIVE GROUP | SUZANNE KUHN

PO Box 211, Evington, VA 24550 | 302-514-7899

www.brookstonecreativegroup.com

Contact: website form

Services: Amazon optimization, social-media assessment and consulting, video interviews, email and digital marketing, search-engine optimization

Books: all

Charges: flat fee, custom rate

Credentials/experience: Suzanne has more than thirty years of book-specific experience. Brookstone is an expansion of her promotion business, SuzyQ, with a team of almost two dozen professionals who bring a wide range of knowledge and experience to help you get published.

CHOICE MEDIA & COMMUNICATIONS | HEATHER ADAMS

231 Public Square, Ste. 300, PMB #45, Franklin, TN 37064-2552 | 404-423-8411

heather@choicepublicity.com | www.ChoicePublicity.com
Kerry Gardner, kerry@choicepublicity.com
Devin Lee Duke, devinlee@choicepublicity.com
Sarah Payton, sarah@choicepublicity.com

Contact: email

Services: media relations, branding and strategy, social media, events

Books: nonfiction

Charges: retainer-based partnership or project fee

Credentials/experience: "Choice Media & Communications is a boutique media and communications business dedicated to providing clients with quality public relations. Choice helps authors create a clear communications plan, gain media coverage, and receive guidance they won't get anywhere else. With more than two decades of high-level professional communications experience across varying industries and with many of today's tastemakers and thought leaders, Choice founder Heather Adams created a public relations business marked with warmth and enthusiasm, strategic development, clear communication, detailed execution, and thorough reporting."

CHRISTIAN INDIE PUBLISHING ASSOCIATION | SARAH BOLME

PO Box 481022, Charlotte, NC 28269 | 704-277-7194
cipa@christianpublishers.net | www.christianpublishers.net

Contact: email

Services: information and tools for publishing and marketing for independent authors, including cooperative marketing, cutting-edge information, and cost savings

Specialty: marketing services

Books: all generes

Charges: membership fee plus costs for cooperative marketing services
Credentials/experience: "CIPA has been providing services for small publishers and independent authors since 2004."

EABOOKS PUBLISHING | CHERI COWELL

1567 Thornhill Cir., Oviedo, FL 32765 | 407-712-3431
Cheri@eabookspublishing.com | *www.eabookspublishing.com*

Contact: email
Services: marketing coaching that includes branding, website and blog, and social media
Books: fiction, nonfiction, children's
Charges: flat fee
Credentials/experience: "Traditionally published author who now owns a self-publishing company that also offers this coaching service because it is what I wish I had: one-on-one coaching."

ENLIVEN YOUR TRIBE | BRIAN ALLAIN

brian@enlivenyourtribe.com | *enlivenyourtribe.com*

Contact: email
Services: platform development, social-media and email marketing
Books: all spiritual genres
Charges: custom rate
Credentials/experience: "We have helped many authors significantly expand their platforms, including Frederick Buechner, Kathleen Norris, Diana Butler Bass, and the Marcus Borg Foundation, as well as many authors just getting started."

JONES LITERARY | JASON JONES

Nashville, TN | 512-720-2996
jason@jonesliterary.com | *jonesliterary.com*

Contact: email
Service: publicity
Books: nonfiction
Charges: custom
Credentials/experience: "Previously led SERVE Literary & Media, which my experience and relationships gave birth to as a division of PR by the Book, LLC. Prior to that, I spent five years with Thomas Nelson. I've been blessed with wonderful clients, have been fortunate enough to have led campaigns for eleven *New York Times* bestselling titles and have worked alongside some of the industry's most successful authors, ministries, and nonprofit organizations."

LOGOS PUBLICATIONS, LLC

PO Box 271, Lampeter, PA 17537 | 717-681-8452
customerservice@logospub.com | *www.logospub.com*

Contact: website form
Service: Catch Fire is a collaborative, subscription-based marketing service that is conducted via our website *FindChristianBooks.com*
Books: fiction, nonfiction, self-help; we reserve the right to reject any book we feel does not fit with our Christian worldview
Charges: six-month minimum subscription
Credentials/experience: "Logos Publications is a trusted ally to both indie and traditionally published authors. We are proud members of the Christian Indie Publisher's Association and the Southern Lancaster County Chamber of Commerce."

MCCLURE/MUNTSINGER PUBLIC RELATIONS |
PAMELA MCCLURE and JANA MUNTSINGER

PO Box 804, Franklin, TN 37065 | 615-595-8321
info@mmpublicrelations.com | *www.mmpublicrelations.com*

Contact: email
Services: customized publicity campaigns, including radio, TV, internet, and social media
Books: any book they like
Charges: customized by campaign
Credentials/experience: "After more than 40 combined years of book publicity, we have long and strong relationships with dozens of editors, writers, and producers. We specialize in knowing how to place religious books in Christian and general-market media, traditional outlets, and online."

MEDIA CONNECT | SHARON FARNELL

301 E. 57th St., New York, NY 10022 | 212-593-6337
Sharon.Farnell@finnpartners.com | *www.media-connect.com*

Contact: email
Services: full-service book publicity firm with TV and radio campaigns, print, online, book tours, etc.
Books: primarily nonfiction but also children's and some fiction
Charges: custom rate
Credentials/experience: "Since joining the company in 1997, Sharon has been instrumental in helping faith-based authors and publishers reach both the Christian and mainstream audience. She has successfully placed her clients in a variety of top media outlets."

SIDE DOOR COMMUNICATIONS | DEBBIE LYKINS

224-234-6699

email through website | www.sidedoorcom.net

> **Contact:** email, phone
>
> **Services:** media relations, working with both Christian and traditional media, as well as online media and bloggers
>
> **Books:** "We focus primarily on Christian nonfiction titles and the occasional novel. We look for well-written, well-edited books on topics that we believe will be of interest to the media. We also consider the author's credentials on the subject. No self-published novels."
>
> **Charges:** custom fee
>
> **Credentials/experience:** More than two decades of experience in marketing, public relations, and communications, with more than fifteen years in Christian book publicity. Authors represented have been featured in numerous media outlets.

VERITAS COMMUNICATIONS | DON S. OTIS

PO Box 1505, Sandpoint, ID 83864 | 719-275-7775

don@veritasincorporated.com | www.veritasincorporated.com

> **Contact:** email, phone, website form
>
> **Services:** schedule radio and television interviews, write and distribute media releases, author training, website representation, travel tracking, select convention representation
>
> **Specialty:** rapid-response releases to the media on newsworthy issues and events
>
> **Books:** primarily Christian nonfiction and selective conservative titles, some fiction if it is issue-driven
>
> **Charges:** flat fee, offers ministry discount
>
> **Credentials/experience:** "Thirty years of publicity work. Traditionally published author of five books with more than 600 radio interviews. Experienced radio and television producer, radio host, and manager for the Voice of Hope Radio Network."

WILDFIRE MARKETING | ROB EAGAR

3625 Chartwell Dr., Suwanee, GA 30024 | 770-887-1462

Rob@StartaWildfire.com | www.StartaWildfire.com

> **Contact:** email
>
> **Services:** Rob Eagar is one of the top experts on all facets of book marketing, including book launches, author websites, email marketing,

social media, public speaking, and author-revenue growth

Specialty: book marketing

Books: all genres

Charges: flat fee

Credentials/experience: "Rob Eagar is the founder of Wildfire Marketing, a consulting practice that has coached more than 450 authors and helped books hit *The New York Times* best-seller list in three different categories: new fiction, new nonfiction, and backlist nonfiction. His company has attracted numerous bestselling authors, including Dr. Gary Chapman, Lysa TerKeurst, DeVon Franklin, Wanda Brunstetter, and Dr. John Townsend."

Christian Writers Institute Courses 2020 Marketing Bundle

Courses in this bundle:
- How to Get Booked as a Podcast Guest
- How to Craft Amazing Blog Posts
- The Art of Persuasion
- 7 Secrets of Amazing Author Websites
- Sell Your Books Like Wildfire
- Book Marketing: How Everything Has Changed and Nothing Is New

Normal price: $355
Savings: 72%
Market Guide price $99.40

https://cwmg.link/mkt2020

How to Scan QR Codes

Use the camera on your smartphone to focus on the above QR code to activate the discount. It will give you the option to visit the site, which you will want to accept. If you are using an older smartphone, you may need to download a QR code scanning app. You can also visit the URL below the code to activate the discount on your computer.

21

LEGAL AND ACCOUNTING SERVICES

CAROL TOPP CPA

10288 Amberwood Ct., Cincinnati, OH 45241 | 513-777-8342
Carol@TaxesforWriters.com | *TaxesforWriters.com*

> **Contact:** email
> **Services:** accounting, taxes, phone consultations
> **Charges:** hourly rate
> **Credentials/experience:** Certified Public Accountant and author.

CHRIS MORRIS CPA, LLC

11209 N. 161st Ln., Surprise, AZ 85379 | 623-451-8182
cmorris@chrismorriscpa.com | *chrismorriscpa.com*

> **Contact:** email
> **Services:** accounting, taxes, contract review
> **Charges:** flat fee, custom
> **Credentials/experience:** "Chris Morris CPA is a firm that has focused its resources on developing a deep understanding of the creative entrepreneur space. We have the privilege of counting photographers, authors, publishing presses, editors, virtual assistants, and bloggers among our clients. In other words, we live and breathe the world of the creative entrepreneur."

TOM UMSTATTD CPA

13276 Research Blvd., Ste. 101, Austin, TX 78750 | 512-250-1090
tom@taxmantom.com | *www.taxmantom.com*

> **Contact:** website form
> **Services:** accounting, taxes
> **Charges:** flat fee, hourly rate
> **Credentials/experience:** More than 35 years of experience.

Christian Writers Institute Courses 2020 Tax & Legal Bundle

Courses in this bundle:

- Tax & Business Guide for Authors
- Ghostwriting & Collaboration
- Understanding Copyright Law
- The Book Contract

Normal price: $117
Savings: 58%
Market Guide price $49.`4

https://cwmg.link/taxlegal2020

How to Scan QR Codes

Use the camera on your smartphone to focus on the above QR code to activate the discount. It will give you the option to visit the site, which you will want to accept. If you are using an older smartphone, you may need to download a QR code scanning app. You can also visit the URL below the code to activate the discount on your computer.

22

SPEAKING SERVICES

ADVANCED WRITERS AND SPEAKERS ASSOCIATION (AWSA)

PO Box 6421, Longmont, CO 80501

ReachOut2Linda@gmail.com | awsa.com

Contact: email, mail

Director: Linda Evans Shepherd

Services: website directory, online prayer group, coaching, online training and community, conference prior to the opening of Christian Product Expo, fall retreat at the Christian Booksellers Expo at Munce

Membership: women only, $40/year

Main membership qualifications: two major forms of communication from this list: national media (column, blog, podcast, radio or TV show), published book, speaking more than twice a year outside your community, making movies, acting; protégé membership for beginning to intermediate communicators

CHRISTIAN COMMUNICATORS ANOINTED & APPOINTED SPEAKER SUMMIT

contact@christiancommunicators.com | www.ChristianCommunicators.com

Contact: email, website form

Directors: Tammy Whitehurst, Sherry Poundstone, Lori Boruff

Service: annual conference to educate, validate, and launch speakers to the next level for beginning or seasoned speakers; March 17-21 in Ridgecrest, NC

CHRISTIAN SPEAKER NETWORK

christianspeaker.net

Contact: website form

Service: web page that is listed in the online database

Fee: $39.95 per year

CHRISTIAN WOMEN SPEAKERS
womenspeakers.com
> **Contact:** website form
> **Service:** web page that is listed in the online database
> **Fees:** free or $29.99 per month/$299 per year for higher ranking, extra features and benefits

DECLARE
info@wearedeclare.com | wearedeclare.com
> **Contact:** website
> **Directors:** Eryn Hall, Kristin Lemus, Michelle Acker
> **Services:** annual conference in October to equip women to be effective communicators, blog, podcasts, community events

NEXT STEP COACHING SERVICES
info@nextstepcoachingservices.com | nextstepcoachingservices.com
> **Contact:** website form
> **Coach:** Amy Carroll
> **Services:** coaching for women speakers to sharpen messages, develop marketing, and gain organizational tools; weekly speaking tips via email

NORTHWEST CHRISTIAN SPEAKERS
2818 Martin Rd., Bellingham, WA | 360-966-0203
Coordinator@NWSpeakers.com | nwspeakers.com
> **Director:** Christie Miller
> **Contact:** email, phone
> **Service:** speakers bureau, not limited to the Northwest
> **Qualifications/requirements:** attend training workshops/evaluation session

SHE SPEAKS CONFERENCE
Sponsored by Proverbs 31 Ministries. See the listing in Chapter 17, "Writers Conferences and Seminars."

SPEAK UP SPEAKER SERVICES
3141 Winged Foot Dr., Lakeland, FL 33803 | 586-481-7661
gene4speakup@aol.com | sussinc.com
> **Contact:** email, mail
> **Director:** Carol Kent

Service: speakers bureau, fee negotiation, contracts for services, speech and TV-interview coaching, SpeakUp Conference (see listing in "Writers Conferences and Seminars")

Qualifications/requirements: at least two books or CDs currently available in the Christian market and regularly speaking nationally; see list of application details to mail

Representation: exclusive, nonexclusive

ULTIMATE CHRISTIAN COMMUNICATORS CONFERENCE
ultimatechristiancommunicatorsconference.com

Contact: website

Director: Felice Gerwitz

Service: annual conference for women to train, coach, and provide networking for beginning and advanced speakers, February 7-8 in Tampa, FL

Christian Writers Institute Courses
2020 Public Speaking Bundle

Courses in this bundle:
- The Art of Persuasion
- How to Become a Successful Speaker
- Public Speaking for the Writer
- Speak So People Will Listen

Normal price: $67
Savings: 56%
Market Guide price $29.48

https://cwmg.link/speak2020

How to Scan QR Codes
Use the camera on your smartphone to focus on the above QR code to activate the discount. It will give you the option to visit the site, which you will want to accept. If you are using an older smartphone, you may need to download a QR code scanning app. You can also visit the URL below the code to activate the discount on your computer.

23

WRITING EDUCATION RESOURCES

ANN KROEKER, WRITING COACH
annkroeker.com/podcasts
> **Type:** podcast
> **Host:** Ann Kroeker
> **Description:** "These writing podcast episodes offer practical tips and motivation for writers at all stages. . . . Tune in for solutions addressing anything from self-editing and goal-setting . . . to administrative and scheduling challenges."

CHRISTIAN EDITOR NETWORK LLC
www.ChristianEditorNetwork.com
> **Type:** organization
> **Owner:** Kathy Ide
> **Description:** "Four organizations committed to serving Christian editors. The Christian PEN: Proofreaders and Editors Network, Christian Editor Connection, PENCON editors conference, and The PEN Institute. (See individual listings in this guide for details.) Our passion is to equip, empower, and encourage editors in the Christian market."

CHRISTIAN PUBLISHING SHOW
www.christianpublishingshow.com
> **Type:** podcast
> **Host:** Thomas Umstattd, Jr.
> **Description:** "The Christian Publishing Show is a podcast to help Christian authors change the world. We talk about how to improve in the craft of writing, how to get published, and how to market effectively. Get expert advice from industry insiders."

THE CHRISTIAN SPECULATIVE FICTION PODCAST
www.buzzsprout.com/324404

Type: podcast

Host: Paul Regnier

Description: "Author interviews and topic discussions about speculative fiction and how faith intersects with stories. Discussions cover writing craft, publishing, promotion, and everything related to the life of a speculative fiction author. Join us as we talk about storytelling in the genres of science fiction, fantasy, paranormal, superhero, and everything in between."

CHRISTIAN WRITERS INSTITUTE
christianwritersinstitute.com

Type: courses

Director: Steve Laube

Description: "The Christian Writers Institute was created to help Christians become proficient in the skills, craft, and business of writing. To build the Kingdom of God word-by-word. It does so by providing audio, video, and pdf courses taught by some of the industry's best teachers. In addition, the Institute publishes a number of books on writing for writers, including *The Christian Writers Market Guide*. Originally founded in 1945, it is estimated that over 30,000 students have been trained by the Christian Writers Institute."

THE COMMUNICATOR ACADEMY PODCAST
www.communicatoracademy.com/podcast-2

Type: podcast

Hosts: Kathi Lipp, Michele Cushatt

Description: "The Communicator Academy Podcast is for those who love God and want to share His story through writing, speaking, social media—and yes—even marketing. Hosts Kathi Lipp and Michele Cushatt are both 'communication nerds' who love talking about God's message and how to share it better. Their refreshing and honest take on the 'industry' do's and don'ts as well as insight on what makes you stand out from the rest, will not only entertain, but will serve in helping you propel your career to the next level. If you are looking to clarify your calling, you will want to hang out with these two."

CREATE IF WRITING

createifwriting.com/podcast-and-show-notes

> **Type:** podcast
> **Host:** Kirsten Oliphant
> **Description:** "Create If Writing is a weekly podcast for writers and bloggers dealing with authentic platform building online. You will hear from experts on list-building, connecting through Twitter, and how to utilize Facebook. But tools for building an audience would feel empty without a little inspiration, so these training episodes are balanced with inspirational interviews with writers who share their creative process, ups and downs, and how they have dealt with success or failure."

DECLARE PODCAST

declareconference.com/declare-podcast

> **Type:** podcast
> **Description:** The mission of Declare is "to equip women to walk in their callings as Christian communicators."

FIGHTWRITE PODCAST

fightingwrite.blogspot.com/p/the-geek-block.html

> **Type:** podcast
> **Host:** Carla Koch
> **Description:** "The FightWrite podcast is another resource for you writers knee deep in writing action scenes."

THE GATECRASHERS PODCAST

www.stitcher.com/podcast/amanda-luedeke/the-gatecrashers-podcast

> **Type:** podcast
> **Hosts:** Amanda Luedeke, Charis Crowe
> **Description:** "Teaming up to talk about both sides of publishing (self-publishing and traditional), Amanda and Charis share their combined twenty years of experience in the industry from both sides of the desk. They offer a glimpse behind the 'gates' as they share the realities, opportunities, and difficulties of the publishing world."

HOME ROW: JUST KEEP WRITING

homerowpod.com

> **Type:** podcast
>
> **Host:** J. A. Medders
>
> **Description:** "Get inspired to write from some of today's best writers. Listen. Learn. Just keep writing. You might learn how to get a book deal, write a best-seller, or quit your day job. Maybe you'll get that nudge you need to . . . write the blog, article, or book you've been thinking on for far too long. As Christians, our aim is to write in such a way that Jesus is made much of and the Church is encouraged to follow our risen Lord."

THE HOPE*WRITERS PODCAST

podcasts.apple.com/us/podcast/hopewriters/id914574328?mt=2#

> **Type:** podcast
>
> **Hosts:** Emily P. Freeman, Brian J. Dixon, Gary Morland
>
> **Description:** "Let's take the next step in your writing life! Maybe you're a beginner stumped about what to do first. Or you're experienced but aren't sure what to do next. Maybe you need help knowing your message or who you're actually writing for. Maybe you want to reach more readers but without becoming a self-promoting robot. Maybe you're an author who's been doing this for years but you long to see how other writers balance the business and marketing side of the writing life. Or you want to know how to write a book or find an agent or just start a regular writing routine.
>
> "Maybe you're afraid of failure, or that you're a bad writer and no one will tell you. Or you think what if I work hard at this and never get published or make even a dollar? What if my spouse or family never understand how much this means to me? What if I share too much and people in my real life get mad? What if I make a fool of myself or break the internet? And what if I'm successful and my life changes and I have to do new things and sacrifice my family?
>
> "The three of us have collectively written a bunch of books, some of them bestsellers, and we know what it's like to have all these questions and more. The Hope*writers Podcast will help you skip the long learning curve we've struggled through and will put you ahead of the game. Each week you get answers to these questions, from us and from interviews with publishing pros, to help you have clarity for what's next for you."

THE JERRY JENKINS WRITERS GUILD

www.JerrysGuild.com

Type: courses

Director: Jerry Jenkins

Description: "The Writers Guild is like a writing conference you can access from anywhere 24/7. Instant access to video training on any writing topic. Additionally, several times each month Jerry answers your questions live, hosts new writing workshops, interviews industry experts, and so much more." Membership is open only periodically; join the waitlist for the next open period. Jerry also offers individual online courses at *jerryjenkins.com/online-creative-writing-courses*.

KICK-START YOUR AUTHOR PLATFORM MARKETING CHALLENGE

christianediting.co.nz/kick-start

Type: class

Director: Iola Goulton

Description: "Forty-day email challenge, with an email each day with a series of tasks to complete. Ongoing support is available via a private Facebook group. Topics: What is Marketing?; Understanding Your Brand; Know Your Genre; Know Your Target Reader; Design Your Visual Brand: fonts, colors, author photo, website logo; Create and Brand Social Media: Facebook, Instagram, Pinterest, Twitter; Create a Social Media Plan; To Blog or Not to Blog?; Create a Mailing List; Set Up, Design, and Configure Your Website."

KINGDOM WRITERS

authors.libsyn.com/podcast

Type: podcast

Hosts: CJ and Shelley Hitz

Description: "CJ and Shelley Hitz are passionate about equipping and empowering Christian writers of all genres to share their unique gifts with the world. This podcast is filled with spiritual encouragement as well as prayers to help you overcome the resistance you face as a writer. Your story matters!

"We believe that you have a specific role to play in the kingdom of heaven to impact lives for eternity. And because of this, we will pour out our lives encouraging writers like you to not only tell your stories but to take the courageous step of self-publishing your stories in books that will outlive you and leave behind a powerful legacy."

NOVEL MARKETING PODCAST

www.novelmarketing.com

> **Type:** podcast
> **Hosts:** Thomas Umstattd Jr., James L. Rubart
> **Description:** "This is the show for writers who hate marketing but still want to become bestselling authors. Our goal is to make book promotion fun and easy by connecting you with innovative marketing strategies that work."

PASTOR WRITER

pastorwriter.com/episodes

> **Type:** podcast
> **Host:** Chase Replogle
> **Description:** "Join me as I interview pastors, authors, and writing experts in my journey to better understand the calling and the craft of writing, reading, and living the Christian life."

THE PEN INSTITUTE

www.PENInstitute.com

> **Type:** courses
> **Director:** Erin Brown
> **Description:** Online courses, lesson packs, webinars, and one-on-one instruction for aspiring and established freelance and in-house editors. Instructors are all experienced industry professionals. Established in 2004.

THE PORTFOLIO LIFE

podcasts.apple.com/us/podcast/the-portfolio-life-with-jeff-goins/ id844091351

> **Type:** podcast
> **Host:** Jeff Goins
> **Description:** "Jeff Goins shares thoughts & ideas that will help you to pursue work that matters, make a difference with your art & discover your true voice!"

THE PROLIFIC WRITER PODCAST

theprolificwriter.net/blog-podcast

> **Type:** podcast
>
> **Host:** Ryan Pelton
>
> **Description:** "The Prolific Writer is about writing fast, writing often, and writing well. Follow writer and publisher Ryan Pelton as he discusses processes and strategies for writing hundreds of thousands of words and sharing them with the world. TPW podcast will also interview fellow writers and discuss their tips and tricks on the craft of writing and share advice on latest trends in publishing."

SERIOUS WRITER, INC.

seriouswriter.com

> **Type:** courses
>
> **Directors:** Cyle Young, Bethany Jett
>
> **Description:** "Serious Writer's mission is to set the industry standard for excellence for the clean and Christian writing markets through online courses, one-day book camps, and writers conferences." The Serious Writer Academy offers recorded classes. The Serious Writer Club offers monthly live classes, recorded classes, chats, and more; registration is open only a few times a year.

WRITE FROM THE DEEP

www.writefromthedeep.com/write-from-the-deep-podcast

> **Type:** podcast
>
> **Hosts:** Karen Ball, Erin Taylor Young
>
> **Description:** "Encouragement, refreshment, and truth from writers, for writers. Every writer, at some point, faces the deep places of crushing trials and struggles. But the deep is also a place where we can learn to abide in God as never before. This podcast reminds writers they're not alone, and equips and helps them to embrace the deep, to discover their truest voice and message, and to share it with refined craft and renewed passion."

THE WRITE HOUR
www.thewritercoach.biz

> **Type:** podcast
> **Host:** Joyce Glass
> **Description:** "How do I start writing a book? Why do I need to write a book? What is the process to write a book? What is next after I have written my book? Are you a personal development leader ready to expand your business with a book? Have your questions answered by Joyce Glass, The Write Coach For Personal Development Leaders. Learn from leaders in the publishing world and begin your writing journey or take your writing career to the next level. Dig deeper with step-by-step instructions and mini-workshops. Joyce's strong point is breaking down the overwhelm and guides you to the next step in your journey. In every episode, she gives practical advice you can implement immediately. Join The Write Hour each week for your dose of writing motivation!"

24

CONTESTS

A listing here does not guarantee endorsement of the contest. For guidelines on evaluating contests, go to *www.sfwa.org/other-resources/for-authors/writer-beware/contests*.

Note: Dates may not be accurate since many sponsors had not posted their 2020 dates before press time.

CHILDREN AND TEENS

CORETTA SCOTT KING BOOK AWARD
www.ala.org/awardsgrants/awards/24/apply

> **Description:** Sponsored by Coretta Scott King Task Force, American Library Association. Annual award for children's books published the previous year by African-American authors and/or illustrators. Books must promote an understanding and appreciation of the "American Dream" and fit one of these categories: preschool to grade 4, grades 5–8, grades 9–12.
> **Deadline:** December 1
> **Prize:** $1,000 and plaque

FIRST EDITION CHILDREN'S BOOK WRITING CONTEST
firsteditionproject.com/childrens-book-contest.html

> **Description:** Sponsored by Southwest Human Development in Arizona, dedicated to early childhood development. Manuscripts appropriate for children from birth to five years old, 600 words or fewer, original, and not previously published in any form or currently under consideration by another publisher. Retellings of

traditional stories, such as fairy tales, will be considered, as long as the manuscript is unique and in the writer's own words.

Deadline: October 15

Entry fee: starts at $50 and varies with submission date

Prizes: publication with $1,000 advance, 8% royalty, and author copies

SOCIETY OF CHILDREN'S BOOK WRITERS AND ILLUSTRATORS

www.scbwi.org/awards/grants/for-authors

Description: Sponsors a variety of contests, scholarships, and grants.

Deadline: varies by contest

Prizes: ten awards for published authors and five for unpublished authors, plus grants for emerging voices and student writers

FICTION

ALLIANCE AWARD

www.realmmakers.com

Description: Sponsored by The Faith and Fantasy Alliance to give readers their say in what speculative fiction novels they enjoyed most in the preceding year. Only readers may nominate books in this contest. Books may be traditionally published or self-published.

Deadline: submit between March 1 and 24

Entry fee: none

Prize: certificate of recognition

AMERICAN CHRISTIAN FICTION WRITERS CONTESTS

www.ACFW.com/contests

Description: Genesis Contest for unpublished Christian fiction writers in a number of categories/genres. First Impressions award for unpublished writers. Carol Awards for best Christian fiction published the previous year.

Deadline: varies by contest

Entry fee: varies by category and membership

BARD FICTION PRIZE

www.bard.edu/bfp

> **Description:** Sponsored by Bard College. Awarded to a promising, emerging young writer of fiction, 39 years or younger and an American citizen. Entries must be previously published.
> **Deadline:** June 15
> **Entry fee:** none
> **Prize:** $30,000 and appointment as writer-in-residence for one semester at Bard College, Annandale-on-Hudson, New York

BOSTON REVIEW SHORT STORY CONTEST

www.bostonreview.net/contests

> **Description:** Previously unpublished short stories no longer than 5,000 words.
> **Deadline:** October 1
> **Entry fee:** $20
> **Prize:** $500 plus publication

BULWER-LYTTON FICTION CONTEST

www.bulwer-lytton.com

> **Description:** Sponsored by San Jose State University English Department. For the worst opening line to a novel. Each submission must be a single sentence; multiple entries allowed. Entries will be judged by categories: general, detective, western, science fiction, romance, etc. Overall winners, as well as category winners.
> **Deadline:** June 30

THE EUPLE RINEY MEMORIAL AWARD

www.thestorytellermagazine.com/contests

> **Description:** Sponsored by *The Storyteller Anthology/Magazine*. Open genre contest but must be about family in some way and suitable for a family magazine. Length: 3,000 words maximum. Can enter multiple stories with separate entry fee for each one.
> **Deadline:** date varies
> **Entry fee:** $5
> **Prizes:** first place, $50; second place, $25; third place, $15; honorable mention, $10

FLANNERY O'CONNOR AWARD FOR SHORT FICTION

www.ugapress.org/index.php/series/FOC

Description: Sponsored by University of Georgia Press. For collections of short fiction. Length: 40,000–75,000 words. Contestants must be residents of North America.
Deadline: submit between April 1 and May 31
Entry fee: $30
Prize: $1,000 plus publication under royalty book contract

GRACE PALEY PRIZE FOR SHORT FICTION

www.awpwriter.org/contests/awp_award_series_overview

Description: Sponsored by Association of Writers and Writing Programs. Short-story collections. May contain stories previously published in periodicals. Length: 150-300 pages.
Deadline: submit between January 1 and February 28
Entry fee: $25
Prize: $5,500 and publication

JACK DYER FICTION PRIZE

craborchardreview.siu.edu/submissions-annual-lit.html

Description: Sponsored by Southern Illinois University Department of English. Annual competition for short stories twenty pages or fewer on a theme.
Deadline: submit between December 1 and January 31
Entry fee: $2
Prizes: $500 each and publication in *Crab Orchard Review*

JAMES JONES FIRST NOVEL CONTEST

www.wilkes.edu/pages/1159.asp

Description: Sponsored by Wilkes University. For a first novel or novel-in-progress by a US writer who has not published a novel. Submit a two-page outline and the first fifty pages of an unpublished novel.
Deadline: March 15
Entry fee: $30
Prizes: first place, $10,000; two runners-up, $1,000 each; a selection from the winning work is published in *Provincetown Arts*

KATHERINE ANNE PORTER PRIZE IN SHORT FICTION

untpress.unt.edu/submitting-katherine-anne-porter-prize-short-fiction

Description: Sponsored by University of North Texas Press. Quality unpublished fiction by emerging writers of contemporary literature. Can be a combination of short-shorts, short stories, and novellas from 100 to 200 pages (27,500-50,000 words). Material should be previously unpublished in book form.

Deadline: submit between May 1 and June 30

Entry fee: $25

Prize: $1,000 and publication by UNT Press

NATIONAL WRITERS ASSOCIATION NOVEL-WRITING CONTEST

www.nationalwriters.shoppingcartsplus.com/f/Novel_Form4.pdf

Description: To encourage development of creative skills and recognize and reward outstanding ability in the area of novel writing. Any genre or category of novel manuscript may be entered. Only unpublished works in the English language. Maximum length: 100,000 words. Must be submitted via USPS.

Deadline: postmarked by April 1

Entry fee: $35

Prizes: first place, $500 and possible representation; second place, $250; third place, $150; fourth through tenth places, book of the winner's choice; honorable mentions, certificate

NATIONAL WRITERS ASSOCIATION SHORT-STORY CONTEST

www.nationalwriters.shoppingcartsplus.com/f/Short_Story_Contest1.pdf

Description: Any genre of story. Length: 5,000 words maximum. Submit only unpublished works in the English language via mail.

Deadline: postmarked by July 1

Entry fee: $15

Prizes: first place, $250; second place, $100; third place, $50; fourth through tenth places, recognition

REALM MAKERS AWARDS

www.realmmakers.com

Description: Sponsored by The Faith and Fantasy Alliance. Realm Makers Genre Awards in these categories: debut, science fiction, fantasy, young adult, supernatural/paranormal, and horror/other (for those who don't feel other categories accurately characterize their speculative work). Realm Award recognizes the most excellent speculative novel written by a Christian author in the previous calendar year. Length: 60,000 words minimum; 50,000 words minimum for young adult. Parable Award for Excellence in Cover Design is awarded to the best overall cover for a speculative novel written by a Christian author.

Deadline: submit between January 1 and 20
Entry fee: $35
Prizes: cash

SERENA MCDONALD KENNEDY AWARD
www.snakenation.press/contests

Description: Sponsored by Snake Nation Press. Novellas up to 50,000 words or short-story collections up to 200 pages, published or unpublished.
Deadline: August 31
Entry fee: $25
Prize: $1,000 and publication

TOBIAS WOLFF AWARD FOR FICTION
www.bhreview.org/contest-submissions-guidelines

Description: Sponsored by Western Washington University's *Bellingham Review*. Length: 5,000 words maximum.
Deadline: submit between December 1 and March 31
Entry fee: $20
Prize: $1,000 plus publication

NONFICTION

ANNIE DILLARD AWARD IN CREATIVE NONFICTION
bhreview.org/contest-submissions-guidelines

Description: Sponsored by Western Washington University's *Bellingham Review*. Unpublished essays on any subject. Length: 5,000 words maximum.
Deadline: submit between December 1 and March 31
Entry fee: $20 for first submission, $10 each additional one
Prize: $1,000

AWP PRIZE FOR CREATIVE NONFICTION

www.awpwriter.org/contests

Description: Sponsored by Association of Writers and Writing
Programs. Open to published and unpublished authors. Book
collection of nonfiction manuscripts. Length: 150–300 pages.
Deadline: submit between January 1 and February 28
Entry fee: $15 for members, $30 for nonmembers
Prize: $2,500 and publication with the University of Georgia Press

THE BECHTEL PRIZE

www.twc.org/publications/bechtel-prize

Description: Sponsored by Teachers & Writers Collaborative. For
unpublished essays that explore themes related to creative writing,
arts education, and/or the imagination. Length: 2,500 words
maximum.
Deadline: January 6
Entry fee: $20
Prize: $1,000 and publication

EVENT NON-FICTION CONTEST

www.eventmagazine.ca/contest-nf

Description: Unpublished creative nonfiction. Length: 5,000 words
maximum.
Deadline: October 15
Entry fee: $34.95, includes a one-year subscription to *EVENT*
Prizes: first place, $1,500; second place, $1,000; third place, $500 plus
publication

GUIDEPOSTS WRITERS WORKSHOP CONTEST

www.guideposts.org/enter-the-guideposts-writers-workshop-contest

Description: Contest is held in even years with a mid-June deadline.
Submit an original, unpublished, true, first-person story (your
own or ghostwritten for another person) in 1,500 words or fewer
about an experience that changed your life. Show how faith made
a difference. Twelve winners will attend an all-expenses-paid,
weeklong writers workshop in Rye, New York, to learn about
inspirational storytelling and writing for Guideposts publications.

JOHN GUYON LITERARY NONFICTION

craborchardreview.siu.edu/submissions-annual-lit.html

Description: Sponsored by Southern Illinois University Department of English. Annual competition. Literary nonfiction, 6,500 words.
Deadline: submit between December 1 and January 31
Entry fee: $2
Prize: $500 and publication online

NEW LETTERS PRIZE FOR NONFICTION

www.newletters.org/writers-wanted/may-writing-contests

Description: For unpublished essays. Length: 8,000 words maximum.
Deadline: May 18
Entry fee: $24
Prize: $1,500 and magazine subscription

RICHARD J . MARGOLIS AWARD

award.margolis.com

Description: Sponsored by Blue Mountain Center. Given annually to a promising young journalist or essayist whose work combines warmth, humor, wisdom, and concern with social justice. Submit at least two examples of published or unpublished work and a short biographical note, including a description of current and anticipated work. Length: 30 pages maximum.
Deadline: July 1
Prize: $5,000 plus a one-month residency at the Blue Mountain Center in Blue Mountain Lake, New York

PLAYS, SCRIPTS, SCREENPLAYS

ACADEMY NICHOLL FELLOWSHIPS IN SCREENWRITING

www.oscars.org/nicholl/about

Description: International contest open to any writer who has not optioned or sold a treatment, teleplay, or screenplay for more than $25,000. May submit up to three scripts, 70-160 pages.
Deadline: submit between March 7 and May 1
Entry fee: $45-85, depending on submission date
Prizes: up to five $35,000 fellowships; recipients will be expected to complete at least one original feature-film screenplay during the fellowship year

AMERICAN ZOETROPE SCREENPLAY CONTEST

www.zoetrope.com/contests

> **Description:** To find and promote new and innovative voices in cinema. For screenplays and television pilots. No entrant may have earned more than $5,000 as a screenwriter for theatrical films or television or for the sale of, or sale of an option to, any original story, treatment, screenplay, or teleplay. Prizes, fellowships, awards, and other contest winnings are not considered earnings and are excluded from this rule. Length: film scripts, 70-130 pages; one-hour television pilot scripts, 45-65 pages; half-hour television scripts, 22-34 pages.
> **Deadline:** September 19
> **Entry fee:** $35-$50, depending on submission date
> **Prizes:** first place, $5,000, plus consideration for film option and development; ten finalists will also get this consideration

AUSTIN FILM FESTIVAL SCREENWRITERS COMPETITION

austinfilmfestival.com/submit

> **Description:** Offers a number of contest categories, including narrative feature, narrative short, documentary feature, documentary short for screenplays, screenplay, teleplay, and scripted digital competition.
> **Deadline:** varies by type
> **Entry fee:** $35-70, varies by type and submission date
> **Prizes:** $1,000-$5,000

KAIROS PRIZE FOR SPIRITUALLY UPLIFTING SCREENPLAYS

www.kairosprize.com

> **Description:** Sponsored by Movieguide. For feature-length screenplays. Judges consider not only a script's entertainment value and craftsmanship, but also whether it is uplifting, inspirational, and spiritual and if it teaches lessons in ethics and morality. Length: 87-130 pages; will accept scripts up to 150 pages (not counting the title page) for an additional $20.
> **Deadline:** October
> **Entry fee:** varies, depending on submission date
> **Prizes:** $15,000 each for first-time and professional screenwriters

MILDRED AND ALBERT PANOWSKI PLAYWRITING COMPETITION

www.nmu.edu/forestrobertstheatre/playwritingcompetition

Description: Sponsored by Forest Roberts Theatre, Northern Michigan University. Unpublished, unproduced, full-length plays. Award to encourage and stimulate artistic growth among educational and professional playwrights. Provides students and faculty members the opportunity to mount and produce an original work on the university stage.

Deadline: submit between June 1 and December 1

Prize: $2,000, a summer workshop, a fully mounted production, and transportation to Marquette, Michigan

MOONDANCE INTERNATIONAL FILM FESTIVAL COMPETITION

www.moondancefilmfestival.com

Description: Offers a variety of awards for films, screenplays, librettos, and features that raise awareness about social issues.

Deadline: May 30

Entry fees: $50-100

Prize: promotion to film companies for possible option

SCRIPTAPALOOZA SCREENPLAY COMPETITION

www.scriptapalooza.com/competition/how-to-enter

Description: Any screenplay from any genre considered; must be the original work of the author (multiple authorship acceptable). Shorts competition: screenplays fewer than 40 pages.

Deadline: submit between December 16 and April 13

Entry fee: $45-65

Prizes: first place, $10,000; each genre winner, $500 (action, adventure, comedy, drama, family, science fiction, thriller/ horror, historical), plus access to more than fifty producers through Scriptapalooza's network

SCRIPTAPALOOZA TV COMPETITION

www.scriptapaloozatv.com/competition

Description: Scripts for television pilots, one-hour dramas, reality shows, and half-hour sitcoms. Length: pilots, 30-60 pages; one-hour program, 50-60 pages; reality show, one- to five-page treatment; half-hour sitcom, 25-35 pages.

Deadline: October and April

Entry fee: $45-50, varies with deadline

Prizes in each genre: first place, $500; second place, $200; third place, $100, plus access to more than fifty producers through Scriptapalooza's network

POETRY

49TH PARALLEL POETRY AWARD

bhreview.org/contest-submissions-guidelines

Description: Sponsored by Western Washington University's *Bellingham Review*. Up to three poems in any style or on any subject.

Deadline: submit between December 1 and March 31

Entry fee: $20; international entries, $30

Prize: $1,000 and publication

ANHINGA-ROBERT DANA PRIZE FOR POETRY

www.anhingapress.org/anhinga-robert-dana-prize

Description: Sponsored by Anhinga Press. For poets submitting a manuscript of original poems in English. Length: 48-80 pages.

Deadline: submit between February 15 and May 1

Entry fee: $28 per manuscript

Prize: $2,000, a reading tour, and publication by Anhinga Press

BALTIMORE REVIEW POETRY CONTEST

baltimorereview.submittable.com/submit

Description: All styles and forms of poetry, directed toward an announced theme. Maximum of three entries.

Deadline: November 30

Entry fee: $10

Prizes: $100-500 and publication

BARBARA MANDIGO KELLY PEACE POETRY AWARDS

www.peacecontests.org/#poetry

Description: Sponsored by Nuclear Age Peace Foundation. Awards to encourage poets to explore and illuminate positive visions of peace and the human spirit. Poems must be original, unpublished, and in English. May submit up to three poems for one entry fee.

Deadline: July 1

Entry fee: adults, $15; youth ages 13-18, $5; none for ages 12 and under
Prizes: adult winner, $1,000; youth winner, $200; ages 12 and under, $200

BLUE MOUNTAIN ARTS POETRY CARD CONTEST
www.sps.com/poetry

Description: Biannual contest. Original poems. May be rhymed or unrhymed, although unrhymed is preferred. Poems also considered for greeting cards or anthologies. Original creations in English only. No limit to number of entries.
Deadlines: June 30 and December 31
Entry fee: none
Prizes: $350, $200, $100

BOSTON REVIEW ANNUAL POETRY CONTEST
www.bostonreview.net./contests

Description: Submit up to five unpublished poems in English; no more than ten pages total. Submit manuscripts in duplicate with cover note.
Deadline: June 30
Entry fee: $20, includes a subscription to *Boston Review*
Prize: $500 plus publication

CAVE CANEM POETRY PRIZE
cavecanempoets.org/prizes/cave-canem-poetry-prize

Description: Sponsored by Cave Canem Foundation. Supports the work of black poets of African descent with excellent manuscripts and who have not found a publisher for their first book. Offered every other year. Length: 48-75 pages.
Deadline: varies, with a spring season date
Entry fee: $15
Prize: $1,000 plus publication by a national press and copies of the book, with a feature reading in New York City

THE COMSTOCK REVIEW CHAPBOOK CONTEST
comstockreview.org/comstock-writers-group-chapbook

Description: Submissions must be unpublished as a collection, but individual poems may have been published previously in journals. Length: 25-34 pages. Poems may run longer than one page.
Deadline: submit between August 1 and October 31
Entry fee: $30
Prize: $1,000 plus publication and author copies

FLO GAULT STUDENT POETRY PRIZE
www.sarabandebooks.org/flo-gault

Description: Sponsored by Sarabande Books. For full-time Kentucky undergraduate students. Submit up to three poems.
Deadline: submit between October 1 and December 1
Prize: $500 and publication

HOLLIS SUMMERS POETRY PRIZE
www.ohioswallow.com/poetry_prize

Description: Sponsored by Ohio University Press. For an unpublished collection of original poems written in English, 60-95 pages. Open to both those who have not published a book-length collection and to those who have.
Deadline: December 1
Entry fee: $30
Prize: $1,000 plus publication in book form by Ohio University Press

THE JAMES LAUGHLIN AWARD
www.poets.org/academy-american-poets/james-laughlin-award-guidelines

Description: Sponsored by Academy of American Poets. To recognize a second full-length print book of original poetry by a US citizen, permanent resident, or person who has DACA/TPS status, forthcoming within the next calendar year. Author must have published one book of poetry in English in a standard edition (48 pages or more) in the United States or under contract and scheduled for publication during the current calendar year; publication of chapbooks (less than 48 pages) does not disqualify. Length: 48-100 pages.
Prize: $5,000 plus publication

KATE TUFTS DISCOVERY AWARD
www.cgu.edu/tufts

Description: Sponsored by Claremont Graduate University. Award presented annually for a first poetry volume published in the preceding year by a poet of genuine promise.
Deadline: June 30
Prize: $10,000

KINGSLEY TUFTS POETRY AWARD

www.cgu.edu/pages/6422.asp

> **Description:** Sponsored by Claremont Graduate University. Presented annually for a published book of poetry by a midcareer poet to both honor the poet and provide the resources that allow artists to continue working toward the pinnacle of their craft.
> **Deadline:** June 30
> **Prize:** $100,000

MURIEL CRAFT BAILEY MEMORIAL POETRY AWARD

comstockreview.org/annual-contest

> **Description:** Sponsored by *The Comstock Review*. Unpublished poems up to 40 lines. No limit on number of submissions.
> **Deadline:** submit between April 1 and July 15
> **Entry fee:** postal: $5 per poem for up to five poems; online: $27.50 for five poems
> **Prizes:** first place, $1,000; second place, $250; third place, $100

NEW LETTERS PRIZE FOR POETRY

www.newletters.org/writers-wanted/may-writing-contests

> **Description:** A single poetry entry may contain up to six poems, and the poems need not be related.
> **Deadline:** May 18
> **Entry fee:** $24 each entry; if entering online, add a $5 service charge to entry fee; includes a one-year subscription to *New Letters*
> **Prize:** $1,500 for best group of three to six poems

PHILIP LEVINE PRIZE FOR POETRY

www.fresnostate.edu/artshum/english/levineprize

> **Description:** Sponsored by California State University Department of English. An annual book contest for original English, previously unpublished, full-length poetry manuscripts. Length: 48-80 pages with no more than one poem per page.
> **Deadline:** submit between July 1 and September 30
> **Entry fee:** $28 online fee; $25 postal fee
> **Prize:** $2,000 and publication by Anhinga Press

POETRY SOCIETY OF VIRGINIA POETRY CONTESTS

poetrysocietyofvirginia.org

> **Description:** More than twenty-five categories for adults and students.

Form and length vary according to the categories. All entries must be unpublished, original, and not scheduled for publication before the winners of the competition are announced.

Deadline: submit between October 15 and January 15
Entry fee: $5 per poem for nonmembers
Prizes: $100, $50, $30, $20, varying according to specific competition

RICHARD PETERSON POETRY PRIZE

craborchardreview.siu.edu/submissions-annual-lit.html

Description: Sponsored by *Crab Orchard Review*, Southern Illinois University, Carbondale Department of English, on an announced theme. Unpublished poems by a United States citizen, permanent resident, or person who has DACA/TPS status. Length: five pages maximum. Limit three entries.
Deadline: January 31
Entry fee: $2
Prize: $500 and publication online

SLIPSTREAM ANNUAL POETRY CHAPBOOK COMPETITION

www.slipstreampress.org/contest.html

Description: Sponsored by Slipstream Press. Entries may be any style, format, or theme. Length: 40 pages maximum.
Deadline: December 1
Entry fee: $20
Prize: $1,000 plus fifty published copies of chapbook

SOUL-MAKING KEATS LITERARY COMPETITION: JANICE FARRELL POETRY PRIZE

soulmakingcontest.us/guidelines-rules/

Description: Sponsored by National League of American Pen Women. Three poems per entry. One poem per page, one-page poems only. Free verse, blank verse, and prose poems.
Deadline: November 30
Entry fee: $5 per entry
Prizes: first place, $100; second place, $50; third place, $25

SUMMERTIME BLUES POETRY CONTEST

www.thestorytellermagazine.com/contests

Description: Sponsored by *The Storyteller* magazine. Poems may be rhyming or nonrhyming and should be about summer, although this topic isn't mandatory. Length: 40 lines maximum. Multiple entries accepted.

Deadline: postmarked by August 31

Entry fee: $5 per three poems

Prizes: first place, $25 plus publication; second place, $15; third place, $10

TOI DERRICOTTE & CORNELIUS EADY CHAPBOOK PRIZE

cavecanempoets.org/prizes/toi-derricotte-cornelius-eady-chapbook-prize

Description: Sponsored by Cave Canem Foundation. Dedicated to the discovery of exceptional chapbook-length manuscripts by black poets. Presented in collaboration with the O, Miami Poetry Festival and The Center for the Humanities at the CUNY Graduate Center.

Deadline: September 30

Entry Fee: $12

Prize: $500, publication, ten copies of the chapbook, a four-day writer residency, and a feature reading

TOM HOWARD/MARGARET REID POETRY CONTEST

winningwriters.com/our-contests/tom-howard-margaret-reid-poetry-contest

Description: Sponsored by Winning Writers. Poetry in any style or genre. Length: 250 lines maximum.

Deadline: submit between April 15 and September 30

Entry fee: $12 per poem

Prizes: Tom Howard Prize, $3,000 for poem in any style or genre; Margaret Reid Prize, $3,000 for poem that rhymes or has a traditional style; $100 each for ten honorable mentions in any style

UTMOST NOVICE CHRISTIAN POETRY CONTEST

www.utmostchristianwriters.com/poetry-contest/poetry-contest-rules.php

Description: Sponsored by Utmost Christian Writers Foundation. Unpublished poems may be rhymed or free verse, up to 60 lines. Need not be religious in content. Maximum of five entries.

Deadline: February 28

Entry fee: $20 per poem

Prizes: $1,000, $500, $300; ten honorable mentions, $100; best rhyming poem, $300; honorable mention rhyming poem, $200

VIOLET REED HAAS PRIZE FOR POETRY

www.snakenation.press/contests

> **Description:** Sponsored by Snake Nation Press. Length: 50-75 pages. Previously published eligible.
>
> **Deadline:** August 31
>
> **Entry fee:** $25
>
> **Prize:** $1,000 plus publication

WERGLE FLOMP HUMOR POETRY CONTEST

winningwriters.com/our-contests/wergle-flomp-humor-poetry-contest-free

> **Description:** Sponsored by Winning Writers. Submit one published or unpublished humor poem up to 250 lines.
>
> **Deadline:** April 1
>
> **Entry fee:** none
>
> **Prizes:** first place, $1,000; second place, $250; ten honorable mentions, $100; plus the top twelve entries will be published online

MULTIPLE GENRES

BLUE RIDGE CONFERENCE WRITING CONTEST

www.blueridgeconference.com/contest-info

> **Description:** Sponsors three book contests for fiction or nonfiction: Foundation Awards, Director's Choice, and The Selahs. Look for details about guidelines, deadlines, and entry fees on the website after January 1.

CHRISTIAN INDIE AWARDS

www.christianaward.com

> **Description:** Sponsored by Christian Indie Publishing Association. This award is designed to promote and bring recognition to quality Christian books by small publishers and independently published authors. Books must be printed in English, for sale in the United States, and promote the Christian faith. Awards are offered in eighteen categories. Publishers and authors may nominate titles, and Christian readers vote to determine the winners.
>
> **Deadline:** November 15
>
> **Entry fee:** $45

COLUMBIA JOURNAL CONTESTS

columbiajournal.org/submit/winter-contest

Description: Fiction and nonfiction, 5,000 words maximum; poetry, five pages maximum.
Deadline: December 1
Entry fee: $15 per submission
Prizes: $500 plus publication in each category

EDITOR'S REPRINT AWARDS

www.sequestrum.org/editors-reprint-award-fiction-and-nonfiction
www.sequestrum.org/editors-reprint-award-poetry

Description: Sponsored by *Sequestrum* journal. Contest open to previously published manuscripts in prose (fiction and creative nonfiction up to 12,000 words) and poetry (up to 50 lines).
Deadline: April 30
Entry fee: $15
Prizes: first prize awarded in both categories, $400 and publication; runners-up, $50 and publication

ERIC HOFFER BOOK AWARD

www.hofferaward.com

Description: Eighteen categories for books from small, academic, and micro presses, including self-published, ebooks, and older books. The prose category is for creative fiction and nonfiction fewer than 10,000 words.
Deadline: January 21
Entry fee: varies by category
Prizes: $2,500 grand prize, other prizes awarded in categories

THE EUPLE RINEY MEMORIAL AWARD

www.thestorytellermagazine.com/contests

Description: Sponsored by *The Storyteller*. Open-genre contest but must be about family—good or bad. Can be fiction or nonfiction (indicate which). Length: 3,000 words maximum. No pornography, graphic anything, New Age, or children's stories will be accepted.
Deadline: June 30
Entry fee: $5
Prizes: first place, $50; second place, $25; third place, $15; honorable mention, $10. Plus an editor's choice award.

EVANGELICAL PRESS ASSOCIATION CONTEST
www.evangelicalpress.com/contest

> **Description:** Higher Goals awards in a variety of categories for periodical manuscripts published in the previous year. Although most submissions are made by publication staff members, associate EPA members may also submit their articles.
> **Deadline:** January 17
> **Entry fee:** $50

EXCELLENCE IN EDITING AWARD
www.ChristianEditor.com/EIE

> **Description:** Sponsored by Christian Editor Connection. This award celebrates newly released books that are superbly written, well edited, and published by a CBA publisher or self-published by a Christian author.
> **Deadline:** December 31
> **Entry Fee:** $35 before November 15, $40 after
> **Prizes:** Winners receive a plaque, print and digital stickers, and promotion through Christian Editor Connection and PENCON.

INSCRIBE CHRISTIAN WRITERS' FELLOWSHIP CONTEST
inscribe.org/contests

> **Description:** Sponsors contests for InScribe members: Fall Contest, Winter Contest, Word Challenge, FellowScript Contests, Barnabas Award, Janette Oke Award, Post Conference Contest.
> **Deadline:** varies
> **Entry fee:** varies
> **Awards:** vary by category

NARRATIVE MAGAZINE CONTESTS
www.narrativemagazine.com/submit-your-work

> **Description:** Biannual contests in a variety of categories, including short stories, essays, memoirs, poetry, and literary nonfiction. Entries must be previously unpublished. Length: varies by category.
> **Deadline:** varies
> **Entry fee:** varies
> **Prizes:** vary by category

NARRATIVE MAGAZINE 30 BELOW CONTEST

www.narrativemagazine.com/node/345528

> **Description:** For writers ages 18-30. Fiction, nonfiction, poetry (up to five poems), essays, memoirs. Length: 15,000 words maximum. Restrictions on previously published works.
> **Deadline:** November 19
> **Entry fee:** $25 per entry
> **Prizes:** $1,500, $750, $300, plus ten finalists will receive $100 each

NATIONAL WRITERS ASSOCIATION CONTESTS

www.nationalwriters.com/page/page/2734945.htm

> **Description:** Sponsors six contests: nonfiction, novel, young writers, poetry, short short, and David Raffelock Award for Publishing Excellence.
> **Deadline:** varies by contest
> **Entry fee:** varies by contest
> **Prizes:** vary by contest

NEW LETTERS AWARDS FOR WRITERS

www.newletters.org/writers-wanted/may-writing-contests

> **Description:** Sponsored by University of Missouri—Kansas City. Entries accepted in these categories: poetry, fiction, nonfiction.
> **Deadline:** May 18
> **Entry fee:** $20 for first entry; $15/additional entry
> **Prizes:** $2,500 for the best in poetry and fiction, $2,500 for nonfiction

NEW MILLENNIUM AWARDS

submit.newmillenniumwritings.org

> **Description:** Sponsored by New Millennium Writings. Fiction and nonfiction: 6,000 words maximum. Flash fiction (short-short story): 1,000 words maximum. Poetry: three poems to five pages total. No restrictions as to style or subject matter.
> **Deadline:** November 30
> **Entry fees:** $20, $45 for three entries, $72 for five entries
> **Prizes:** $1,000 plus publication for each category

OREGON CHRISTIAN WRITERS CASCADE AWARDS

oregonchristianwriters.org

> **Description:** Contests for novels; nonfiction books; memoir; young adult/middle grade fiction and nonfiction books; poetry;

children's chapter and picture books; articles, columns, and blog posts; short stories/flash fiction; and devotionals. Separate divisions for published and unpublished authors. Awards are presented at the summer conference in Portland, Oregon.
Deadline: submit between February 14 and March 31
Entry fees: $30-35 for members, $40-45 for nonmembers

PROMISING BEGINNINGS CHRISTIAN WRITERS' CONTEST

www.KathyIde.com

Description: This contest is open to both published and unpublished writers. Submit the first five pages of an unpublished or self-published book manuscript, fiction or nonfiction (any genre except poetry), for YA or adult readership (no children's). Must follow the formatting guidelines on the Promising Beginnings blog at *www.KathyIde.com*. Submissions will be judged on whether the quality of the writing shows promise.

Deadline: November 30

Entry fee: none

Prize: full scholarship to Mount Hermon Christian Writers Conference (including meals and economy lodging) or to SoCalChristian Writers' Conference (including meals, dorm lodging, and travel expenses up to $300)

SOUL-MAKING KEATS LITERARY COMPETITION

www.soulmakingcontest.us

Description: Sponsored by National League of American Pen Women, Nob Hill, San Francisco Branch. Categories include flash fiction, short story, memoir vignette, humor, novel excerpt, intercultural essay, creative nonfiction, religious essay, young-adult poetry, and young-adult prose.

Deadline: November 30

Entry fee: $5

Prizes in each category: first place, $100; second place, $50; third place, $25

TENNESSEE WILLIAMS/NEW ORLEANS LITERARY FESTIVAL

tennesseewilliams.net/contests

Description: Tennessee Williams gained some early recognition by entering a writing contest. The festival that bears his name now sponsors writing contests in poetry, fiction, very short fiction, and one-act playwriting.

Deadline: varies according to genre
Entry fee: varies
Prizes: vary by category

THE WORD GUILD CHRISTIAN WRITING AWARDS

thewordguild.com/contests

Description: The Word Awards recognize the best work published in the previous year in thirty-five categories of writing, including novels, nonfiction books, articles, columns, poems, song lyrics, scripts, and screenplays. Fresh Ink Student Writers Contest for never-before-published student writers. In the Beginning for unpublished novice and emerging writers. The Grace Irwin Prize for Canadian writers who are Christians; recognizes the best book published in the previous year. The Leslie K. Tarr Award celebrates a major career contribution to Christian writing and publishing in Canada. The Partnership Award recognizes an individual or organization that has shown exceptional support and encouragement for Canadian writers and editors who are Christians.

Deadline, entry fees, prizes: vary according to the award and its guidelines

WORDS AND MUSIC WRITING COMPETITION

wordsandmusic.org/contest

Description: Sponsored by The Pirate's Alley Faulkner Society, Inc. Seven categories: novel, novella, book-length narrative fiction, novel-in-progress, short story, essay, poetry, and short story by a high-school student. For previously unpublished work only.

Deadline: May 15
Entry fee: varies by category
Prizes: $250-7,500, depending on category

WRITER'S DIGEST COMPETITIONS

www.writersdigest.com/writers-digest-competitions

Description: Every other month, *Writer's Digest* presents a creative challenge for fun and prizes, providing a short, open-ended prompt for short-story submissions based on that prompt. Winner receives publication in *Writer's Digest*. Also sponsors annual contests for feature articles, short stories (multiple genres), poetry, personal essays, and self-published books (categories vary).

Deadline: varies according to contest

Entry fee: varies

Prizes for annual contest: first place, $500; second place, $500; and more places for each contest; grand prize, $2,500

THE WRITERS' UNION OF CANADA AWARDS & COMPETITIONS

www.writersunion.ca/awards

Description: Short Prose Competition for Developing Writers for fiction or nonfiction by an author who has not yet published a book. Length: 2,500 words maximum. Danuta Gleed Literary Award for the best first collection of short fiction.

Deadlines: Short Prose, March 1; Danuta, January 31

Entry fee: $29

Prizes: Short Prose, $2,500; Danuta, $10,000, plus two finalist awards for $500 each

WRITERS-EDITORS NETWORK ANNUAL INTERNATIONAL WRITING COMPETITION

www.writers-editors.com/Writers/Contests/Contest_Guidelines/contest_guidelines.htm

Description: Nonfiction and fiction: 4,000 words maximum; children's literature (story, fiction-book chapter, poem, magazine article, or nonfiction-book chapter targeted to a specific age group): 4,000 words maximum. Poetry may be traditional or free verse. All entries must be unpublished or self-published and not accepted for publication by a traditional publisher at the time they are entered in the contest.

Deadline: March 15

Entry fees: poetry, $5 for members, $10 for nonmembers; prose: $10 for members, $20 for nonmembers

Prizes: $200, $150, $100, $75, plus one-year membership in Writers-Editors Network

RESOURCES FOR CONTESTS

These websites are sources for announcements about other contests.

DAILY WRITING TIPS
www.dailywritingtips.com/25-writing-competitions

FREELANCE WRITING
www.freelancewriting.com/writingcontests.php

FUNDS FOR WRITERS
fundsforwriters.com/contests

NEW PAGES
www.newpages.com/classifieds/big-list-of-writing-contests

POETS & WRITERS
www.pw.org/grants

TETHERED BY LETTERS
tetheredbyletters.com/resources/contest-list

THE WRITE LIFE
thewritelife.com/writing-contests

THE WRITER
www.writermag.com/writing-resources/contests

DENOMINATIONAL PUBLISHERS

ANGLICAN
The Anglican Journal

ASSEMBLIES OF GOD
God's Word for Today
LIVE
My Healthy Church
Take 5 Plus

BAPTIST
The Alabama Baptist
B&H Publishing
The Brink
CommonCall
Facts & Trends
HomeLife
Judson Press
Love Lines from God
Mature Living
On Mission
Parenting Teens
ParentLife
Point
Randall House Publications
The Secret Place
Word&Way

BRETHREN
BMH Books
GraceConnect

CATHOLIC
America
American Catholic Press
The Arlington Catholic Herald
Ave Maria Press
Catholic Book Publishing Corp.
Catholic Digest
Catholic New York
Catholic Sentinel
Celebrate Life
Christ Our Hope
Columbia
Commonweal
Franciscan Media
Image Books
LEAVES
Liguorian
Liturgical Press
Loyola Press
Our Sunday Visitor Newsweekly
Paraclete Press
Parish Liturgy
Pauline Books & Media
Paulist Press
Resurrection Press
Scepter Publishers
St. Anthony Messenger
St. Mary's Messenger
U.S. Catholic

CHARISMATIC
See Pentecostal.

CHRISTIAN CHURCH/ CHURCH OF CHRIST
Christian Standard
College Press Publishing
Leafwood Publishers

CHURCH OF GOD
Bible Advocate
The Church Herald &
Holiness Banner
The Gem
Gems of Truth
Now What?
Pathways to God
Pentecostal Messenger
Warner Press

EPISCOPAL
Forward Day by Day
Forward Movement
The Living Church

EVANGELICAL COVENANT
The Covenant Companion

LUTHERAN
Augsburg Fortress
Beaming Books
Canada Lutheran
The Canadian Lutheran
Christ in Our Home
Concordia Publishing House
Fortress Press
The Lutheran Digest
Lutheran Forum
The Lutheran Journal
Lutheran Witness
Northwestern Publishing House

The Word in Season

MENNONITE
Canadian Mennonite
Christian Leader
The Messenger
Purpose

MESSIANIC
The Messianic Times

METHODIST
Abingdon Press
Christian Living in the
Mature Years
Good News
Light + Life Magazine
Methodist History
Pockets
The Upper Room

NAZARENE
The Foundry Publishing
Holiness Today
Reflecting God
Standard

OPEN BIBLE
Message of the Open Bible

ORTHODOX
Ancient Faith Publishing

PENTECOSTAL/CHARISMATIC
Charisma
Charisma Leader
Empowered Publications, Inc.
Ministry Today
Whitaker House

PRESBYTERIAN
byFaith
Presbyterians Today

These Days
Westminster/John Knox Press

QUAKER/FRIENDS
Friends Journal
Friends United Press

REFORMED
Christian Courier
Faith Alive Christian Resources
P&R Publishing

SALVATION ARMY
Faith & Friends
New Frontier Chronicle
Peer
SAConnects

War Cry

SEVENTH-DAY ADVENTIST
Guide
Journal of Adventist Education
Ministry
Our Little Friend
Pacific Press
Primary Treasure
Vibrant Life

UNITED CHURCH OF CANADA
United Church Observer

WESLEYAN
Light from the Word

PUBLISHING LINGO

My first week working in a bookstore I learned a valuable lesson. I had a stack of books in my arms that I had taken from a shipment in the back room. My boss walked by and said, "Steve, please put those in the dump," and kept walking.

I paused and thought, *Why should I throw these away? They are brand new books!* To my chagrin, I discovered that, in bookstore lingo, a dump was a cardboard display in the front of the store.

The lesson I learned is that knowing the lingo can keep you from being confused or potentially misunderstanding some instructions. Like bookstores, writing and publishing have their own lingo. The following definitions will acquaint you with some of the more important terms.

ABA: American Booksellers Association. This acronymn has come to mean the general market, as opposed to CBA, the Christian market.

Advance: Money a publisher pays to an author up front, against future royalties. The amount varies greatly from publisher to publisher and is often paid in two or three installments (on signing the contract, on delivery of the manuscript, and on publication).

AE: An abbreviation for Acquisitions Editor. Not all publishing houses use this abbreviation, but they all have acquisitions people in their editorial departments.

All rights: An outright sale of a manuscript. The author has no further control over any subsidiary rights or reusing the piece.

Anecdote: A short, poignant, real-life story, usually used to illustrate a single thought. It need not be humorous.

ARC: Advance Reader Copy. An early paperback (or ebook) version of a book sent out for reviews around four to six months prior to publication.

Assignment: When an editor asks a writer to create a specific manuscript for an agreed-on price.

As-told-to story: A true story you write as a first-person account about someone else.

Audience: The people who are expected to be reading your manuscript, in terms of age, life experience, knowledge of and interest level in the story or subject. Publishers want to be sure writers understand their assumed audiences well.

Audiobooks: Spoken-word books available on compact disc, MP3 file, or streaming via the internet.

Backlist: A publisher's previously published books that are still in print a year or more after publication.

Bible versions:
AMP—*Amplified Bible*
ASV—*American Standard Version*
CEB—*Common English Bible*
CEV—*Contemporary English Version*
CSB—*Christian Standard Bible*
ESV—*English Standard Version*
GNB—*Good News Bible*
GWB—*God's Word Bible*
HCSB—*Holman Christian Standard Bible* (replaced by CSB)
ICB—*International Children's Bible*
KJV—*King James Version*
MEV—*Modern English Version*
MSG—*The Message*
NAB—*New American Bible*
NABRE—*New American Bible Revised Edition*
NASB—*New American Standard Bible*
NEB—*New English Bible*
NET—*New English Translation*
NIrV—*New International Reader's Version*
NIV—*New International Version*
NJB—*New Jerusalem Bible*
NKJV—*New King James Version*
NLT—*New Living Translation*
NRSV—*New Revised Standard Version*
RSV—*Revised Standard Version*
TEV—*Today's English Translation* (aka *Good News Bible*)

TLB—*The Living Bible*
TNIV—*Today's New International Version*

Bio: Brief information about the author.

Bluelines: The last printer's proofs used to catch errors before a book or periodical is printed. May be physical pages or digital proofs in PDF format.

BOB: Back-of-Book ad for the author's previous book(s) or a similar book released by the publisher. It uses the blank pages in the back of a book or extra pages at the end of an ebook.

Book proposal: Submission of a book idea to an agent or editor. It usually includes a hook, summary and purpose of the book, target market, uniqueness of the book compared to similar ones in the marketplace, chapter-by-chapter summaries or plot synopsis, marketing and promotion information, your credentials, and delivery date, plus one to three sample chapters, including the first one.

Byline: Author's name printed below the title of a story, article, etc.

Camera-ready copy: The text and artwork for a book that are ready for the press.

Category romance: Novels of around 50,000-60,000 words that are published in categories and according to strict guidelines. An example is Love Inspired novels.

CBA: Christian Booksellers Association. The acronym has come to describe the Christian market as opposed to ABA, the general market.

Chapbook: A small book or pamphlet containing poetry, religious readings, etc.

Circulation: The number of copies sold or distributed of a periodical.

Clips: Copies of articles you have had published in newspapers or magazines.

Colophon: The publisher's emblem or imprint used on the title page or spine of a book or a statement at the end of a book with information about its production, such as the type of font used.

Column: A regularly appearing feature, section, or department in a periodical with the same heading. It's written by the same person or a different freelancer each time.

Comp copies: Complimentary copies given to the author by the publisher on publication.

Comps: Shorthand for "comparable." The publisher may have comps on cover designs or titles to help position the book in the marketplace.

Concept statement: A 50- to 150-word summary of your proposed book.

Contributing editor: A freelance writer who has a regular column or writes regularly for the periodical.

Contributor's copy: Copy of an issue of a periodical sent to an author whose work appears in it.

Copyright: Legal protection of an author's work. A manuscript is automatically copyrighted in your name when you produce it. You don't need to register it with the Copyright Office unless you are self-publishing a book or other publication.

Cover copy: Or "copy." The text on the back cover of a book, in the online description, or in marketing materials. For a hardcover, it can also include flap copy, the text on the inside dust-jacket flaps.

Cover letter: A letter that accompanies some manuscript submissions. Usually it's needed only if you have to tell the editor something specific, to give your credentials for writing a manuscript of a technical nature, or to remind the editor that the manuscript was requested or expected. Often used as the introduction to a book proposal. Rarely used for an article submission; query letters are used instead.

Credits, list of: A listing of your previously published works.

Critique: An evaluation of a manuscript.

Defamation: A written or spoken injury to the reputation of a living person or organization. If what is said is true, it cannot be defamatory.

Derivative work: A work derived from another work, such as a condensation or abridgment. Contact the copyright owner for permission before doing the abridgment, and be prepared to pay that owner a fee or royalty.

Developmental edit: Usually the first round of editing done on a manuscript. The editor helps "develop" the book by shaping its content and structure.

Devotion: A short manuscript based on a Scripture verse or passage that shares a personal spiritual discovery, inspires to worship, challenges to commitment or action, or encourages. A book or periodical of devotions is called a devotional.

Ed board: Editorial board meeting. The editors meet to discuss the new proposals they received to determine which ones should go to the pub board.

Editorial guidelines: See "Writers guidelines."

Em dash (—): Used to create a break or set off material in a sentence instead of using a comma. *The Chicago Manual of Style* calls this punctuation mark "the most versatile of the dashes."

Endorsements: Flattering comments about a book, usually printed on the back cover or in promotional material.

Epub: Term for a specific file format used by ebooks. Mobi is used for Kindle (Amazon). Epub is used by everyone else (Nook, Kobo, Apple, Google Play, etc.).

Essay: A short composition expressing the author's opinion on a specific subject.

Evangelical: A person who believes that one receives God's forgiveness for sins through Jesus Christ and believes the Bible is the authoritative Word of God. This is a broad definition for a label with broad application.

Exegesis: Interpretation of a Scripture passage.

Feature article: In-depth coverage of a subject, usually focusing on a person, an event, a process, an organization, a movement, a trend, or an issue. It's written to explain, encourage, help, analyze, challenge, motivate, warn, or entertain, as well as to inform.

Filler: A short item used to "fill" a page of a periodical. It could be a joke, anecdote, light verse, short humor, puzzle, game, etc.

First rights: A periodical editor buys the right to publish a manuscript that has never been published and to do so only once.

Foreign rights: Selling or giving permission to translate or reprint published material in another country.

Foreword: Opening remarks in a book to introduce the book and its author.

Freelance: Supplied by freelance writers.

Freelancer or freelance writer: A writer who is not on salary but sells his or her material to a number of different periodicals and publishers.

Galley proof: A typeset copy of a book or magazine used to detect and correct errors before printing.

General market: Non-Christian market, sometimes called secular market.

Genre: Refers to a type or classification, as in fiction or poetry. For instance, westerns, romances, and mysteries are fiction genres.

Glossy: A photo with a shiny, rather than matte, finish. Also, a publication printed on such paper.

Go-ahead: When an editor tells you to write or submit your article.

Hard copy: A printed manuscript, as opposed to one sent via email.

Independent book publisher: A book publisher who charges authors to publish their books or buy a certain number of copies, as opposed to a royalty house that pays authors. Some independent publishers also pay a royalty. Sometimes called a subsidy, vanity, or custom publisher.

ISBN: International Standard Book Number, an identification code needed for every version of a book.

Journal: A periodical presenting information in a particular area, often for an academic or educated audience.

Kill fee: A fee paid for a completed article done on assignment that is subsequently not published. The amount is usually 25-50% of the original payment.

Libel: To defame someone by an opinion or a misquote that puts his or her reputation in jeopardy.

Little/Literary: Small-circulation periodicals whose focus is providing a forum for the literary writer, rather than on making money. Often they do not pay or pay in copies.

Mainstream fiction: Other than genre fiction (such as romance, mystery, or fantasy). Stories of people and their conflicts handled on a deeper level.

Mass market: Books intended for a wide, general market, produced in a smaller format, usually with smaller type and sold at a lower price. The expectation is that their sales will be higher.

Mobi: Term for a specific file format used by ebooks. Mobi is used for Kindle (Amazon). Epub is used by everyone else.

Ms: Abbreviation for manuscript.

Mss: Abbreviation for more than one manuscript.

NASR: Abbreviation for North American serial rights. Permission for a periodical targeting readers in the US and Canada to publish a manuscript.

New-adult fiction: A developing fiction genre with protagonists ages 18-25. In the general market, these novels often explore sexual themes considered too "adult" for the YA or teen market. They tend to be marketed to older teen readers.

Novella: A short novel, usually 20,000–35,000 words. The length varies from publisher to publisher.

On acceptance: Editor pays a writer at the time the manuscript is accepted for publication.

On assignment: Writing a manuscript at the specific request of an editor.

On publication: Publisher pays a writer when his or her manuscript is published.

On speculation/spec: Writing something for a periodical editor with the agreement that the editor will buy it only if he or she likes it.

Onetime rights: Selling the right to publish a manuscript one time to more than one periodical, primarily to nonoverlapping audiences, such as different denominations.

Over the transom: Unsolicited manuscripts sent to a book editor. Comes from the old transom, which was a window above the door in office buildings. Manuscripts could be pushed "over the transom" into the locked office.

Overrun: The extra copies of a book printed during the initial print run.

Pen name/pseudonym: A name other than your legal name used on a manuscript to protect your identity or the identities of people included or when you wish to remain anonymous. Put the pen name in the byline under the title and your real name with your contact information.

Perfect binding: When pages of a paperback are glued together (bound) on the spine and the cover is then attached.

Periodical: A magazine, newsletter, or newspaper.

Permissions: Asking permission to use text or art from a copyrighted source.

Personal experience: An account based on a real-life experience.

Personality profile: A feature article that highlights a specific person's life or accomplishments.

Plagiarism: Stealing and using the ideas or writing of someone else as your own, either as is or rewriting slightly to make them sound like your own.

POD/Print-on-demand: A printing process where books are printed one at a time or in small numbers instead of in quantity. The production cost per book is higher, but no warehousing is necessary.

POV: Point-of-view. A fiction term that describes the perspective of the one telling the story, such as first person or third person.

Press kit: A compilation of promotional materials for a book or author, used to publicize a book.

Pub board: A formal meeting where people from editorial, marketing, sales, finance, and management meet to discuss whether or not to publish a book.

Public domain: Work for which copyright protection has expired. Copyright laws vary from country to country; but in the US, works published before 1925 have entered the public domain.

Recto: The right-hand page in printing.

Running head: The text at the top of each page that can show the author's name, book title, chapter, or page number.

Query letter: A letter sent to an editor about an article or book you propose to write and asking if he or she is interested in seeing it.

Reprint rights: Selling the right to reprint an article that has already been published. You must have sold only first or onetime rights originally and wait until it has been published the first time.

Response time: The number of weeks or months it takes an editor to get back to you about a query, proposal, or manuscript you sent.

Review copies: Books given to reviewers or buyers for bookstore chains and online sellers.

Royalty: The percentage an author is paid by a publisher on the sale of each copy of a book.

Running head: The text at the top of each page that can show the author's name, book title, chapter, or page number.

SASE: Self-addressed, stamped envelope. Always send it with a hard-copy manuscript or query letter.

SASP: Self-addressed, stamped postcard. May be sent with a hard-copy manuscript to be returned by the editor to indicate it arrived safely.

Satire: Ridicule that aims at reform.

Second serial rights: See "Reprint rights."

Secular market: An outdated term for the non-Christian publishing market.

Serial: Refers to publication in a periodical, such as first serial rights.

Sidebar: A short feature that accompanies an article and gives additional information about the topic, such as a recommended reading list. It is often set apart by appearing within a box or border.

Signature: All books are printed in 16-page increments or signatures (occasionally in 32-page increments for large books like Bibles). A large sheet of paper is printed, then folded multiple times. Three sides are cut (top, side, and bottom). The fourth side holds eight double-sided pages. The signatures are compiled and bound into the finished book.

Simultaneous submissions: Sending the same manuscript to more than one editor at the same time. Usually this action is done with nonoverlapping periodical markets, such as denominational publications or newspapers in different cities, or when you are writing on a timely subject. Most periodical editors don't accept simultaneous submissions, but they are the norm in the book market. Be sure to state in a cover letter that it is a simultaneous submission.

Slander: The verbal act of defamation.

Slanting: Writing an article to meet the needs of a particular market.

Slush pile: The stack of unsolicited manuscripts that arrive at an editor's desk or email inbox.

Subsidiary rights: All the rights, other than book rights, included in a book contract, such as translations, audiobooks, book clubs, and movies.

Subsidy publisher: See "Independent book publisher."

Synopsis: A brief summary of a work, ranging from one paragraph to several pages.

Tabloid: A newspaper-format publication about half the size of a regular newspaper.

Take-home paper: A small periodical given to Sunday-school students, children through adults. These minimagazines are published with the curriculum.

Think piece: A magazine article that has an intellectual, philosophical, or provocative approach to a subject.

Trade book: Describes a 5½" x 8½" paperback book (sometimes 6" x 9"). This is a typical trim size for a paperback. Mass-market books are smaller, around 4" x 6".

Trade magazine: A magazine whose audience is in a particular business.

Trim size: The size of a book after being trimmed in the printing process. (See "Signature" for more information.)

Unsolicited manuscript: A manuscript an editor did not specifically ask to see.

Vanity publisher: See "Independent book publisher."

Verso: The left-hand page in printing.

Vignette: A short, descriptive literary sketch of a brief scene or incident.

Vita: An outline of one's personal history and experience.

Work-for-hire: A manuscript you create for an agreed payment, and you give the publisher full ownership and control of it. You must sign a contract for this agreement to be legal.

Writers guidelines: Information provided by an editor that gives specific guidance for writing for the publication or publishing house. If the information is not offered online, email or send an SASE with your request for printed guidelines.

INDEX